Teaching for a Tolerant World, Grades K-6

Teaching for a Tolerant World, Grades K-6

Essays and Resources

Judith P. Robertson, Editor,

and the Committee on Teaching about Genocide and Intolerance of the National Council of Teachers of English

National Council of Teachers of English
1111 W. Kenyon Road, Urbana, Illinois 61801-1096

The poem "Weaving Home" on page 80 is used with permission, ©1991 by Michael J. Caduto, All Rights Reserved. Written permission is required from the author before copying this poem in any form. The poem is from page 34 of *Keepers of the Animals: Native American Stories and Wildlife Activities for Children* by Michael J. Caduto and Joseph Bruchac (Golden, Colorado: Fulcrum Publishing, 1991). For copies of this book, as well as related books and music, contact: Michael Caduto, P. O. Box 1052, Norwich, VT 05055, USA. Telephone/fax: (802) 649-1815.

Staff Editor: Kurt Austin

Interior Design: Doug Burnett

Cover Design: Jenny Jensen Greenleaf

NCTE Stock Number: 51833-3050

Library of Congress Cataloging-in-Publication Data

Teaching for a tolerant world, grades K–6: essays and resources/
  Judith P. Robertson, editor, and the Committee on Teaching about
  Genocide and Intolerance of the National Council of Teachers of
  English.
      p. cm.
    Includes bibliographical references and index.
    ISBN 0-8141-5183-3 (pbk.)
      1. Toleration—Study and teaching (Elementary)—United States.
  2. Prejudices—Study and teaching (Elementary)—United States.
  3. Genocide—Study and teaching (Elementary)—United States.
  4. Discrimination—Study and teaching (Elementary)—United States.
  5. Multicultural education—United States. I. Robertson, Judith P.,
  1951–   . II. National Council of Teachers of English. Committee on
  Teaching about Genocide and Intolerance.
  HM1271.T43 1999
  372.83—dc21   99-16881
                                                               CIP

לבעלי

אברהם

באהבה

Contents

Acknowledgments

In addition to the contributors, I would like to thank the following individuals for their contributions to this volume: Carol Danks, for having the vision and patience to lead the project; Allan Kathnelson, Roger Simon, and Tim Stanley for their assistance in reviewing manuscripts; Rita Gero for her unrelenting tenacity in the pursuit of elusive citations; members of the NCTE Committee on Teaching about Genocide and Intolerance for the lengthy discussions we had at various stages in the process: Marjorie Bingham, Jean Boreen, Grace Caporino, Carol Danks, Galene Erickson, Joseph Hawkins Jr., David Haynes, Caroline Heller, Claudia Katz, Thomas Klein, Rochmanna Miller, Sybil Milton, Joan Peterson, Leatrice Rabinsky, Becky Reimer, Rose Rudnitski, and Samuel Totten; and NCTE staff who provided guidance and support. Marlo Welshons and my editor at NCTE, Kurt Austin, have been particularly helpful and gracious in their suggestions.

I Guidelines on Teaching about Genocide and Intolerance through Language Arts/English Studies Education

Editor's Introduction: On Constructing Memory and Hope in Childhood

Judith P. Robertson
University of Ottawa

In an article entitled "Meandering in a Moral Maze" (*Radical Philosophy* 83: 45–46), Anthony Arblaster makes the point that we have lived through what reasonably has been called "a long century of violence," which, as far as killing, cruelty, and suffering are concerned, is by no means over. Yet education has been oddly reluctant to investigate violence, whether the concept, its nature and causes, or its implications for learning. *Teaching for a Tolerant World, Grades K–6* asks what it means to take seriously pedagogy's obligation to construct memory and hope in children through uses of literary texts about violence, and to examine this ideal against the articulations of teachers and children who struggle to define and to delimit the representations that best capture the meaning of extreme-limit mass suffering. The volume is intended for elementary language arts teachers and teacher educators, and presents multiple and sometimes conflicting perspectives on the following issues: the uses of picture books and novels for children about intolerance and genocide; the terms and conditions of constructing social memory through commemorative narratives written for children; the pedagogical uses or abuses of discourses of "readiness" for maintaining boundaries on questions of what level of horror and how to represent survivor testimonies to children; and the problem that education's desire to "enlighten" children with knowledge as a way of freeing them from the inhibiting power of myth or silence must give way to the fact that children and teachers may have internal resistances to knowledge that "says more" than knowledge itself can grasp.

The pedagogical imperative that this volume tries to answer emerged from an NCTE resolution at the 1993 Annual Convention in Pittsburgh in which the group's charge stated:

> To develop and submit for publication materials on the literature of genocide and intolerance; to include in the materials components such as compilations of resources (e.g., bibliographies, visual media, lists of agencies and associations) and materials on how to teach pertinent literary works.

The eighteen-member Committee on Teaching about Genocide and Intolerance was created in response to this resolution, with Carol Danks as Chair. The committee began its work at the 1994 Annual Convention in Orlando, presented its emerging framework at a half-day workshop in San Diego in 1995, and met again in Chicago in 1996, in Detroit in 1997, and in Nashville in 1998 to review, debate, and struggle with the pedagogical issues involved in the charge to educate about genocide and intolerance. As a result of these efforts, members developed a conceptual scheme for the three books in this series—one for elementary teachers, one for middle school teachers, and one for secondary teachers. Editors for each volume served as committee members and solicited contributions from teachers and teacher educators across North America. The resulting volumes present guidelines, essays, and resource sections that explicitly explore the imperative and means by which memory and possibility may be bequeathed to children and adolescents through the study of literary texts now and in the future.

Following the Editor's Introduction in Section One of this volume is an essay entitled "Guidelines for Teaching about Intolerance and Genocide." Grace Caporino and Rose Rudnitski co-authored this piece with input from other committee members. The guidelines are meant to underscore the idea that public understanding even in young children gets aired, transferred, and shaped through literature and art, and that the task of transmitting the memory of those who are no longer "here" must be engaged thoughtfully and with care by educators. Issues pertaining to the particular difficulties of this legacy with elementary children get addressed in the Guidelines and in subsequent sections of the volume.

Section Two is entitled "Learning about Intolerance and Genocide: Questions of Pedagogy." This section explicitly addresses the uncertainties confronted by educators who seek to shape collective memory through its inscription in literature and other media for young children. Contributors to this section write from experiences that resonate with the observation of Efraim Sicher and others that literature gives space in the imagination for what cannot be said otherwise, and for what has not been experienced directly but must be reconstructed or even invented (Sicher 1998, 169). Problematically, what becomes disconcertingly clear in teacher accounts of classroom work is that in spite of the transformative potential that survivor stories and testimonies offer, their use in learning experiences with elementary children is anything but straightforward. In worst-case scenarios, the act of pedagogical stumbling (through ignorance of history, through the outright repression of knowledge, through the invasion of the space of children's subjectivity by telling them too much or too little about the horror, or through the illusion that we can possibly fully know the event of intolerance or genocide we are teaching about) can actually betray our ethical intentions.

The articles in this and other sections connect with one another through their emphasis on the pedagogical experience of doubt, uncertainty, and hope when teaching children about genocide and intolerance. Difficulties presented include the obvious ones of when and how to respond to children's questions about histories of mass suffering or murder. They include recognition of the widespread availability of curricular materials that may deform or naturalize historical truth. They address the danger of deadening children's senses through burdening them with unrelenting images of loss or horror. They provide grounded instances of dealing educatively as teachers and parents with "the question child" whose natural and spontaneous curiosity may provoke in adults a jumbled hansard of emotion that feels like anything but mature or self-assured response. And they perhaps worry too little about the possibility of muting the moral gravity and complexity of genocide through well-intentioned emphases on rescuing and salvation. Center stage within this pedagogical arena of hope, error, and struggle is a theme that appears to contest the very NCTE initiative that this book was intended to embody: that is, to develop guidelines for elementary teachers on teaching about genocide and intolerance. Most of the contributors to this text strongly refuse the notion that genocide education should be introduced in early elementary years (i.e., primary grades, or grades K–3). Others engage in a careful questioning and critique of the notion of educating for tolerance—an impulse that they expose as implicitly constituted by a conceptual/moral error that is in itself stubbornly elitist in effect.

Notwithstanding the controversies embodied in these important discussions, historical accuracy and representation are key terms to the opening contribution of Section Two. Samuel Totten's "Defining Genocide: Words Do Matter" provides a thoughtful history of the use of the term *genocide,* and warns against the premature introduction or careless misuse or conflation of this term in elementary education. In "A Letter to My Children: Historical Memory and the Silences of Childhood," Timothy Stanley reflects on the personal conflicts that ensued when he was asked by his eight-year-old daughter, "Daddy, what are Nazis?" He provides a conflicted and passionate account of the need to respond to children's difficult questions, and what might constitute an ethical response.

If Tim Stanley's piece reminds teachers that children's psyches are formed in and through the social, Yeuk Yi Pang's contribution, "To Know Me, Read My Story. To Respect Me, Read It Well," builds on the claim through its emphasis on how narratives can serve as a foundation to children's moral learning. She shows how well-known children's books can be used to provide classroom-based interventions for teaching children to reason ethically about just interactions with others. Two other pieces in this section return to this theme. In "Rights, Respect, and Responsibility: Toward a Theory of Action in Two Bilingual (Spanish/English) Classrooms," Beth Yeager, Irene Pattenaude, Louise Jennings, and María Fránquiz describe bilingual elementary-grade classrooms in which Holocaust study through literature became the instigator for children's moral insight and action. Following this essay, Debbie Miller and Anne K. Goudvis discuss their use of stories to develop primary school children's understanding of concepts related to the value of human life and practices of community action.

One of the hard dilemmas I experienced in putting together this text was my awareness of the danger of appearing to naturalize the terrible and inhuman losses experienced by the victims of particular genocides by placing these together in one volume. Another obstacle was that by including contributions that illustrate the importance of teaching young children respect for all living things, I would be seen to be endorsing a perspective that subsumes an event like the Holocaust under a discourse that reflexively links it with infractions of a less particular or heinous kind. In attempting to remain true to the principle of human decency and respect for the particularity of human sufferings, as well as to my insights about young children's learning through language, I drew on the following principles.

The contributors to this volume argue that literary education for young children needs to focus on showing how stories can organize the world in ways that entrench certain interests over others (Stuckey 1991); that literary education needs to be sustained by moral concerns that involve how the language of texts acts as an instrument—one that can enact or deny justice, equality, mercy, and love (Purpel 1989; Shannon 1989; Courts 1991); that language ultimately has the capacity to produce what it names (Butler 1994); and that through repetition, stories and representations can either support or disrupt oppressive ways of being with people and the environment (Haraway 1989). This theoretical paradigm is admittedly broad. It is my hope and desire that its inclusions do not show a disrespect for the tragic dimensions of loss or memorialization within any community.

It is in the spirit of such reasoning that Section Two includes an important contribution by Anne C. Bell and Constance L. Russell entitled "Life Ties: Disrupting Anthropocentrism in Language Arts Education." Here, the authors show how language and stories divide humans from natural worlds and structure ways of thinking which naturalize for young children the idea of the inevitability of human domination and aggressivity. Respecting a similar imperative, beginning teacher Christine Connelly in "Inviting/Supporting Critical Praxis through Picture Books: 'Possibility' in Monica Hughes's *A Handful of Seeds*" envisions a literary/environmental study unit for elementary children that uses a picture book and illustrations to focus on concepts related to how people can debase one another, how dictatorial governments can participate in the legislation and authorization of violence against particular groups, and the resultant effects of impoverishment, disenfranchisement, or death for some children. Connelly's piece focuses on critical pedagogy through language arts, and on the possibilities of hope as the politicization of young consciousness occurs through identification with the protagonist as a source of radical resistance and renewal.

As suggested above, the uncertainty that had to be confronted as an essential part of the experience of envisioning this text is inextricably entangled with the uncertainty that has to be faced in teaching about issues of genocide and intolerance. For teachers working in elementary settings, resistances to uncertainty in teaching continually get mobilized in disheartening ways. There is the stubborn tendency for others not to be able to imagine conceptual clarity in those of us who work with young children. There is the reality that school culture does not always make conceptual clarity a necessary part of everyday elementary school life. There is the impulse to flee when we are asked as elementary teachers to clarify our thoughts on issues. There is the defensive appeal of imagining that the realms of educational theory and practice exist somehow as separate entities from each other, and the tendency to ascribe a higher truth value to one or the other. Even more pronounced is the difficulty of accepting that in the process of teaching ourselves difficult knowledge in order to support the learning of others, there is a great deal of self-righteous posturing, denial, or ignorance that must be faced. At the heart of the issue of what to tell children, then, is the difficult acknowledgment that in the aftermath of histories of horror, knowledge of genocide is impossible to assimilate at a certain level because its lessons of indifference, cowardice, stupidity, moral detachment, and cruelty fly in the face of who we believe we are and who we want to be (Avni 1995, 215).

This volume dedicates itself to working with children through literature to address the ensuing moral and historical imperatives of

these predicaments. In the spirit of offering a critique of facile answers, April Nauman in "Re-Reading the Bad Guys: Sixth Graders'
Understanding of Nazi Soldiers in *Number the Stars*" describes a time
in which literary study of the Holocaust became the focus of difficult
historical and moral learning for upper elementary children, and a
wrenching odyssey for herself. Similarly, Michele Dunlap "talks
back" by exposing the investments that teachers bring to particular
beliefs that may be injurious in effect for children. In "Tolerance and
Intolerance for African American Children and Families: Lessons
from the Movie *Crooklyn*," Dunlap presents a disturbing study in
which she found fantasies of authority and stereotype in white
beginning teachers who watched a movie about a black family.
Dunlap exhorts us to examine our own thinking before we set out
narrowly to educate children about intolerance.

Sharon Todd also reminds readers that teachers inhabit a social
world in which we struggle within a network of stories and images
that create psychological fictions whose effects can be deleterious. In
"Educating beyond Tolerance: Reading Media Images of the *Hijab*,"
she draws on psychoanalytic notions of learning to explore how
readers make meaning through interactions with media images of
Muslim women's headdresses. She proposes educational strategies
for disrupting the oppressive social and psychological relations
associated with racist and nationalist discourse. Similarly, in "Nightmare Issues: Children's Responses to Racism and Genocide in Literature," Vicki Zack uses excerpts of children's responses to literature to
reflect on the complexities of their and her learning as they explore
stories relating to the mass destruction of European Jewry (the
Shoah), and the black African diaspora and experience of slavery. In
"Daniel Pinkwater's *Wingman*: Exploring Conflict-Resolution Strategies through Multiethnic Literature," Belinda Yun-Ying Louie and
Douglas Louie describe how fourth-grade students engaged with the
notion of conflict through novel study. Their contribution serves as a
reflection on how a short novel may be used to engage preadolescent
children in voicing and developing alternative practices of representation and problem solving.

Section Three of the book is called "On Facing Uncertainty in
Teaching." It differs from Section Two in the ways in which contributing authors attempt to conceptualize not so much the "how to" of
education about genocide and intolerance, but rather the "why to" in
the formulation of pedagogical responses to uncertainty. Contributing authors in this section attempt to illumine the principles that
organize lived response to traumatic learning in the classroom. P. J.
Nomathemba Seme opens with "South African Teachers' and Students' Resiliency in Combating Apartheid Violence." In a brave first-
person retelling of classroom-based research, Seme examines the

effects on teachers and first-grade students of learning to read within a racist war-zone, and emphasizes the principles of resistance, solidarity, hope, and spirituality.

In "Teaching Risky Stories: Remembering Mass Destruction through Children's Literature," Roger I. Simon and Wendy Armitage Simon explore such key terms as shadow texts, pedagogical responsibility, and invasion of the space of childhood subjectivity through education about genocide. The authors make painfully clear the psychological risks for children reading picture books and novels about historical incidents of loss, and present pedagogical principles for assisting learners to work through questions and pain in risky stories such as *Daniel's Story* or *Faithful Elephants*. Working from a slightly different perspective, Judith P. Robertson's essay, "Teaching about Worlds of Hurt through Encounters with Literature: Reflections on Pedagogy," presents evidence of how beginning elementary language arts teachers experience the dangers and possibilities of working with Gary Paulsen's *Nightjohn*. She utilizes concepts from psychoanalysis to illumine how unconscious resistance to unbearable knowledge about human behavior plays itself out in instances of reading and learning to teach.

Section Three thus underscores the pedagogical point that before undertaking to teach students about worlds of hurt through story, educators need to anticipate the difficulties they will encounter along the way. Readers may respond to disturbing knowledge about the human condition by showing signs of emotional regression, social divisiveness, psychological paralysis, or grief. The knowledge that genocides unfold within general conditions of betrayal and absence of coordinated rescue may cause learners unwittingly to seek repose in myths of salvation or redemption. It is this theme that gets examined by Deborah Britzman in "Dimensions of a Lonely Discovery: Anne Frank and the Question of Pedagogy." Britzman studies the history of *The Diary of Anne Frank* in order to make the painful observation that testimonies of loss confer significant difficulties to inheritors who are charged with the task of interpreting and passing down the story to future generations; and that education is not best served through work in elementary classrooms that reproduces in children naive fantasies of rescuing or idealism.

Section Four of the text is entitled "Additional Resources," and it is here that the contributors to this volume acknowledge that teaching must be viewed not as transmitting but as accessing knowledge. According to Shoshana Felman, "Each great subject has a turning point contained within it, and that turning point has to be met. The question for the teacher is, then, on the one hand, how to access, how *not to foreclose* the crisis, and, on the other hand, how to *contain it*, how much crisis can the class sustain" (Felman and Laub

1992, 54). Elementary teachers must personally incorporate or inhabit the texts of difficult knowledge before making decisions about which of these texts to share with children.

Sarah-Hope Parmeter opens with "Uncloseting the Classroom Library: An Annotated Bibliography of Teacher Resources," in which she reviews available picture books and novels for teaching about sexual difference, and she illumines her grounds for selection. She includes a comprehensive list of educational resources for addressing issues related to gay, lesbian, and bisexual affectional identity. Dona J. Helmer, in "Mirror, Mirror on the Wall, Who Is the Fairest One of All? Using Children's Literature to Teach about Aging," addresses the issue of the marginalization of elderly persons in North America. She proposes resources and strategies for working with difficulties presented by particular narratives, e.g., those that access knowledge about loneliness, neglect, sickness, or impending death.

Joseph A. Hawkins Jr. and Glenda Valentine are teacher activists who have worked at the Southern Poverty Law Center. Editors of *Teaching Tolerance*, these author-activists and reformers propel us into a world of human, paper, cinematic, and virtual resources for teaching elementary children about past and present African American history and life during the Middle Passage, Reconstruction, and the Civil Rights Era. Similarly, Judith P. Robertson and Bernard W. Andrews present information on accessing pedagogical resources for disrupting sexism and stereotypical gender identifications in young children. Their chapter is entitled "How Long Will Dennis Still Be a Menace? Teacher Resources for Deregulating Gender Roles in Elementary Classrooms." Elspeth Ross follows with "From Cupboard to Classroom: First Nations Resources." Social activist, writer, and adoptive parent of Aboriginal children, Ross presents a comprehensive discussion (complete with annotations, addresses, and phone numbers) of anti-racist books and books without bias about Native people. Finally, Karen Shawn's "What Should They Read, and When Should They Read It? A Selective Review of Holocaust Literature for Students in Grades 2 through 6," presents selection criteria and annotations for novels, photo essays, autobiographies, memoirs, and short story collections recommended for elementary Holocaust education. These chapters are tied together by the insistence that in order to reclaim or help children reclaim their ties to community and memory, it is necessary as a teacher to inscribe oneself into its shared narratives (Avni 1995, 213).

I wish to express my appreciation to the editors and committee members at the National Council of Teachers of English, and to the contributing authors of *Teaching for a Tolerant World, Grades K–6* for joining with me to confront all of the difficult vulnerabilities in bringing to fruition this project. May the lives of all of those who have struggled for justice in the world be an ongoing source of blessing and inspiration to the teachers and children whose wakefulness is touched by this book.

Works Cited

Arblaster, Anthony. 1998. "Meandering in a Moral Maze." *Radical Philosophy* 83: 45–46.

Avni, Ora. 1995. "Beyond Psychoanalysis: Elie Wiesel's *Night* in Historical Perspective." In *Auschwitz and After: Race, Culture and "The Jewish Question" in France,* edited by Lawrence D. Kritzman, 203–218. New York: Routledge.

Butler, Judith. 1994. "Gender as Performance." *Radical Philosophy* 67: 32–40.

Courts, Patrick L. 1991. *Literacy and Empowerment: The Meaning Makers.* New York: Bergin & Garvey.

Felman, Shoshana, and Dori Laub. 1992. *Testimony: Crises of Witnessing in Literature, Psychoanalysis, and History.* London: Routledge.

Haraway, Donna. 1989. *Primate Visions: Gender, Race, and Nature in the World of Modern Science.* New York: Routledge.

Purpel, David E. 1989. *The Moral and Spiritual Crisis in Education: A Curriculum for Justice and Compassion in Education.* New York: Bergin & Garvey.

Shannon, Patrick. 1989. *Broken Promises: Reading Instruction in Twentieth Century America.* Granby, MA: Bergin & Garvey.

Sicher, Efraim. 1998. "In the Shadow of Memory: Second Generation Writers and Artists and the Shaping of Holocaust Memory in Israel and America." *Judaism: A Quarterly Journal of Jewish Life and Thought* 186 (47:2): 169–85.

Stuckey, J. Elspeth. 1991. *The Violence of Literacy.* Portsmouth, NH: Boynton/ Cook.

General Guidelines for Teaching about Intolerance and Genocide

Grace M. Caporino
Carmel High School, Carmel, New York

Rose A. Rudnitski
State University of New York at New Paltz

Rationale
The opposite of goodness is not evil; it is indifference to evil.

Elie Wiesel

Why Use Literature, Language, and Composition to Teach about Genocide and Intolerance in the English/ Language Arts Classroom?

The NCTE Committee on Genocide and Intolerance endeavors to acknowledge and affirm the role of the English and language arts teacher in developing curriculum for teaching about genocide and intolerance. Fundamental to this pedagogy is the need to examine the social and linguistic dynamics of intolerance and to promote tolerance and acceptance of all racial, religious, ethnic, and social groups. We salute our colleagues who take up the challenge to engage students in the study of this complex topic. We advance the view that literature can be morally powerful, and through the refractory lens of discourse or of writing, we can help our students understand life as it should be. Literature gives space to the human imagination to configure what has not been experienced directly, and moves individuals to act in the interest of the common good. In alluding to its potency, Nel Noddings states,

> Not only does literature provide a possible starting point for critical thinking, it also gives a place to passion and to passionate commitment . . . We have to feel something that prompts us to ask, "What

A slightly different version of this essay also appeared in *Teaching for a Tolerant World, Grades 9–12: Essays and Resources* (Urbana, IL: NCTE, 1999).

are you going through?" and we have to feel something again when we hear the answer, if we are to respond appropriately. (161)

We face a new century with the belief that English and language arts teachers perform a vital role by meeting the challenge of teaching about intolerance and genocide, and by evoking the requisite passion in young people to reflect and to act in the interest of the common good.

History shows us that acts of intolerance can escalate and may, in extremity, culminate in genocide. Even in instances where escalation does not rise to the level of genocide, its harmful effects erode the principles of freedom and the inalienable rights of all people. Curriculum and instruction geared toward teaching acceptance and valuing others helps de-escalate the progression toward violence and helps to humanize rather than dehumanize targets of intolerance. Without dehumanization, genocide is impossible. With humanization, genocide is less likely.

A fundamental principle of this committee is that teaching about acceptance and value for others sensitizes students to events of intolerance and genocide. Reading, discussing, and writing about texts that deal with intolerance and genocide help students learn about human deeds of violence throughout history, and illumine parallels existing in human behaviors that make hatred and suffering possible today. Engaging with this material in these ways enables students to clarify and articulate their questions, thoughts, and feelings about intolerance. This pedagogy promotes the idea that suffering inflicted by humans on humans is *not* inevitable and that transformative behavior *can* be an expected outcome. These curricular approaches foster attitudes that strengthen the fibers of a democratic society and inspire in students an awareness of their essential roles as citizens in the global community.

It is in the English/language arts classroom that students encounter linguistic and literary experiences that elevate and debase our humanity. It is through the medium of language that intolerance initially manifests itself. Language is used in propaganda and in influencing public opinion. It is basic to the development of values, the institution of laws, as well as the formation of public policy. Language has the potential to liberate or to imprison. The language arts teacher facilitates both an understanding of and a critical response to such language as it occurs in student surroundings and through the critical analysis of literature. The aim of the English studies/language arts classroom is to invite informed dialogue and reflection on language and literature so that students and teachers examine the ways persons and groups build respect for differences or contribute to the forces of hate.

Curricular Premises

Language has been used throughout history in the service of deception, manipulation, and domination of individuals and groups. It can also be used by victims, advocates, and activists as a means of resistance, education, and liberation.

Language thus functions as a social and historical medium that can limit or expand human possibility, depending on the way language is organized to mark, mythologize, or delimit what it means to be human.

Literature goes beyond representing a culture or a period. It is universal, transcending time and place, and as such has a lasting, shaping influence on readers.

Similarly, other media such as newspapers, films, art, and music can be used to influence human activity. In classrooms they can also be used to examine the context of a historical event and the factors that helped to shape it.

Literature teaching therefore can be viewed as a transformative social practice through which students (along a developmental continuum from primary through secondary levels) can imagine how things could be otherwise and come to recognize that the possibility exists for a better world.

Literature functions not only as an aesthetic form, but also as social discourse. Texts play with meanings in a way that reflects and shapes cultural practices and, in many ways, represent the emotional and cultural memory of humankind.

For older elementary learners (i.e., grades 4 to 6), emphasis is placed on nonfiction and testimony for the literary responses to genocide, as eyewitness accounts mediate student challenges to truthfulness of events that by their nature are unbelievable. For younger elementary students (i.e., grade 2 and up), historically accurate fictional renderings that do not overburden the reader with graphic images of suffering and loss are suitable.

Literature engages the human character. It not only evokes a response, it also helps to illuminate history because it frequently serves as a response to it. Literature responds to this human record of history and evokes further responses in young readers by bringing people to life and by putting a human face on the history. It also helps us to see what might be.

Literature resonates, helping us to see and know ourselves. It often does more, but it should not do less.

Through writing, students can express, analyze, refine, and clarify their own emotional responses to issues of difficult knowledge and engage in the critical reflection that leads to personal transformation.

Film and electronic media use techniques of editing, narrative, and image construction to create meanings in ways that are similar to printed texts. Students' analysis of media deepens their understanding of the human condition at a given time. It also helps students learn how stories can be framed in multiple ways that have different effects.

Pedagogical Guidelines

Our basic premise is that teacher judgment is central to teaching about genocide and intolerance. It is only through systematic observation, assessment, and instruction that elementary teachers can determine what is appropriate for students and what is not. These guidelines are offered in support of such assessment and instruction as suggestions for implementation based on the classroom teacher's professional judgment. Teacher discretion informs the application of these guidelines before, during, or after reading, viewing, writing, or discussion. Teacher judgment determines which guidelines are developmentally appropriate for elementary, middle, and secondary school levels. Young children should not be burdened with images of horror, nor should they be made to learn about the world in ways that diminish hope. At the same time, age appropriateness for educating about genocide and intolerance has less to do with chronological age than with the emotional readiness children demonstrate as evidenced directly by their questions and observations.

In the following presentation of guidelines for teaching about genocide and intolerance, the proposed stages of language arts instruction are given after each guideline. "B" designates that the activity should occur *before* the learning experience, "D" designates *during*, and "A" designates *after*.

Explore with students reasons for studying intolerance and genocide. Build on student initiatives and understandings at the beginning of the study in order to give them greater ownership of the subject matter. **B**

Determine what purpose you have in mind when selecting readings for a unit. **B**

Recognize that your ability to explain your purpose for studying intolerance and genocide will help you explain the merits of such learning to students, parents, administrators, and fellow teachers. Before planning each learning experience, set a clear purpose. Keep in mind that there are two levels of purpose setting: setting the purpose for choosing the literary piece, and setting the purpose for learning activities. **B**

Ascertain through discussion and observation what students appear to know and what they do not know about particular groups of people and their cultural, religious, and historical experiences. **B, D**

Communicate with supervisors, colleagues, and parents throughout the unit. Be open to input from parents and the community. Be prepared to dialogue with others beyond the classroom about how to support the children's learning and difficult questions during this time. **D, B, A**

Begin teaching this topic with the belief that you will learn along with your students. **B**

When selecting picture books or novels, consider authenticity, literary merit, and age appropriateness. For age appropriateness, readings with a youthful narrator voice or sensibility are generally more suitable. The presentation of story should not overwhelm the young reader with senseless or graphic images of hopelessness or destruction.
  Considerations of literary merit include:

(1) richness of detail in scenes and characterization

(2) the existence of young characters and situations with which reader can identify

(3) poetic or figurative language that is accessible in terms of the child's reading ability

(4) coherent narrative organization in which the structure of the story is understandable

(5) descriptive density in the storytelling that evokes a powerful response in readers or listeners

(6) themes of struggle, hope, compassion, love, dignity, help, survival, and difficulty that stimulate the senses of young readers and provoke their curiosity and desire to learn more because the story works in qualifying ways on issues that resonate. **B, D**

For children in grades 4 to 6, eyewitness accounts—i.e., survivor memoirs, autobiographies, testimonies, documentaries, or fiction—that are of verifiable origin or authorship are of primary importance. **B, D**

Having students read fewer works deeply and thoughtfully, giving ample time for discussion and writing, supports the development of ideas and the expression of uncertainties. **D**

Help students understand that momentous events are experienced and integrated in different ways by different people. Allow children to read various versions of events in order to help them develop skills of reasoning, careful listening, and concerned emotional response. **B, D, A**

Provide older elementary students (i.e., grades 4 to 6) access to different genres, voices, and primary documents during the course of study. This provides a variety of narrative perspectives and entry points to issues. **B, D**

Research and try to clarify in your own mind the meanings of the following terms. Be prepared to define and redefine them with children: prejudice, stereotyping, blind obedience, genocide, racism, discrimination, antilocution, homophobia, persecution, anti-Semitism, intolerance, justice, community, listening, dialogue, hope. These words associate with meanings that provide the basis for conceptual frameworks upon which children build understandings. **B, D, A**

Without reducing the singularity and uniqueness of different instances of mass suffering or murder, emphasize the universal patterns inherent in intolerance and in the paths to genocide. Some patterns that include characteristics that are thought to be possible precursors of acts of genocide are:

(1) antilocution

(2) scapegoating

(3) out-group considered outsider

(4) racist ideology

(Frelick, 75–76) **B, D, A**

Provide an accurate historical context in which to situate the literature, the writing, the media, and the language study. **B, D**

Teach about these issues and events with the resolve that education may prevent their recurrence if those who experience this education are willing to embrace their civic and moral responsibilities. **B, D, A**

Recognize that student response—i.e., verbalization, questions, dialogue—is an integral part of the pedagogy. **B, D, A**

Avoid comparisons and ranking of pain which propose that any one group suffered more than another. **D, A**

Connect issues of intolerance to both past and current North American experiences. **D, A**

Avoid simulations. When students imitate or recreate historical events such as the Middle Passage, selection, or deportation, they are susceptible to a false premise. The underlying assumption is that the shift from the cognitive to the experiential bridges a gap and brings students closer to knowing the event. Yet English and language arts teachers dwell in the land of words, and processing knowledge through verbal learning is a distinctive hallmark of our discipline with time-honored supremacy over the "make-believe" style of presentation. While reenactment and role-play may arise spontaneously in the classroom, exploration through reading creates a deeper and more lasting learning experience. Further, the activity of simulation flies in the face of the research which shows that survivors of traumatic episodes of intolerance and genocide often grapple with their own choice of language to convey or to relive these events, as the nature of trauma is such that it shocks and numbs so much that it admits no reenactment. The experience of reading texts differs fundamentally from simulations which inject a "hands-on," sporty feel to a topic that is inherently serious. Student reading of selections and analyses of media responses with varying perspectives of events of intolerance and genocide can do more to facilitate understanding than reductive attempts at recreation or simulation. **D**

The above guideline does not exclude the use of the genre of drama. For children in upper elementary classrooms, plays read aloud or enacted by students are appropriate pedagogical activities. Here, the guideline above on text selection and literary merit applies. **D**

Encourage students to reflect, orally and in writing, on what they have read or viewed so they can articulate for themselves and others what it means. **D, A**

Emphasize critical thinking in discussions and activities. **B, D, A**

Be prepared for any response. Responses may include grief, silence, outrage, depression, indifference, paralysis, and denial. These responses signal the chance to engage with and to support children's learning. **D, A**

Silence or refusal to read a particular text is an appropriate and honest response in elementary children that deserves acknowledgment and respect. **D, A**

Analyze the ways that language is used to corrupt and subvert human rights and human dignity, and also the ways in which language can promote intolerance. Relate to euphemisms (word substitutions) currently employed to diminish the qualities attributed to groups of people. **D, A**

Analyze the roles of victim, murderer, perpetrator, resister, voyeur, collaborator, bystander, advocate, and rescuer/activist, which evoke the question, "Which are we most likely to have become?" (Cynthia Ozick xi). Emphasize that like all categories, these categories are not rigid and inflexible. **B, D, A**

Refrain from simplifying the complex issues which arise from studying examples of intolerance and genocide. Human behavior is often complicated by historical and social forces. Beware of easy answers. Many questions raised have pedagogical merit in themselves and may not require or have definitive answers. **D, A**

Differentiate gratuitous violence from deliberate violence. Students may have a desensitized view of violence because they have been exposed to so much in the media. Teacher response to typical student comments about images of brutality inherent in this study such as "pretty neat" or "ugh" are important. Such comments should not be ignored and present an opportunity to listen to the student's intended meaning, and to challenge his or her assumptions if necessary. **D, A**

Provide closure, while at the same time understanding that knowledge of human suffering can open emotional wounds that do not close easily. **A**

Help students take measure of what they have learned. **D, A**

Literature reflects the emotional memory of humankind. It engages human character with all its grandeur, anguish, weaknesses, and depravity, and provides us with the most profound understanding of the human and experiential dimensions of existence.

Our Commitment

Teaching about genocide and intolerance is not easy. Perhaps that is why many of us avoid it. However, we are committed to bringing these concepts into the classroom precisely because they matter, despite their difficulty. It is a challenge to survive in this world as a whole human being with principles and integrity, especially when immersed in an environment rife with unprincipled, intolerant behavior. Incidents of intolerance and genocide are occurring with more frequency worldwide than at any other time in history. How we respond to these events is a measure of our own humanity. How we teach our children is another. Perhaps we can create a better world through our teaching. Perhaps we can stop just one intolerant act. That possibility is our inspiration.

References

Charny, Israel, and Alan Berger. *Genocide: A Critical Bibliographic Review.* New York: Facts on File Publications, 1988–1991.

Frelick, Bill. "Teaching Genocide as a Contemporary Problem." *Social Science Record* 24.2 (Fall 1987): 74–77.

Noddings, Nel. "Ethics and the Imagination." *A Light in Dark Times: Maxine Greene and the Unfinished Conversation.* Ed. W. Ayers and J. Miller. New York: Teachers College Press, 1998.

Ozick, Cynthia. "Prologue." *Rescuers: Portraits of Moral Courage in the Holocaust.* New York: Holmes & Meier, 1992.

II Learning about Intolerance and Genocide: Questions of Pedagogy

Defining Genocide: Words Do Matter

Samuel Totten
University of Arkansas, Fayetteville

A major concern of many scholars and activists in the field of genocide studies is that there is no overall consensus in regard to how the term *genocide* should be defined. This is a vitally significant issue, for without an agreed-upon definition, combating genocide becomes just that much more difficult. This chapter in no way advocates the introduction of genocide education within early elementary classrooms. Rather, the discussion is intended to alert educators working at the upper elementary levels about the history of struggle around the naming and determination of genocide as a human rights abuse of heinous proportion, and the historical considerations that surround the use of the concept of "genocide" in children's literary learning about mass murder.

Ever since Raphael Lemkin coined the term *genocide* in 1944, various scholars, activists, and governmental officials have been wrestling with the concept in an effort to develop something that is not so inclusive that it is meaningless, but not so exclusive that it denies protection to targeted groups of people. As a result, over the past forty-five years or so scholars have repeatedly recast the definition of genocide in an attempt to either make it more workable, manageable, "analytically rigorous" (Chalk and Jonassohn 1990, 15), and/or to fit within their concept or typology of genocide. At the same time, other terms have been coined in an effort to differentiate between the intent and scope of various types of crimes against humanity. Among these are *ethnocide, cultural genocide, selective genocide, genocidal process*, and *genocidal massacres*. Efforts by scholars to develop a theoretically sound *and*, at the same time, practical definition of genocide, continue to this day.

Portions of this essay appeared previously as "Genocide: Definitional Issues" in *The CSERV Bulletin: Journal of the Center for the Study of Ethnic and Racial Violence* 3(1), 1994. The essay also appears, in a slightly different form, in *Teaching for a Tolerant World, Grades 9–12: Essays and Resources* (Urbana, IL: NCTE, 1999).

Lemkin, a Polish Jewish émigré and a noted law professor at Yale and Duke Universities who waged a one-man crusade for establishment of an international convention against the perpetration of genocide, formed the term *genocide* by combining the Greek *genos* (race, tribe) and the Latin *cide* (killing). In *Axis Rule in Occupied Europe,* Lemkin defined genocide in the following manner:

> Generally speaking, genocide does not necessarily mean the immediate destruction of a nation, except when accomplished by mass killings of all members of a nation. It is intended rather to signify a coordinated plan of different actions aiming at the destruction of essential foundations of the life of national groups with the aim of annihilating the groups themselves. The objectives of such a plan would be the disintegration of the political and social institutions of culture, language, national feelings, religion, economic existence of national groups and the destruction of the personal security, liberty, health, dignity, and even the lives of the individuals belonging to such groups. Genocide is directed against the national group as an entity, and the actions involved are directed at individuals, not in their individual capacity, but as members of the national groups . . . Genocide has two phases: one, destruction of the national pattern of the oppressed group; the other, the imposition of the national pattern of the oppressor. (1944, 79)

In regard to Lemkin's definition, Chalk and Jonassohn have noted that, "Even nonlethal acts that undermined the liberty, dignity, and personal security of members of a group constituted genocide if they contributed to weakening the viability of the group. Under Lemkin's definition, acts of ethnocide—a term coined by the French after [World War II] to cover the destruction of a culture without the killing of its bearers—also qualified as genocide" (1990, 9). Those who have argued against the inclusion of ethnocide under the rubric of genocide suggest that there is a distinct difference between those situations in which people are outright slain and when aspects of a people's culture are destroyed.

Following World War II and the annihilation by the Nazis and their collaborators of approximately six million Jews and five million other people such as the Gypsies, the mentally and physically disabled, Russian prisoners of war, Poles, and other Slavs, the United Nations adopted a resolution on December 9, 1946, calling for international cooperation on the prevention and punishment of genocide. It was the terrible and systematic slaughter perpetrated by the Nazi regime that provoked the United Nations to formally recognize genocide as a crime in international law.

From the outset, however, the development of the UN Genocide Convention was enmeshed in controversy. As Leo Kuper has written, nations with vastly different philosophies, cultures, and "historical experiences and sensitivities to human suffering" (1985, 10) presented various interpretations as to what constituted genocide, and argued in favor of a definition and wording in the Convention that fit their particular perspective(s). The arguments and counterarguments resulted in what can best be described as a "compromise definition."

On December 11, 1946, the United Nations General Assembly passed this initial resolution:

> Genocide is a denial of the right of existence of entire human groups, as homicide is the denial of the right to live of individual human beings . . . Many instances of such crimes of genocide have occurred, when racial, religious, political, and other groups have been destroyed entirely or in part . . .
>
> The General Assembly therefore, affirms that genocide is a crime under international law which the civilized world condemns, for the commission of which principals and accomplices—whether private individuals, public officials or statesmen, and whether the crime is committed on religious, racial, political or any other grounds—are punishable. (Kuper 1981, 23)

Of the utmost significance here is that while this resolution "significantly narrowed Lemkin's definition of genocide by downplaying ethnocide as one of its components, . . . at the same time, it broadened the definition by adding a new category of victims—'political and other groups'—to Lemkin's list" (Chalk and Jonassohn 1990, 10).

However, the Soviet Union, Poland, and other nations argued against the inclusion of political groups, claiming that their inclusion would not conform "with the scientific definition of genocide and would, in practice, distort the perspective in which the crime should be viewed and impair the efficacy of the Convention" (Kuper 1981, 25). The Soviets feared that if political groups were protected under the Convention then the Soviet Union could be found culpable for the millions of people it murdered due to their political beliefs. The Poles also asserted that "the inclusion of provisions relating to political groups, which because of their mutability and lack of distinguishing characteristics did not lend themselves to definition," would weaken and blur the whole Convention (Kuper 1981, 26).

The upshot is that political and social groups were excluded from the Convention. The sagacity of excluding such groups has been questioned, and in some cases outright criticized, by numerous scholars. Others, however, believe that the exclusion of political groups from the Convention was a sound move. For example, Lawrence LeBlanc supports the exclusion of political groups because of the "'difficulty inherent in selecting criteria for determining what constitutes a political group,' their instability over time, the right of the state to protect itself, and the potential misuses of genocide-labeling of antagonists in war and political conflict" (1988, 292–94). (For a more detailed discussion of the debate surrounding the UN Convention on Genocide, see the chapter entitled "The Genocide Convention" in Leo Kuper's (1981) *Genocide*, pp. 19–39.)

On December 9, 1948, the Convention on Genocide was approved by the General Assembly of the United Nations. The Convention on Genocide defines genocide as follows:

> In the present Convention, genocide means any of the following acts committed with the intent to destroy, in whole or in part, a national, ethnical, racial or religious group, as such:
>
> a. Killing members of the group;
> b. Causing serious bodily or mental harm to members of the group;
> c. Deliberately inflicting on the group conditions of life calculated to bring about its physical destruction in whole or in part;
> d. Imposing measures intended to prevent births within the group;
> e. Forcibly transferring children of the group to another group.

As Kuper perspicaciously notes, "The Genocide Convention . . . draws no distinction between types of genocide, because it seeks to define the elements they share in common: it differentiates only the means" (1985, 150).

Frank Chalk and Kurt Jonassohn (1990), a historian and sociologist respectively, have written a solid critique of some of the key concerns scholars have with the United Nations' definition of genocide. In addition to addressing the exclusion of political and social groups, they also note that "it makes no distinction between violence intended to annihilate a group and nonlethal attacks on members of a group. 'Killing members of the group' and 'deliberately inflicting . . . conditions of life calculated to bring about its physical destruction in whole or in part' are commingled in the definition with causing 'mental harm to members of the group' and 'forcibly transferring children of the group to another group'" (11). Here, again, of course, is the issue as to whether or not ethnocide should be subsumed under the larger definition of genocide.

In his role as Special Rapporteur to the United Nations Sub-Commission on Prevention of Discrimination and Protection of Minorities, Ben Whitaker (1985) has made a number of key recommendations regarding changes that he and others think need to be implemented in order to strengthen the Genocide Convention's definition of genocide. It is their hope that such changes will ultimately strengthen the efforts of intervention and prevention when genocide rears its ugly face. These changes include but are not limited to re-consideration by the UN as to whether cultural ethnocide should be included under the Genocide Convention (17); re-consideration by the UN as to the possibility of including political and other groups under the Genocide Convention or "in the absence of consensus [the inclusion of] this provision in an additional optional protocol" (19); and, at the end of Article II of the Convention the addition of such words as "In any of the above conduct, a conscious act or acts of advertent omission may be as culpable as an act of commission" (20). As Whitaker (1985) stated earlier in the report, "In certain cases, calculated neglect or negligence may be sufficient to destroy a designated group wholly or partially through, for instance, famine or disease" (20). (For a more thorough discussion of these points and others see Whitaker's (1985) *Revised and Updated Report on the Question of the Prevention and Punishment of the Crime of Genocide.*)

Revised and/or New Definitions of Genocide

In a major study of the UN Convention on Genocide (*The Crime of State*), Pieter N. Drost (1959), a Dutch law professor, was extremely critical that political and other groups were excluded from the UN definition of genocide. He argued that the following definition replace the latter one: genocide constitutes "the deliberate destruction of physical life of individual human beings by reason of their membership of any human collectivity as such" (2:125).

In 1974, Vahakn Dadrian was the first sociologist to put forth a new definition of genocide: "Genocide is the successful attempt by a dominant group, vested with formal authority and/or with preponderant access to the overall resources of power, to reduce by coercion or lethal violence the number of a minority group whose ultimate extermination is held desirable and useful and whose respective vulnerability is a major factor contributing to the decision for genocide" (123). In regard to Dadrian's "definition," Helen Fein, a sociologist, has commented that "Here explanation has usurped definition; furthermore, it is not clear what is to be observed and classed as genocide except that the perpetrator is a representative of the dominant group and the victims are a minority group. This elementary distinction was later outmoded by the Khmer Rouge genocide in Kampuchea" (1990, 13).

In 1980 Irving Horowitz, a sociologist and political scientist, published *Taking Lives: Genocide and State Power*, wherein he argues that genocide is a totalitarian method for gaining national solidarity. His suggestion for revising the UN's definition is as follows: "Genocide is herein defined as a structural and systematic destruction of innocent people by a state bureaucratic apparatus" (17).

In 1985 Israel Charny, a psychologist, developed what he calls a humanistic definition of genocide: "The wanton murder of human beings on the basis of any identity whatsoever that they share—national, ethnic, racial, religious, political, geographical, ideological" (4). Some have argued that this definition is much too broad to be of use in scholarly research and analysis; others, however, agree with Charny that there is a need to focus attention on the need to protect *all* victim groups.

After developing a number of preliminary and working definitions of genocide from the late 1970s on, Fein has settled—for the time being at least—with the following "sociological" definition: "Genocide is sustained purposeful action by a perpetrator to physically destroy a collectivity directly or indirectly, through interdiction of the biological and social reproduction of group members, sustained regardless of the surrender or lack of threat offered by the victim" (1990, 24). Fein comments that her use of the phrase "sustained purposeful action" would exclude single massacres, pogroms, [and] accidental deaths.

After examining all of the above definitions and typologies as well as others, Chalk and Jonassohn (1990) rejected them and developed their own definition and typology. Their definition is as follows: "Genocide is a form of one-sided mass killing in which a state or other authority intends to destroy a group, as that group and membership in it are defined by the perpetrator" (23). As for the rationale for their definition, they state that "We have rejected the UN definition as well as others proposed because we want to confine our field of study to extreme cases. Thus, we hope that the term *ethnocide* will come into wider use for those cases in which a group disappears without mass killing. The suppression of a culture, a language, a religion, and so on is a phenomenon that is analytically different from the physical extermination of a group" (23).

While Fein (1990) applauds the wealth of case studies researched by Chalk and Jonassohn, she has difficulty with some aspects of their definition. For example, she finds the phrase "a state or other authority" too limiting a description of a perpetrator.

In 1991 Charny delivered a paper entitled "A Proposal of a New Encompassing Definition of Genocide: Including New Legal Categories of Accomplices to Genocide, and Genocide as a Result of Ecological Destruction and Abuse" at the first Raphael Lemkin Symposium on Genocide at Yale University Law School in which he presented a new "generic definition" of genocide and a series of subcategories. His "generic definition" is as follows: "Mass killing of substantial numbers of human beings, when not in the course of military action against the military forces of an avowed enemy, under conditions of the essential defenselessness and helplessness of the victims" (18). In making an argument for such a definition, he says: "I propose that at all times our first loyalty be to honoring the significance of the lives of all human beings. Let us take all of the human race as our basic communality . . . How sad and corrupt we become if our scholarly definition of genocide cannot encompass events where hundreds of thousands and millions of human beings lie in the graves of humanity's obvious genocidal cruelty!" (Charny 1991, 19). Such a definition would include "any cases of mass murders of any human beings, of whatever racial, national, ethnic, biological, cultural, religious, political definitions, or totally mixed groupings of any and all of the above" (Charny 1991, 18).

As the field of genocide studies continues to grow, new and clearer distinctions are bound to be made in regard to that which does and does not constitute genocide. At the same time, various scholars are bound to disagree over what constitutes a reasonable approach to such issues. For instance, quite recently Charny cautioned against "obsessive definitionalism" (1991, 6), while Fein issued a concern about the concept of genocide becoming a "superblanket of generalized compassion" (1991, 8). Regardless of different perspectives, all the scholars mentioned in this essay are searching for ways to understand and prevent genocide. As Charny states, "one can look with some satisfaction on the increasing emergence of scholarship and scientific study of genocide as a process whose origins and lawful development can be tracked with some measure of understanding and also predictability, and therefore one may also dare begin to think of possibilities for some day preventing genocide" (1988b, 1).

If humanity is to develop sound—and more important—workable conventions and genocide warning systems in order to stave off genocide, then scholars, activists, governmental officials, et al. need to come to a general consensus in regard to how genocide should be defined. Until this is done, the debate over definitional issues is bound to interfere with efforts of intervention and prevention.

Misuse of the Term by the General Public, Activists of Various Causes, and the Press

Disturbingly, the misuse of the term *genocide* is rampant. It is often misused and abused on a regular basis by various groups that want to draw dramatic attention to their plight. Concomitantly, as Jack Nusan Porter, a sociologist, has noted: "Since 'genocide' has become such a powerful catch-word, it is often used in political and cultural rhetoric" (1982, 9).

Among the more outlandish examples of the misuse of the term/concept of genocide are President Reagan's policy on AIDS research, and thus the insinuation that he was purposely "targeting" homosexuals; the Israelis' actions against the Palestinians during the

Intifada; "government policies letting one race adopt the children of another" (Simon 1995, 3); the practice of birth control and abortions among Third World people (Porter 1982, 9); rampant drug availability, use, and sales in the inner cities of the United States; and the rate of abortions in the United States. Recently, during NATO air attacks on Bosnian Serb military targets in 1995, "Russia charged that the Serbs were facing 'genocide' from the West" (Associated Press 1995, A5). When genocide is used in such a loose and irresponsible manner, not only does it distort the true meaning of the term, but it diminishes and minimizes those actions that are truly genocidal in nature. Such misuse and over-use of the term may also contribute to inuring some to the horror of the reality of genocide.

It is also worth noting that some school curricula on the Holocaust and genocide have a tendency to incorrectly define genocide. For example, in *The Holocaust: A North Carolina Teacher's Resource* (Scher 1989, 109) and *A Study Guide on the Holocaust* (Georgia Commission on the Holocaust 1994, 7) *genocide* is defined in the following way: "Term created after World War II to describe the systematic murder of an entire political, cultural, or religious group . . . ." The major problem here is the use of the term *entire*. The most technically correct definitions include such wording as "in whole or in part." By using "or in part," it prevents those responsible from making the disingenuous claim that since some members of the targeted group were not killed, genocide was not committed. The definition in the aforementioned works also neglects to include key groups that are protected under the UN Convention on Genocide: national, ethnical, racial.

In the Connecticut State Department of Education's resource guide *Human Rights: The Struggle for Freedom, Dignity and Equality* (1987), the following definition of *genocide* is used: "The word 'genocide' originally meant the total destruction of a national group as the result of some intentional policy. The meaning of the term genocide has now been broadened to include all official [that is, carried out by a recognized government] actions to harm, in whole or in part, various types of human groups" (15). Under this definition virtually any civil or human rights infraction committed by the government would constitute genocide. This is a classic case of watering the term down to where it becomes meaningless.

In order for students to gain a true understanding as to what does and does not constitute genocide, the definition to which students are introduced *must be accurate*. When this is not done, students may be apt to perceive genocide as being synonymous with "murder," "massacres," "pogroms," or some other violent and deadly situation. While each of the latter is a serious offense, none of them constitutes genocide.

Incorporating Issues of Genocide into Literature Units and Programs: Some Concerns and Precautions

There are several concerns and precautions that teachers should consider when incorporating issues of genocide into their literature units and programs. Among the most significant are the following:

Use such terms as *Holocaust, holocaust, genocide, massacres, pogroms,* with accuracy and care. Provide students with correct and complete definitions of each as well as examples of each in order to help them differentiate between the various types of infractions.

Select and use pieces that truly focus on genocide and not on a situation that constitutes a different type of human rights infraction. (Obviously, if a teacher wishes to focus on other aspects of human rights violations, that is legitimate; the key here is not to "pass something off" as genocide when it is clearly not "genocidal" in nature.)

Select and use pieces that highlight a significant aspect of the genocidal act.

Select literature that portrays the genocidal act in an accurate manner.

Avoid literature that romanticizes any aspect of a genocidal situation.

Avoid literature that provides a simplistic view/perspective of the genocidal situation.

Provide the students with a solid and accurate historical overview of the genocide under study. This can be easily, quickly, and accurately done by showing a noted film on the genocide under study and/or having the students read and discuss a key article or essay on the genocide prior to discussing a piece of literature.

Select literary works that constitute outstanding pieces of literature.

Avoid pieces of literature that contain gratuitous violence.

Do not select genocide as the focal point for literary learning in early primary (K–2) grades.

For additional concerns, caveats, and advice see *Guidelines for Teaching the Holocaust* (Parsons and Totten 1993) issued by the United States Holocaust Memorial Museum. While these guidelines, as the title suggests, focus exclusively on the Holocaust, many of the caveats and suggestions are equally germane to other genocides.

References   Associated Press. 1995. "NATO Strikes Again, Russians Decry Attacks."
                   Northwest Arkansas Times 13 Sept.: A5.

Chalk, Frank, and Kurt Jonassohn. 1990. *The History and Sociology of Genocide: Analyses and Case Studies.* New Haven and London: Yale University Press.

Charny, Israel W. 1985. "Genocide, the Ultimate Human Rights Problem."
Social Education Special Issue on Human Rights. Edited by Samuel
Totten. 49(6): 448–52.

———, ed. 1988a. *Genocide: A Critical Bibliographic Review.* New York: Facts
on File.

———. 1988b. "Intervention and Prevention of Genocide." In *Genocide: A
Critical Bibliographic Review.* Edited by Israel W. Charny. New York:
Facts on File.

———. 1988c. "The Study of Genocide." In *Genocide: A Critical Bibliographic
Review,* edited by Israel W. Charny. New York: Facts on File.

———. 1991. "A Proposal of a New Encompassing Definition of Genocide:
Including New Legal Categories of Accomplices to Genocide, and
Genocide as a Result of Ecological Destruction and Abuse." Paper
presented at the Raphael Lemkin Symposium on Genocide, February, Yale University Law School.

Connecticut State Department of Education. 1987. *Human Rights: The
Struggle for Freedom, Dignity and Equality.* Hartford, CT: Author.

Dadrian, Vahakn N. 1974. "The Structural Functional Components of
Genocide: A Victimological Approach to the Armenian Case." In
Victimology. Edited by Israel Drapkin and Emilio Viano. Lexington,
MA: Lexington Books.

Drost, Pieter. 1959. *The Crime of State.* Vol. 2. Leyden: A. W. Sythoff.

Fein, Helen. 1990. "Genocide: A Sociological Perspective." *Current Sociology*
38(1): 1–126.

———. 1991. "Genocide: Life Integrity Violations and Other Causes of Mass
Death: The Case for Discrimination—A Reply to Israel Charny's
Critique." *Internet on The Holocaust and Genocide* 30/31: 7–8.

Georgia Commission on the Holocaust. 1994. *A Study Guide on the Holocaust.*
Atlanta, GA: Author.

Horowitz, Irving Louis. 1980. *Taking Lives: Genocide and State Power.* New
Brunswick, NJ: Transaction Publishers.

Kuper, Leo. 1981. *Genocide: Its Political Use in the Twentieth Century.* New
Haven, CT: Yale University Press.

———. 1985. *The Prevention of Genocide.* New Haven, CT: Yale University
Press.

LeBlanc, Lawrence J. 1988. "The United Nations Genocide Convention and
Political Groups: Should the United States Propose an Amendment?"
Yale Journal of International Law 13(2): 268–94.

Lemkin, Raphael. 1944. *Axis Rule in Occupied Europe: Laws of Occupation, Analysis of Government, and Proposals for Redress.* Washington, D.C.: Carnegie Foundation for International Peace. [Reprint, New York: Howard Fertig, 1973.]

Parsons, William S., and Samuel Totten. 1993. *Guidelines for Teaching about the Holocaust.* Washington, D.C.: United States Holocaust Memorial Museum.

Porter, Jack Nusan. 1982. "Introduction." *Genocide and Human Rights: A Global Anthology.* Edited by Jack Nusan Porter. Washington, D.C.: University Press of America.

Scher, Linda, ed. 1989. *The Holocaust: A North Carolina Teacher's Resource.* Raleigh, NC: North Carolina Council on the Holocaust and North Carolina Department of Public Instruction.

Simon, Thomas. 1995. "Grading Harms: Giving Genocide Its Due." Paper presented at the International Conference on Genocide, April, University of Nebraska at Lincoln.

Whitaker, B. 1985. *Revised and Updated Report on the Question of the Prevention and Punishment of the Crime of Genocide.* New York: United Nations Economic and Social Council. E/CN.4/Sub.2/1985/6, 2 July.

2 A Letter to My Children: Historical Memory and the Silences of Childhood

Timothy J. Stanley
University of Ottawa

D addy, what are Nazis?" the older of you asked. "Are they bad guys?" the younger wanted to know. You were about eight years old and six at the time. We had been watching *The Sound of Music*. Your mother and I hadn't seen the film in many years, and we had remembered its singing and laughter more than its Nazis. You wanted to know, because Liesl's boyfriend in the movie, Rolfe, was a Nazi, and you could not understand why he turned out to be a bad guy. Rolfe's character hardens during the movie as he throws his lot in with the Nazis. At the dramatic climax of the film, he betrays the family, almost resulting in their undoing. Like all the really important questions of childhood, yours were matter-of-fact, and I wanted my answers to be matter-of-fact, too.

Your questions made perfect sense. Amid much singing, the orphaned Maria becomes the governess for the aristocratic Von Trapp family. Eventually Maria and the widowed father, a captain in the Austrian navy, fall in love. This idyll is destroyed when the Nazis occupy Austria and order Captain Von Trapp to report for service in the newly integrated German navy. As an Austrian nationalist, Captain Von Trapp finds his new position untenable, so he and his family (still singing) flee across the Alps to Switzerland. The film does not make clear why Captain Von Trapp does not like Nazis, nor what he risks in resisting them. It both articulates Nazism and is silent on it. While it represents nationalist opposition to the Nazi/German occupation of Austria, it shows neither the totalitarian-

I would like to thank Judith P. Robertson for her encouragement in pursuing this essay. I would also like to thank Frances Boyle for her ongoing support and careful proofreading. Finally, I would like to thank my children for teaching me what it is to be human.

terrorist nor the racist natures of Nazism. Anti-Semitism is never even mentioned, nor overtly depicted. Indeed, had the film portrayed these things, I doubt that your parents would have let you watch it at such tender ages. In the absence of explanation, Captain Von Trapp's decision to flee Austria with his family seems disproportionate. Hence, "What are Nazis?" is a perfectly logical question. It even makes sense to ask the question in the present tense because the film populates a quasifictive location. Is this a docudrama or a "fact-based" account? Or is it a complete work of fiction? Did it happen long ago or more recently?

Yet, this straightforward and eminently logical question left me feeling utterly inadequate. I found it almost unanswerable, both in my own terms and in terms that I thought you could understand. As someone who has devoted most of his adult life to anti-racist work, as a historian of racisms and a supposed expert in critical multicultural/anti-racist education, I was especially troubled. Who is better placed to give a full and appropriate answer? And if I cannot, who can?

What are matter-of-fact answers here, I wondered? "The Nazis, or National Socialists, were the ruling party in Germany, 1933–1945," and, "Yes, they are bad guys," would have explained nothing. As answers they would also have been profoundly mistaken. National Socialism was an international movement.[1] Its international nature was even represented in the movie: Rolfe and his friends were Austrian Nazis who, like those of many other European countries, connived and collaborated in the German occupation of their countries, and actively worked to effect the genocide of the Jewish and other populations and to create "the Aryan race." Nor was Nazism just European. There were Nazis in the United States and in Canada too.[2] The "was" is wrong, too. Nazism is not merely historical. Today there are Nazis, sometimes mistakenly called neo-Nazis as if in fact they are something new, in many countries, including our own. Indeed, the growing respectability of white supremacist and fascist groups is one of the emerging crises of our time.[3] To have given a "safe" answer suggesting that Nazism is far removed from the realities of our lives, by both time and distance, would have been simply wrong.

I also wondered, do I tell you about the central facts of Nazism: the Holocaust, the mass, industrialized, assembly-line murder of millions, many of them women and children, some no older than yourselves? Do I tell you about the systemic terror and its willing accomplices? Even if I knew how to explain these things, matters that I find barely comprehensible myself, I am not sure that you are old enough to carry such knowledge. At my patriarchal best, if that's not an oxymoron, I want to keep you innocent of such knowledge—

along with knowledge of the other terrors of my postmodern existence including thermonuclear destruction, global warming, and
psychopathic rapists—until when? Age twelve? Sixty-five? Someday,
I know you must know, or you will be unarmed to meet the future.
But not now, not while you are so young. When?

Your questions troubled my desire to keep you innocent of
such knowledge. I am well aware that creating a space in which you
can grow up in selective silence constitutes my power, my masculinity, my location in the metropolis, and my ability to silence difference. To have given you full answers would have screamed difference, decentered my location, destabilized my manliness, established
my powerlessness. It would have challenged the categories of my
existence. Yet to have given lesser answers would also have constituted my incompetence both as a parent and as a witness to history.
Your questions caught me, because I knew that my fantasy of your
childhood innocence was just that, a fantasy. To really protect you
from such knowledge is itself impossible. Nazism and its realities
surround you. They surround you with silences, with hidden meanings, with limited possibilities.

These are not the only historical silences that surround your
childhood. You live among people about whose pasts and whose
conditions you know nothing. Some of this is the result of your age
and your lack of experience with the world. Some comes from the
deliberate efforts of your parents and the other adults around you to
keep you insulated from certain realities. Still other silences come
from the social structures that shape your lives. At the school that
your parents send you to, you participate in lessons recreating
"pioneer times," as if the human past of our city only begins with the
arrival of Europeans. The same school unapologetically fosters
loyalty to the very institutions that obliterated Aboriginal people
from our memory as well as from the land we now occupy. Like all
other public schools in Canada, this school fosters a nationalism that
exists in relation to vast silences and their exclusions from our
collective memory.[4] Even the language that we now speak, English
(with some help from French), has displaced and silenced the languages of the people who had populated the land on which our
house now sits. You know that some of your classmates speak
neither English nor French, but you do not know that some people
see this as proof that they are not, and can never be, "Canadian."[5]
Cantonese, for example, the language of one set of your great-
grandparents, has been spoken in parts of what is now Canada as
long as any nonaboriginal language, yet it is still seen as a "foreign"
language, in a way that English in most parts of Canada never is.[6] In
our city are people who speak many languages. You can barely even
imagine the stories that they have to tell. Yet, almost all of the time,

what you learn in school, in books, and on television celebrates only some of these stories, those of Europeans.[7] Such institutional silences are the stuff of racisms.[8]

I am well aware that not all children are privileged to live in such silence. Remember in kindergarten when one of the boys in your class came to school, his face swollen and bandaged? We found out that he had been beaten up by a group of bigger kids who had gone around the playground assaulting anyone who was nonwhite. You said the class laughed at him, because he looked so funny. I wonder where the real damage was. Which assault will he live with, maybe for the rest of his life? I know that the response of your doubtless well-meaning teacher, first trained in the sixties and now close to retirement age, was inadequate. Would my response have been any better? I can't even tell you matter-of-factly what Nazis are. How could I spontaneously deal with something really important in a kindergarten class of twenty-five?

When we watched the movie, "What are Nazis?" didn't occur to me the way it did to you. In his second scene in the movie, Rolfe gives Captain Von Trapp a Nazi salute. I automatically read this, and the Captain's reaction, as a foreboding of trouble. Of course, Rolfe was a Nazi (and an almost certain bad guy), while the Captain as an anti-Nazi was a good guy, even if it took him three-quarters of the movie to hook up with Julie Andrews's character, Maria. Only your questions made problematic what I took for granted.

Why didn't these questions occur to me? In large part because the portrayal of Nazis in *The Sound of Music* is conventional. I have seen countless movies and television shows in which the appearance of Nazis has signaled trouble. Nazis were part and parcel of the mass culture of my childhood. There were Nazis on *Combat*, on *Hogan's Heroes*, on countless war (i.e., World War II) movies (the first movie that I went to see without adult accompaniment was *The Longest Day*). All of these taught me that the Nazis are always the bad guys.[9]

Your questions also made me wonder how old I was when I first knew about the Holocaust. It seems to me that I have always known, but knowledge must have come in increments. I think awareness came from television. Unlike your parents (who see TV as an evil, brain-destroying device for thought control and mass con- sumerism), my parents—your grandparents—thought it was a blessing. It brought the world into the living room, they said. It meant that their children knew so much more about things than they did. It also meant that the only censorship of TV your father experi- enced as a child was at bedtime. (I even did my homework in front of the TV.)

Maybe they were right. I have memories of seeing archival footage of the mass disposal of bodies in the newly liberated concentration camps, and of my big brother asking my father, "Are they Jews?" and of him swallowing hard and nodding. I am not sure how old I was at the time, but I don't think I was that much older than you are now. Even though I was horrified at the images, I remember thinking, "Of course they are Jews." I think I already knew, in general terms, about the Holocaust.

Unlike you, I grew up in a neighborhood that was largely Jewish. The Holocaust and its consequences were part and parcel of the stories and silences of my friends' families. Holocaust survivors included my friends' parents. The Holocaust was the reason, although I didn't know it at the time, so few had aunts and uncles, unlike me. But these are things we discussed as teenagers, not as children. Knowledge may have come from my parents' talk, from my asking "What are Nazis?", but I don't think so.

All of this made me wonder, can I use your mass culture to explain Nazis? Are Nazis like Darth Vader and the evil Empire? Are they similar to Cruella De Vil in *101 Dalmations*? The jackals in *The Lion King*? Yes, and no, I thought.

Some scenes in *The Lion King* represent the jackals in terms of stock images of storm troopers, their triumphant march past Scar harkening back to Leni Riefenstahl's 1934 propaganda portrayal of the Nuremberg rallies, *Triumph des Willens* (*Triumph of the Will*). In some ways, the logic of Nazism is also the logic of *The Lion King*. Both rest on biologistic notions of difference, and on uncritical acceptance of racialized and racist logic. In *The Lion King* the jackals are evil because of their evil essences. There is no texturing of this. Apparently they do what they do because they are jackals. Simba's essence, inherited genetically from his father, is noble and kingly. His true self emerges when he rediscovers this essence. These essences are marked by the beauty of the lions and the ugliness of the hyenas. By contrast, Scar, Simba's uncle who usurps the throne, is flawed, both morally and physically. In this movie, essences are fixed, unchanging and inherent. They are presented as a simple binary of nobility/beauty and corruption/ugliness, and a religious conviction that the former must win out over the latter (an all-too-frequent theme in Disney movies). A similar binary was one of the central tenets of Nazism.

But at the same time, Nazis are not like the hyenas of *The Lion King*. Nazis are not Nazis because they inherited their Nazism from their parents. Unlike being a hyena, being a Nazi does not have a genetic basis. Rather, Nazi propaganda spreads its mythology of an "objective" scientific basis to its creed. Like all racisms, it creates the categories of "race" that it polices.[10] The thought crossed my mind that the Nazi occupation of Austria was like the Empire's takeover of Luke Skywalker's home planet in *Star Wars*. But the evil Empire, for all of the special effects, did not constitute its dominance along "race" lines. In the *Star Wars* universe, entire civilizations may be destroyed as means to the end of imperial dominance, but such destruction is not the ultimate goal of its dominance. Like *The Lion King*, *Star Wars* also presents Manichean images of good and evil. Evil is all-powerful, corrupted and merciless. This evil can only be opposed by a good that is similarly powerful, but corruptible. Good can become evil, it seems, but not the other way around.

While *Star Wars* can supply analogies for the occupation of a country by Nazis, for the power that this involved, it cannot account for the characters of Nazis themselves. Nazism and its minions have been disturbingly banal. Hitler, unlike *Star Wars'* emperor who had mastered the secrets of the "dark side of the Force," was not all-powerful. Rather, he was merely the head of a vast bureaucracy whose members were significantly distanced from the human consequences of its actions, at the same time that they competed with each other on how best to implement the Nazi program. The perpetrators of the Holocaust, unlike the fictional perpetrators of the evil Empire, were more like me than I would care to admit.

I even momentarily thought that the Holocaust might be explainable in terms of Cruella De Vil and the puppies from *101 Dalmatians*. Despite its comic relief, *101 Dalmatians* is about the ruthless, mass murder of iconic children. At heart it is a terror movie for children. In this sense Cruella's plotted extinction of the Dalmatian puppies is like that of the Nazis' plot against Jewry. But I realize that this analogy quickly breaks down. First, the puppies escape; millions of Jews did not. Second, unlike the Nazis and their "Final Solution," Cruella, for all her faults, did not want to kill all Dalmatians. Third, the Nazis who perpetrated the Holocaust were not incompetent buffoons.

Indeed, as I thought about the mass culture of your childhood, nowhere could I find an analogy for Nazism and its evils. Nazis are not like anything else that has been represented to you. Thus, your questions probe an enormous and dangerous silence. Even as your mass culture articulates reality, it displaces it. In representing Nazism, *The Sound of Music*, for example, displaces its victims. How many other families fled over the Alps, only to be turned back by Swiss border guards, their stories never to be made into movies? Children's television (and most adult television, for that matter) is filled with depictions of good and evil as fixed, and mutually exclusive, essences. It is replete with redemptive narratives in which somehow evil is in the end redeemed by good. The drearily mundane reality of ordinary people doing evil things, without redemption, is silenced, displaced by a glamorized world of radical essences.

Such Manichean depictions gave rise to the question whether

Nazis are bad guys. In *The Sound of Music,* they seem rather ordinary people, yet they are also the bad guys of the plot. I wanted to answer that Nazis are indeed bad guys. To me Nazism is the epitome of evil. This sense is so deeply ingrained within me that I can remember years ago, half a lifetime really, when I was visiting a friend in Hong Kong, feeling violently ill as I looked out his window and saw a building covered in swastikas. It took me a moment or two to realize that it was a Buddhist temple—the swastika, reversed in its corrupted Nazi form, is an age-old symbol for life—but I was never entirely comfortable in its shadow. My visceral reaction testified to my sense that Nazism is the essence of evil.

But my mature understanding is not that Nazism is an evil of fixed and radical essences. Rather, I understand it as an evil based on what Hannah Arendt called "loneliness." According to Arendt, "loneliness is at the same time contrary to the basic requirements of the human condition *and* one of the fundamental experiences of every human life" (Arendt 1951, 475, original emphasis). Writing in the sexist idiom of the 1950s, she argued that loneliness violates human beings' contact with others, and undermines common sense "which regulates and controls all other senses and without which each of us would become enclosed in his own particularity of sense data which in themselves are unreliable and treacherous. Only because we have common sense, that is because not one man, but men in the plural inhabit the earth, can we trust our immediate sensual experience" (475–76). With the severing of common bonds and myriad links between human beings, cause and effect become separated from each other. It then becomes possible to follow the logic of an idea to its ultimate conclusion or to implement a political program to the point where it defies common sense.

And yet, the very Manicheanism of mass culture fosters such separation. It thrives on loneliness. After all, the lonely person can be sold anything. The underlying message of the million commercials you will see in your lifetime is that buying this product will end your loneliness. By representing evil as an essence, radically different and removed from our selves, as Other, mass culture furthers disconnection. Mass culture then becomes our popular culture, the shaper of meanings in our day-to-day life. It replaces others with whom we are connected with Others whom we fear. It encourages the folly of abandoning the public sphere for the dubious safety of private fortresses. By reducing us to mere consumers, rather than producers of communal cultures, it makes us parties to our own loneliness.[11]

Understood in this way, I see my own implication in the conditions that foster Nazism. Every time I distance myself from the social phenomena of my times, every time I give in to my postmodern fears, I construct loneliness. In myriad small ways, I tear what Arendt called "common sense" and the totalitarian condition is furthered. This does not mean that I am responsible for all the ills in the world. It *does* mean that I am not as removed from them as I would sometimes like to imagine.

As a parent, this leaves me torn between a sense of powerlessness and an awareness of my responsibility to keep you safe until you are old enough to take care of yourselves. Nazism does not belong only to some faraway time and place, something to be remembered, perhaps, but not to be relived. Its dangers surround you: the essentialist logic of the mass media, the growing atomization of our social world, the deepening inability of political forces to meet our needs, the racist and fascist groups waiting for their moment. At the same time, I know that it is also my responsibility to give you hope, to provide you with reasons to embrace life and its possibilities.

Education is the only solution that I know to these dilemmas. Education, understood not as technique or training, not as schooling, but as part and parcel of "the engagement of being human," i.e., the shared act of making meaning of meanings inherited from others.[12] For it is education, and not mass culture, that has the potential to counter disconnection. Only an educated understanding can critically engage with the essentialism of mass media. Only the remaking of meanings can build our connections to others and overcome loneliness. These connections necessarily are not just to the things that we like, or would choose for ourselves. They also include our connections to things we would rather forget or rather not know. Education understood in this way is rarely easy, often dangerous, but through its dialogue with others always affirms our humanity.[13]

Your questions made for the teachable moment and demanded answers. The answers could not come from elsewhere. They had to come from me, because I was the one you asked. They needed to be truthful, and open-ended, for I also knew that like all other truly important questions, these are questions that you will ask many times as you mature as members of a human community.

So I answered: "Nazis were, are [I corrected myself], people who believe that if you are blond-haired and blue-eyed, and especially white-skinned, you should rule the world, and that everyone else should either be your slave or be killed. In the 1930s after coming to power in Germany, they took over Austria, and many other countries in Europe. This resulted in the Second World War in which both your grandfathers fought against the Nazis. Although they do not control governments anymore, Nazis are still around. And no, Nazis are not 'bad guys' like Darth Vader or Cruella De Vil. They were pretty well ordinary people like you and me. But what they did was murder millions of people, mainly Jewish people, because they weren't blond-haired and blue-eyed, and what they did was evil. Indeed it is the essence of evil."

It was the first time I had used the term *evil* in describing something to my children. And as I answered, I mourned.

Notes   1. My understanding of the history of Nazism is largely taken from Michael R. Marrus, *The Holocaust in History* (New York: Penguin, 1987).

2. On Canadian Nazis, see Lita-Rose Betcherman, *The Swastika and the Maple Leaf* (Toronto: Fitzhenry & Whiteside, 1975) and Marilyn F. Nefsky, "The Shadow of Evil: Naziism and Canadian Protestantism," in *Anti-Semitism in Canada: History and Interpretation*, ed. Allan Davies (Waterloo, Ontario: Wilfrid University Press, 1992). On Canadian complicity in the Holocaust, see Irving Abella and Harold Troper, *None Is Too Many: Canada and the Jews of Europe, 1933–1948*, 3rd ed. with a new epilogue. (Toronto: Lester Publishing, 1991).

3. An obvious example is the rising respectability of David Duke in the United States. For his Canadian connections, see Julian Sher, *White Hoods: Canada's Ku Klux Klan* (Vancouver: New Star Books, 1983). On racist and fascist groups in Canada, see Stanley R. Barrett, *Is God a Racist? The Right Wing in Canada* (Toronto: University of Toronto Press, 1987) and Warren Kinsella, *Web of Hate: Inside Canada's Far Right Network* (Toronto: HarperCollins, 1994).

4. See Timothy J. Stanley, "'Chinamen, Wherever We Go': Chinese Nationalism and Guangdong Merchants in British Columbia, 1871–1911," *Canadian Historical Review* 77.4 (1996): 475–503.

5. The role of historical narratives in articulations of popular racisms is explored in Leslie G. Roman and Timothy J. Stanley, "Empires, Émigrés and Aliens: Young People's Negotiations of Official and Popular Racism in Canada," in *Dangerous Territories: Struggles for Equality and Difference in Education*, edited by Leslie G. Roman and Linda Eyre (New York: Routledge, 1997).

6. Cantonese has been continuously spoken in Canada's westernmost province, British Columbia, since before that territory "joined" the Canadian confederation. On the significance of this population to that territory's history in the middle of the nineteenth century, see Robert Galois and Cole Harris, "Recalibrating Society: The Population Geography of British Columbia in 1881," *The Canadian Geographer* 38.1 (1994): 37–53. On racialization of the category "Chinese," see Kay Anderson, *Vancouver's Chinatown: Racial Discourse in Canada, 1875–1980* (Montreal and Kingston: McGill-Queen's University Press, 1991).

7. For critiques of the imperialist and racist underpinnings of Western culture, see Edward W. Said, *Orientalism* (New York: Pantheon, 1978); and Edward W. Said, *Culture and Imperialism* (New York: Knopf, 1993). See also Paul Gilroy, *The Black Atlantic: Modernity and Double Con-*

sciousness (Cambridge: Harvard University Press, 1993). On the curricular implications of such critiques, see George J. Sefa Dei, *Anti-Racism Education: Theory and Practice* (Halifax: Fernwood, 1996). See also William F. Pinar, "Notes on Understanding Curriculum as a Racial Text," in *Race, Identity and Representation in Education,* edited by Cameron McCarthy and Warren Crichlow (New York: Routledge, 1993); and Ali Rattansi, "Changing the Subject? Racism, Culture and Education," in *"Race," Culture and Difference,* edited by James Donald and Ali Rattansi (London: Sage Publications, 1992), 11–48.

8. David Theo Goldberg, *Racist Culture: Philosophy and the Politics of Meaning* (Oxford, England, and Cambridge, MA: Blackwell, 1993).

9. While being silent on the international nature of Nazism, many of these representations I grew up with differentiated between Nazis and "good" Germans, i.e., those patriots distastefully serving their country and the perpetrators of the Holocaust. Indeed the conflict between the two was often a device for dramatic tension. The effect of such representations was to rescue nationalism as a worthwhile project.

10. Robert Miles, *Racism* (London: Routledge, 1989). See also Goldberg, *Racist Culture.*

11. As it becomes popular, mass culture also produces possibilities. Thus, it both constrains and defines possibilities in teaching. For examples, see Henry A. Giroux, *Disturbing Pleasures: Learning Popular Culture* (New York: Routledge, 1994) and Peter M. Appelbaum, *Popular Culture, Educational Discourse, and Mathematics* (Albany: SUNY Press, 1995).

12. My conception of education comes from Michael Oakeshott, "Education: The Engagement and Its Frustration," in *The Voice of Liberal Learning: Michael Oakeshott on Education,* edited by Timothy Fuller (New Haven: Yale University Press, 1989) as reworked by Maxine Greene, "What Counts as Philosophy of Education?" in *Critical Conversations in Philosophy of Education,* edited by Wendy Kohli (New York and London: Routledge, 1995), 3–23.

13. See Charles Taylor, "The Politics of Recognition," in *Multiculturalism: A Critical Reader,* edited by David Theo Goldberg (Oxford, England, and Cambridge, MA: Blackwell, 1994), 75–106.

Works Cited

Arendt, Hannah. 1951/1973. *The Origins of Totalitarianism.* New edition with expanded prefaces. San Diego, New York, and London: Harcourt Brace Jovanovich.

The Lion King. 1994. Directed by Roger Allers and Rob Minkoff. 88 min. Walt Disney Co. Distributed by Buena Vista Home Video Dept. CS, Burbank, CA 91521. Videocassette.

The Longest Day. 1962. Produced by Elmo Williams. Directed by Den Annakin, Andrew Marton, and Bernard Wicke. 180 min. Twentieth Century Fox Film Corporation. Distributed by Foxvideo, Inc., P. O. Box 900, Beverly Hills, CA 90213. Videocassette.

101 Dalmatians. 1961. Produced by Ken Anderson. Directed by Wolfgang
     Reitherman, Hamilton S. Luske, and Clyde Geronimi. 79 min. Walt
     Disney Co. Distributed by Buena Vista Home Video Dept. CS,
     Burbank, CA 91521. Videocassette.

The Sound of Music. 1965. Produced by Argyle Enterprises, Inc. Directed by
     Robert Wise. 174 min. Twentieth Century Fox Film Corporation.
     Distributed by Foxvideo, Inc., P. O. Box 900, Beverly Hills, CA 90213.
     Videocassette.

Star Wars. 1977. Produced by Gary Kurtz. Directed by George Lucas. 121
     min. Twentieth Century Fox Film Corporation. Distributed by
     Foxvideo, Inc., P. O. Box 900, Beverly Hills, CA 90213. Videocassette.

To Know Me, Read My Story. To Respect Me, Read It Well

Yeuk Yi Pang
University of British Columbia

The transition from what we think of as more primary (because "real") to the experience of stories about it is so automatic and frequent that we risk losing our sense of just how astonishing our story worlds are, in their power to add "life" upon "life"—for good or ill.

Wayne C. Booth, *The Company We Keep*

The study of literature cannot bring about moral excellence nor prevent moral degeneracy, yet without literature I think that we would find it more difficult to live well and act virtuously.

Andrew J. Auge, *Literature and Moral Life*

Introduction

Reading "good" stories will lead people to become good themselves. Such is a commonly held and seldom examined expectation that leads many educators, searching for a way to help students to resist forces that may lead them to intolerant attitudes, to look to perspectives such as those espoused by William J. Bennett in *The Book of Virtues* (1993). Yet we need not dispute the goodness of the message that, say, an enormously popular story like "Beauty and the Beast" embodies to recognize that reading this story will not necessarily inspire every child to the virtues it recommends. In fact, most teachers will have experience with children who can read this story without getting any of the intended moral messages, or who, recognizing one form of message, will find its meaning and significance totally alien to their world.

I will argue that stories are, in fact, one of the best ways to help children understand intolerance, think through their own positions in relation to it, and consider imaginatively the range of responses they might take toward it. Stories can give readers a sense of life as lived. Teachers can use stories to nurture compassion, imagination, and a sense of fellowship with other human beings. They can use stories to teach about the human implications of intolerance, the dignity of respect, and how students might act as agents resisting the former while promoting the latter. But to tap into this potential, teachers need to understand why they cannot naively use a story such as "Beauty and the Beast" to promote virtues such as acceptance and compassion, or to teach about the imprudence of quick judgments and preconceptions. Teachers need to ask probing questions about how stories actually can educate human feeling and moral intelligence.

The naive view sees literature as a blunt tool, and moral education as the inculcation and indoctrination of moral virtues and codes into children. This view takes little notice of the part that children play as readers and listeners in the construction and interpretation of stories, and as agents in the development of their moral perspectives and the direction of their moral lives. It also fails to consider how a teacher's pedagogy with a story can affect student learning. In this essay, I suggest a more sensitive understanding of the interplay between student and text in the act of reading and thus creating a story. I also draw on a reciprocal notion of how the story read might influence the moral life of a reader. In light of these understandings, I discuss the role that teachers can play in helping students to interact more profoundly with the narrative texts they engage toward ethical ends.

It is important to remember that stories have the power to influence for ill as well as for good. Educators need to be clear about their ethical responsibility here and to consider carefully the goals they seek. By encouraging and helping students to read narratives with sensitivity, teachers can offer students educational experiences that are ethically sound. By helping students to read narratives in a way that calls forth compassion and imagination, teachers promote respect and understanding. By helping students to engage with their readings in a way that develops moral voice, teachers foster a sense of responsibility and integrity.

Tolerance Is Not Enough

Before looking at how teachers can nurture ethical and educational transactions between child and narrative text, I will look briefly at one moral outcome we may seek through literary education. Here, I suggest that educators promote respect rather than mere tolerance because promoting tolerance is an inadequate response to the problem of intolerance. Tolerance cannot, by itself, form the basis for developing meaningful relationships among people. It serves more as a safety measure that reminds human beings of our own limits and ensures a constraint on our biases. It is when our understanding and compassion fail that we call on tolerance to restrain our actions. While intolerant actions and views occur when this "safety valve" is either missing or weakened, they do not originate from the faulty valve. We know that no safety valve alone can stem the tide of fear, anger, and hatred that expresses itself in intolerance and genocide. Moreover, tolerance has its limits. When a situation demands that people work out their differences, merely being tolerant will not be enough.

While it is important to develop tolerant attitudes, educators seeking to prevent intolerance and genocide need to take a more fundamental approach by promoting the compassion and empathy that ground respect. Certain narratives can help to nurture this compassion by inviting us, through engaged reading, to enter the worlds of others and thereby perceive them more fully and generously. By encouraging students to read widely and to enter empathically into the worlds of many people apparently different from themselves, teachers can help students to develop a more fluid sense of self and others (Dyson 1996, 493). Students who are able to see the apparent boundary between themselves and others as problematic can better resist drawing the kinds of sharp distinctions between "us" and "them" that allow people to dehumanize and perpetrate atrocities on each other. Teachers can help students achieve this perception by helping them to imagine many alternative, intelligent, and viable ways of life. Finally, they can illuminate the many different ways that intolerance (and genocide) can be challenged, and inspire students toward responsible actions from the best in themselves. But as mentioned earlier, stories do not automatically achieve these ends. This is where teaching can make a difference.

In addition to all the direct pedagogical strategies and lessons that teachers can devise, educators wanting to help students develop compassion, empathy, and respect must also understand that student beliefs, attitudes, and actions, while not completely imported from outside, are also not developed or sustained by each individual alone. In fact, to recognize the importance of narrative literature is to recognize the social nature of moral life. This has significant implications for teaching. If story reading is to result in moral growth, then teachers must provide the right classroom atmosphere and community conditions for this growth. I return to this point later in the essay.

Using Literature's Conservative and Subversive Potentials

Depending on their perspective, different people have championed different potentials of literature to enrich moral life. Literary narrative, most prominently in the form of fables, can be used to reaffirm conventional views and ways, or it can (as parables do) call into question common ways of understanding and proceeding, urging new insights. An educator may foster either or both kinds of outcomes for moral enlightenment. Depending on the location of the reader, either affirmation, or questioning, or some complex combination of both may be required to stimulate moral sensitivity and to nurture moral voice. The way a teacher encourages a child to read the story can determine the nature of the experience, and thus influence the kind of effect it produces.

Related to these two ethical effects, there are three ways teachers can help students relate to paradigmatic individuals depicted in stories. By paradigmatic individuals I mean to include heroes/heroines and other kinds of positive characters, but also villains and other kinds of generally negative characters. Teachers can help students relate to these characters ethically by (1) helping them to see such characters as exemplars to emulate (or not, in the case of villains) in their particulars; (2) helping them to be inspired by such characters to put forward effort in the pursuit/support of virtue or avoidance/alleviation of vice; and (3) helping students to question some of the characterizations in stories to reveal a more complex understanding of just what makes a hero or a villain (Dyson 1996, 490, 494).

While teachers' desire to develop autonomy in students may lead them ultimately to seek development of the third kind of relation, the other two kinds can have significant educational effects as well. Through emulating someone we admire, we can (now and again) discover something of value in ourselves. For some students, this may be exactly what they need.

Reading to Subvert Intolerance and Affirm Respect

Three different factors interact in a reading performance to produce an effect: the text which embodies the story, the reader's orientation while reading, and the reader's background knowledge, attitudes, and skills. The third factor involves the intellectual, emotional, and ethical location of the reader in relation to the story and the text, as well as the interpretive and critical capacities that the reader brings to the reading performance. Teachers need to understand how these factors interact in the reading experience if they are to make informed judgments about how and where their teaching can effectively enhance students' abilities to access ethical enrichment through reading.

Qualities of the Text

The qualities of particular texts and stories are factors teachers often consider first when choosing books for students. While there are other factors influencing the reading outcome, teachers should recognize that certain textual qualities can invite meaningful reading performances. In particular, Jerome Bruner has argued for the educational value of texts that leave room for the reader to construct meaningful connections as they transform the text into a story (1986, 25–27). As the following examples illustrate, it is often the implicit messages and insights embedded in a story that have the greatest impact on readers. These are the insights that the reader helps to construct as part of her or his reading. Moreover, texts do not only invite certain reading performances, they also tolerate a certain range of interpretations and resist readings that violate the integrity of their stories. By asking questions about how texts invite, tolerate, or resist different readings, teachers can enhance their ability to choose appropriate texts for students.

In assessing the potentials of texts, teachers ask questions about the quality of the writing: whether the narrative engages readers, whether the characters are believable, sympathetic, or inspirational, and whether the potential messages in the story and the experiences the story invites are ones we consider relevant and worthy. For example, *Charlotte's Web* (White 1980) has many of these desirable qualities, and its enduring appeal attests to the power of these qualities. The story may be fantasy, but it nevertheless draws readers into its narrative quest to save Wilbur, which Charlotte's extraordinary efforts inspire in the rest of the barnyard community. Readers will find the characters variously inspirational (Charlotte, the spider), sympathetic (Wilbur, the pig) and believable (Templeton, the rat). They may extract from (or build into) this story many potential messages. One of the most central and compelling messages comes across through the character of Charlotte. She embodies in her perspective a compassionate and accepting stance toward others. In her matter-of-fact estimation, while different "persons" have different characteristics, none are judged as intrinsically bad.

White's portrayal of Charlotte is effective largely because it is understated. The spider's perspective comes across spontaneously as part of the story rather than through protracted orations explaining how she sees others. Even Templeton, who starts out living on the margins of the barnyard community, and who is perceived as the embodiment of vices, is brought to participatory membership in the community through Charlotte's inclusionary leadership. Initially, "The rat had no morals, no conscience, no scruples, no consideration, no decency, no milk of rodent kindness, no compunctions, no higher feeling, no friendliness, no anything" (46). Charlotte, however, invites him to share in the community's quest and contribute his particular abilities (going to the dump to bring back words for new messages in the web) toward achieving their common goal. This allows the rest of the community to see value where they once saw only vice. Through this change in the community's perception of him, Templeton gains acceptance and a kind of respect. A space opens for him to see himself differently as well. Always merely selfish before, Templeton ends up saving Wilbur at the county fair with an unprompted act of pure unselfishness. Saving Wilbur had become *his* goal.

Not all texts weave such an engaging tale with subtle though powerful characters carrying such clearly virtuous messages. Besides watching out for textually blunt and superficial stories, teachers seeking to educate about intolerance need to be aware of a more specific hazard. Stories that take the reader into the world of intolerant and hate-filled souls pose such a danger. Wayne Booth (1988) examines how the "company we keep" can either nourish or poison our moral life. Booth warns that getting on the inside of intolerant and hate-filled characters can influence us in potentially unpredictable ways. There are no fast and easy rules about when it is safe or beneficial to expose oneself or one's students to this company, or when it would be necessarily harmful. There are, however, important questions teachers can ask in order to clarify the potential harm reading such stories may pose. Surely, it is not simply that the story introduces intolerant characters, but how such characters are introduced and how the story proceeds to illuminate, explain, and use the characters as it unfolds. Teachers need to consider these aspects in order to determine the nature of the company they are contemplating for their students (or that students may be choosing for themselves). Whose voice, whose stance does the story authorize? Does the story invite compassion, encourage outrage, resist intolerance, tolerate moral ambiguity, or evoke ethical relativism?

An example may prove helpful here. Consider the character Gordy in *Stepping on the Cracks* (Hahn 1991). The story is set in 1944, where the war forms a constant background concern in the lives of College Hill residents. Margaret and Elizabeth are two friends preparing to enter the sixth grade. Their greatest nemesis is Gordy, the neighborhood bully who constantly terrorizes them. As the story unfolds, the girls, and the reader, begin to get a glimpse of the turmoil that characterizes Gordy's life. His father beats him and terrorizes his whole family, and Gordy is hiding his brother Stuart, a deserter, from the authorities. These revelations about Gordy's life open up new possibilities for understanding Gordy's conduct and attitude, but readers are never brought fully inside his world. The text leaves to the initiative of the reader either to investigate that world further (imaginatively) or not.

Yet this little glimpse is enough to shake the comfortable perceptions of the two protagonists in the story. They begin to view Gordy in a more sympathetic light and even make extraordinary efforts to help him. The story never makes Gordy's character transparent. When Margaret and Elizabeth offer to help him with Stuart, Gordy is anything but thankful. "What are you jerks hanging around here for? . . . You want a punch in the face or something?"(103). Even when he accepts their aid, he continues to resort to threats in his interactions with them: "'Go on,' he said, 'before I change my mind and sock you a good one.' He pedaled toward school, glancing back from time to time to scowl at us" (110). Gordy's ambivalence reveals some of the real chaos in his world, but primarily in a way that encourages compassion. Although readers do not completely understand his pain, they can identify enough to want his dilemma solved. It is difficult to say how this might affect a reader whose own world is similarly confused and chaotic. It may prove comforting or frustrating, depending on the prospects for relief in the particular reader's own life.

A further concern comes from stories that take readers, say, into the inner world of a Nazi prison camp leader or a Somalian warlord, who may commit great atrocities in the afternoon and sleep undisturbed by conscience at night, without providing the ethical resources within the story to keep readers from losing their sense of ethical integrity. Teachers must take care with young children, who may have less sophisticated conceptual and ethical resources. The chaos, confusion, and bitterness of a character like Gordy may prove difficult for these less mature students. I believe that it is best to begin children's education about intolerance with less traumatic stories, and help them to develop the critical resources that will aid them in dealing with more serious cases.

Angel Child, Dragon Child (Surat 1983) may serve as such a story. In it Hoa Nguyen, or "Ut" as she likes to be called, and her sisters are newly arrived in America from Vietnam. Their dress and language are strange to the kids at their new school, and they are unmercifully teased. In particular, Raymond taunts Ut, calling her clothes "pajamas" and laughing at her words and ways. Ut gains strength from her mother, whose picture she keeps in a matchbox in her pocket. Her mother has been unable to travel with the family from Vietnam, but thinking of her gives Ut strength to endure the teasing. Things come to a head when Raymond and Ut are caught fighting and the principal orders them to spend time together and learn about each other.

> "Hoa, you need to speak with Raymond. Use your words. Tell him about Vietnam." Raymond glared. "And you, Raymond, you must learn to listen. You will write Hoa's story." (18)

The story demonstrates that an impasse between two children can be overcome. Raymond becomes a champion of Ut and her family, helping the rest of the community to learn about Vietnam and rallying them to help Ut bring her mother from Vietnam. In this story, Raymond is not a difficult character to understand. His intolerance is still superficial and apparently easy to overcome. In real life this is not always the case, and some teachers may be concerned that this story makes friendship seem too easy. Children who have experienced much more resistant forms of intolerance may also have a hard time finding this story credible. Yet, it has merit nonetheless. Part of what educators hope reading stories will do for children is to expand and to enhance their imaginative capacity, to help them get beyond their own limited experiences, and consider a wider range of possibilities. "[W]e discover the powers of any narrative only in an act of surrender" (Booth 1988, 32). Thus, to view this story as simply naive would be to miss its pedagogical power. In deciding whether or not to use a story in the classroom, teachers need to keep in mind the full context in which the story will be received.

In doing this, however, teachers need to consider another potential problem with this story. This is a criticism not so much of the story in its particularity, but in the fact that it may be part of a repertoire of stories that serve to reinforce certain stereotypes about people that may ultimately work to support intolerant attitudes toward them. In the story, Ut's family needs help to bring the mother to America. The story portrays Raymond as the person who initiates the community's efforts to come to the rescue. Reading too many stories that reinforce this image of the ultimately kind and generous dominant group can desensitize students to those not infrequent situations where this is not the case. Thus, it is important for teachers to think about not only the individual merits and potentials of particular stories, but to consider the mix of stories that students read both inside and outside the classroom, and how, together, they might contribute to students' ethical development (Schwartz 1995).

This leads us to another aspect teachers should consider when choosing a story to use with a group of children of various back-grounds, sensitivities, and abilities. Certain texts can invite different levels of meaningful interaction. Most of us will have experienced reading a story again many years after having first encountered it, and finding quite a different story in the same text. Folktales often have this dimension. *Taro and His Grandmother* is one such tale (East 1986). It is a story that is set in the distant past, and for many North American readers, it is set in an unfamiliar culture. Because of this, it takes on many of the fantastic qualities of a fairy tale. Partly for this reason, such tales can speak to us at many different levels. As Marina Warner (1995) puts it in *From the Beast to the Blonde,*

> all the wonders that create the atmosphere of fairy tale disrupt the apprehensible world in order to open spaces for dreaming alterna-tives. . . . The dreaming gives pleasure in its own right, but it also represents a practical dimension to the imagination, an aspect of the faculty of thought, and can unlock social and public possibilities. Paradoxically, the remoteness of their traditional setting . . . under-pins the stories' ability to grapple with reality . . . the magic enter-tainment helps the story look like a mere bubble of nonsense from

the superstitious mind of ordinary, negligible folk. The enchantments also universalize the narrative setting, encipher concerns, beliefs and desires in brilliant, seductive images that are themselves a form of camouflage, making it possible to utter harsh truths, to say what you dare (xvi–xvii).

Taro and His Grandmother signals many of these fairy-tale aspects with its beginning: "Long ago, so they say, in Japan, there was a village at the foot of a tall snowy mountain . . ." (East 1986, 1). It goes on to tell of how a drought leads the headman of the village to banish all old people to the mountains to fend for themselves. Taro's attachment to his grandmother makes him very reluctant to carry out this plan, but his grandmother's loving care for him inspires him to disobey the headman. This act of compassion and responsibility proves also to be prudent when Taro's grandmother solves the three riddles that a powerful warlord makes his condition for helping the village. While the message is simply stated in the text, "Old people have had time to grow wise," a reader's understanding of this message and the story as a whole will depend on his or her experiences with old people or with changing perceptions of old people (25). Because many simple tales leave much room for the reader to make meaning in reading and interpreting the story, readers can continue to enjoy these stories after repeated readings.

At the other end of the reality continuum lie historically situated tales, those that we tell children are based on things that really happened. *My Name Is Seepeetza* (Sterling 1992) narrates the experiences of author Shirley Sterling, a member of the interior Salish Nation, who as a child was sent to a residential school for Native people in British Columbia. Its historical authenticity has a distinctive impact on children. That the story claims to tell of real events affects the way readers digest its contents. Thus, the quality of the reader's surrender is different from the case of fairy tales. Teachers explicitly aware of these differences will be more adept in planning reading lessons and responding to children's various interpretations and reactions.

Sterling's narrative gains its depth and multidimensional appeal from the author's honest, simple, and gentle approach. She draws the reader into the world of Seepeetza (or Martha Stone, as she is renamed at the school) by relating the feelings and perceptions of this child as she experiences residential school life: the pain of leaving her family, the confusion, the fear, but also the joy of returning home, of sharing the lighter and less oppressive moments in the residential school. If one has not experienced forced removal from family and incarceration in an institution of "learning," it is difficult to fathom the pain that residential schools inflicted. The unsophisticated style makes this story accessible to a fairly young audience (eight- to ten-year-olds). At the same time, the complex historical and social context of the events narrated can offer the reader with more background knowledge and understanding chances to find the most profound meanings. Without bitterness, melodrama, or reproach, this story tells of pain and entrusts the rest to the reader's heart. It is a book that invites and rewards a sensitive reading and by so doing, helps readers to develop sensitivity.

The authenticity of Seepeetza's story poses the question of authorship. This is another consideration that teachers should address when choosing books that tell of the special experiences of a minority people. If literary educators wish to help students gain a broader and deeper understanding of others (and thereby themselves) by having them read narratives that draw them into the world of others, it is important to ask who is authoring these narratives. The extreme example of how a former KKK member was able to write and widely sell a book called *The Education of Little Tree* (Carter 1991) underscores my concern. Carter's book claims to tell the "true story" of Little Tree, an orphan who goes to live with his Cherokee grandparents and learns a considerable amount about the "Indian Way" (Marker 1992). One of the main criticisms of the book is not that it was written by an ex-KKK member, but rather that it nurtures a perception of Native people and cultures that non-Natives find comfortable, while at the same time missing many important issues. That the book was authored by a non-Native, ex-KKK member cannot be dismissed as irrelevant to this point.

To address these concerns, another criterion should be used in evaluating the suitability of books to nurture understanding and respect. Teachers seeking to educate themselves and their students about a certain group need to look for books written by people from that group. Although being from a certain culture can never alone be sufficient to validate the cultural perspective an author puts forth in a story, teachers who ignore the stories a people tells about itself will send a clear message to students about their own perception of this group. Moreover, teachers seeking to develop students' moral voices need to help students listen respectfully to marginalized voices and not merely take paternalistic stances toward them. Compassion rooted in respect, not pity or paternalism, is the orientation that counters intolerance. Helping students listen to others (and to each other) tell their own stories about themselves may be a fundamental step in promoting respectful relations among them (Thomas 1993).

At the same time, however, I would not recommend that teachers avoid all authors narrating on or from a perspective not their own. To corroborate this point, I offer as an example the recent book *The Dream Carvers* (Clark 1995). The story is not told from a Native American perspective, but it does offer a look into a Native people's world. Joan Clark is a non-Native writer, yet she writes with sensitivity for cultural difference and displacement. The book tells the story of a young Greenlander, Thrand, who is captured by the local Osweet people after one of their sons is killed by the Greenlanders. Thrand is brought into the Osweet family to replace their lost son, Awadasut. Thrand, renamed Wobee by the Osweet, comes to feel a part of the Osweet people through their generosity, trust, slow acceptance, and inclusion of him in their way of life.

At first Thrand tries to understand his captors by using his past experiences as a Greenlander. Hence, he thinks they will either kill him or use him as a "thrall" (slave) because that is what Greenlanders would do. When this perspective fails to explain the way the Osweet treat him, he begins to open himself to a different perspective in order to fully understand and appreciate the actions of the Osweet. Yet, there are some concepts his Greenlander perspective clearly shares with the Osweet perspective: a general appreciation for kindness, trust, and helping one's family. These very basic values form the foundation for the bridge that Thrand/Wobee eventually builds to the world of the Osweet people; these, and the experience of sharing their way of life, of working, hunting, eating, and celebrating with them, struggling with them, feeling with them, and of sharing their stories. He continuously compares what the Osweet do and feel with how Greenlanders would react. The Osweet also try to understand Wobee better by asking him about his people and by listening to his stories. Although they take him to replace the slain Awadasut, they do not expect him to be Awadasut.

The story possesses many of the qualities that will engage a broad audience. For a general North American audience, it shows how two distant cultural perspectives interact in the mind and heart of a boy. It does not belittle cultural difference nor does it overly romanticize Native cultures while demonizing the "White Man." It shows how Thrand is transformed by his life with the Osweet, how his understanding and perceptions of his relations with people and the environment change as he comes to see things from the Osweet point of view and comes to be Wobee, a member of the Osweet people. This transformation is not without confusion and conflict, however, as throughout the story until the very end he is watching for an opportunity to escape and to return to his people. Whether his transformation is totally voluntary remains in question as he returns to the Osweet after effecting an escape.

Reading Orientation

The second factor for teachers to consider in assessing how they might influence the educational potential of reading literature is how children read the stories. Stories can give us *information* about other perspectives and ways of life, thereby exploding stereotypes and superficial preconceptions, and they can give us a chance to *experi-ence* (vicariously) what it is like to actually take on a different perspective or live according to a different way of life. While the former can be very important, the latter is the unique offering of stories. How can teachers help children read in a way that gives them access to this experience?

Louise Rosenblatt (1978) describes two different orientations that readers can take in reading: an "efferent" and an "aesthetic" orientation. These orientations indicate where readers direct attention when reading. Efferent readings are guided by external concerns. When reading efferently, the primary goal is gathering information to "take away" for some outside purpose(s). Most education assessment and evaluation practices tend to support and encourage efferent reading (Rosenblatt 30–40; Noddings and Shore 1984, 104–9). But it is the aesthetic orientation that gives students access to experiencing a story. This orientation requires readers to give their attention to the full range of responses that the particular text evokes in them. In a way, it requires that they open the floodgates and give themselves fully to the task of constructing and experiencing meaning through the text. Only when teachers encourage this kind of reading can they expect students to engage with the text in a way that fosters appreciation for different perspectives.

Reading *Angel Child, Dragon Child* from a purely efferent perspective would cause readers to miss the most important and effective aspects of this story. The tone it sets, the rhythm and sound of the Vietnamese words, the sense of passing time, the sound of Ut's whisper, the anticipation of Mother's arrival—the experience of all this would be lost on the purely efferent reader. One who reads efferently may come to *know* the story, but would not *experience* it. An aesthetic orientation, on the other hand, opens the reader to being touched by a story, allowing for a compassionate response. Teachers need to understand, however, that while aesthetic reading makes this response possible, it cannot guarantee that readers will emerge from the reading experience with tolerant or respectful attitudes. In other words, learning of value depends quite significantly on the location of the reader and the pedagogy used to develop the reading transaction.

Consider, for example, a child who has been raised with a narrow and biased image of Native peoples. If this image is further reinforced by unconscious fears, anger, low self-respect, low self-confidence, and a general self-absorption or insensitivity to the plight of others, the experience of reading the gentle story of Seepeetza, even with an aesthetic orientation, could simply reinforce the negative stereotype the child already holds. Potential responses might be: "How stupid of her to be so affected by this experience";

"So what if you are taken away from your parents; that could be fun"; "A bit of hardship is good for building character." These may not be very sensitive responses, but they could be genuinely aesthetic ones for someone who has not developed the intellectual and emotional resources to successfully comprehend and appreciate Seepeetza's plight. Teachers need to be prepared for this kind of unanticipated response. They need to find ways to help students achieve critical distance from and reflective understanding of their own biases that will allow a compassionate reading to emerge.

Reader's Background or Location

This raises a crucial consideration for educators interested in using literature to subvert intolerance and to nurture respect: the location of the reader. When assessing the qualities of a text, teachers often forget about the readers, but in fact this is misleading. The assessor must always keep in mind the reading audience. The teacher may imagine the implicit audience as more innocent (as opposed to worldly) and homogeneous than the actual reading audience the teacher may face in his or her classroom. In considering the location of the reading audience, teachers must not forget to include questions about how their own location influences their reading of a text and thus their assessment of it.

Bias, interest, and past experiences will affect the way a reader interprets the story in a text. Highly intolerant people will not easily surrender their biases to stories that assume an innocent audience. Such stories would more likely elicit scorn than compassion in these readers. No matter how educationally sensitive teachers are, they cannot guarantee that their choices will never result in a child's intolerance being aggravated, or a child's vulnerability challenged. The risk of aggravating intolerance needs to be taken seriously. It does not affect only the particular reader or readers who may react in this way. The rest of the classroom community may also suffer from such a response.

Highly vulnerable readers are at risk when reading narratives that tell stories too close to their own, or when they belong to the group the story highlights. Having the story discussed in the public forum of a classroom may make such students feel doubly exposed. This is when the classroom atmosphere becomes crucial. Without a supportive classroom climate, where respect is the norm, and where the students feel they can trust the teacher to be sensitive to their learning needs and interests, the educational potential of reading narrative literature diminishes and the risk to vulnerable readers increases. (For an interesting case study where a teacher was able to create the needed environment and choose the appropriate literary catalysts for students to examine a controversial and sensitive issue, see Athanases 1996.) Educators must ever be aware of the contextual (environmental) influences that interact with their teaching and begin to make the learning atmosphere in their classrooms a part of their conscious educational concern.

In addition to nurturing a supportive and respectful climate in the classroom, teachers can lessen the risk to vulnerable readers by choosing stories that include a sense of hope and the possibility of compassion, even as they depict disturbing incidences of great human cruelty and destructiveness. Teachers cannot expect to keep children innocent by completely circumventing education about intolerance and genocide, but they can choose materials with sensitivity and give students the necessary support and coping resources, at best, to benefit from literary experiences but, at least, not to be harmed by them.

The influence of past experiences, individual likes, dislikes, biases, and such on a person's experience of a story can be very strong, but aesthetic interaction is more than a matter of stimulus-response. The character of the interaction between reader and text can be influenced directly by the reader as he or she reads. Among the range of possible feelings, insights, and reactions that a text may elicit in the reader, he or she must choose a meaningful path or interpretation. What is involved in this beyond instinct, individual tendencies, the automatic-unconscious influence of past experiences and situational factors? What is involved, that is, in the conscious search for meaning? This is where a child's interpretive and critical capacities come into play, and where teachers can contribute most crucially.

A reader's interpretive capacities are greatly influenced by past experience with reading and making sense of stories. But they are influenced not only by one's own, personal experiences. Being part of a reading community whose interpretive capacity supports and nurtures one's own can significantly direct the growth of a reader's interpretive resources. When teachers encourage the practice of sharing and studying interpretations in their classrooms, help students to question interpretations by providing an atmosphere of attentiveness and curiosity rather than authoritarianism or competition, and encourage students to find and share their own meaning in texts rather than expecting them to look for the "correct" interpretations, readers have the chance to hone their interpretive capacities and become less vulnerable to purely reactive readings. By giving students experience with a wide variety of texts and interpretations, encouraging them to struggle for meaningful engagement, helping them to complement their reading with understanding garnered from lived experiences, guiding their struggle with their own search for meaning, and by providing students with a rich interpretive community, teachers contribute invaluably to students' interpretive growth.

Already reflective interpretations can be further developed by a student's more sophisticated and explicit critical capacities. From an immediate aesthetic reading to a more self-conscious interpretive reading, teachers should encourage students to move toward a critical reading of narratives. This is especially important with texts particularly effective at drawing readers in and carrying them along seemingly without much effort. These texts often make us feel very good—as *The Education of Little Tree* apparently did. A critical reading requires that readers distance themselves from their reading to question or examine the motives and intentions of the author, the assumptions of the story or characters, the impact of different literary devices on their reading, and the influence of their own biases.

Some stories have the capacity to help readers examine their own biases as they challenge readers to find a meaningful interpretation. *Smoky Night* (Bunting 1994) could provide such an opportunity. It is a simple story that takes place in a controversial context, the 1992 Los Angeles riots. Deep-seated but often hidden racial biases that touch every reader exert themselves powerfully as each person struggles to make sense of the disturbing events surrounding the riots. Contradictory urges to expose and hide the ugliness of racism lead to surprising and frightful revelations about humans and society. The racial background of Daniel, the narrator of the story, is never clear. Readers know that he and his mother are not Korean like Mrs. Kim; that perhaps they are like Mr. and Mrs. Ramirez, but perhaps not. The ambiguous racial identity of the main characters allows a wide range of audiences to identify easily with the narrator, without the divisiveness of racial identification inhibiting engagement.

Teachers can help students to access the transformative potential of such stories by encouraging them to reflect on their interpretations and to seek more justified and compassionate readings. They can do this by encouraging dialogue about how different interpretations make sense or not in light of different assumptions, emphases, and understanding of motives and intentions. Looking at the story critically, teachers may ask students to consider how the story might be different for them if they were to imagine the narrator as an African American, a Mexican immigrant, or of some other cultural or ethnic origin or experiential background. Another line of questioning that might evoke critical reflection involves asking students to consider how Daniel and Mrs. Kim are able to get past the biases and preconceptions that stood like a wall between them. How did they begin to see and treat each other like fellow human beings? Students may consider situations where they have had similar opportunities, how they took advantage of these opportunities, or why they did not. Teachers can encourage students to speak candidly about their own biases by offering the same themselves, and by helping students to see how engaged and critical reflection through the story can lead to enriched understanding of self and others. The more a story stimulates this kind of reflection, the more teachers encourage students to play with the story material to illuminate the ethical dimensions it portrays, the more reading can help promote students' moral agency.

Here, taking a critical perspective is not an end in itself. Rather, it provides a perspective on the text that can inform our aesthetic transaction with it. This is why the critical stance should not be evoked too early and why it should never be overemphasized to the point of overwhelming aesthetic engagement altogether. When readers take a critical stance, they enhance their capacity to engage in meaningful interaction with the text; the critical stance should improve their aesthetic experience rather than replace it. When teachers place too much emphasis on critical aspects, they can force students into an efferent orientation toward the text and thereby frustrate their deeper literary and ethical intentions.

By helping students develop their critical capacities, teachers can also help to protect students from engaging with texts that offer dubious ethical experiences, and give students the tools that can warn them of narratives that might take them where they are not ready to go. Helping students gain access to transformative experiences must always be paired with helping them to acquire the critical capacities to judge when it is best for them to pursue those experiences, as well as which to pursue. Part of taking this critical development seriously is respecting (although not always acquiescing to) students' judgments when they find a story too personally disturbing to engage.

I have argued that teachers need to attend to three factors specific to reading stories. As my discussion shows, these factors interact with each other so that any attempt to examine the influence of one such factor on the reading experience leads one to questions about the influence of the other two. It should come as no surprise that no simple pedagogy emerges from these insights. Yet the following heuristic, stripped of details, may prove helpful. Essentially, teachers must *choose* appropriate texts, *invite* engaged (aesthetic) reading, *promote* an atmosphere of respect and community that *fosters* the sharing of interpretations, *encourage* dialogue, and *guide* students in their critical examination of the messages offered by the stories.

Some Suggestions on Strategies

In what follows, I offer some strategies teachers can use to help students access the ethical and educational benefits of reading narratives. I begin by looking at how teachers can prepare preliterate children for this achievement. I go on to discuss strategies that help children as their literacy grows. At every level, the point is to make story reading an engaged critical challenge (Daniels and Case 1996), allowing students to exercise and develop the full range of capacities and resources I have discussed.

Primary Pre-Readers

Even before children start learning to read and write, adults prepare them for literacy by reading to them. By what we read and the way we read it, we teach children what to expect from engagement with a story, and we give them their first flavor of literacy. Through our vocalization of a story, we help children learn to interpret. We may, by the way we read, invite children to engage with the story and stimulate their imaginations, compassion, and willingness to entertain different worlds and possibilities, or we may bore them, stimulate their fears and anxieties, and otherwise give them cause to turn away from engaging with the story. Through tone, pitch, emphasis and inflection, rhythm, and dialogue about the story, we help children to enter the mood of a story, imagine the voice of different characters, feel the emotions elicited by the words in the text, and think about the messages the story offers. This is an introduction to what it means to read, not just a matter of word recognition or following and remembering a plot, but aesthetically engaging in the life-world offered by the story. It is common wisdom that reading to children helps with their growth toward literacy. Attention to the way we read can act like fertilizer, contributing significantly to the quality and strength of that growth.

Another strategy to use with pre-readers (and also with students at all levels of literacy) is to have them retell a story. Perhaps one of the reasons why young children seem to enjoy this activity so much stems from its educational virtue. Although no retelling is ever equal to reading the original text, both teachers and students can learn from retelling and hearing others retell a story. Asking students to reconstruct a story gives them a task that requires them to examine their interpretation and understanding of the story from a different point of view. This allows students to test the coherence of their interpretations, and in the retelling to reconstruct interpretations that better meet their sense criteria. It also allows for resistance and objection to interpretations that violate the integrity of the story or to stories that violate readers' sense of compassion or justice (Dyson 1996, 472, 480–83, 491–93). The task of telling a meaningful story imposes its own set of criteria that guides the construction of an adequate/conscientious interpretation. The purpose is to get someone else to understand and experience the story you tell. There is a feeling of accomplishment when others who have read the same story agree that your retelling is accurate, and your interpretation viable and illuminating. There is a feeling of ethical empowerment when resistance or objection is respectfully considered and acknowledged.

The teacher can learn a great deal from the way a student retells a story. A mere summary of the plot can indicate a tendency toward an efferent orientation in reading. This, however, could also be a response to the kind of question teachers use to elicit the retelling. If teachers ask, "What happened in this story?", students will more likely respond with a run-through of the plot than if teachers ask, "What is this story about?" or "Can you tell me this story in your own words?" or "Imagine you wanted to tell this story to your friend but you didn't have the book with you; how would you tell it?" To encourage a more aesthetic stance toward a story, teachers can also ask certain kinds of questions about the quality of experiences depicted in the story or how the actions or situations in the story made students feel when they were reading it. Teachers can also frame questions in a way that encourages students' active participation in interpreting and making sense of the story.

To give an example of how this might work with a more complicated story, I will look at Jane Leslie Conly's *Crazy Lady!* (1993). This story narrates the experiences of Vernon, a boy with his own set of problems complicated by the mildly traumatic experience of entering junior high school. Vernon's life changes when circumstances bring Maxine, the "crazy lady," and her son Ronald, a boy with special needs, into Vernon's life. Although his friendship with this odd pair includes conflicts and complications, it brings Vernon a level of self-confidence he had never known before. The reader shares Vernon's frustrations as he tries to help Maxine and Ronald through difficult times. Maxine constantly challenges Vernon's loyalty by her untameable spirit and her alcoholic binges. Vernon simply cannot understand this part of Maxine which works against his every attempt to establish a "normal" friendship.

The story narrates many struggles between Maxine and Vernon as well as within each of the characters. Students can interpret and understand these struggles with varying levels of insight and sensitivity. Asking students to retell in written, spoken, or dramatic form any of the key conflicts in the story gives them the opportunity to negotiate an interpretation, and to communicate it meaningfully to others. Reconstructing Maxine and Ronald dramatically also proves to be a significant ethical challenge for students and a pedagogical challenge for teachers. Experiencing this challenge themselves can sensitize students to authors and works which are particularly good at revealing the humanity in all their characters. It can help them to appreciate the difference between such stories and those which depend on one-dimensional stereotypes.

Reinforcing and Enriching Literacy through Reading Aloud

After children learn to read for themselves, adults tend to read to them less and less. Teachers can support students in their private reading by continuing the practice of sharing stories through reading aloud. Through this reading performance, teachers can offer students alternative perspectives on character voice, and through their unique emphasis in reading, potential new interpretations. Vocalizing a story makes explicit and reinforces the importance of voice in the aesthetic experience of a story, helping students to become more aware of how voice influences a story. Sharing voice interpretations can support the development of range and variation in the voices students call forth in their silent reading. It can also give them the opportunity to imaginatively experience what it is like to take on different moral voices.

Story performances of this kind offer new possibilities of interpretation to students. Having read a story one way, hearing a different interpretation expressed through a vocal performance of the text presents students with a different interpretation in a far more persuasive way than when someone tries to describe his or her different perspective. This is because it requires the listener to be active in creating that interpretation by participating in it.

Having Students Write Stories of Their Own

Teachers can give students a chance to develop their independent moral voices by having them write stories of their own about tolerance, intolerance, or respect. This strategy gives students a chance to take a stand by authoring a narrative that meaningfully claims that stance as valid (Tappan and Brown 1989). Authoring also gives students a chance to ask and explore important questions in their imaginations, to work through these questions and test out different ways for answering them.

Teachers must be careful in using this strategy, as there are children who are too vulnerable to write stories for public consumption. Teachers need to exercise judgment in assigning this kind of work. But there are seldom cases where a sensitive modification of the assignment would not be able to significantly alleviate the risk to the student. Teachers might make sharing a voluntary rather than a mandatory part of some assignments. Even allowing children time to write stories that they need share with no one (not even the teacher) could be an option. This would give students a chance to write freely and to gain confidence through exercising their moral voice in writing. Teachers can also introduce students to literary devices such as allegory, situating stories in the past, future, or in fantasy settings, and using animal or other nonhuman characters that allow them to write about sensitive matters in powerful yet subtle, less threatening and self-exposing ways. With particularly vulnerable children, it takes time to nurture a trusting relationship where the child feels comfortable sharing personally revealing stories with the teacher and others. Teachers cannot force this process without causing trauma to the student.

Despite this caution, it is important that teachers try to give students access to a public forum for expressing their ethical views, where students can take public stances in supporting or resisting other public stances. As Dyson (1996, 492–93) argues in support of the "author's theater" she observed and studied, this is where students gain the resources, skills, and confidence to exercise responsibility and where they come to appreciate the living force of integrity. It is also a forum where teachers can foster the building of and participation in a community.

As children's experience with narrative literature increases, they learn different and more subtle ways of incorporating ethical positions within a story. Having them write stories sharpens the literary sensitivity that supports moral sensitivity. The expressive literary experience of writing stories can be a crucial avenue for the development of a child's moral voice. Authoring a story is an act of taking responsibility for the ethical stance taken by the story. To author it is to say you stand by it (Tappan and Brown 1989, 190–92). As children are always telling stories anyway, helping them to develop this art sharpens their awareness of the ethical dimension of storytelling. The chance to speak in strong moral voices through the characters they create gives children a way to build confidence and develop social responsibility and integrity.

Moving from Story to Story, and to Lived Experience

Stories possess the power to make significant points about the devastating effects of intolerance and the great promise and dignity of respectful relations. Such power inheres in the concreteness of story language and narrative. However, it is stories that say something significantly meaningful beyond the particulars they narrate that occasion the development of moral sensitivity and responsibility. Teachers can help children appreciate this capacity of stories by making reference to familiar stories when discussing new ones, and making reference to familiar stories to help children understand and deal with situations encountered in daily life (and vice versa). Children constantly use the resources of stories to make sense of their world. They appropriate story material to situate themselves and construct their social worlds (Dyson 1996, especially 475–76). As Dyson also makes clear in her study and analysis of how children "played with" the story material of popular culture, they also use this material in ways that allow them to resist and negotiate the roles and relations that the stories (in particular, their characters) offer. Teachers can encourage this kind of critical "playing" by giving students space to do it and by guiding them to negotiate with respect (Dyson 1996, 493). They can also introduce students to concepts that will help them to articulate their positions more precisely and persuasively. In this way, students will come to see how stories can be meaningful beyond themselves, and they can learn to call forth the stories they have read to help them to better understand and live their lives.

Conclusion

If teaching about intolerance is to be educationally worthwhile and ethically transformative, teachers need to understand the roots of intolerance. I have argued that stories offer a unique advantage in educating children's moral intelligence in a way that gets at these roots. For teachers to make the most of this advantage, they must understand the connection between stories and lives, and how pedagogy can give students access to the transformative power of stories along with the critical resources to direct this power toward educational and ethical enrichment. I have argued that this pedagogy must attend to five factors: (1) the quality of the texts, both literary and ethical, individually and as a group; (2) the orientation of the readers; (3) the background knowledge, attitudes and skills of the readers, including their critical resources; (4) the way these first three factors interact to influence the reading experience; and finally (5) the classroom community available to support the readers in interpreting and reflecting on their reading. I have suggested that the teacher influences each of these factors with potentially significant ethical consequence for the reader and his or her reading experience.

Teachers can use the perspectives and strategies I have offered in this chapter to help students develop the compassion, respect, sense of community and fellowship, critical resources, spirit, and ways of life that will contribute to a strong, mature moral voice. By providing a repertoire of appropriate texts, necessary skills and concepts, a respectful and participatory environment, and practical and emotional support, teachers can open the way for ethically enriching reading transactions to become a way of life.

A class that has shared a number of stories (like a generation, society, or culture that has grown up on a common set of stories), shares a repertoire of perspectives, sensitivities, resources, paradigmatic characters, and memories with which to make meaning of life together, interactions with each other, agreements, disagreements, conflicts, and celebrations. Helping children gain access to community through narratives and helping them to acquire the necessary sensitivities to transform that access into an avenue for genuine ethical participation is to empower them to understand and resist intolerance.

Works Cited

Athanases, Steven Z. 1996. "A Gay-Themed Lesson in an Ethnic Literature Curriculum: Tenth Graders' Responses to 'Dear Anita'." *Harvard Educational Review* 66(2): 231–56.

Bennett, William J., ed. 1993. *The Book of Virtues: A Treasury of Great Moral Tales.* New York: Simon & Schuster.

Booth, Wayne C. 1988. *The Company We Keep: An Ethics of Fiction.* Berkeley: University of California Press.

Bruner, Jerome. 1986. *Actual Minds, Possible Worlds.* Cambridge, MA: Harvard University Press.

Bunting, Eve. 1994. *Smoky Night.* San Diego: Harcourt Brace.

Carter, Forrest. 1991. *The Education of Little Tree.* 1976. Reprint, Albuquerque: University of New Mexico Press.

Clark, Joan. 1995. *The Dream Carvers.* New York: Penguin.

Conly, Jane Leslie. 1993. *Crazy Lady!* New York: HarperCollins.

Daniels, LeRoi, and Roland Case, eds. 1996. *Critical Challenges for Primary Students.* Burnaby, British Columbia: The Critical Thinking Cooperative, Field Relations and Teacher In-Service Education, Faculty of Education, Simon Fraser University.

Dyson, Anne Haas. 1996. "Cultural Constellations and Childhood Identities: On Greek Gods, Cartoon Heroes, and the Social Lives of Schoolchildren." *Harvard Educational Review* 66(3): 471–95.

East, Helen. 1986. *Taro and His Grandmother: A Japanese Folktale.* London: Macdonald. (Retold from an original by Chia Hearn Chek).

Hahn, Mary Downing. 1991. *Stepping on the Cracks.* New York: Clarion Books.

Marker, Michael. 1992. "*The Education of Little Tree:* What It Really Reveals about the Public Schools." *Phi Delta Kappan* 74(3): 226–27.

Noddings, Nel, and Paul J. Shore. 1984. *Awakening the Inner Eye: Intuition in Education.* New York: Teachers College Press.

Rosenblatt, Louise M. 1978. *The Reader, the Text, the Poem.* Carbondale: Southern Illinois University Press.

Schwartz, Elaine G. 1995. "Crossing Borders/Shifting Paradigms: Multiculturalism and Children's Literature." *Harvard Educational Review* 65(2): 634–50.

Sterling, Shirley. 1992. *My Name Is Seepeetza.* Vancouver: Douglas & McIntyre.

Surat, Michele Maria. 1983. *Angel Child, Dragon Child.* New York: Scholastic.

Tappan, Mark B., and Lyn Mikel Brown. 1989. "Stories Told and Lessons Learned: Toward a Narrative Approach to Moral Development and Moral Education." *Harvard Educational Review* 59(2): 182–205.

Thomas, Lawrence. 1993. "Moral Flourishing in an Unjust World." *Journal of Moral Education* 22(2): 83–96.

Warner, Marina. 1995. *From the Beast to the Blonde: On Fairy Tales and Their Tellers.* London: Vintage.

White, E. B. 1980. *Charlotte's Web.* New York: Harper & Row.

4 Life Ties: Disrupting Anthropocentrism in Language Arts Education

Anne C. Bell
York University

Constance L. Russell
York University

To voice concern for nature in the context of a pedagogical discussion about genocide and intolerance is anything but straightforward.[1] The very term *genocide* denotes specifically human oppressions, and any gesture which promises to stray from the implied focus is suspect. Why, after all, should educators devote time and energy to the plight of nonhuman beings when so many people are suffering? More to the point, perhaps, why should space be devoted to such considerations in this book? These are troubling questions which we, as environmental activists and educators, have little choice but to raise and address. Not only are they representative of the skepticism that has met many of our efforts as nature advocates, but they point as well to the widespread assumption that humans are separate and qualitatively distinct from the rest of nature. Indeed, these questions are intelligible only within an institutional framework that upholds such a distinction.

Like other deeply rooted dualisms based on race, gender, class, and sexuality, the human/nature divide has served to explain and even vindicate acts of hatred and violence. As Neil Evernden contends, the absolute separation of humans from nature has allowed us to claim the unique qualities which justify our domination of the Earth (1992, 96). Our intent here is both to elucidate this dynamic and to suggest how it might be challenged through language education activities that honor and foster affinities for all life. Working from the understanding that forms of oppression intersect, overlap, and feed on each other, we argue that it is a mistake to consider issues of human welfare and justice without regard for nonhuman beings and in isolation from our broader life context.

This argument can be and indeed has been made on a variety of grounds. To begin with the obvious, since human life is interwoven with the larger web of life on Earth, we are implicated in the severing of any thread. Hence, as 80,000 square miles of forest are cut each year, as species go extinct at a rate 1,000 to 10,000 times higher than ever before (Leakey and Lewin 1995, 237; Wilson 1993, 36), and as landscape after landscape is poisoned and bulldozed for the sake of "progress," it is little wonder that human communities and, in some cases, entire cultures are unraveling. A recent feature article in a Toronto daily newspaper described, for instance, the impacts of oil development in the Mexican state of Tabasco (Diebel 1996, F5). Oil spills, toxic effluents, and industrial alterations to the landscape have resulted in an ecological catastrophe where twenty years ago the rivers and lagoons teemed with life and the human inhabitants lived well from fishing and farming. Poverty, sickness, and their attendant miseries are rampant, and social unrest ferments. When thousands of peasants blocked roads to oil wells to draw attention to their suffering, the Mexican army was sent to quell the uprising and many of the protesters were badly beaten.

Scenarios comparable to the one in Tabasco play out the world over. They bear sorry witness to the fact that the domination of humans and the domination of the rest of nature go hand in hand.[2] The global ecological crisis *is* a social and political crisis, and for this reason, many social change advocates, including ecofeminists and environmental justice activists, are calling for mutual awareness and support.[3] Sensitive attention to the needs of others (human and nonhuman), and to the ways in which one's social change agenda might help or hinder those of another, is deemed essential (Bullard 1993, 23; Taylor 1993, 57; Heller 1993, 236; Lahar 1993, 96). As Vandana Shiva (1989) suggests, people involved in ecology movements, women's movements, and peace movements need to draw inspiration from each other in order to challenge the ruling powers that imperil all life.

David Selby calls for a similar alliance among anti-racist, anti-sexist, and humane[4] educators on the grounds that all are concerned with "counteracting negative and repressive attitudes that fuel discrimination and injustice." Pointing to studies that have established a strong link between cruelty to animals and acts of violence against people, he urges educators to acknowledge and work from an understanding of interconnectedness (1995, 21, 26).[5] Anticipating resistance to the idea of humane education, he reminds us that it is not a question of focusing on animals *over* humans, but of recognizing the systemic iniquities that threaten humans and other animals alike.

We share Selby's view that concern and compassion for all forms of life should coalesce in efforts to educate for tolerance. Like him we also wonder whether educators will rankle at efforts to correlate human and nonhuman oppressions (1995, 22). After all, the very notion of "human rights" is predicated on the belief that humans are unique and therefore merit special consideration.[6] In the recent past, women and people of color were often denied rights because of their perceived similarity to animals (Selby 1995, 17–18). Are we really prepared, then, to blur the boundaries with talk of interconnectedness, especially given the ongoing struggles and torment of so many people?

It seems not, for the most part.[7] As Chet Bowers contends, many of the most progressive and critical thinkers in education today are silent about the ecological crisis (1993, 135). Schools, likewise, remain mute (Beigel 1996, 105). It is our contention that this silence speaks volumes about attitudes to nature, and points plainly to the anthropocentric bias that pervades educational theory and practice in the West.

Anthropocentrism is the belief in the primacy of the human enterprise and hence in the inherent superiority of humans over all other species and thereby the right to dominance.[8] Like sexism, racism, classism, and heterosexism, anthropocentrism orders relationships according to a hierarchical value system based on difference. Industrial society's relentless ravaging of nature is evidence of anthropocentrism, as is the physical, conceptual, emotional, and spiritual segregation of humans from the rest of nature in North American schools. Indeed, from kindergarten onward, educational institutions play an important role in organizing teaching and learning experiences along anthropocentric lines. Disciplinary boundaries, curriculum, teaching locales, and teaching tools all serve to reinforce the human/nature divide and the anthropocentric biases which it legitimates.

For instance, it is generally the case that children study "nature" as part of a science curriculum where learning experiences are mediated and controlled through human-made devices (books, computers, videos, laboratory equipment), and where nonhuman beings are described "objectively" in terms of physical attributes, functions, and various statistical measurements and calculations. In other words, children may learn in a setting which excludes any direct interaction with the subjects of study, and in a language which likewise denies reciprocity with the rest of nature by defining it as mechanical and determinate (see Abram 1996, 71). A further problem, as Bowers explains, is that the explanatory framework of science treats ethical concerns as lying beyond its legitimate domain of inquiry (1996, 7). Thus, even though there may be some discussion of environmental topics, as Jennifer Beigel points out, there is little deliberation about human participation in and responsibilities toward the natural communities of which we are a part (1996, 107–8). Both Bowers and Beigel propose that such discussions should be included in the nonscience areas of the curriculum, where a more explicit cultural emphasis could be brought to bear. Bowers, in particular, stresses the importance of educating students about the ways that language shapes our taken-for-granted patterns of thought and behavior, with potentially adverse consequences for the rest of nature.

Below we examine the constitutive role that language plays in human/nonhuman relationships and consider how such insights might be taken up in an elementary school language arts program. The challenge, as we see it, is to move toward a counterdiscursive education that disrupts prevailing assumptions about what it means to be "natural," "human," "animal," and so on. Creating space to attend to the quality and moral dimensions of our relationships with nonhuman beings and to voice and explore alternative understandings of those relationships is key. Before proceeding to a discussion of classroom strategies and activities, however, we feel that it is important to dwell a little longer on the "why" of educating for life ties. Because this issue is so rarely considered in educational circles, we extend the general commentary in order to make better sense of the notions of genocide and intolerance with regard to nonhuman beings, and of the ways in which language is centrally implicated.

Genocide, Biocide, Ecocide

The term *genocide* was first applied to the murder of Jews and members of other ethnic groups by Nazi Germany, and refers to the systematic annihilation of a national or ethnic group. It was coined by Raphael Lemkin (1944/1973) from the Greek word *genos* (race, tribe) and the Latin *cide* (killing) "to denote an old practice in its modern development."[9] Integral to the concept are connotations of intent, method, and choice of victims on the basis of their membership in a group (1973, 79). Genocide is no happenstance; it is willful destruction aimed at the eradication of the target, and the very deliberateness with which it is perpetrated highlights the heinous depravity of the act.[10]

We do not propose here to extend the notion of genocide to include the organized decimation of nonhuman species (although this has been done, for example by Richard Ives, who writes of the genocidal campaign against tigers and the genocidal war against the world's oldest forests (1996, 180, 297)). It is not that we shy away from comparing the two phenomena, but rather that we hold both the similarities and differences to be of consequence. The term *genocide* is one of many words that mark the culturally produced human/nature dualism, and the boundaries implied can best be investigated if they are acknowledged rather than ignored.

How then might we name the express slaughter of nonhuman groups? There exists, in fact, no English word perfectly suited to this purpose, but the terms *ecocide* and *biocide* will do. While *ecocide* refers explicitly to the destruction of one's home or habitat and is understood to include both human and nonhuman victims (Grinde and Johansen 1995; Marcuse 1972, 10), *biocide* evokes more directly the living beings that are killed. Neither expression signifies a persecuted group per se, yet both connote lethal acts that are purposeful and methodical. Often, ecocide and biocide are so closely intertwined as to be virtually synonymous.

A heartrending example of this phenomenon is detailed by Erwin A. Bauer in his book *Wild Dogs*. Since the implementation in 1909 of a national pest and predator control program in the United States, writes Bauer, billions of dollars have been spent on the "control" of wild animals. With regard specifically to coyotes, the goal has been utter eradication through the use of traps, guns, aircraft, poisons, military electronic technology, and synthetic hormones (for birth control). In 1989, the latest year for which he was able to gather statistics, government hunters killed 86,052 coyotes, an increase of 10,000 over the previous year (1994, 53).[11]

This and other "institutional wars" against wildlife are rationalized on the grounds that the victims pose a threat to people and domesticated animals (who merit protection from wild animals because of their status as property). As Bauer explains, however, such campaigns often defy even the most cold-blooded logic:

> In 1962, the ADC [the Animal Control Branch of the U.S. Department of Agriculture] reported killing two hundred thousand predators, including opossums, skunks, badgers, black bears, and cougars, but mainly coyotes, to save a few head of cattle and sheep. That same year, at immense cost, the ADC befouled 3 million acres of overgrazed public and private land in the West with 700 tons of poison and 350,000 lethal gas cartridges to kill rodents (prairie dogs, hares, ground squirrels, gophers, and mice) that stockmen claimed were devouring the grasslands their sheep and cattle needed. If left alone, the coyotes would have recycled the rodents for nothing. (1994, 53)

The vilification of target groups or species is often key to the rationalization of massive extermination efforts, and thus to the exoneration of their perpetrators. The very expression *predator control* defines its victims as threatening, and therefore as undesirable. The word *pesticide* functions in a similar manner by marking particular plants and animals as deserving of human contempt and enmity. A telling contemporary example is the dandelion, whose fall from favor is recounted by Des Kennedy in *Living Things We Love to Hate*. Once "the darling of society," cultivated for its nutritional value and medicinal properties, the dandelion was prized in many cultures for millennia. Its time-honored virtues have been all but forgotten in North America, however, where intolerance for this so-called weed expresses itself through the annual application of millions of litres of 2,4-D, a carcinogenic (causing cancer) and teratogenic (causing birth defects) herbicide. The dandelion, explains Kennedy, is "poisoned and despised because it dares defile the manicured perfection" of our lawns (1994, 56–60,62).

Terms like *pest, weed, vermin,* and *varmint* set fatal contours to our relationships with creatures so designated. Nonhuman beings labeled as objects of abhorrence cannot be tolerated, and so must be eradicated. The words themselves call out for a particular response. This is true not only of expressions that explicitly signify aversion, but even of those which do not. John Livingston maintains, for example, that the standard vocabulary of conservationists and environmentalists often casts living, breathing nonhuman beings as objects to be controlled and exploited by humans. Typically, those who speak in terms of stewardship, wise use, wildlife husbandry, sustainable harvest, natural heritage, and so on portray nature as a commodity, an asset over which humans have absolute jurisdiction (1981, 24–31; 1992). His analysis of the term "natural resources" is indicative of his general argument:

> Traditionally, "resources" (including wildlife) have been perceived in an entirely utilitarian light. Someone has observed insightfully that resources do not exist in and of themselves; they *become*. The moment we see usefulness in something—anything—that thing becomes a resource. . . . But we see in wildlife and other "resources" more than utility. Just as important, perhaps more so, is the unstated but implicit assumption that the use, whatever it is, is vested solely and exclusively in the human interest. The ownership and proprietorship are ours alone. (1981, 16–17)

Metaphors of utility and ownership underlie all discussions about the management and disposition of natural entities. Far from neutral, words like *stock, game, furbearer, timber,* and *natural capital* privilege user relationships and assert the authority of economic interests. As numbers and equations are bandied about and "sustained yields" calculated, those who "manage" nature create an illusion of detachment and control. There is no mystery, nothing beyond the human grasp, but instead only demands for more precise information and more efficient technique. Meanwhile, euphemisms like the "harvesting" of forests and the "culling" of wildlife conceal the slaughter. Shrouded in silence is any sense of nonhuman beings as experiencing subjects of a life, any recognition of their rightness or integrity. Their "radical otherness," as Evernden puts it, is "obscured by explanation and neglect" (1992, 122).

In light of this broader social dynamic, educating for tolerance with regard to nature becomes first and foremost a project of recovery. It requires bringing forth, into our sensed awareness, the emotional and ethical dimensions of our relationships with other life. At the same time, it involves recuperating meanings that have been trivialized or forgotten through common rhetorical usages. Searching for words and stories that better accommodate the wild diversity of human and nonhuman being also entails a critical exploration of dominant and alternative articulations and of the reasons for and implications of representing nature in particular ways. What we propose is that teachers and learners begin with the wonder, longing, fear, and affinity that they feel in their bones. It is here, in the thick of lived experience, that we can begin to acknowledge and give voice to partial, complex, and often contradictory understandings.

Bearing Witness to Other Life

The planet Earth is currently in the throes of a mass extinction due almost exclusively to the undertakings of our own species (Leakey and Lewin 1995). Most of us, however, are only dimly if at all aware of the crisis. We are ignorant not only of the destruction that is taking place, but of the very existence of its casualties, even those living closest to us. For the most part, few of us notice, much less know anything about our wild nonhuman neighbors, and in this customary inattention the seeds of destruction germinate.

To be sure, victims of intolerance are often marked and deliberately targeted, yet the opposite is also true: when the lives and interests of any group are deemed unworthy of consideration, another form of discrimination—a sort of intolerance by omission—can result. With reference to the absence of women, the poor, and non-Europeans from Western historical accounts, Stephanie Lahar writes that invisibility and violence are "strangely and intimately related": "refusing to perceive or acknowledge another person is one end of a continuum whose other is murder and genocide" (1993, 93). Nonhuman beings are similarly at risk when neglectfully written out of our lives. Indeed, a number of authors suggest that our failure to bear witness to the diversity of life around us has much to do with its eradication (Ehrenfeld 1993, 115; Weilbacher 1993; Nabhan and St. Antoine 1993; Abram 1996, 27–28).

Contending with the systematic erasure of nonhuman beings from formal learning experiences is crucial to efforts to educate for tolerance. For the two of us, the need to do so informs our every undertaking as environmental educators. Below we present a list of recommendations for teachers who share similar concerns and aspirations. The list is in no way definitive, but rather represents work in progress. It is offered as a point of entry for practice and further reflection.

1. Call into Question the Us/Them, Human/Nature Divide. This divide is a dominant, experiential reality for many of us, especially in schools. What experiences, appropriate to language arts, can we make available to challenge it? One possibility, suggested to us by professor Leesa Fawcett (York University), is to ask students to keep a natural history journal where they record their observations of/ interactions with a plant or animal over time. (Teachers of younger students might want to keep one journal for the entire class.) Whether children focus on a pet, birds at a feeder, or a tree in the schoolyard, the simple fact that they are paying attention and according importance to nonhuman beings is an important step, one which has the potential to surprise and inspire.

Students should be encouraged to share their journals, and so to participate in storytelling where all of the actors are not human. Discussions could highlight instances of animals thinking, feeling, and communicating, or of plants responding to sun, rain, changing seasons, and other living beings. The point is to create a space for talking about the purposeful yet ultimately mysterious lives of our earthly companions. Discussions could also provide a forum to acknowledge the difficulty of interpretation, including its arbitrariness and indeed impossibility in some cases.

2. Try to Work from and Convey an Understanding of the Ways That Oppressions Are Connected. Oppression is not a topic customarily dealt with in elementary schools, although older students will have heard of racism, sexism, and the environmental crisis. The point is not to conduct in-depth analyses of these phenomena, but to gently probe examples when they arise in curriculum materials, in the media, and in the students' lives. A simple means of highlighting the links between various forms of intolerance, for example, is to ask the students to compile a list of common insults based on comparing people to other animals. The words *pig, cow, rat, dog, weasel, chicken,* and so on will likely emerge, at which point the class could discuss how their use is demeaning to both people and other animals.

History, past and current, provides many examples of the links between oppressions, especially environmental destruction and the consequent harm to disenfranchised groups. Lynne Cherry (1992) documents one example in her environmental history of the Nashua River (for children ages 6–10). Her story begins with the river as it once was, sparkling clear, and tells of its place in the lives of humans and other animals for thousands of years prior to European colonization. Cherry then describes the changes brought about by European settlers, including the felling of forests, the decimation of wildlife, and the dislocation of the Native people. Industrialization spells the "death" of the river itself, a calamity which is reversed when concerned citizens lobby industry and government and work toward the river's restoration. Our one reservation about the book is that in the end, the hawks, owls, and deer return to the river, but no mention is made of the Native people. Their absence should be noted and discussed with students.

The story of the Nashua River could serve as a catalyst for student research about the histories of their own home place. By delving into the past and becoming more aware of what has changed, what has been lost, and who has come and gone, students will be able to consider and assess the "progress" of modern industrial society from a more critical perspective. In addition to text-centered research and writing, students can interview/converse with older people in the community. Such encounters will not only add depth and insight to their research, but also invite reflection on the importance of transgenerational communication and relationships which tend to be undervalued if not disparaged in mainstream culture (see Bowers 1996, 9).

3. Draw Attention to the Ways That Words Shape Our Understanding and Experiences. Attitudes to nature are embedded in and perpetuated through language. An activity well suited to investigating the way that words hide or highlight particular viewpoints and interests is David Selby's "Animal Adjectives" (1995, 121–22). We adapted it for a grade 5/6 workshop on wolves and coyotes where we asked students, working in groups of three or four, to list words that they associated with wolves, coyotes, dogs, and foxes. Once their lists were drawn up, we asked them to mark with a plus or minus sign those words that revealed positive or negative feelings about the animals. This step called on them to attend to implicit meanings and clarify their own interpretations. Afterward a representative from each group presented their word lists to the rest of the class, providing a further opportunity to probe and elucidate meanings and to link words and feelings to humankind's treatment of these animals.

Some words did not fit easily into the positive or negative categories. In three groups, for example, the wolf was described as *wild*, which was considered neither a positive nor negative trait. Many others, however, clearly expressed implicit judgments. The diverse and often dissonant characterizations of the animals led the students to question and challenge each other and, ultimately, to realize that their opinions might be surprisingly different. The exploration of the rationale behind their various representations was particularly fruitful. For instance, a number of groups associated the fox with the expression *thief* based on the perception that foxes steal food, usually chickens, from farmers. One boy, however, countered with the view that foxes need food to survive and that they are not stealing, but simply feeding.

When we asked students to recount their personal experiences with these animals, it became evident that while all had interacted with dogs, few students could recall encounters with foxes, even fewer with coyotes, and none with wolves. Their lack of experience with wild canines thus became a starting point for discussion about the sources of their words and feelings. It became evident that these were rooted in stories they had heard, films they had seen, and books they had read. One group, for example, playfully associated coyotes with the words *ACME, chases roadrunners*, and *dumb cartoon*, thus highlighting the power of popular culture to infuse their representations.

4. Help Students to Recognize and Move beyond Stereotypes. Deeply ingrained stereotypes about particular animals can condone and perpetuate intolerance. In modern North American society, for example, fear and hatred of snakes, rats, leeches, spiders, and certain large carnivores are part of the dominant cultural heritage. While there are good reasons to fear some plants and animals, misconceptions abound, fueling hysteria and violence. Working out appropriate relationships with other beings thus requires that we question the grounds for belief and action.

In a grade 5/6 workshop on "bugs,"[12] we brought to the fore the possibility that some commonplace assumptions might be ill founded. We distributed a list of statements which students were to evaluate as either true or false. Included were such facts as flies can transmit diseases; bedbugs bite; only female bees have stingers; and such fallacies as tarantula bites are deadly to humans; and earwigs crawl into people's ears. The exercise was helpful, not only in dispelling misconceptions, but especially in posing as a problem our intolerance for other life. Where students felt a particular creature's presence would be disturbing, then alternatives to killing it (e.g., removing it from one's immediate space) were considered; and where killing was deemed necessary, the ethical and ecological implications of doing so were discussed.

5. Acknowledge Diverse Cultural Perspectives and the Fact That All Cultures Have Not Interacted with Nature in the Same Way. When talking about human intolerance toward nonhuman beings, it is easy to forget or dismiss cultural and historical differences. This is a grave oversight in that it unfairly portrays all humans as equally uncaring, disrespectful, and obtuse, and dulls our sensitivity to contextual subtleties, both cultural and ecological. It is important, for example, to distinguish between the hunting of a wild animal for subsistence and hunting for sport or commercial purposes. By drawing attention to the reasons for the hunt, the rituals surrounding it, the technologies involved, the numbers killed, and the uses made of the animals afterward, it becomes possible to move beyond hard and fast rules and blanket condemnations.[13] It also becomes easier to perceive and acknowledge that some cultures (or subcultures) have given rise to more ecologically appropriate ways of being than others.

The "Keepers" series of Native stories and environmental activities by Michael Caduto and Joseph Bruchac (1989, 1991) offers a means of foregrounding other cultural perspectives. Each chapter begins with a traditional story from one of the Native American nations; the story provides a starting point for activities that reflect an interdisciplinary approach to environmental education.

6. Encourage Students to Question the Modern Linear View of Progress and Technological Change. The equation of technology with progress is a cultural given in modern industrial societies (Bowers 1996). Even though recent technological developments have spelled disaster for many species and for the humans who have depended on them, we seem singularly unwilling or unable to call into question the desirability of such "advances." We accept whatever comes along, seldom asking whether something that *can* be done *should* be done (Pivnick 1997b).

The story *My Grandpa and the Sea* by Katherine Orr (1990) brings precisely this question to the fore, and in a manner that elementary students ages four to eight can readily appreciate. The tale takes place in the Caribbean and is told by a young girl whose grandfather is a fisherman. The old man teaches his granddaughter about loving the sea, and when younger fishermen arrive with new power boats and big nets, he refuses to join them. "Times are changing, old man, and this is the way of the future," his nephew tells him. He nevertheless resists this vision of technological progress and material plenty, correctly foreseeing that their greed would soon deplete the sea of fish. Instead, he discovers a way to make a simple living from harvesting sea moss, taking only from the sea what it is able to give.

7. Try to Increase Awareness of the Links between Lifestyle Choices (Particularly Consumer-Oriented Ones) and Ecocide/ Biocide. Teachers should work from the understanding that consumer habits in overdeveloped nations are driving the "liquidation" of natural "resources" in ways and at rates that threaten all life on

Earth. While it is impossible to completely dissociate ourselves from the consumer culture in which we live, we can learn to distinguish between needs and wants, and to question whether and when particular wants should be satisfied.

Dr. Seuss's *The Lorax* (1971/1991) illustrates this point. From the bright-colored tufts of the Truffula trees, the greedy Once-ler creates the "thneed" which no one has ever heard of but everyone suddenly needs. With a few phone calls, the thneed business is rolling, and in no time results in the fouling of air and water and the denuding of the landscape. The situation becomes so intolerable that the area's inhabitants, the Bar-ba-loots, the Humming-Fish, and the Swomee-Swans, must leave. The Once-ler proceeds to ignore the pleas of the Lorax (who speaks for the trees) until there is nothing left of the Truffulas, except one tiny seed.

This fanciful tale follows the storyline of many contemporary environmental issues, and in so doing provides valuable insight into destructive, self-centered beliefs, values, and behaviors. *The Lorax* invites a critical exploration of the links between consumerism, the profit motive, "resource" extraction, ecocide, and genocide.

8. Anticipate and Try to Mitigate the Trauma That Children May Experience as They Delve into Environmental Issues. As Cathie Kryczka maintains, "disturbing pictures and stories of a poisoned world and uncertain future lead to feelings of fear and powerlessness." It is important, therefore, to present material in ways that children can cope with, and, where possible, to give them a sense that there is something they can do to help (1992–93, 16). Look for stories with hopeful endings, like *My Grandpa and the Sea* or *A River Ran Wild*. When dealing with a worrisome, yet unresolved, issue, encourage students to imagine both probable and preferred outcomes, and then to think of ways to move toward the preferred one(s). Most important, indulge fully and frequently in the beauty and wonder of nature—take time with students to enjoy fall colors, fresh snow, and the return of frogs and flowers in the spring.

In southern Ontario, for instance, when milkweed goes to seed and monarch butterflies migrate, the time is right to talk about this particular plant's role in sustaining the beautiful, familiar, yet vulnerable insect. The current situation is in many ways perturbing. The monarchs must journey thousands of miles to Mexico where their wintering grounds, a few hectares of forest, have been and continue to be logged. Closer to home, the milkweed, the monarch caterpillar's primary food source, is commonly eradicated as a noxious weed. Still, the story is not without hope, thanks to the efforts of many nature advocates and to the resilience of both plant and butterfly. Moreover, since the milkweed and monarch can be readily encountered in fields and roadside ditches, students can participate in the story's unfolding—as witnesses, admirers, well-wishers, and sowers (blowers) of seed.

9. Try to Work from and Convey an Understanding of Other Beings as Experiencing Subjects of a Life, in Some Ways Similar to and Some Ways Different from Us. Seek out stories and poems which suggest nondestructive ways of responding to "otherness." The poem "Weaving Home" by Michael Caduto (Caduto and Bruchac 1989, 34) is admirably suited to this purpose:

Weaving Home
Michael J. Caduto

Spider in dark nook hiding
     on tangled dust string insect net,
    buzzing bug on the cob is the corn
     for your table.

Sometimes I dream
     of one broom strike . . .
home no more
     for eight legs on high.

But then,
     we share this place
     and each day I stare upwards
     to see your larder grow.

Patient on silken threads,
     your friends who would spare you are few
     among those you protect
     from becoming mosquito meals.

Eight legs perch on aerial warp.
Eight eyes look down at two
     and ask
"What are you doing in *my* home?"

     "Weaving Home" is used with permission,
     ©1991 by Michael J. Caduto.

A difficult but rewarding piece for grade 5/6 students, it depicts a human/spider relationship in a way that invites an examination of our ambivalent and often lethal interactions with other life. It can be taken up as a meditation on tolerance and on the interplay between words, attitudes, and actions.

We asked students to identify expressions that described where the spider lived, and then discussed what the images revealed about the poet's feelings toward the spider. The progression from "dark nook" and "tangled dust string" to "silken threads" and "home," they realized, signalled a shift from aversion to tolerance. With some prompting on our part, the students also noticed a parallel shift in point of view from that of the poet to that imagined of the spider, whose voice sounds in the final line.

Caduto represents the spider not only as a companion, but as a speaking presence whose interests match and challenge his own. Through poetry, he is able to make room for possibilities quite inaccessible to or through scientific accounts of reality. Unconstrained by expectations of precision, method, and objectivity, his words do not transfix the spider, but instead reveal a willful and intelligent self. It is a use of language which supports and complements a thematic discussion around tolerance, in that it acknowledges an other-than-human perspective.[14]

10. Encourage Students to Remember Their Deep-Seated Connections with Other Life. The notion of the autonomous individual is one of the profoundly unecological "myths of modernity" (Bowers 1996) that must be challenged if we are to recognize, understand, honor, and sustain our life ties. Much environmental education theory posits that teachers must *instill* such a sense of connection in students. Yet, as Janet Pivnick (1997a) contends, these connections already exist, although they may indeed be clouded, obscured, or misted over. Our task, in that case, is to draw children's attention to the small incidents in their lives "which are already bursting with signs of connection."

One approach, again suggested by Leesa Fawcett, is to invite students to write an environmental autobiography. With pictures and words they can recall and reflect on the events, encounters, people, and places that have influenced their relationships in a more-than-human world. Feelings, values, beliefs, and actions with regard to nature are brought to the fore. Because the environmental autobiography features the local, the particular, and the personal, it can also serve as familiar grounding of an appropriate scale from which to respond to larger crises (see Ehrenfeld 1993, 123).

11. Bring More Fully Embodied, Sensual Experiences into the Language Arts Curriculum. As David Abram contends, modern Western civilization's neglect of the natural world and its needs "has clearly been encouraged by a style of awareness that disparages sensorial reality, denigrating the visible and tangible order of things . . ." (1996, 94). We need, then, to cultivate another style of awareness, one that is "susceptible to the solicitations" of the nonhuman presences that surround and influence our daily lives (20). This means venturing outside on occasion and seeking inspiration in "the depths of our ongoing reciprocity with the world" (56).

Since students tend to associate the outdoors with "play" rather than "school," outings require added attention to organizational matters and should have an identified focus. The trick is to establish parameters while nevertheless remaining open and alert to the possibilities that present themselves. For example, on a recent leaf-collecting excursion with a group of grade 1 students, one little girl discovered the velvety softness of a staghorn sumac branch. Her exclamation of delight brought the other students running. All wanted to touch. With a little encouragement, they then tasted the hairy, somewhat sour berries. Some immediately spat them out while others reached for more, and a discussion spontaneously ensued about their differing reactions and about the flavor and feel of the berries in their mouths. The fact that they could interact with the rest of nature not only through sight but also through touch and taste surprised and pleased them. It was a valuable and unanticipated lesson.

If we are to understand our life ties as something other than mere conceptual abstractions or physical constraints, then we must work at reconnecting words and experience, values and emotions, heads and bodies, stories and life worlds. We need to make room for the intimate, sensual, and surprising dimensions of knowing nature and ourselves as part of nature. Grounding our accounts in experience, in the sights, sounds, odors, and flavors from which stories are made, is vital.

Disrupting Anthropocentrism

We recognize that the issues and recommendations outlined above may be difficult to appreciate, much less act upon, given an educational framework which emphasizes human interests, individual achievement, technological progress, and indoor, book-centered learning. The adequacy of such a framework, in turn, is difficult to challenge because it reflects, upholds, and reproduces the cherished beliefs and values of mainstream culture. Consider this chapter then a plea for understanding and support. Despite the best efforts of nature advocates everywhere, species are being pushed to the brink of extinction at unprecedented rates, and the tide of destruction seems only to be gaining momentum.

Ecocide and intolerance have deep cultural roots, which is why calls for a greater cultural emphasis when educating about them make sense. Language arts programs have an important role to play in this effort, particularly in fostering greater sensitivity to and awareness of the language practices that give shape and meaning to our relationships with other life.

Notes   1. We would like to express publicly our gratitude to Judith Robertson for her decision to include the nonhuman realm in this discussion of genocide and intolerance. Efforts to bridge the human/nonhuman divide are exceedingly rare in critical education literature, and for this reason alone merit appreciative recognition. In addition, we would like to thank Blain Horsley and his grade 5/6 students at Macphail Memorial Elementary School in Flesherton, Ontario, for having given us the opportunity to test out many of the activities described above. Their responses and observations, both enthusiastic and critical, have been crucial to the development of this essay. David Lewis and his grade 1 students at Woodland Park Public School in Cambridge, Ontario, also provided insight and inspiration. Many thanks also to Roger Simon and David Selby for their careful reading of this paper and their astute editorial suggestions. Anne Bell gratefully acknowledges the financial support of the Social Sciences and Humanities Research Council of Canada.

2. David Abram brings another enlightening perspective to this dynamic. He looks at the forced relocation of oral peoples from their traditional lands due to clear-cutting of forests and so on, and argues that it is an instance of cultural genocide: "The local earth is, for them, the very matrix of discursive meaning; to force them from their native ecology (for whatever political or economic purpose) is to render them speechless—or to render their speech meaningless—*to dislodge them from the very ground of coherence*" (1996, 178). A court case is currently being fought in Canada on those very grounds. The company Daishowa Inc. has sued the Friends of the Lubicon, a group attempting to assist the Lubicon Cree of Northern Alberta, on the grounds that (among other things) the Friends are inaccurately characterizing their forestry operations on Lubicon land as constituting cultural genocide.

3. Ecofeminism is a theory and a movement which makes explicit the links between the oppression of women and the oppression of nature in patriarchal culture. The environmental justice movement refers to the quests and struggles of people of color which "unite environmentalism and social justice into one framework" (Bullard 1993, 7).

4. Humane education refers to efforts to educate for compassion, kindness, respect, and responsibility toward wild and domesticated animals.

5. We are somewhat uneasy with possible interpretations of this position. Like Selby, we believe it is crucial that the premise of interconnectedness not obscure the integrity and intrinsic value of nonhuman beings. In other words, an acknowledgment of our ties with others must not lead us to forget that they matter in and for themselves. The prediction that as many as 50 percent of the Earth's species may disappear by the end of the next century (Leakey and Lewin 1995, 233) cannot and must not be translated into terms of human interest alone. We cannot begin to fathom the horror of such an eventuality if we concentrate primarily on its adverse ramifications for ourselves.

6. Humans *are* unique, of course, but no more so than any other species. We need to keep in mind that claims to human uniqueness are tied not only to human rights, but also to claims of human superiority, useful in rationalizing acts of violence and disregard toward other living beings. Numerous reasons have been invoked to support claims to human uniqueness, including our manipulation of tools, our modification of the environment, our self-awareness, our creativity, our capacity for empathy and compassion, our reasoning abilities, and our use of language; and while such thinking continues to hold sway in virtually every aspect of modern existence, it has been either disproven or hotly contested on all such grounds (Griffin 1992; Noske 1997).

7. There are, of course, exceptions. For example, in her discussion of racist propaganda which portrays blacks as irrational brutes, Marjorie Spiegel notes that the stereotyping of blacks rests upon the stereotyping of animals which is "false" in its own right (1988, 31). There have been many notable attempts to extend rights to nonhuman animals. These have generated mixed responses, usually hostile, derisive, and uncomprehending, though sometimes passionately supportive. Yet, even dedicated nature advocates question whether extending rights to other animals is appropriate. They argue that rights are not adequate to all judgments (Ehrenfeld 1993, 129–30) and that the very act of granting rights requires bringing nature into human moral and legal systems which assume hierarchy and domination (Livingston 1994, 174).

8. In formulating this definition of anthropocentrism, we deliberately mimicked the wording of Audre Lorde's definitions of racism, sexism, and heterosexism (1984, 45).

9. Lemkin explains that expressions used at the time of the Second World War, such as "Germanization" and "Italianization," were inadequate since they treated mainly the cultural, economic, and social aspects of what was taking place, leaving out what he calls the "biological" aspect—that is, the physical extermination of the people involved (1973, 80). His detailed analysis of the concept and techniques of genocide merits careful reading by anyone interested in exploring this topic further. See also Totten (Chapter 1), this volume.

10. Genocide occurs in autocratic, militaristic situations, and often crimes against nature do as well. For feminist examinations of the connection between militarism and environmental degradation, see Enloe (1990) and Seager (1993). We should remember too, that even at times of relative peace among humans, wars are waged against nonhumans. Consider, for example, the military metaphors used to describe and rationalize the use of pesticides.

11. In a wonderful twist of fate, coyotes are now more abundant in North America than ever, despite the death squads. This is cause for hope, but not for complacency, for we must bear in mind the suffering of the individual victims. Neither should we forget that abundance is no guarantee of survival. After all, hunters contributed to the extinction of what was once perhaps the most abundant bird in the world: the passenger pigeon (Day 1989, 32–36; Ehrlich, Dobkin, and Wheye 1988, 273–77).

12. We used "bug" in the colloquial sense, including all sorts of insects that are not, scientifically speaking, bugs, and even some creatures, like spiders, that are not insects.

13. In 1995, with our friend and colleague Rachel Plotkin, we conducted a series of workshops on whales for high school and elementary students (grade 5). For the final workshop, the older students designed and facilitated activities. Three of the students focused on whale hunting and invented a game to illustrate the differences between traditional subsistence and commercial whaling.

14. See Sean Kane (1994, 191, 142–44, 231) and Neil Evernden (1992, 116) who differentiate between language that seeks to frame and domesticate nature, and that which allows other voices to emerge.

Works Cited

Abram, David. 1996. *The Spell of the Sensuous: Perception and Language in a More-than-Human World*. New York: Pantheon.

Bauer, Erwin A. 1994. *Wild Dogs: The Wolves, Coyotes, and Foxes of North America*. San Francisco: Chronicle Books.

Beigel, Jennifer. 1996. "Literature and the Living World: Environmental Education in the English Classroom." *Isle: Interdisciplinary Studies in Literature and Environment* 2(2): 105–118.

Bowers, Chet A. 1993. *Critical Essays on Education, Modernity, and the Recovery of the Ecological Imperative*. New York: Teachers College Press.

———. 1996. "The Cultural Dimensions of Ecological Literacy." *The Journal of Environmental Education* 27(2): 5–10.

Bullard, Robert D. 1993. "Introduction" and "Anatomy of Environmental Racism and the Environmental Justice Movement." In *Confronting Environmental Racism: Voices from the Grassroots*, edited by Robert D. Bullard, 7–13, 15–39. Boston: South End Press.

Caduto, Michael J., and Joseph Bruchac. 1989. *Keepers of the Earth: Native Stories and Environmental Activities for Children*. Saskatoon, Saskatchewan: Fifth House Publishers.

———. 1991. *Keepers of the Animals: Native Stories and Wildlife Activities for Children*. Saskatoon, Saskatchewan: Fifth House Publishers.

Cherry, Lynne. 1992. *A River Ran Wild: An Environmental History*. San Diego: Harcourt Brace.

Day, David. 1989. *Vanished Species*. New York: Gallery Books.

Diebel, Linda. 1996. "A Paradise Lost to Oil Pollution." *Toronto Star*, 25 February. F5.

Ehrenfeld, David. 1993. *Beginning Again: People and Nature in the New Millennium*. New York: Oxford University Press.

Enloe, Cynthia. 1990. *Bananas, Beaches, and Bases: Making Feminist Sense of International Politics*. Berkeley: University of California Press.

Ehrlich, Paul R., David S. Dobkin, and Darryl Wheye. 1988. *The Birder's Handbook*. New York: Simon & Schuster.

Evernden, Neil. 1992. *The Social Creation of Nature*. Baltimore: Johns Hopkins University Press.

Griffin, Donald. 1992. *Animal Minds*. Chicago: University of Chicago Press.

Grinde, Donald A., and Bruce E. Johansen. 1995. *Ecocide of Native America: Environmental Destruction of Indian Lands and People*. Santa Fe, NM: Clear Light.

Heller, Chaia. 1993. "For the Love of Nature: Ecology and the Cult of the Romantic." In *Ecofeminism: Women, Animals, Nature*, edited by Greta Gaard, 219–42. Philadelphia: Temple University Press.

Ives, Richard. 1996. *Of Tigers and Men: Entering the Age of Extinction*. New York: Doubleday.

Kane, Sean. 1994. *Wisdom of the Mythtellers*. Peterborough, Ontario: Broadview Press.

Kennedy, Des. 1992. *Living Things We Love to Hate: Facts, Fantasies, and Fallacies*. Vancouver: Whitecap Books.

Kryczka, Cathie. 1992–93. "Children's Books: How to Choose Children's Books about the Environment." *Earthkeeper* 3(2): 16–17.

Lahar, Stephanie. 1993. "Roots: Rejoining Natural and Social History." In *Ecofeminism: Women, Animals, Nature*, edited by Greta Gaard, 91–117. Philadelphia: Temple University Press.

Leakey, Richard, and Lewin, Roger. 1995. *The Sixth Extinction: Patterns of Life and the Future of Humankind*. New York: Doubleday.

Lemkin, Raphael. 1973. *Axis Rule in Occupied Europe*. 1944. Reprint, New York: H. Fertig (page references are to reprint edition).

Livingston, John A. 1981. *The Fallacy of Wildlife Conservation*. Toronto: McClelland and Stewart.

———. 1994. *Rogue Primate: An Exploration of Human Domestication*. Toronto: Key Porter Books.

Lorde, Audre. 1984. *Sister Outsider: Essays and Speeches*. Trumansberg, NY: Crossing Press.

Marcuse, Herbert. 1972. "Ecology and Revolution." *Liberation* 16: 10–12.

Nabhan, Gary Paul, and Sara St. Antoine. 1993. "The Loss of Floral and Faunal Story: The Extinction of Experience." In *The Biophilia Hypothesis*, edited by Stephen R. Kellert and Edward O. Wilson, 229–50. Washington, DC: Island Press.

Noske, Barbara. 1997. *Beyond Boundaries: Humans and Animals*. Montreal: Black Rose Books.

Orr, Katherine. 1990. *My Grandpa and the Sea*. Minneapolis: Carolrhoda Books.

Pivnick, Janet. 1997a. "A Piece of Forgotten Song: Recalling Environmental Connections." *Holistic Education Review* 10(4): 58–63.

———. 1997b. "Speaking from the Deep: The Problem of Language in Deep Ecology Education." *The Trumpeter: Journal of Ecosophy* 14(2): 53–56.

Seager, Joni. 1993. *Earth Follies: Coming to Feminist Terms with the Global Environmental Crisis.* New York: Routledge.

Selby, David. 1995. *Earthkind: A Teachers' Handbook on Humane Education.* Oakhill, Stoke-on-Trent, UK: Trentham Books.

Seuss, Dr. 1991. "The Lorax." In *Six by Seuss.* 1971. Reprint, New York: Random House.

Shiva, Vandana. 1989. *Staying Alive: Women, Ecology, and Development.* London: Zed Books.

Spiegel, Marjorie. 1988. *The Dreaded Comparison: Human and Animal Slavery.* London: Heretic Books.

Taylor, Dorceta E. 1993. "Environmentalism and the Politics of Inclusion." In *Confronting Environmental Racism: Voices from the Grassroots,* edited by Robert D. Bullard, 53–61. Boston: South End Press.

Weilbacher, Mike. 1993. "The Renaissance of the Naturalist." *Journal of Environmental Education* 25(1): 4–7.

Wilson, Edward O. 1993. "Biophilia and the Conservation Ethic." In *The Biophilia Hypothesis,* edited by Stephen R. Kellert and Edward O. Wilson, 31–41. Washington, DC: Island Press.

Resources

The following is a list, in alphabetical order, of resource books that teachers might find helpful.

Brand, Jill, Wendy Blows, and Caroline Short. 1991. *The Green Umbrella: Stories, Songs, Poems and Starting Points for Environmental Assemblies.* London: A & C Black and World Wide Fund for Nature.
Explores various environmental issues (e.g., water, air, endangered species, waste, food). Useful not only for school assemblies but within the classroom.

Keaney, Brian. 1993. *English in the School Grounds: Learning through Landscapes.* Crediton, UK: Southgate.
Offers suggestions for using school grounds as an inspiration and practical resource for storytelling, poetry writing, drama and language skills. Includes photocopiable worksheets.

Moses, Brian. 1992. *Somewhere to Be: Language and the Environment.* Surrey, UK: WWF.
Explores environmental issues through language arts activities. Uses original poetry and prose as starting points for discussion. Emphasizes the development of research skills, weighing various sides of an argument, preparing group presentations, engaging in constructive debate, and writing. Also includes a bibliography.

Opposing Viewpoints, Junior series, various authors. San Diego: Greenhaven Press.
Presents two sample views on various controversial issues and suggests ways of identifying bias in each; offers excellent activities for language arts. Primary goal is to encourage critical thinking. Relevant titles in the series include *Animal Rights, Endangered Species, The Environment, Forests, Pollution,* and *Zoos.*

Orion Society. 1995. *Bringing the World Alive: A Bibliography of Nature Stories for Children.* New York: Orion Society.
A bibliography of children's picture books "that reflect and celebrate the realm of the child and the natural world while presenting ecological information in ways children can relate to and appreciate." (To order call 212-758-6475).

Palmer, Martin, and Esther Bisset. 1985. *Worlds of Difference.* Glasgow: Nelson and WWF.
Explores the implications of various religious perspectives and belief systems on perceptions of nonhuman nature. Includes creation stories from nine different cultures.

Selby, David. 1995. *EarthKind: A Teacher's Handbook on Humane Education.* Oakhill, Stoke-on-Trent, UK: Trentham Books.
Explores and develops the theory and practice of humane education and suggests a range of activities, many of which are appropriate for language arts. Also contains a bibliography and annotated list of humane organizations.

Sheehan, Kathryn, and Mary Waidner. 1994. *Earth Child: Games, Stories, Activities, Experiments and Ideas about Living Lightly on Planet Earth,* Revised Edition. Tulsa, OK: Council Oak Books.
Each chapter is built around a theme (e.g., wetlands, trees, endangered species, day and night) and offers a wide range of activities to foster connections with the nonhuman. There is a "Dream Starter" in each chapter, a simple story designed to help children imagine the life and feelings of another animal, insect, or plant. In addition, the authors recommend a number of useful books. Sprinkled throughout and at the end of each chapter are descriptions of children's books particularly suited to each theme. Also contains an excellent bibliography of even more children's books, as well as resources for teachers and parents. A Teacher's Guide, CD-ROM, and audiotape are also available.

Many of these books are available through Green Brick Road, a nonprofit, nongovernmental resource center and clearinghouse for global, environmental, and energy education materials. For more information, call 1-800-GREEN38 or check out their homepage (http://www.io.org/~greenbr). Environmental education resources are also available through the Acorn Naturalists. For their annual catalogue, call 1-800-422-8886 or visit their homepage (http://www.acorn-group.com).

In addition, there are two journals that regularly describe a variety of activities that are appropriate for use in the language arts classroom. *Green*

Teacher is exemplary in this regard. Write 95 Robert St., Toronto, M5S 2K5; call 416-960-1244. *Pathways: Ontario Journal of Outdoor Education,* while not in wide circulation, has published articles on the use of narrative in outdoor education. In particular, see Volume 7(5). With its emphasis on storytelling, it provides an interesting counterpoint to the prevailing privilege given to the written word in language arts. (Contact Bob Henderson, 905-525-9140).

5 Inviting/Supporting Critical Praxis through Picture Books: "Possibility" in Monica Hughes's *A Handful of Seeds*

Christine D. Connelly
University of Ottawa

In/forming Readings of Hegemony and Difference in *A Handful of Seeds*

It is never easy to attend to the stereotypes in children's picture books about genocide and intolerance, but it is feasible to bring new hope to the moral, historical, sociocultural, and political texts of genocide and intolerance. In this essay, I address possibilities for inviting/supporting students in grades 4 to 6 to engage in critical analysis of genocide and intolerance, as seen in such picture books as *A Handful of Seeds,* which depicts the struggles of homeless Haqe children to survive poverty and starvation on the margins of urban Bolivian society. *A Handful of Seeds,* written by Monica Hughes and illustrated by Nicaraguan-Canadian artist Luis Garay, is a text published by UNICEF with the endorsement of children's entertainers Sharon, Lois, and Bram. I suggest a framework for inviting/supporting young readers of *A Handful of Seeds* to participate in activities related to women's studies, Bolivian history, human rights, geography, politics and current affairs, primary health care, community gardening, and community service for young readers in their immediate neighborhoods.

Through somber images and third-person omniscient narrative in *A Handful of Seeds,* Garay and Hughes detail the story of a young Haqe[1] girl/woman named Concepcion who struggles to survive by planting, tending, and sharing a community garden with other children who are as destitute and marginalized as she is herself. Upon the death of her grandmother, her only remaining guardian, Concepcion is evicted from the small, plain mud-floored bungalow with its cracked yellow walls where she has lived. She has little alternative but to leave her community with a cartful of belongings, a bundle of corn, beans, and chilies, and her grandmother's wise counsel to "save enough seed for the next planting." She descends barefoot along stony and muddy paths from the high plains with the hope of finding new opportunity in the city. Concepcion ends her journey at the periphery of the city, settling into exacerbated marginality on the edge of the dump with a "delinquent" gang of young men and women; she quickly realizes that she cannot access the city as beautiful place of possibility.

However, she does not despair. Concepcion remembers the legacy left by her grandmother: a handful of seeds. Soon, she conscientiously sets to laboring the earth to nurse bountiful bean and chili bushes to life for her survival and for the sustenance of the neighborhood's orphan young people. Using the materials available in the dump, she carefully plants what soon burgeons into a seemingly magical garden, nurturing the young people with sustenance and hope for community sustainability and well being. The collaborative community garden becomes emblematic of the hope inherent to collective action and mutual aid, particularly as an alternative to the alienating systemic controls instituted and enforced by representatives of state authority.

A Handful of Seeds reflects a commitment to making the struggles of Haqe peoples accessible to privileged North American aid communities who could intervene to change the present situation. In order for young North American readers to appreciate the meaning of this intervention, however, it is important for educators to attend to the sociohistorical context of Haqe struggles for life and freedom in Bolivia. Educators and young people must be aware that the Haqe peoples were at times abused in horrific ways by state policies and their enforcement. Archer and Costello (1990) comment on the abject dehumanization of Haqe peoples by successive imperial regimes:

> Both Aymara and Quechua people were forcibly re-located to work in the mines at Potosi where conditions were so appalling that thousands died of suffocation, accidents, diseases and malnutrition. Communal lands were taken over by the Spanish and *campesinos* were forced to work on large estates in conditions akin to slavery. . . . In post-colonial wars . . . the indigenous *campesinos* and mineworkers were used as cannon-fodder. (155)

Archer and Costello (1990) describe how Haqe culture resisted decimation even under the brutality of Spanish colonization, forced displacement, slave labor in the dehumanizing conditions of tin and silver mines, and legislated marginalization by the Bolivian government. Similarly, Rivera Cusicanqui (1986) documents how the oligarchic monopolization of collective goods and resources, land, the market, and political power/domination was carefully rationalized in official policy by such statements as that made in 1864 by J. V. Dorado:

> To yank away these lands from the hands of the ignorant or backward indigenous man without means, capacity or will to cultivate [them], and to pass them on to the entrepreneurial, active and intelligent white race, avid of property and fortune, full of ambition and of need, is effectively the most healthy conversion in the social and economic order of Bolivia [my translation]. (13)

Almost a century later, by 1976, 48 percent of La Paz was comprised of Aymara-speaking inhabitants, half of whom had been forcibly displaced by the revolution (1952) and state-imposed agrarian reform (1953).

A Handful of Seeds does not adequately pay tribute to the collective action taken by Haqe peoples for their deliverance from the state's tactics of genocide and oppression. Rivera Cusicanqui acknowledges that Haqe peoples did not tolerate the state's racist containment initiatives:

> For its type of insertion in the urban environment, the Aymara is especially sensitive to the foul aftertaste of the dominant colonial and racist mentality in the creole layers of the population and [the Aymara] live daily phenomenons of discrimination and exclusion with intensity. . . . [my translation]. (13)

Rather, as Rivera Cusicanqui elaborates, the post-revolution generation of young Haqe people, mitigated by rural education, seasonal migration, castellanization,[2] and entry into urban society, developed a strong collective consciousness of the paternalistic and manipulative features that prevailed in the management of the so-called "campesino problem." With this acute awareness of colonial discourse, young Haqe peoples recognized their marginality and exclusion and saw that with false rhetoric of being "free and equal" citizens, only the defense of their own culture (*la cultura propia*) would resist their manipulation by unions. Radio communications bridging rural and urban areas of La Paz became an effective mechanism to contest the antidemocratic character of the official union system. The participants in this movement made public statements recognizing the tyranny of homogenizing political, educational, and socioeconomic systems that had operated to alienate Haqe peoples through Western capitalist cultural assimilation practices to the extent that rural Haqe populations had to cope with deficient health conditions, unequal income distributions, and discriminatory price-setting politics. Road blockades were set up throughout the valleys of Cochabamba in protest; however, efforts were quickly abated by brutal military intervention with the January 29, 1974, massacre in the Tolata, Epizana, Sacaba, Suticollo, and Aroma/La Paz, where undocumented numbers of Haqe men, women, and young people were murdered, "disappeared," or were injured by Bolivian military convoys of armored vehicles.

Educators working with *A Handful of Seeds* should also be aware that there are profound paradoxes in this text that betray the possibility of Concepcion's "heroine-ism" as a young Haqe woman. Not only is the young reader insulated or distanced by several layers of silence around the tyranny of colonialism and patriarchal domination, but he or she is also obliged by the author's language regarding such concepts as "poverty" or "marginality" to adopt a naive complicity in constructing the subordination and alienation of Native peoples and in normalizing "poverty" as pertaining to "them." In this text, women are often defined in relation to the men they serve, for example, "the neighbor's wife." Concepcion's socioeconomic participation is subject to the discretion of the male authority figures, "the man who owned the land," Tomas, or the male police officer who brutalizes the young people, for instance, who determine whether and how she will be a part of the community. These men control Concepcion's space: the man who owned the land determines that she must leave the little house, Tomas decides that Concepcion can stay with the gang, the police yell and hit Concepcion's friends with their sticks. Moreover, the men are stoic and tough in the face of male violence. Only Concepcion cries in despair at their situation; she is positioned as a weak yet resilient marginal member of patriarchal and colonial Bolivian society. How to begin to invite/support young readers to consider and transform the narratives and silences at work in texts such as *A Handful of Seeds*? How to engage in the text in such a way as to honor and pay tribute to the humanity of the Haqe peoples?

Working out Problematics and Possibilities with Young Readers

The following section constitutes a suggested framework for working with primary to junior students with and beyond such texts as *A Handful of Seeds*. This unit is grounded in ongoing group discussions around the issues of genocide and intolerance as addressed through *A Handful of Seeds*, bridging three weeks of forty-five-minute integrated language arts periods. During this time, plenary activities are mediated through ongoing consensus-based decision-making processes. This approach is intended to invite/support young people to claim an active voice in negotiating the curriculum and personal/collective participation in the unit.

In this unit, the work with *A Handful of Seeds* begins from the learners' world knowledge with a plenary discussion about genocide and intolerance to invite/support the young people to conceptualize and voice their questions and assumptions. I suggest that points of conversation be recorded on chart paper or other available media (chalkboard, whiteboard, projected computer screen, etc.) by the young people or by the teacher with the support of the young people, to facilitate visual learners' participation in discussion. This set of discussion points can serve as an important resource for the class to revise and elaborate emergently throughout this unit. The teacher asks such questions as, "How do you know about . . . ?", or "Where did you learn about . . . ?" to begin to root out the layers of knowledge(s) to which the young people have had access. At the beginning and end of each plenary session, sitting in a circle, the group is invited/supported to participate in a voluntary and confidential "check in" or "check out," a process which means that each learner has the opportunity to either "pass," or to speak about whatever he or she thinks is important to add to the discussion. During "check in" or "check out," the educator also invites the young people to comment about the way they feel about the process of the unit, or the changes they see. During this process, one person facilitates and another person takes notes, if this is desirable; the following time, the notetaker becomes the facilitator and someone else volunteers to act as the notetaker.

Reading begins to take place through collaborative or turn-taking plenary read-aloud and group discussion, in small groups with discussion as the need emerges, in pairs, or individually. Part of the challenge of facilitating the reading of this text is to support young people to find a language to talk about hegemony and difference. The following types of initial questions demonstrate the specific phrasing of potential inviting and supporting questions that permit the teacher-facilitator to suggest framings without imposing any particular ideology.

> How have anthropology and history represented the experience of intolerance in Haqe communities? What does it mean to examine these stories from the perspective of privileged "outsider"? How can outsiders "aid" oppressed people without imposing ideology?
>
> How can we revolutionize our lives through our readings and healings of such hi-stories?
>
> How can we begin at the grassroots to end poverty and social inequity?

A wide variety of resources exist to support these readings/activities. In extension of pre-established classroom centers such as the art studio, the quiet reading area, or the publishing center, one possibility is for the class to collaboratively set up a community resource center documenting hegemony and suggestions for transformative activities, a women's studies center, a Bolivian information center, a human rights center (for a critical look at UNICEF and other similar projects), and a collaborative community garden, among other possibilities. The young people could also have the option to view particular videos, such as Goldtooth (Street Kids International) and to have space to communicate personal reflections on those videos in relation to their concepts about *A Handful of Seeds* and as grounded in their personal experiences and emerging concepts about hegemony and social transformation. Copies of the book and other resources could be made available to the young people for consultation and sign-out to take home. The teacher could also offer to hold conferences with each student or with small groups of students on an ongoing basis during reading activities. Students should date, sign, and store their work in their learning portfolios. As Figure 1 illustrates, this classroom arrangement allows sufficient space for wheelchair access to all areas of the room.

Potential Whole Group Activities

viewing Street Kids International's video "Goldtooth" (see http://www.web.net/~ski/goldtooth.html for publication and ordering information)

visit from guests from the Canadian International Development Agency's Women in Development Branch and CIDA's Multilateral Food Aid Branch (call CIDA at 819-997-5456)

video: "Friends of the Family" (1982), produced by Bernard Gérin, Derek Lamb, and David Verral with co-producer UNICEF, directed

Figure 1.
A possible layout for accessible student-centered working groups.

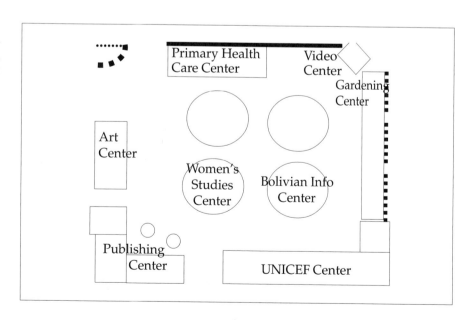

by Yossi Abolafia: An animated film for young people explaining the purpose of raising funds for foreign aid by showing, in a simple way, the kinds of projects the money is used for in developing countries.

video: "Keep the Circle Strong/Par la Force du Cercle" (1990), directed by Luc Côté, Robbie Hart, and Joël Bertomeu, produced by Luc Côté and Robbie Hart with ADOBE Foundations and CIDA: a 28-minute film documenting the five-month journey of Mike Auger of Cree heritage to live and work with Haqe peoples in Bolivia as part of his quest to reclaim his Native culture.

video: "To See the World/Voir le Monde" (1992) produced by Thérèse Descary: Seeing the poverty, hunger, sickness, and homelessness suffered by young people around the world, a young traveler decides to take action.

video: Meena series (from UNICEF Canada) (see http://www.unicef.org/meenicdb/)

Possible Learning Centers

The following suggests possible activity centers where young people collaborate toward consciousness-raising around issues pertaining to difference, intolerance, and genocide. The activities elaborated as part of each learning center offer potential starting points for young people to reconsider the layers of text at work in *A Handful of Seeds*.

The Human Rights Center

This center includes support materials to invite the reader of *A Handful of Seeds* to consider the rights of the child as identified through the Convention on the Rights of the Child. Documents available at this center include:

for wired classrooms:

- the UNICEF animation links: http://www.awn.com/unicef/index.html or http://www.unicef.org/meenicdb/
- the UNICEF information link: http://www.unicef.org/subinfo.htm
- Children Now homepage: http://www.dnai.com/~children/
- Centre of the Future of Children Web site: http://www.futureofchildren.org/cap/index.htm

other documents available through UNICEF:

- "Convention on the Rights of the Child" (booklet and poster)
- "The Canadian Committee for UniFem"
- "Status of the Convention on the Rights of the Child"
- "Canadian Coalition for the Rights of Young People"
- "Rights Now!" (most current edition)
- "First Call for Young People"

- "Communiqué"
- "Help UNICEF Ensure a FUTURE for Today's Young People"
- "Facts and Figures" (annual)
- "Splash" (issues 7 and 8 or later editions, with photocopies of pp. 4–5 of issue 7)
- "The State of the World's Young People 1996"
- "Within Our Reach" with copies of "Student Activity Sheets" for "The Paper Bag Game," "The Child Protectors," "What a Team: 100 Million Farmers and Ten Canadians," "Anx Vrnwu Iziaw: Listening for Literacy," "Word Power," "Student Reporters Set the Record Straight," and "No Kidding: Kids Stop a War"

UNICEF documents are available from a number of centers located internationally. The folks at the Ottawa UNICEF store were extremely helpful when I explained about this project. They are located at 379 Bank Street, Ottawa, Ontario, Canada, K2P 1Y3, fax: 613-235-3522, phone: 613-233-8842. The book *A Handful of Seeds* is also available from this store (ISBN: 1-895555-27-2).

Other possible activities at the human rights center include:

1. You are a member of a Doctors Without Borders team and you have heard about the innovations of the Haqe community in coping with tuberculosis and other illnesses. You and your team travel to a small Haqe community to learn about Haqe medicinal/faith practices. You want to support the community, but not in a way that would be imposing your cultural ideas. Would you bring medical supplies (limit: up to 10 kg per person flying internationally) to support the community? (Hint: see page 12 of "Communiqué" for other ideas, or consult your pharmacist or doctor)

2. You are a human rights observer traveling with a team through the outskirts of major Bolivian cities and rural areas in the Altiplano (Andes mountain range). What strategies could you use to support Haqe peoples to address the intolerances brought against them by the Bolivian military police? How have human rights groups dealt with these injustices in the past?

3. You are very worried about soil erosion in Potosi. During rain storms, the hillside dwellings are often washed away. Many of the people living in these dangerous locations were forced to move there from their lands in the countryside. Many of their former lands are now owned by the state or by powerful members of Bolivian society. What strategies would ensure that the community would have safe, dry, secure shelter?

4. What do you know about the experiences of young people living in the street? How are the lives of "street kids" portrayed in international development agency media such as *A Handful of Seeds* or "Goldtooth"?

5. How are aid organizations in Bolivia trying to help young people overcome poverty? What does it mean to fight poverty? How is environmental racism related to power? How do social and political power relate to poverty? Also, read *Fly Away Home* and *Uncle Willie and the Soup Kitchen*. In *Fly Away Home*, how does Andrew cope with his lifestyle? In *Uncle Willie and the Soup Kitchen*, would any of the strategies to fight poverty apply to your area? Create a collaborative partnership or join an existing anti-poverty coalition to fight poverty in your neighborhood. (Hint: see the National Anti-Poverty Organization for more information.)

6. You are part of a watchdog organization in La Paz. Your job is to make sure that street kids are safe from the police. The Bolivian government has not really cracked down on police brutality. What could you do to create a community where street kids are safe from the police or other dangers? (Hint: some Canadian organizations have established shelters for street kids and have strict procedures for investigating reports of child abuse on the streets. Also, see the Street Kids International support material, e.g., "The Making of 'Goldtooth.'" How do these materials represent the "Third World child"?)

7. What aspects of the UNICEF-sponsored book *A Handful of Seeds* do you find problematic? Write a letter (or e-mail) to UNICEF or to another source (newspaper, magazine, etc.) describing your concerns and suggesting other possibilities.

Women's Studies Center

This center will focus on the representation of women in texts such as *A Handful of Seeds*. Through the support documents available in this part of the room, young people begin to wonder about the scripting of Concepcion's "role" as caregiver-nurturer in Hughes's *A Handful of Seeds* or the portrayals of the Haqe mother and grandmother. Support documents could include portions of Trinh Minh-Ha's text, *Framer Framed*, with appropriate contextualization. Young women and men could be supported to reflect on their representations of women and race/class/age/ability/body, family, religion, labor, social participation (e.g., voice/silence, in/visibility). Topics include the feminization of poverty and sex-role stereotyping. Suggested supplemental activities include the following:

1. The Haqe language is partly based on oral tradition. If you were Concepcion's grandmother, what would you say about your life if you were telling your story to Concepcion beside an evening fire? (Record a monologue in some way.) (Hint: One way for women to enjoy equity is to have the same rights as men, but also to have an active voice in social, economic, political, and personal-political life. What have been the experiences of Haqe women in terms of equity?)

2. You are a photographer in Bolivia. You live in the Altiplano (Andes mountain range) close to Concepcion and her grandmother. Concepcion and her grandmother agree to help you to document their lives. You show them how to use your camera equipment and they take photographs of themselves to represent their experiences. Using words and pictures, create a "photo" essay recording the lives of Concepcion's grandmother and her ancestors and descendants. (Hint: What significant obstacles might she and the other women in her family have overcome?)

3. In Canada, society is moving toward greater gender equity. In Bolivia, a similar process is slowly emerging among upper-class society. What is the significance of Concepcion's social position in this story as a young girl, and what is her relationship to the men in the story? How will Concepcion view gender equity as she grows up? What factors would enable her to live with equal status to the men in her community? How can Concepcion fight so that women share power equally?

4. You are the Bolivian Minister of Education. UNICEF Canada has expressed some concern over the fact that Concepcion is not at school. Is UNICEF Canada justified in its concern or is it imposing an irrelevant set of values upon the Bolivian context? You must take action quickly. How do you ensure that Concepcion and her friends in the barrio have the same access to education as wealthier Hispanic children? (Hint: Read "Education of the Girl-Child" on the front page of the summer 1995 edition of "Rights Now!" Also, you should know that in Bolivia, "[t]he lack of opportunity begins early. In rural areas, parents may not see any value in an extensive classroom education for a girl. Despite laws that require eight years of school for every Bolivian child, many receive much less, and a girl is especially likely to get just a few years. As a result, nearly half of Bolivia's women are illiterate, whereas three quarters of its men can read" (Blair 1990, 143). What are the layers of hegemony at work in this statement? How would this cultural condition affect Concepcion's life? What evidence of her subordination do you see in the story?

What educational opportunities do street children receive? If Concepcion had been a boy, would her life have been different following her grandmother's death? For further reading, please see "Word Power: The Story of Nasim" on pages 37–40 in "Within Our Reach" (grades 5–8).

Bolivian Information Center

Young people contribute to building this center into a mini-library of reference materials critiquing texts relating to the socioeconomic, political, and cultural contexts of Bolivia. The young people will be invited/supported to read critically to hear whose voice is being documented and what generalizations and stereotypes are represented in available information. This process invites/supports students to ask questions about the framing of Concepcion, her heritage, and her urban environment represented by Hughes and Garay; Sharon, Lois, and Bram; and UNICEF. Some of the problematic resources available at this center include:

Internet addresses for wired classrooms: http://jaguar.pg.cc.md.us/websites.html

Bolivian daily newspaper, La Razon: http://la-razon.com/

In Spanish, Radio Loyola from Bolivia (requires a G2 RealPlayer or better for access): http://www.nch.bolnet.bo/WelcomeTexto.html

Other texts to be read with a critical eye in terms of representations of difference:

Blair, David Nelson. 1990. *The Land and People of Bolivia.* New York: Lippincott.

Griffiths, John. 1985. *Let's Visit Bolivia.* London: Burke.

Kohler, Fred. 1979. *Bolivie.* Paris: Vilo.

Lerner, Harry Jonas. 1987. *Bolivia in Pictures.* Minneapolis: Lerner Publications.

Morrison, Marion. 1988. *Bolivia.* Chicago: Young Peoples' Press.

St. John, Jetty. 1986. *A Family in Bolivia.* Minneapolis: Lerner Publications.

Learners wonder how "Bolivia" is represented in these texts: who has decided what information is relevant or important? Do Haqe peoples have a voice/voices in these texts? Other interesting resources for students and educators include:

Carter, W. E. 1965. *Aymara Communities and the Bolivian Agrarian Reform.* Gainesville: University of Florida Press.

Film: "The Aymaras of the Altiplano" 1997. Directed by Francisco Gedde, produced by Sur Imagen LIDA and Earthscape Lifestyle. Montreal, PQ: Multimedia Group of Canada.

The following constitute possible activities to supplement the Bolivia Information Center:

1. How do the media (e.g., online newspapers, RealAudio radio programs, travel brochures, etc.) represent Bolivia? Is any information omitted from the descriptions or photographs? What messages are conveyed by the brochures about Bolivian society? Using a map and any resources from the Bolivian Information Center and the UNICEF Center, research the points of interest noted on the itineraries and make notes about the socioeconomic and cultural groups represented in the tours. If you were a tourist, what would you see if you took one of these tours? What would you NOT see? Create two "photo albums" using art, music, and/or drama to illustrate (1) what you would see as a tourist on one of these tours, and (2) what you would NOT see on one of these tours.

2. Create a greeting card for UNICEF Canada that reflects multiculturalism/anti-racism and socioeconomic equity of entitlement in Bolivia. How can you represent Bolivian people with dignity? Use the resources from this center to learn about the groups of peoples that comprise the Bolivian population.

3. Create a topographic map of Bolivia indicating sources of water, food, and natural resources. Show where Concepcion, her friends, and her grandmother might live. What is the population of Bolivia? Where are the majority of people concentrated? Do you notice any patterns to the population distribution in Bolivia (e.g., by social status, ethnic origin)? What might be some of the reasons for this distribution?

Community Gardening Center

This learning center will enable the young people to collaboratively plan and grow a garden of corn, beans, and chilies with only minimal soil and only a broken kettle handle for a hoe, in reflection of Concepcion's circumstances in *A Handful of Seeds*. The young people may allocate resources in terms of producing sufficient food for everyone's nourishment/enjoyment, or for a particular purpose (e.g., foodbank or communal kitchen donations). The materials available to the young people at this activity station include soil such as that found at the edge of the dump where Concepcion and her acquaintances established their garden, rain water (or else clean water from the primary health care station workshop on water purification), and commercial packages of corn, bean, and chili seeds.

Additional activities could include:

1. Team up with a few friends to plan and care for a community garden. What symbolic value might this garden have as a memorial to Haqe/minority peoples in Bolivia and minorities around the world? Remember: you only have a limited number of seeds to last you for the rest of your life! Think ahead to the needs of your classmates in view of producing sufficient food for everyone's nourishment and enjoyment. Be sure to clear away the rocks and other debris from the poor soil and use clean water obtained from the water purification workshop at the Primary Health Care Center.

2. Given the resources available to Concepcion, create a plan for an alternate growing method for these street children. On the edge of the dump where Concepcion lives with her friends, there is likely less than 40 cm deep of arable soil for planting and no clean drinking water. If the children consume corn, beans, and chilies produced with water contaminated by the poor sanitation systems of the barrio and the pollution from the city and the dump, the children may develop bacterial infections, diarrhea, and diseases. Furthermore, the soil will lose its nutrients if reused too soon after a crop has grown and will not yield the same vegetation a second or third time. What can Concepcion and her friends do to ensure the sustainability of their crops? How else could Concepcion grow beans, corn, and chilies from seed?

3. Read the instructions on the back of the bean, corn, and chili seed packages. How long would it take for the seeds to grow? What conditions (soil, light, water, temperature) would the seeds require in order to germinate? Concepcion didn't get her seeds from a package. How did she know how long it would take for her beans to grow? Would the instructions on your seed packets apply to the conditions in Bolivia? What might happen if your seeds were planted in Bolivia? Would pesticides be necessary? What effect would they have in Bolivia? Compare the climates of your region and Concepcion's area of Bolivia. Draw a graph to show when the growing season begins in your region and when it begins in Bolivia. Show how quickly the seeds would grow in each environment. Use the resources at the Bolivia Information Center for information about Bolivia's growing climate.

Primary Health Care Center

This center invites/supports young people to wonder about arbitrary standards such as "nutrition," "normal growth" patterns in young people, disease prevention methodology including immunization and water purification, and the environmental conditions in which Concepcion and her friends lived and worked. Suggestions for activities include:

1. You work in a clinic in Potosi and go to visit Concepcion and her friends to make sure that they are healthy. What are Concepcion's basic survival needs? What comprises Concepcion's diet? How old is she? Is she meeting her daily nutritional requirements? What effect does Concepcion's climate have on her health needs? Complete a patient's chart to show how Concepcion's daily food intake compares with nutritional requirements for her age group. If she is not meeting her daily requirements, create a nutritional plan to account for her health needs based on the energy and food sources available to her in her environment. Compare this new diet with your own daily food intake.

2. Water in Potosi is not drinkable, yet Concepcion and her friends need water for their gardens of beans, corn, and chilies. Why is their water polluted? What would happen if they consumed the contaminated water? What could Concepcion and her friends do to protect themselves from disease? Read "The Clean Water Girl" in "Within Our Reach" (grades 1–4), then create your own "Solar Water Cleaner" either by following the directions on p. 25 of "Within Our Reach" (grades 1–4), or else by inventing your own machine. If you invent your own machine, think carefully about the materials that would be available to Concepcion and her friends in the barrio. (Hint: What materials from the list of things required to build the "Solar Water Cleaner" might NOT be available to Concepcion and her gang?)

Evaluation

The young peoples' work in this unit will be evaluated according to formative, process-based assessment which will include peer evaluation, teacher evaluation, and self evaluation. The young people will be invited/supported to become actively involved in goal setting and self monitoring as part of their metacognitive learning processes. A chart such as this can be completed by each child at certain intervals as necessary, or perhaps at the beginning of every language arts period, to be reviewed after every conference:

Table 1.
An example of a student-designed format for self-direction.

Goal	Strategy	Reflections

Goals can be as general as "I will try to listen when my group members are talking" or "I will try to work for forty minutes with my group" or as pointed as "I will draw about 'voice.'" One possible way of evaluating young people in their participation in learning activities surrounding this unit is to negotiate with the class the completion of a certain number of "points" worth of activities as a rough target. In this way, learners are able to focus on whatever activities they choose to complete as long as their process of exploration leads them through activities worth, for example, fifteen points. Alternatively, during conferencing, the teacher talks with each young person about the way in which he or she would like to be evaluated for progress. Learners talk about the sorts of activities that they plan to work on and how they would like their work to be weighted. Educators also suggest various possibilities for evaluation. For example, one option is to show a young person a few evaluation schemas and to discuss the ways in which they might be synthesized into an evaluation rubric appropriate for his or her work. One example of this sort of rubric looks like this:

Table 2.
Possible evaluation criteria for a final product.

Criteria	Descriptors	Evaluation
Content	• conducts extensive research (notes, personal dictionary and journal entries)	20%
	• answers learning center questions with richness of relevant supporting detail (evidence of emergence of thought through prewriting and process writing)	10%
	• writes with technical accuracy; uses appropriate and precise vocabulary, spelling, grammar (evidence of prewriting, drafting, and editing in writing)	5%
	• completes required number of questions	5%
	• develops coherent arguments	5%
	• writes originally and creatively, demonstrating interesting and thoughtful presentation of new ideas; asks interesting and provoking questions to theorize about poverty as evidenced in *A Handful of Seeds*	20%
Task Commitment	• sets reasonable (attainable) daily goals to structure work periods	15%
	• progresses conscientiously toward established goals	10%
Interpersonal Skills	• collaborates and cooperates harmoniously with peers and teacher/facilitator	10%

Educator Self-Evaluation Rubrics

The success of this unit is assessed based on several indicators. First, the educator seeks feedback from pupils on their enjoyment of the book *A Handful of Seeds,* and requests feedback on the value of the learning center activities in terms of interest and process. Second, the educator reflects on his or her own progress through ongoing field notes, considering students' anonymous suggestion box entries, or according to qualitative observation.

A Pedagogy of Hope

As Simon (1992) argues, the register of historical possibility—a possibility for hope and transformation—is distinct from the register of secular history, which defines the present. Simon claims,

> Clearly we all live in an empirical present that must be grasped and acknowledged. However, we also live within an ethical present whose forward-pressing hopefulness is its most precious feature. A critical educational practice that suppresses either register cannot help but fall prey to either a cynical deconstructionism or a wishful futurism. (149)

Thus, the activities in this unit are intended to support a collaborative edification of human dignity through an ongoing commitment to hopeful critical praxis. In the conclusion of this unit, young people can be invited/supported to join a plenary discussion to wonder about hope and history in the context of the class activities that have the potential to transform views of the past and ever-shifting present. In reconsidering this chapter, I return to the pressing question: What sort of transformative reading is possible through the critical reading of hegemonic representations of difference? How, I wonder, do we move beyond the colonial view of the Other toward the possibility of a genuine dialectic around the collective responsibilities to support social justice, locally or globally, in a way that does not intrude or impose particular ideologies, but which registers the possibility of difference?

Notes

1. Osborne (1973) and others have documented the colonial implications of the term *Aymara,* illustrating that the name Aymara was "applied in error" to designate all of the inhabitants of the lacustrine basin and the Bolivian Altiplano speaking the language Aymara:

> These people have never called themselves Aymaras but either collectively *Haqe,* or "men" or by the names of the various territorial groups into which they were organized. The *Aymaraes* were originally a people of the Quechua group established about a hundred miles north of Cuzco, Bolivia; at some time after their incorporation

into the Inca empire a colony, or *mitmac*, of these Aymaras was settled by the southern shores of the lake. Much later, when the Jesuits began their missionary work at Juli, they came across some of these old colonists of the Aymaraes and quite mistakenly transferred their name to all the peoples of the southern shores of the lake and the Altiplano whom we now call Aymaras. (13)

I use the name *Haqe* in reflection of the overgeneralization of ethnicity in *A Handful of Seeds*, but also as an indication of the problematic of the imposed categorization "Aymara" and as a demonstration of respect for the right to self-determination.

2. *Castellanization* refers to the colonial or imperial imposition of Spanish (Castellano) language/culture, especially upon indigenous peoples, as the only legitimate means to "civilization" or socioeconomic inclusion.

Works Cited

Archer, David, and Patrick Costello. 1990. *Literacy and Power: The Latin American Battleground.* London: Earthscan.

Blair, David Nelson. 1990. *The Land and People of Bolivia.* New York: Lippincott.

Hughes, Monica. 1993. *A Handful of Seeds.* Toronto: Lester.

Multiculturalism and Citizenship Canada. 1991. *Convention on the Rights of the Child.* Ottawa: Human Rights Directorate.

Osborne, Harold. 1973. *Indians of the Andes: Aymaras and Quechuas.* New York: Coopers Square Publishers.

Rivera Cusicanqui, Silvia. 1986. *Oprimidos pero No Vencidos: Luchas del Campesinadoaymara y Qhechwa de Bolivia, 1900–1980.* [*Oppressed but Not Defeated: The Struggles of the Aymara and Quechwa Rural Peoples of Bolivia, 1900–1980*]. Geneva: United Nations.

Simon, Roger I. 1992. *Teaching against the Grain: Texts for a Pedagogy of Possibility.* Toronto: OISE Press.

Trinh, Thi Minh-Ha. 1992. *Framer Framed.* New York: Routledge.

Suggested Readings

Apple, M. W. 1990. *Ideology and Curriculum.* New York: Routledge.

Bhabha, Homi. 1994. *The Location of Culture.* London: Routledge.

Corrigan, P. 1987. "In/forming schooling." In *Critical Pedagogy and Cultural Power,* edited by D. W. Livingstone et al. Toronto: Garamond.

Foucault, Michel. 1972. *The Archaeology of Knowledge.* London: Routledge.

Freire, Paulo. 1994. *Pedagogy of Hope.* New York: Continuum.

Spivak, Gayatri C. 1990. *The Post-colonial Critic: Interviews, Strategies, Dialogues.* New York: Routledge.

Trinh, Thi Minh-Ha. 1991. *When the Moon Waxes Red: Representation, Gender and Cultural Politics.* New York: Routledge.

Re-Reading the Bad Guys: Sixth Graders' Understanding of Nazi Soldiers in *Number the Stars*

April D. Nauman
University of Illinois at Chicago

Ten years ago, I went to see the concentration camp at Dachau. I went alone. I rode a train from Munich and transferred to the "Concentration Camp" bus—a regular municipal bus full of children coming home from school. Inside the compound, tourists snapped pictures of one another in front of the guard towers, as though they were at some national monument. I walked through the museum building near the entrance, intending to go quickly but not able to: the black-and-white photographs on the walls would not be simply glanced at, and I spent a long, silent time looking at one series of four photos—three close-ups of the suffering face of a young man subjected to a medical experiment, the fourth a picture of his dissected brain. At the other end of the camp, I crept through the buildings that housed the gas chamber and crematorium, crept out, then realized that I had stayed too long in this place, and I faced the heavy task of walking back across the compound, across a gray open space of crushing air—air that felt visceral, weighted, so that each step I took was slower and harder.

These impressions have stayed with me for ten years. The most prominent, however, both then and now, is this: When the Dachau bus first pulled up at the gates of the concentration camp, I didn't realize that I was there. It was not what I had expected. Without the dramatic camera angles and haunting background music, this concentration camp did not appear as the dark and looming place of infamy that I had seen in so many images. In fact, it looked ordinary. It looked modern, small, and suburban—a place anyone anywhere might pass on his or her way to work every day. For me, this became the dominant metaphor of the place: that extreme human cruelty can occur in any collection of ordinary buildings, which simply blend in, *anywhere*.

This impression has strengthened my conviction that new generations need to learn about the Holocaust. In addition to re-membering and honoring the victims of the Holocaust, students must learn to recognize the dangers of growing intolerances in their own country and lives. Students need to know about the Holocaust not only as a unique historical event, but also to provide them with a context for understanding modern-day acts of genocide and intoler-ance as well as the sociocultural environments in which such crimes become possible.

Unfortunately, an organized study of the Holocaust is often not a part of predetermined late elementary or middle school cur-ricula. How, then, can busy, overburdened teachers with too little time expose their students to the important lessons of the Holocaust?

For years I thought that one answer to this dilemma lay in the use of historical children's literature. "Good books" such as Lois Lowry's *Number the Stars* (1989) could be assigned or recommended (to children aged nine or ten to twelve years) for outside reading or sustained-silent reading periods. To me, a devotee of integrated instruction, the lure of this approach was irresistible. Giving students literary works set during World War II accomplishes several objec-tives: exposure to the rich language and exciting stories of good writers, historical information, *and* the humanitarian themes that are so important to children's growth as socially responsible beings.

However, a recent experience has revealed the pitfalls of such an approach. Through this experience I learned that not only is an "incidental" use of historical literature (i.e., the use of such literature without specific pedagogical support) inadequate for conveying historical facts, it may actually *undermine* educational attempts to convey humanitarian themes by reinforcing patterns of simplistic and intolerant ways of thinking about others. In this essay I share the lessons that I learned from a group of sixth graders' understanding of Nazi soldiers in *Number the Stars*.

Students' Understanding of Lowry's Nazi Characters

I recently spent a semester in an elementary school in a middle-class Chicago suburb collecting data for my doctoral dissertation, a study of how girls and boys understand and are influenced by fictional characters, with a focus on gender issues (Nauman 1997).[1] As part of that study, six sixth graders and I read and discussed *Number the Stars* in a small-group setting. This novel—a popular Newbery Award–winner about a ten-year-old girl (Annemarie) who helps her family smuggle Jews out of Nazi-occupied Denmark—was one I knew well and often recommended to fifth- and sixth-grade children. I included it in my study primarily because I felt it was a typical example of a story about a brave girl. However, I was also cognizant of the value of its historical content. By having my students read this book, I felt that I was contributing to their education about past genocide and intolerance and heightening their sensitivity to such issues.

The three girls and three boys in the group had volunteered for it partly because of their interest in reading *Number the Stars*. Thus, they were all motivated to read it. In addition, all were adept readers and students. Two girls and one boy had been selected for the advanced language arts program at the school. All the girls and one boy read avidly outside of school. I got to know these students (and their classmates) well during my time with them, documenting their reading preferences and histories and learning about their personalities and lives.

Our first activity after reading *Number the Stars* was a worksheet asking for their interpretations of various characters' motivations at different points in the book. Again, I was looking mainly for differences and similarities in the girls' and boys' understandings of the male and female characters, being most interested in whether they thought Annemarie's actions were brave. I had also included questions about the motivations underlying various other major male and female characters' actions. In addition, I had a question about the motivations of a group of Nazi soldiers in one particular scene. I recall not being terribly interested in how the students would respond to this question; I assumed I knew how they would. Mainly I put it in so the worksheet would have exactly ten questions. Their responses to it, however, surprised me greatly.

In this scene, the Nazi soldiers and their dogs intercept Annemarie when she is on an important mission to deliver a package to her uncle, a fisherman who ferries hidden Jews across to Sweden. The package is concealed in a picnic basket. While searching the basket, the Nazis take out a piece of bread, look it over, then, rather than putting it back in the basket, throw it to their dogs to eat. On the worksheet, the students were asked to explain why the Nazis threw the bread to their dogs rather than giving it back to Annemarie.

To me, the reason for the Nazis' action was obvious: they were just plain *mean*. Surprisingly, most of my intelligent, adept students "missed" this obvious answer—"misread" the *author's intention*. Their responses truly puzzled me: they seemed to be looking for complex, rational explanations for the Nazis' behavior. They seemed to be "thinking too hard" about why the Nazis did this. The responses of the students were:

Paula: Because they were suspicious about it [the bread] and maybe there was also a bread shortage.

Julia: Maybe because they thought she was hiding something in the bread.

Carrie: So he could make sure there was nothing in it.

Ted: Annemarie had no power to stop them.

Kardik's response was closer to what I had expected:

Kardik: They'd rather steal than be polite.

After reading these seemingly odd responses, I was even more surprised by the last one, because it was, *word for word,* what I had expected:

David: They are mean.

Why was this particular student's response *identical* to mine, when all the others seemed so off to me? And why weren't the girls' interpretations closer to mine (as I might have expected in my study of gender issues)? Other forces were at work here, and I began to consider what David and I had in common that the other students and I did not.

One commonality was obvious: David was the only student in the group whose background, like mine, was Judeo-Christian. The other five students were first generation Asian Americans, none Christian. Julia was Pakistani; Kardik, Indian; Ted and Paula, Korean; and Carrie, Taiwanese. Many of the students in this sixth-grade class were Asian American, many first generation. (David, like me, was not first generation European American.)

When we talked informally about the book in our small group, I discovered that the Asian American children had very little prior knowledge of the Holocaust. (I had not presented any prereading activities about it.) None of the children had learned about the Holocaust in school; thus, whatever knowledge they had came from their families, friends, and the culture at large. Because the Holocaust, being part of World War II in Europe, had not affected these (non-Japanese) Asian Americans' family histories or national histories in the same ways that it affected European Americans, it seemed likely that the Asian American children would not have had family discussions of the Holocaust. Nor would they have had the same type of exposure to artistic portrayals of it (in books, movies, and documentaries sought out by family and friends) that the European American Jewish and Christian children had.

I had the opportunity to pursue my questions and hypotheses about these interpretive differences in another small group. This second small group consisted of girls only, its main purpose being to talk about the way girls and women are portrayed in children's books in general and in *Number the Stars* in particular. Seven girls had volunteered for this group, which met only twice. Four girls were non-Christian first-generation Asian American; one was Jewish and very invested in her religious heritage; one had one Christian parent and one Jewish parent but attended Hebrew school; and one was Christian of German heritage. The families of the three European American girls had been in the United States for more than one generation.

The girls read *Number the Stars* (again with no prereading activities about the Holocaust) before our first meeting, at which time I asked them to complete a questionnaire on their previous learning—formal and informal—about the Holocaust, World War II, and the Nazis. The questionnaire included a free-associating task in which the students wrote down anything that came to mind on these topics during a timed minute. The students then answered the same question about why the Nazis gave Annemarie's bread to their dogs instead of returning it to the picnic basket.

As in the other small group, none of these girls had studied World War II or the Holocaust in public school. None of the Asian Americans said they had learned about it from their parents or friends, although one girl said she'd seen a movie about World War II (Wise 1965). Michelle and Susan, the Jewish girls, had studied the Holocaust in Hebrew school and had also learned about it from their families, friends, movies, and documentaries. Kim, the Christian girl, also said she had learned about the Holocaust from her family and friends.

On the free association task the students wrote down seven to ten terms. Susan became frustrated, blurting out that there was "too much to write." The Asian American girls came up with an average of 4.5 facts and 2.5 evaluative statements, compared with 5 facts and 3.7 evaluative statements written by the Jewish and Christian girls. Susan, who was apparently concerned with doing this activity "correctly," wrote only facts (e.g., Germans, concentration camps, uniforms, Hitler). The other six girls wrote at least one evaluative statement, all of which included "mean" or "bad people." Thus, although the Jewish and Christian girls had learned more about the Holocaust, all the girls had learned something about it from American culture at large, and they associated meanness or badness with the Nazis. As I expected, however, almost all the Asian American girls (three of four) gave "more considered" explanations for the Nazis' behavior when they threw Annemarie's bread to their dogs, whereas almost all the Jewish and Christian girls (two of three) said that, basically, the Nazis were mean. Interestingly, Michelle, who was so deeply invested in her Jewish heritage, misremembered

Annemarie as being Jewish: "Maybe [the Nazis] knew that Annemarie was Jewish and they thought that Jews don't deserve food or anything. So, since the dog wasn't Jewish, they gave it to the dog." (Annemarie is in fact a Christian girl who helps her Jewish friend escape.)

Thus, the differences in these sixth graders' interpretations clearly related to their prior, culturally determined knowledge of the Holocaust. Likewise, my own interpretation of Lowry's Nazi characters, which I took to be the "correct" reading of the author's intentions, also strongly related to my culturally determined prior knowledge. This observation illustrates not only *how* such knowledge affects interpretation of characters, but *what* that knowledge is. Both, as it turns out, have important implications for teaching about the Holocaust, genocide, and tolerance in general.

Sensing the Meaning

Reader-response theorist Louise Rosenblatt defines reading as a "transaction between the reader and what he [sic] senses the words as pointing to" (1978, 21). This wonderfully vague definition captures the importance of reader factors (e.g., previous experience and individual psychology) in the interpretation of fictional characters as well as that of cultural and educational forces. To "sense" what the words are "pointing to" in a particular character portrayal, the reader must draw on his or her knowledge of people, which is culturally determined. The Judeo-Christian cultural construction of Nazis is distinct and evident in the Jewish and Christian students' (as well as my own) interpretation of fictional portrayals of Nazis. Such readers draw from a well-etched Nazi schema that readers of other cultural backgrounds have not—or *not yet*—developed. The Asian American students in my study had not yet learned that the Nazis were simply *monsters*.

Reader-response theorists have illustrated that a text cannot be thought of as separate from a reader's interpretation of it. However, the words in a text, or, to be truer to reader-response theory, the meanings of the words that we as a cultural collective have assigned to them, influence our final interpretations or beliefs about what the text is saying. Readers begin a book with a set of culturally determined preconceptions about types of people, and when the author's words seem to match those preconceptions, readers "sense" what they are pointing to without experiencing dissonance. Lowry's portrayal of the Nazi soldiers in *Number the Stars* is highly consistent with Judeo-Christian Americans' culturally learned construction of Nazis. Their acts seem to indicate that they are monsters—just what we thought they would be. Imagine what we would make of a Nazi character who shines a flashlight into a dark corner, discovers a

Jewish family hiding, looks into their terrified eyes, then quietly walks away. We might predict that he's sneaking off to lay some terrible trap for the family, his treachery doubled for having first pretended to have compassion. But what would we think if, in the end, he really *does* let them go? We may think of this character as someone only *pretending* to be a Nazi, but in essence "not-Nazi," as it so defies our preconception of this type of person. Alternatively, those of us who have learned to read critically may become suspicious of the author's intention, checking to see if he or she is some terrible revisionist. In either case, the sense of dissonance is a problem that we must resolve, because we all know that Nazis are simply *monsters*.

Thus the meaning that we make of, or collectively assign to, character portrayals reflects our cultural preconceptions of people. However, a circular process is at work in the act of such interpretation: part of what etches out those cultural schemata are the representations of types of people most prevalent in a certain culture's literature and other fictions. In my study I learned that fictional characters (and adults' interpretations of them) provide a source of children's learning about *real* people. This knowledge of real people—which is to some extent based on their culture's fictional portrayals of people—is in turn used to understand *other* fictional portrayals of people, which reinforces readers' notions of what different types of real people are like. When this cycle is allowed to continue without a challenge, we end up with a collection of ready-made labels for real and fictional people alike, which we affix with little or no critical awareness.

The danger of this cycle is clear when we think of stereotypic portrayals of persecuted minority groups—the Jews, for example. However, we are unaccustomed to thinking that stereotypic portrayals of Nazis are a problem. But my findings suggest that it is a problem, both in educating children about the Holocaust specifically and about genocide and intolerance in general.

Messages Received

In my study, I found that, in addition to prior cultural knowledge, the students' reading and media-viewing preferences and histories influenced their interpretations of Lowry's Nazis. Susan, for instance, immersed in stories about animals and pets and their loving owners, wrote this seemingly bizarre response to the bread question: "So that, they wouldn't be mean to the dogs."[2] By contrast, Ted's interpretation of the Nazis' action—"Annemarie had no power to stop them"—reflects his immersion in his favorite genres—"anything with fighting in it." To Ted, the central issue was who could overpower whom.

My findings also showed that reading and media-viewing preferences and histories differed between the sexes. Not surprisingly, boys sought out fiction about boys, whereas most girls sought out fiction about girls. (Some girls but no boys said they liked reading books and watching shows about the opposite sex.) This had important consequences, because the books and shows about boys tended to be generically different from those about girls. The boys in my study tended to immerse themselves in the genres of action/ adventure, superhero fiction, horror, and science fiction, whereas the girls read realistic stories, often series, about friendships and romances. The boys' genres were more plot-centered and fantastic, often classifying characters into the simple dichotomous scheme of good guys and bad guys. Conflicts between such characters were usually physical. By contrast, the girls' genres were highly character-centered, evoking emotional responses (e.g., books about girls dying of cancer) and exploring the complexity of interpersonal relationships (between female friends or romantic partners). Thus the girls generally were not as heavily exposed as the boys to the simple good guy/bad guy schema. And in fact, in the original small group reading *Number the Stars*, the boys' interpretations of the Nazis' actions reflected this: all three boys, regardless of cultural heritage, tapped into the good guy/bad guy schema more easily than the girls did, better able to recognize that the Nazis fit the definition of "bad guys."

Because these children used fictional characters as a source for understanding real people, especially those unlike themselves, these different types of characterization have very important implications. Equally important, fictional characters provided these children with a source of learning about *themselves*. Given these observations, the differential styles of characterization in fiction marketed for boys versus girls have the power to affect the development of the two sexes in "societally useful" ways. Girls learn that people—fictional and real—are complex beings, capable of caring and compassion, deserving of forgiveness. Girls' genres are designed, knowingly or not, to socialize girls into caregiving roles, teaching them the skills they will need to be successful mothers and wives.

What, then, do genres designed for boys teach? That some people are simply good and some simply bad? That some are strong, brave, and deserving, while others are weak, cowardly, and of less value? That some are just right and others just wrong? These notions are useful when a society must justify going to war. These notions also underlie acts of intolerance and genocide. It is how the Nazis portrayed the Christians and the Jews. In the good guy/bad guy schema, *we—whoever we are*—are never on the bad-guy side. Therefore the other guy—the "not-we," the one who is different—must be.

The notion that there are easily identifiable bad guys and good guys is part of what enables humans to commit acts of violence against others, which is why it is useful in the socialization of future soldiers. The "enemy," whoever they are, may be viewed as Other, perhaps not quite as human as *we* are, which may work to diminish an individual's moral objections to killing. But the good guy/bad guy schema is not only applicable to "outside enemies"; the "Other" is all around us. This schema is just as useful to propagandists and charismatic leaders seeking to turn one group of citizens against another. Thus any reproduction of the good guy/bad guy schema must be critically questioned.

Because *we* can never be *not-we*, simplistically casting Nazis as the "bad guys" opposite "us," on the other side of a neat slash, also undermines one of the most important themes in Holocaust education. As long as North American culture retains the view of Nazis as simple bad guys, children will learn that once upon a time far away there lived evil monsters called the Nazis, and students will never grapple with the reality that, somehow, not long ago, a nation of people not terribly unlike us *became* Nazis. How did this happen? Could it happen again? Could it happen to us? How can we prevent it? These are the essential questions raised when we think deeply about the Holocaust.

Reading Characters Critically

Characters portrayed as "good guys" or "bad guys" are flat characters, as are the Nazi soldiers in *Number the Stars*. A flat character, according to E. M. Forster's original definition, is an easily recognizable type whose character "can be expressed in a single sentence" (1927, 41). By contrast, a round character is one who is "capable of surprising in a convincing way" (Forster 1927, 41). A flat character has no real human motivation—a person acts mean because he is just mean (Russ 1973).

Learning to read fictional characters critically includes being able to identify which portrayals are flat and questioning why they are that way. Before educators can teach children how to do this, however, we need to examine our own understanding of how characters are created, which may be limited in part by the awe we often feel toward literary authors, who seem magical in their creative abilities and insights into the human psyche.

Forster (1927) writes that the nature of characters is "conditioned by what [the author] guesses about other people, and about himself, and is further modified by the other aspects of his work" (44). Forster's use of the word *guess* here is important, because it allows us to see that literary authors are, indeed, mere mortals, and as such are creatures of culture whose notions about people are guided by the same cultural beliefs and forces that affect the rest of us. In learning their craft, literary authors are taught that characters should be "convincing" (Gardner 1991), consistent (Macauley and Lanning 1964), with a "realistic psychology" (Macauley and Lanning 1964, Phelan 1989). These concepts deeply embed and are embedded in cultural understandings of what various people are like. Thus, even the characters of gifted authors such as Lois Lowry require critical reading.

In addition, the writer's process of characterizing can range from sympathetic to unsympathetic, knowledgeable to unknowledgeable (Nauman 1997). For example, an author creating a character like himself or herself will probably do so with a great deal of personal knowledge and sympathy. However, when authors base a character on a neglectful parent, an unfaithful lover, an irresponsible sibling, or a fickle friend, they will probably not feel much sympathy toward that character and end up creating an unflattering portrayal (Cornillon 1973, Ellman 1968). Authors attempting to create a character from a cultural group of whom they have no first-hand knowledge are likely to fall back on culturally bound stereotypes, often without intending to, but nevertheless with a negative effect. Of course, authors can also *intentionally* portray groups in negative ways. A propagandist who despises Jews will portray a cruel stereotype to foment hatred.

I believe the best way to introduce the concepts of characterization to elementary-school-aged children is through writing exercises. Students are asked to invent a fictional character based on someone they know well and like, and to write a character sketch or story. They then write about a character based on someone they either dislike or are angry with (within appropriate parameters, of course; siblings are a likely source of material for this exercise). Finally, they write in a sympathetic way about an imagined character from a cultural group of whom they have little personal knowledge. This last exercise may require more teacher modeling and support through prompts, such as, "Try to imagine how a Native Alaskan girl might spend her day, what her concerns may be," and so on. Though I would not then ask the children to write about a member of a group they *disliked* (as this would encourage students to think of others in negative ways and perhaps even provide rehearsal for future intolerant behavior), I would have a discussion about an imaginary author who disliked or was angry at some group and what his characterizations of those group members may be like.

These writing exercises form the basis for examining how different authors portray different characters. Such analysis can easily become a part of the discussion about every book that the students read during the school year. Questions for discussion can include, "Are the different characters round or flat?", "What details has the author used to portray the different characters?", "Do you think the author knows a lot about her characters?", "What is the author's attitude toward the different characters?" And, most important, "*Why* has the author portrayed the different characters in these ways?"

In *Number the Stars,* as well as in some other books and movies about the Holocaust, the reason for the authors' negative manner of characterizing the Nazis is clear: they abhor what the Nazis did and want future generations to abhor it also. Such character portrayals are an expression of moral outrage. By portraying Nazis as incomprehensible monsters who commit evil acts simply because they are evil, authors make it easy to hate Nazis. However, these easy-to-hate flat characters contain no clue that the Germans at that point in history were ever anything but evil, and the question of how a nation of people *becomes* fascist never arises.

Beginning with an analysis of character portrayals, books such as *Number the Stars* become excellent introductions to the study of the history of the Holocaust. The class discusses Lowry's portrayal of all the characters, including the Nazis, and her reasons for such portrayals, then moves into the more difficult question of how the German people could have come to commit such monstrous acts. *Why* were they so susceptible to Hitler's rhetoric of hatred? What were the economic conditions of Germany in the 1920s and 1930s, and how did that nation's struggles contribute to its citizens' vulnerability to fascism? What role did the Treaty of Versailles play in the conditions of Germany at that time? Why were the Jews singled out for persecution? What is the history of anti-Semitism in Germany and in other Christian cultures? How did Hitler's totalitarian fascist regime attempt to exact obedience from German citizens?

Through such questions, discussed in the context of clearly focused history lessons, students and teachers together can begin to probe the cultural and psychological underpinnings of anti-Semitism, intolerance, and genocide, leading to broader questions. Where does group hatred come from, and what fuels it? What is the relationship of feelings of fear, powerlessness, and hopelessness to the intense anger that can overwhelm reason and morality and lead to hate crimes? If genocide is at one end of the spectrum of intolerance, what lies on the other end? Who actively commits hate crimes, and who allows them to happen? Where else have and do genocide and other crimes of intolerance occur? (Through the difficult coming to terms with the Holocaust, European American students will be better able to hear stories of genocide and intolerance from other cultures, contributed by non-European American students.) Finally, what are examples of intolerance toward groups of others in the

United States today (especially attacks against gays and lesbians, the burning of African American churches, violence against women)? What can the students do to protest such incidents? Could there be a Holocaust in North America, and, if not, what will prevent it?

To deeply engage students in the question of how unthinkable acts of cruelty can occur, teachers need to open up space for wondering, to see even Nazis not as flat characters. Exploring how people become Nazis necessitates a deeper study of that history than can ever be achieved by the incidental learning we hope will occur through historical fiction. Unless educators provide children with the fullest possible historical context of the Holocaust, their understanding of fascism will remain flat, and the connection between them and us—past atrocities and current North American intolerances—will never be made.[3]

A Final Reflection

My trip to the concentration camp at Dachau ten years ago was motivated by more than the disturbing stories I'd read and movies I'd seen. The Holocaust has been with me for as long as I can remember. My parents, who were children during World War II, made sure that my sister and I knew about it. I still sometimes have nightmares about Nazis. My deep-felt connection with this tragedy, however, is not because I am Jewish; it is because I am Christian, of German heritage. My motivation for going to Dachau was a lifelong, dread-filled, painful need to somehow come to terms with my own connection to "this horror"—to *genocide.*

How could *my relations* have done such a thing, allowed it to happen? By what accident was I born to the American Naumans instead of the German Naumanns? What would I have done, or not done, had I been there? Such questions are still troubling to Christian children of German heritage when they begin to learn about the Holocaust. I cannot imagine how Jewish children feel; I have not yet found the courage to reflect on my recent discovery that, in Germany, my surname appears to have been Jewish.

For me, and for the millions of other North Americans who are the relatives or descendants of the victims or the persecutors (or both), the Holocaust is not something that happened long ago and far away; it is unbearably close. Partly because this strong connection is felt by so many, the Holocaust remains in North American cultural consciousness as the worst example of intolerance and genocide. As such, it continues to be the subject of fiction and nonfiction, and children in the United States, Canada, and elsewhere will encounter it in various ways: in Newbery Award–winners, Hollywood movies, news stories about survivors.

As I learned through my experiences with this group of sixth graders, what children "absorb" from the culture at large about the Holocaust may not increase their understanding of it or enable them to see the danger in certain patterns of thinking about others. It may, in fact, leave them with the impression that Germany was full of monsters in the 1930s and 1940s; that we—the good guys—put them in their place; and that to ensure a safe society in the future, all we need to do is identify the bad guys and protect ourselves from them—through aggression if necessary.

Only through an organized historical study of the Holocaust and the events preceding it can teachers help children see *why* such a horror happened, how a nation of people not unlike us *became* capable of committing monstrous acts, and how citizens can acquire the knowledge and skills needed to create a world in which such atrocities do not occur. Learning about the Holocaust can give students a better appreciation of the seriousness of what earlier Americans did to the peoples of Africa and indigenous peoples of North America. Through a study of how Nazi propagandists characterized the Jews, students may better appreciate the implications of how Native Americans have been characterized in Hollywood Westerns, and how other minorities and women are currently characterized in the media. These lessons, too, provide a richer context for telling and hearing the stories of what life has been like for African Americans, Native Americans, Latinos/Latinas, Asians, gays and lesbians, women and girls, and all the others who have long been and continue to be the victims of intolerance in our own troubled society.

Notes

1. My dissertation, titled *Reading Boys, Reading Girls: How Sixth Graders Understand and Are Influenced by Fictional Characters,* was completed in January 1997. Data were collected in the spring of 1995. Parental consent was received for all children before their participation in accordance with University of Illinois-Chicago requirements. The children's names have been changed.

2. This was the first of three responses that Susan wrote, all of which reflected various knowledges that she accessed in an attempt to find the "right" answer to the question.

3. For another perspective on this issue, see Stanley (chapter 2), this volume.

Works Cited

Cornillon, Susan K., ed. 1973. *Images of Women in Fiction: Feminist Perspectives.* Bowling Green, OH: Bowling Green University Popular Press.

Ellman, Mary. 1968. *Thinking about Women.* New York: Harcourt. Forster, E. M. 1927. *Aspects of the Novel.* San Diego: Harcourt Brace Jovanovich.

Gardner, John. 1991. *The Art of Fiction: Notes on Craft for Young Writers.* New York: Vintage Books.

Lowry, Lois. 1989. *Number the Stars.* New York: Dell.

Macauley, Robie, and George Lanning. 1964. *Technique in Fiction.* New York: Harper & Row.

Nauman, April D. 1997. *Reading Boys, Reading Girls: How Sixth Graders Understand and Are Influenced by Fictional Characters.* Ph.D. diss., University of Illinois-Chicago.

Phelan, James. 1989. *Reading People, Reading Plots: Character, Progression, and the Interpretation of Narrative.* Chicago: University of Chicago Press.

Rosenblatt, Louise. 1978. *The Reader, the Text, the Poem.* Carbondale: Southern Illinois University Press.

Russ, Joanna. 1973. "What Can a Heroine Do? Or, Why Women Can't Write." In *Images of Women in Fiction: Feminist Perspectives*, edited by Susan K. Cornillon, 3–20. Bowling Green, Ohio: Bowling Green University Popular Press.

Wise, Robert (Director). 1965. *The Sound of Music.* Film. 174 min. Distributed by Twentieth-Century Fox Film Corporation.

7 Tolerance and Intolerance for African American Children and Families: Lessons from the Movie *Crooklyn*

Michelle R. Dunlap
Connecticut College

There is no single face in nature, because every eye that looks upon it, sees it from its own angle. . . . So every man's spice-box seasons his own food.

Zora Neale Hurston, *Dust Tracks in the Road*

W*ebster's Desk Dictionary* defines *tolerance* as "a fair and permissive attitude toward those whose race, religion, beliefs, etc., differ from one's own" (1993, 473). *Intolerance* is defined as "not tolerating beliefs, manners, etc., different from one's own, as in religious matters" (Webster's 1993, 239). Borrowing from these definitions, *tolerance* is defined for the purpose of this chapter as an effort to examine people or situations from multiple and culturally appropriate perspectives. *Intolerance* is defined as a failure to attempt to examine people or situations from multiple perspectives, resulting in premature judgment and possible rejection based upon premature judgment.

The lack of equal-status interactions with others from diverse backgrounds is associated with intolerance and inaccurate stereotyping in our thoughts and opinions toward others (Stephan 1985; Stephan and Brigham 1985). The lack of diversity in service provision, and intolerance toward those being served, are major challenges in many societal arenas, especially in education. Many schools fail to offer diverse teaching and support staffs and little or no exposure to cultural/racial diversity, even in schools where the majority of the students are of color.[1] Trends such as these are found across the United States and are associated with inappropriate practices such as "racial tracking" of students of color into lower-level course sections and white children into higher-level sections (Kirchner 1995; Schofield 1986).

Tolerance and intolerance are not only a matter of what and how we think about others, their behavior, and their circumstances, but also a matter of how we treat people. When misunderstanding occurs, people are less likely to be treated in a manner that is appropriate or relevant to their situation. Hale (1994) and others (Collins and Tamarkin 1990; Gibbs and Huang 1989; Hale-Benson 1986; Shade 1989) have long acknowledged that children of color and their families are often misunderstood by people who dwell outside the culture, and they are often subjected to inequitable practices. For example, it has been noted by Allen and Majidi-Ahi (1989) that when cases of African American children are presented in therapeutic situations, there is little agreement among white diagnosticians regarding the appropriate diagnoses. There is often a lack of understanding of the meaning of particular behaviors and modes of cross-cultural communication. Allen and Majida (1989) also noted that, problematically, teachers' perceptions and opinions of African American children often do not match those of the children's parents, and those opinions and perceptions are often negative in comparison to the relatively more positive ones that the children's own families have of them. In order to gain a better understanding of the nature of the perceptions and misperceptions that exist about families of color, the movie *Crooklyn* was used as a material to promote discussion about parenting, discipline, communication, and relationships regarding the African American family that it portrays.

Crooklyn

The movie *Crooklyn* is a major-release film that was written and directed by acclaimed American writer/actor/director Spike Lee and his siblings, Joie Susannah Lee and Cinque Lee. The movie is based in part on their lives as children, but is "not to be read as straight autobiography" (Ebert 1994). Noted movie critic Roger Ebert wrote about *Crooklyn:*

> They say it isn't literal autobiography, but was "inspired" by their memories. Some of those memories have the specificity of real life, however, including a showdown between [the mother] Carolyn and a son who will not clean up his plate of [food]. (1994, 39)

During the 114 minutes of *Crooklyn,* a wide variety of slices of African American life are offered from Spike Lee's and his siblings' perspectives. The opening scenes depict an African American mother and father in intense interaction with their five children, who appear to range in age from seven to thirteen years. During these scenes, the mother, the children, and their father engage in a variety of modes of communication, including the mother firmly disciplining the children and the children reacting.[2] Many of the scenes appear very passionate verbally, or perhaps even explosive, depending upon one's perspective.[3]

The use of movies as a psychosocial projective technique has been used in other studies (Richard 1996; Robertson 1997a and 1997b). Richard (1996) used movies to assist students in their learning about and discussing racial identity development. Robertson (1997a and 1997b) used participant responses to movies such as *Stand and Deliver* as a technique to elicit and explore beginning teachers' desires and fantasies about what it means to be a good teacher. She finds it useful to examine and to work pedagogically with moments of film engagement in preservice classrooms in order to help novice teachers come to terms with their own fantasies and expectations regarding their teaching careers. In the current study, *Crooklyn* is used projectively, but more for the purpose of documenting the variety of perceptions or readings that can occur for one African American family, and using those readings as beginning points for discussion and education regarding children and families of color.[4]

Design of the Discussions Using *Crooklyn*

Recently, thirty-three undergraduate students participated in a focus-group discussion as part of a multiculturally focused social science course. These participants were enrolled in a teacher certification program at a coeducational, privately supported, liberal arts college in the Northeast United States, one of several colleges where the author consults and educates on the topic of multicultural issues. Prior to the focus-group discussion, the participants watched the entire movie *Crooklyn* with instructions to treat the movie scenes as re-enactments of real-life events (these students will be referred to as the "focus-group" participants). Four months later, an additional set of fourteen social sciences students of similar background and from a similar course at the same college responded to the first fifteen minutes of the movie in writing rather than verbally in their course critical-reflection journals (these participants will be referred to as the "journal-group" participants).[5] In the focus group, the facilitator of the discussion (and current author) was an obviously bi-racial woman who is of African American and European American ancestry. In the journal group, there were two female facilitators. One was European American, and the other was of unknown, but apparently mixed, heritage.

After observing the film, the thirty-three novice teachers, most of whom were female, European American,[6] and between the ages of eighteen and twenty-two, participated in the focus-group discussion and offered their perceptions of the parents and the children depicted in *Crooklyn*. The critical reflection comments of the similar journal group were also analyzed. This essay will explore and elaborate on some of the issues and specific concerns that emerged as the participants engaged with particular scenes in the film. Another purpose of this essay is to relate participant responses to theories and literature regarding African American cultural styles in order to put them into additional perspectives. Explanations that are more culturally appropriate will be offered regarding the communication interactions depicted. Because the majority of the participants in the study were teacher certification candidates, this essay will also include recommendations for assisting teachers and future teachers in examining, interpreting, and responding to the behavior of black children and families in a more tolerant and culturally relevant manner.

Intolerance and Responses toward Others

Limited and unequal-status interactions with those whose race, religion, beliefs, and customs are different from our own make fair interpretations of their behavior difficult. Cultural influences, family upbringing, power dynamics, and cognitive and personality styles are all intricately interwoven and play a significant role in how we orient to, perceive, and interpret behaviors and interactions observable in others (Bowman and Stott 1994; Fiske 1993). Studies document that for a variety of sociological reasons, cognitive distortions and misperceptions are commonplace and have negative impacts on traditionally disenfranchised racial ethnic minorities. For example, African American adults and children, who traditionally have been politically, economically, and otherwise disenfranchised, are inaccurately perceived as being more aggressive than whites when engaging in identical acts such as accidentally bumping others (Duncan 1976; Kirchner 1995; Pettigrew and Martin 1987; Sagar and Schofield 1980). Recent studies also suggest other trends: wealthier and more powerful members in a society may be more likely to stereotype others (Fiske 1993); and blacks are more likely to be misdiagnosed as mentally ill (Barnes 1992).

The perceptions of teachers and other service providers are of crucial importance because of the very nature of their work, which often requires them to make judgments about children and families in day-to-day situations. Some teachers and other service providers make these judgments extremely well and equitably, but others do not (Wilson et al. 1995a). As Wilson et al. (1995a, 85) states, "Unfortunately, many programs aimed at reducing the problems and obstacles of family life fall short of measurable success when confronting family problems in the African American community." An expanded knowledge of perceptions of children and families of color can have crucial implications in practice and policy for schools, social service agencies, and criminal justice systems as they attempt to improve upon cultural understanding and competency between individual service providers and clients (Wilson et al. 1995a). Although specific stereotypes have been studied regarding various cultures, there is very little research available regarding the manner in which African American *children* and *families* are perceived in *everyday, real-life* situations (such as debating or arguing during dinner, adults disciplining children, or children responding to the discipline of an adult).

The movie *Crooklyn* is not real in the sense that movies are usually artistic constructions of reality and/or fantasy. However, *Crooklyn* offers representations of daily life occurrences that may, like any stimulus, be open to the interpretations of the viewer. Because research participants often fear talking about racial matters, the professional literature does not as yet offer profiles of the nature of the judgments that exist regarding children and families, particularly those of color, in everyday situations (Stephan 1985). Nor does the literature offer the observer characteristics associated with these different types of day-to-day interaction judgments. The movie *Crooklyn,* though not a flawless stimulus, was used to engage participants to talk about an African American family. Participants were then invited to offer their readings or interpretations of the behaviors that they witnessed. Although the methodology uses a representation of events rather than real events themselves, it does offer the advantage of providing a comfortable stimulus (a feature film) rather than an experimental or contrived stimulus. It offers a relatively comfortable means by which observers can express, react to, and explore judgments regarding African American children and families who are in challenging domestic situations.

Responses to the *Crooklyn* Family

A variety of themes emerged with regard to the students' perceptions of the parents and children depicted in *Crooklyn*. Although some of the participants who viewed the film had favorable impressions, most of the responses regarding the family were negative. The major themes that emerged regarding the *Crooklyn* family were (1) the family is dysfunctional; (2) the mother is aggressive and violent; (3) the parents are irresponsible; (4) the children are uncontrollable; and (5) the community is barren and threatening. These themes are outlined fully below. The alternative explanations that will be offered will suggest that (1) the family communication may not be dysfunctional, but rather may be straightforward and vibrant; (2) the mother's discipline style may not be the best but may be difficult to classify as abusive; (3) rather than the parents being irresponsible, the parents and children may engage in more sharing of household responsibilities, which may be both necessary and functional for this family; (4) the children, rather than being out of control, may be energetic, outspoken, and responsible; and (5) rather than threatening and barren, the community may be culturally rich, creative, and resourceful.

Theme #1: "The Family Seems Dysfunctional"

Many of the observers expressed strong feelings regarding the functioning of the family. Common descriptions included *dysfunctional behavior, inefficient communication, non-respectful children, chaotic home life*, and *a tense and stressful household*. Several focus-group discussants expressed concern about the volume and intensity of the communication among the family members: "They just kept yelling and screaming at each other all the time"; "The volume of the conversations was very high, much higher than what I am used to"; and "I can't see bringing that into my family or my classroom." As examples, three journal-group participants articulated their perceptions of the dysfunctional nature of the family in response to the discipline scene:

> The communication between the family members was not strong. I kept wondering how this all was affecting the children. They were not learning to communicate effectively. . . . They probably did not feel good about themselves. Most language directed at them was negative. (female[6])

> I gathered that this household is run very inefficiently. The mother did not act appropriately to her children, and as a result her children did not respect her. . . . Although all of us were obviously not raised up in "perfect" families, we all were given the opportunity to go to college, which shows that we were treated with respect, unlike the children in the movie clip. (female)

> The children, developing in a chaotic microsystem, were starting their day with turmoil, anxiety and lack of self-esteem. They were probably not feeling cared for. Unfortunately children usually think their parents are always right, which then gets internalized, "I must be a bad kid." (female)

The students' use of terms such as *negative, inefficient, chaotic, turmoil*, and *lack of self esteem* suggests a tendency to see the family in pathological terms. As another example, in the scene where the daughter (who appears to be about eight years old) urinates in a corner of her brother's room, some of the participants interpreted her behavior as pathological. For instance:

> Since this is just a movie, it is hard to say how this type of discipline might affect the life of a child, but one scene proved to me that these

children were suffering as a result of what I viewed to be poor parenting. When the little girl urinated on the floor, it indicated to me that she was either never taught how to sleep through the night without going to the bathroom, or that this was a form of rebellion due to all of the anger and pain inside of her. (female)

Other participants seemed to struggle with their perceptions concerning the functioning of the family. Rather than making direct judgments of parental discipline, they appeared to struggle with feelings of ambivalence:

The family functioned to the extreme, but did not function improperly. The mother's behavior was both proper and improper. She would discipline her children when necessary and she would smile when the situation was fitting. However, her disciplinary methods were rather extreme. Yelling excessively and spanking the children is hardly a method of choice for most parents. It was an irrational form of punishment. The father's behavior was both good and bad. A laid back individual, the father could be both good and bad at his job at the same time. . . . My direct opinion [is that the family was] not dysfunctional. I just wouldn't raise *my* family that way. (male, his emphasis)

The movie showed a family that was definitely having problems. There was hardly any communication in the family and a little bit of violence and a lot of yelling and misbehaving by the children. The parents seemed burnt out and frustrated. I think these are common scenarios for many families today. I know that this a problem in many of my friends' families. (female)

These passages illustrate that some of the participants noted what they perceived as both favorable and unfavorable characteristics of the family, or they indicated both compassionate and uncompassionate judgments about them. Thus, some participants did not see the family as all bad or as all good, but as a complex mixture of both.

Another issue that emerged was concern about the roles of the members of the family: confusion regarding the children being responsible for a portion of the cleaning, caregiving, and shopping; the father not being authoritarian enough; and the mother being too authoritarian. There seemed to be a disgust with the father's permissive parenting style:

It appeared that the mother did not have good parenting skills. A lot of the expectations she had, regarding what children should be responsible for, could lead to parentification [or the children inappropriately accepting adult responsibilities and behaving as parents to their siblings or even to their parents]. (female)

As they sit down for their meal, the first thing that they do is pray. The father leads the prayer, but he makes a joke of it and all of the children laugh. The mother, not amused with her husband's antics, makes the family again bow their heads and recites a more respectful prayer. *This is the first evidence that suggests that the mother is the head of the household, as opposed to the father.* While they are eating dinner, the children begin to misbehave, and while the father plays along with it and makes no attempt to stop it, the mother is the one to put a halt to their disobedience. *Again, this is another example of how the mother is the leader of the family.* (male, my emphasis)

The father was a horrible role model and father for his children. His manners at the dinner table were abominable. He showed no responsibility for the discipline of the children. He also did not support the mother in her discipline of the children and therefore did not respect her decisions . . . it was easy to see that . . . he would not be the one to help raise his children correctly. (female)

These examples of the participant comments suggest an annoyance with the parents' sharing of family responsibilities with the older children in the family, as well as frustration with the mother who seemed to be usurping the traditional authority of the father. To help put these comments into perspective, we must acknowledge that the students who attend the college from which the participants were recruited tend to be from economically privileged backgrounds and two-parent, nuclear family households. They may have little familiarity and experience with people from cultures, socioeconomic backgrounds, and family structures that are different from their own. Stephan and Brigham (1985) have noted that equal-status contact with others who are different from us is a prerequisite for true intergroup understanding and acceptance. All of the above comments, when taken together, suggest that many of the participants interpreted the family as dysfunctional or as not meeting their own cultural norm for marriage and parenting. Alternative cultural perspectives regarding the "dysfunctional family" theme will now be offered.

Alternative Perspectives Concerning the First Theme: The "Dysfunctional Family"

Black children and families disproportionately suffer from almost every social ill that exists in American society (Billingsley 1992). This trend can be accounted for by differences in socioeconomic and educational opportunities for African Americans, although it is often mistakenly assumed to be due to built-in cultural deficits (Wilson et al. 1995a). As Billingsley (1992, 70) pointed out, the African American culture, like any other culture, has both strengths and weaknesses. But often the strengths are overlooked in favor of a "deficit model" approach that offers inadequate attention to understanding the strengths and competencies of families of color (Wilson et al. 1995a, 93). Some of these strengths include strong extended family and kinship bonds, strong achievement and work orientations, adaptability of family member roles, and spiritual orientation (Hale-Benson 1986; Hill 1972). These strengths are often overlooked and are not employed in the intervention plans that are designed to assist people of color. The stereotype that African Americans are uniquely disorganized and dysfunctional is not supported by fact (Willis 1992; Wilson et al. 1995a).

It seems that the focus-group and journal-group participants in this study adopted a negative model regarding the *Crooklyn* family, not unlike what many clinical and social services agents do (Allen and Majidi-Ahi 1989; Barnes 1992). As noted by Wilson et al. (1995a, 93–94), "[African American cultural] history . . . must be understood in order to understand how [African American people] deal with problems. . . . African American culture is separate, strong, and thriving." Hale-Benson (1986) also underscores the distinctiveness and resiliency of African American culture; she emphasizes the impact upon the functioning of their descendants of Africans having been captured, tortured, and forced into enslavement. It is important to note that many of the characteristics that African Americans still exhibit, such as strong kinship bonds and matriarchal influences, have West African cultural roots, and have been transmitted from generation to generation through the socialization process (Hale-Benson 1986).

Several participants in the focus group either mentioned or prefaced comments with a statement such as "I haven't lived that kind of lifestyle." These kinds of statements do not suggest that these observers lack the potential for empathy, but they do suggest that relative to their own experiences, some of the observers saw the *Crooklyn* family as foreign rather than familiar. There were two journal-group participants, however, who wrote that they could relate to the family and to the mother's parenting style. Both of these comments were from males; the first was European American, and the second was the only African American participant in the journal group:

> I felt that the [video clip] really made me think a lot of how I grew up. I felt that the video itself was very telling. The way that the mother raised them was really not too wrong to me. I think that this is a lot like how I was raised. Their mother motivated them by threatening them. She really never hurt or even abused them, she just got them moving to do what they were supposed to do earlier. . . . Many of the questions made me feel real confident of how my mother raised me. Without actually hurting us we always knew when she was serious about us doing something. I think that this is what the mother in the clip of the movie did. (European American male)

[The clip] had clearly defined parent roles and responsibilities, [understood] by each child. I think the study will allow students to see a brief life experience of a black family . . . showing family values and a beautiful culture. (African American male)

The two favorable comments offered above indicate that relating to the positive aspects of the family and their discipline styles may not simply be a matter of ethnic background, but of shared or similar positive experiences with particular forms of family communication. Shared experiences such as family socialization play a role in our interpretation of events.

Participants also expressed a great deal of concern about the "yelling" among the family members depicted in *Crooklyn*. Willis (1992, 133, 143) addresses this issue when she observes a continuous presence of words and music in African American life. She notes that some observers interpret the communication styles of African Americans as "loud or shallow" because some white people do not understand the value of, and preference for, oral/verbal communication in black culture. Hecht, Collier, and Ribeau (1993) have noted that the volume and style of speaking in the African American culture are often misperceived as heading toward violent action when they are not.

Regarding the concerns expressed about the seemingly mixed-up partnership roles between the mother and the father in *Crooklyn*, research has shown that there is a greater egalitarian sharing of roles and role adaptability in African American families than in European American families (Hale-Benson 1986; Hill 1972; Wilson, Greene-Bates, McKim, Simmons, Askew, Curry-El, and Hinton 1995b). There is also more sharing of what are classically thought of as parental roles with the older siblings in African American families (Hale-Benson 1986, Hill 1972). The African American culture is as much matriarchal as it is patriarchal (Hale-Benson 1986, 47; Hill 1972). In addition, historically, all responsibilities have had to be spread and shared among family members as blacks were required to meet the needs of whites first, which often meant that blacks were not, as individuals, as available to meet the needs of their own families. Thus, roles had to be shared across gender, and between parents, siblings, extended family, and community members in order for the needs of the entire family to be met.

Theme #2: "The Mother Seems Aggressive and Violent"

The second concern to emerge among the participants focused on the mother, who was seen as aggressive and violent, especially with respect to her disciplining of the children:

I could not believe how [the mother] was treating her children. Her household was very tense because she, the mother, was always screaming. They could not even sit down and have a relaxed meal because the mother nit picked at the kids and yelled at them but she did not discipline them. It makes me crazy thinking about how stressful her house would be. I also thought she was too physical with the children. She tore them out of bed and dragged them to the kitchen meanwhile emotionally abusing them. I can easily see how the kids could have no self-esteem. . . . I believe it is important for a child's development to have a parent that is emotionally stable. (female)

The method [of discipline the mother] used in getting her kids out of the bed is a controversial one. She seems to be extremely physical with them, and some might see this as borderline abusive. . . . The segment of the movie that I saw appeared to emphasize the lack of a father figure, and a mother figure who must be abusive to her children in an attempt to maintain control of the household. . . . The effect on the children was that they were afraid of their mother, and could not turn to her, and their lack of respect of their father as a parental figure meant that they could not turn to him either. (male)

The specific role of the mother is one that I did not agree with. I feel that she had a detrimental effect on the children. . . . She would yell negative things at her kids and threaten to hurt them. She slapped them around as well. I am not saying that things were not hard for her but I feel that this type of violence and verbal abuse is not necessary in any circumstances. (female)

The clip that I saw made me very angry. The mother was so mean to the children, mocking the way they ate, threatening them, while the father was passive. There were so many mixed messages being sent out. . . . For me, the worst part was when the mother woke the children up at four o'clock in the morning, making them clean the kitchen. What a horrible way to wake up. (female)

The participants' use of words such as *tore, dragged, abused, slapped, mocked, detrimental, horrible,* and *unstable* suggest that they saw the mother as physically and emotionally aggressive, violent and abusive toward her children. Before concluding that this is the only or the best interpretation of the mother's behavior, alternative explanations need to be considered.

Alternative Perspectives Concerning the Second Theme: The "Violent Mother"

Perceptions of the *Crooklyn* mother as aggressive and violent may, in part, be a matter of shared experiences such as class, income, socio-economic status (SES), generational cohort, and ethnic and gender socialization. Eleanor Maccoby (1980) found that low-SES and high-SES parents differ in their parenting styles, with low-SES parents being more restrictive, power-assertive, or authoritarian than high-SES parents, who tend to be more permissive. On studies conducted with white, middle-class children, authoritarian parenting was shown to be associated with aggressiveness in children, while less restrictive styles such as the authoritative and permissive styles were associated with these children having an internal sense of self-control (Shaffer 1994).

Parenting styles and their effects on children may also vary ethnically. Research has shown that "Black mothers tend to be more firm and physical in their discipline than White mothers" (Hale-Benson 1986, 68). Other studies have also shown that certain forms of corporal and firm punishment when combined with "warm" parenting styles are associated with politeness and self-control in black children, but aggression and a lack of self-control in white children (Deater-Deckard, Dodge, Bates, and Pettit 1996). This firmer style of discipline among black parents may be due to caregiver attempts to teach their children responsibility (Deater-Deckard et al. 1996). It may also be indicative of their desire to prepare their children for, and protect their children against, disproportionate surveillance by others and inequitable punitive practices from a society that is often racist (Collins 1990; Hale-Benson 1986; hooks 1993; Lassiter 1987). White families have significantly less pressure on them in this regard because they do not usually have to deal with individual and shared experiences of racism, particularly from those in authority (Feagin and Sikes 1994).

Nonetheless, among even black scholars there is little consensus on how to view or to judge the appropriateness of the authoritarian methods that often characterize some black women's style of disciplining. Some have argued that such a style of discipline is that of an outdated child-abusing "legacy" of harsh parental control that began during the enslavement socialization process (hooks 1993; Lassiter 1987). Others have argued that these firm styles of discipline still are necessary, and for the most part are harmless, containing an element of warmth and humor wherein "the bark is worse than the bite" and the seemingly harsh discipline "border[s] on play" (Hale-Benson 1986, 172). In addition, the myth of the black woman as domineering, angry, and violent, rather than as strong and resilient, contributes to many of the misperceptions that occur regarding her (Collins 1990; Ladner 1971; West 1995). As mentioned earlier, Hecht et al. (1993, 105) pointed out that compared to European Americans, African Americans are often more assertive and direct in their communications with each other, and that "European Americans may interpret African American behavior as signaling physical confrontation when none is intended." Hecht et al. (1993) argued that some African American threats, even set to music, are taken literally by European Americans, but when African Americans interpret them they are seen only as "wolfing" or "signifying" (see Foster 1986, 188), which are forms of kidding or venting with no intended action. Nonetheless, threatening children, as in *Crooklyn,* with "I'll slap the black off of you" and "I will knock you into tomorrow" most likely is not an optimal method of discipline regardless of the different ways that such comments may be interpreted. Acknowledging that such verbal threats may not be the best, and in some cases may be emotionally detrimental (hooks 1993; Lassiter 1987), there is still the issue of whether the mother's behavior portrayed in the movie *Crooklyn* was actually physically "violent" and "child-abusive."

Child abuse is defined as the maltreatment of a child or "the intentional harm to, or avoidable endangerment of, anyone under the age of eighteen" (Berger and Thompson 1995, 308). According to child abuse experts, behaviors that may signal that a parent is physically or emotionally child-abusive may include having a history of abusing their children in the past; using excessively harsh discipline that is not age appropriate; not being able adequately to explain children's injuries or trying to hide injuries; seeming unconcerned about a child or a child's problems; tending to misperceive a child as bad, monstrous, evil, etc.; being psychotic or psychopathic; misusing alcohol or drugs; blaming or belittling a child; being cold and rejecting; withholding love from a child; and/or treating siblings inappropriately unequally (Community Council on Child Abuse and Neglect, Inc. 1982). Children's reactions to physical abuse can include being wary of physical contact with adults; being apprehensive when other children cry; demonstrating extremes in behavior; seeming frightened of their parents and other adults; and/or reporting that their parents injured them (CCCAN 1982). Children's reactions to emotional abuse can include appearing overly compliant, passive, and undemanding; being extremely aggressive, demanding, or rageful; showing overly adaptive behaviors, either inappropriately adultlike or inappropriately infantile; lagging in physical, emotional, and intellectual development; and/or attempting suicide (CCCAN 1982). We need to reexamine these criteria and consider whether the behavior depicted in *Crooklyn* signals a child-neglectful, endangering, or abusive environment.

Criteria for child maltreatment may vary from one community to another and from one jurisdiction to another. But using as an example the kinds of criteria offered for child maltreatment by the Community Council on Child Abuse and Neglect, Inc. (1982), it is necessary to reconsider whether the mother's behavior depicted in *Crooklyn* qualifies as child-abusive. It is also important to reconsider whether the children's reactions to her resemble those of abused children. The important lesson in this is for teachers to remember that if we are not at least familiar with alternative world views regarding disciplining behavior, then we may be more likely to impose one narrow view when judging such a situation.

Willis (1992) argues that in the African American community a high premium is placed upon the honoring of, and obedience to,

parents and elders of the family. This makes sense given the extended family and kinship networks that exist in these families.
According to Willis (1992, 135), "The learning of respect for elders is
the child's earliest contribution to family maintenance and cohesive-
ness." Many African American parents believe that to follow European American middle-class discipline practices, which are relatively
more permissive in style (e.g., Shaffer 1994), would leave African
American children vulnerable to "confrontations with [racist] authorities" in the mainstream American society (Willis 1992, 138; see
also Hale-Benson 1986 and Wilson 1995b). Thus, some parents may
feel that the firmer styles of discipline may be necessary and adaptive for their African American families when surviving in American
society (Deater-Deckard et al. 1996).

Theme #3:
"The Parents Seem
Irresponsible"

Another concern that emerged among the participants was that of
the parents leaving their children for several hours during the
evening to attend the father's music recital (the *Crooklyn* father is a
jazz musician). Though some participants felt uncertain about
predicting the children's ages, many were appalled that the parents
left five children home apparently unattended. For example:

> I could be mistaken but I thought the oldest child was at the most ten
> years old. The children were too young to be left home alone and
> they were also expected to do too much on their own. (female)

> I must admit that I was surprised at the scene where the children
> stayed home alone. First of all, I was appalled that their parents
> would leave them home alone. But secondly, I was surprised that
> they stayed there and peacefully watched TV. There were no huge
> arguments between them, and they seemed content to be alone
> together. Obviously this was not the first time they had been left in
> this situation. (female)

Thus, some of the students' comments suggest that they felt that
the children were ill equipped for being left at home alone for the
evening. Related to this issue were participants' judgments that too
much was expected of the children in terms of chores and household
responsibilities. For example, some thought that the independence of
the children was not age-appropriate and was indicative of the
parents' irresponsibility. It also was thought that these expectations
may lead to pathological responses such as anxiety and parentification of the children.

The participants interpreted the mother's desire to send her
daughter to Southern relatives for two weeks during the summer as
follows: (1) she had no control over her kids; (2) she didn't want to
be bothered with her children; and (3) she didn't want her daughter

to be "on the streets" with her brothers. As one participant writes in his journal:

> [The mother] emphasizes how she does not want her to stay here and hang out all Summer with her brothers, indicating that they do nothing productive, like her father. (male)

Comments such as the one above indicate that not only was the community perceived as inadequate for raising children, but that the mother was looking for a quick means by which to rid herself of at least one child for the summer.

*Alternative
Perspectives
Concerning the
Third Theme:
The "Irresponsible
Parents"*

Not all of the participants agreed with the perspective that the children were left all alone by irresponsible parents. For example, one participant noted that she had the impression that the children were not alone at all; that the community was there to help look after them, including the neighbors upstairs within a fairly close-knit neighborhood. This perspective is consistent with research on the black community that points to the strength and functioning of the extended family and kinship networks that stretch far beyond blood relations. This network is also associated with members of a given kinship network living in close proximity to one another and sharing in child-rearing responsibilities (Billingsley 1992; Hill 1972).

In responding to the theme of irresponsible parenting, we return to the issue of the adaptability of family roles and the sharing of family responsibilities that is common in African American and lower socioeconomic families (Billingsley 1992; Willis 1992; Wilson 1995b). Hale-Benson (1986) points out that African American children, particularly girls, are expected to be more emotionally mature than their European American counterparts, are given more responsibilities at earlier ages, are very independent, and possess outstanding competencies in novel situations and in situations that require responsibility. These children are expected to assist in the child-rearing responsibilities of the younger siblings, out of necessity, if for no other reason. Thus, for younger siblings to be left in the care of older siblings who are pubescent is not so much a signal of the parent's irresponsibility as much as it is a sign of the children's necessarily mature and responsible nature.

Regarding the *Crooklyn* mother's desire to send her only daughter away for two weeks during the summer, Willis (1992) points out that it is not uncommon for African Americans to send their children away periodically to visit for extended periods of time with relatives in order to help maintain and strengthen the extended family kinship ties. This practice has been extremely common ever since the great migrations of blacks to the North from the Southern states during the industrial revolution in the earlier part of this century. Children from the North were sent to visit relatives in the South, and likewise, children from the South were sent to visit relatives in the North (Billingsley 1992; Hale 1994). This practice continues even to this day among many African American families.

Theme #4: "The Children Seem Uncontrollable"

There was a strong consensus that the mother had no control over the children, as demonstrated by their not following her instructions and their "mouthing off" and "talking back." Some participants thought that the mother was losing control of her children to the streets and to television because of her apparently inept parenting and the uncontrollable nature of the children. The participants saw the need for management and control of the children as vitally important. This concern related particularly to the children's volume of speech, movements, and communication style. Participants felt that these aspects of their behavior needed to be more carefully managed in order to reduce the appearance of their being threatening to others:

> The children's manners and actions reflected their parents' horrible parenting skills. The children were rowdy and unmanageable. They refused to follow their mothers orders and treated her disrespectfully. . . . I feel that this is not all of the children's fault though. I believe it is because of how they were raised and that they did not learn respect to begin with. (female)

> What I didn't understand was why the children failed to clean up the dishes. If they knew their mother would behave that way, why would they deliberately defy her? Perhaps that is my biggest unanswered question. (female)

Thus, descriptions such as *rowdy, unmanageable, disrespectful,* and *deliberately defiant* suggest a perception of the children as out of control.

The focus group was asked what they thought might happen if the *Crooklyn* children were to attend school with middle-class European American children. Some participants again indicated that they saw the *Crooklyn* children as aggressive and potentially threatening to other children. They stated that these children are "loud" and "aggressive" and that other children would run and retreat and would not be able to "stand up for themselves" against them. One participant remarked ethnocentrically, "These aggressive children will not know how to deal with the [self-controlled] children from the other culture(s)." Viewers thought that these children needed to be encouraged to adapt and "tone down" their "aggressive" styles to more acceptable or "appropriate" norms rather than teaching methods being adapted to the children's own styles. Participants thought that if the *Crooklyn* children did not adjust their behavior, their classrooms would be in chaos, and there would be "no control whatsoever."

Alternative Perspectives Concerning the Fourth Theme: The "Uncontrollable Children"

Kunjufu (1986), Hale-Benson (1986), and Hale (1994) explored the issue of African American children being perceived as difficult to manage. One reason offered for the concern is that many teachers do not understand African American children's "verve," which is an excitable energy and interest in their surroundings (Hale-Benson 1986, 78–79, 85–86; Kunjufu 1984, 1986). Teachers may attempt to squash this energy in an effort to gain total control over a child's behavior. Another issue may be misunderstandings that occur regarding African American children's body language and nonverbal communication styles. For example, the children's tendency either to gaze, or to avoid eye contact, may be misperceived as threatening or disrespectful (Cooper 1996; Hale-Benson 1986; Hecht et al. 1993; Kunjufu 1986; Shade 1989). And finally, there may be a mismatch in the firm disciplining style of the African American child's caregivers and the more passive style that may characterize their European American teachers. This can result, as Hale-Benson (1986, 68, 178–79) explains, in the African American children appearing to "run all over" the European American teachers as these teachers try to employ all of the "techniques learned in college," which do not make the best use of the African American cultural style.

Theme #5: "The Community Seems Barren and Threatening"

When participants in the focus group discussed the strengths of the community, there was a general consensus that the community was deficient and that it had nothing to offer. One participant of Latino background made the observation that, from his perspective, the *Crooklyn* movie may be inaccurate because the children don't seem to have anything available to them in their community, whereas "the *Cosby Show* children could at the least go to the mall." He also acknowledged that he wasn't sure that either medium's portrayal accurately reflects African American life.

Another participant voiced concern about meeting the needs of children who are in communities plagued with street violence. This fits some of the participants' notion that the *Crooklyn* mother desired to send her daughter away primarily to get her off of the neighborhood streets. A European American participant in the focus group said, "Yes [it's nice to explore these strengths of the black community and all], but I need to know how we handle situations where, for example, kids are coming to school afraid to walk down the street—afraid that they will be killed."

In contrast to the participants above, some viewers easily identified the strong sense of community as a strength:

> First, there was so much playing [outside], and maybe this is not reality, but it appeared that there was a strong sense of community. (female)

A strong sense of community has been one of the greatest strengths of the African American culture, as outlined by a number of scholars (Billingsley 1992; Hale 1994; Hill 1972; Willis 1992; Wilson 1995a, 1995b). No one movie by itself can portray accurately all of the diversities of African American life any more than one movie could portray European American life and its diversities. However, as an African American woman raised in an African American community environment, I would argue that *Crooklyn* portrayed a number of strengths found in the African American community. For example, *Crooklyn* portrays formal and informal extended kinship networks, extensive and passionate communication styles, adaptability of family roles, responsible and appropriately mature children, and parents who were far from perfect, but who attempt to instill important values in their children. The fact that African American children today are at greater risk than any other group in the United States (Wilson 1995a and 1995b) should not be minimized in this discussion. African American children disproportionately struggle with issues of joblessness, poverty, drugs, the breakdown of family cohesion, and community violence (Billingsley 1992). Unfortunately, mainstream forms of media inappropriately make socially constructed conditions such as these in the black community synonymous with the black culture itself (Chideya 1995), by portraying violence in the black community as unique and as representative of the entire community of black people. The media give the impression that African Americans and other people of color exclusively experience such challenges; in general are failing; and have made few contributions to society. The fact is that many children of color and their families are struggling, even against incredible historical and socially produced pressures, challenges, and odds, and yet the majority are surviving and contributing to their communities. As one example, there is a tendency to share as a community and to assist others, as exemplified by a historical legacy of rearing other peoples' children as well as one's own, a tendency that continues in the African American community to this day (Billingsley 1992; Feagin and Sikes 1994; Wilson 1995b).

Regarding the children who are facing dangers in their homes and/or in their surrounding communities, research shows that teachers who capitalize on the extended family kinship network model are more successful with these children. Incorporating opportunities to include kinship models into their teaching style is associated with greater classroom effectiveness. For instance, successful teachers of African American children tend to treat students as if they are extended family (Foster 1994; Ladson-Billings 1994). Studies suggest that for these children, it is extremely important to use pedagogical approaches that include or acknowledge the children's culture, life issues and stories, struggles, and creative problem-solving (Allen and Butler 1996; Foster 1994; Ladson-Billings 1994; Shade 1989). Successful teachers of African American children have a clear understanding of the importance of this, and employ African American cultural styles, history, and sociology in their pedagogical philosophies and techniques (Collins and Tamarkin 1990). According to Ladson-Billings (1994), children's lives, their issues, their struggles, and their concerns and fears can be used as a bridge to help them express their feelings and knowledge through writing, singing, rapping, and empowering themselves with ideas about pre- and post-enslavement African history and culture, survival and coping.

Thus, the five major themes that emerged in discussions and writing about the children and family in *Crooklyn* can be reconsidered in light of the alternative perspectives offered in research literature written by African American scholars, advocates, and community members.

Conclusion

I have shown that the movie *Crooklyn* proved fruitful as a projective technique for eliciting discussion among pre-certification teacher candidates and social science students. It must be noted that in the focus group, participants may have been hesitant to vocalize positive or favorable impressions about the *Crooklyn* family against the steady flow of negative comments that were being offered. However, confidential written comments did not prove much more favorable among the journal-group participants. It may be necessary to ask participants very specific questions about the family rather than relying on their overall, more general impressions of the family. It will also be important to interview or survey a more culturally, racially, experiential, and economically diverse group to examine any differences that may emerge in their perceptions.

The comments collected from these participants indicate that their past experiences or a possible lack of diverse equal-status experiences may be crucial determinants of intolerant views regarding African American children and their families. In order to illuminate the biased knowledge that may be at work in the viewers' perceptions, I offered alternative perspectives that take into account previous research regarding African American and lower socioeconomic cultural and communication styles. This study points to the urgent need for North American schools and communities to achieve greater diversity within their teacher and social service provider pools in order to better meet the needs of diverse student or client populations. Diversity in teachers and service providers is crucial in terms of ethnic, gender, age, differential/handicap ability, and experience if children's educational and developmental needs are to be met.

I have argued, likewise, that it is important for teachers and service providers to be adequately trained in the variety of ways and styles of diverse cultures and communities. Moreover, it is essential that teachers explore and challenge their own feelings, experiences, perceptions, and misperceptions regarding children and families of backgrounds different from their own (Bowman and Stott 1994).

Intolerance is a behavioral issue as well as a perceptual issue. How we think about others may influence how we treat them. If we do not know intimately those who are from backgrounds that differ from ours, then we may easily misunderstand or misjudge their behavior. Gaining knowledge, exposure, and better understanding with respect to other cultures is analogous to a carpenter increasing her repertoire and usage of tools from her toolbox so that she does not rely excessively upon a limited set of tools for a diverse range of jobs. According to Stephan and Brigham (1985), equal-status experiences with members of diverse communities is the best method for facilitating intercultural learning and appreciation. Throughout this essay I have cited other researchers who show that experiential diversity can also be achieved through learning, studying, and exposing oneself to other cultures, and challenging conventional notions regarding other cultures and the pedagogy of children of color (e.g., Foster 1994; Hale-Benson 1986; Ladson-Billings 1994).

To conclude, methods exist for improving cultural competency in relation to African American children and families. These include (1) being sensitive to and acknowledging familial and cultural strengths in addition to challenges and weaknesses; (2) providing a more appropriate balance of positive media images and role models to children; and (3) being aware of and prepared to acknowledge and incorporate African American cultural interactive and communication styles into activities and interventions with children and their families.

Some of the interactive and communication styles that may exist in African American families that are often misunderstood by those outside of the culture include (1) passionate and assertive verbal and nonverbal communication styles; (2) strong kinship bonds and extended family networks and associated visitation and habitation practices; (3) the sharing of and adaptability in family roles between caregivers and children; and (4) different needs for, meanings of, and expectations regarding behavior toward family and community elders and discipline. It is also important to note that African American teachers and service providers who have not shared experiences similar to those of the children they serve also need to experience equal-status experiences in, and training about, the children of color with whom they will work. Research demonstrates that even teachers of color who have been socialized in the dominant mainstream, predominantly white culture may be likely to think inaccurately and stereotypically about children of color (Foster 1994; Schofield 1986). Thus, teachers of all backgrounds can benefit from cross-cultural training and experiences.

Teachers need to engage in the practice of learning about, searching for, and appreciating cultural strengths and competencies which will also enable them to raise their expectations of the children with whom they work or serve. To embrace these strengths is the most important component in perceptual and behavioral tolerance, and can help reduce the kinds of educational inequities that have been found regarding the treatment of children of color. As Wilson (1995a, 94) reminds us, "Presuming cultural and familial strengths will necessarily lead to different strategies of assistance." Thus, gaining a better understanding of our own weaknesses with respect to our feelings and thoughts about others, learning about other cultures through equal-status experiences, and respectfully investigating and studying other cultures are initial steps toward education about tolerance and intolerance.

Notes   1. For example, in the U.S. state of Connecticut, the majority of schools offer no exposure to cultural/racial diversity among their K–12 teaching faculty, as demonstrated by the fact that students from minority groups (e.g., African American, Hispanic/Latino, Asian American, and Native American) make up nearly 28 percent of the student population, yet teachers of color make up only 6 percent of the faculty (Connecticut Advisory Council for Teacher Professional Standards 1995). In addition, 70 percent of the school districts have two or fewer teachers of color; 31 percent of all Connecticut schools have only one teacher of color, and another 34 percent of all Connecticut schools have no teachers of color. In many of these all-white or nearly all-white teacher districts, students of color make up more than 70 percent of the student population (Connecticut Advisory Council for Teacher Professional Standards 1995).

2. *Crooklyn* opens with scenes of African American children playing in their neighborhood. During the first fifteen minutes of *Crooklyn*, five of the children, four brothers and their sister, ages about seven to thirteen, are called home to a nutritious meal in an apparently clean and comfortable

brownstone home. As they sit down to dinner, the children seem bubbly and are chattering. The mother admonishes her children to be quiet for grace. The father offers a short prayer. The mother seems to disapprove and says grace also. A stream of conversations begins which includes various forms and intensities of chatter, banter, complaints, discipline, questions, and remarks that occur among the family members. For example, one of the boys tells his siblings to get their elbows off the table. The mother lightly slaps at her daughter's hand and tells her to quit biting her nails. Then she tells one of her sons to close his mouth. He "eats like a pig . . . chews like a cow . . . he's greedy," she remarks. She tells another son that he is going to have his "head pulled off" if he does not put down the salt. She admonishes one other son to eat his food. The children are also warned by the mother to be sure to have the kitchen clean by the time that she comes home after attending their father's "gig." She says that she expects to come home to sleep and relax, and should not have to "run around after them." The father is relatively relaxed during these activities. The father belches, much to the disapproval of the rest of the family. He says that it is a compliment to his wife's good cooking. He appears disturbed only by their neighbor's loud attempt to perform a song, and bangs on the wall in hopes that the amateur performance will stop.

There is then a change in scene, and the movie shows the children watching television while lying across a bed. Another scene shows the daughter waking in the night and walking sleepily to her brothers' room, where she squats and urinates. A change in scene occurs again, and suddenly, lights are on and the mother is pulling the sleeping children from their beds, and slapping them about their bottoms. It is four o'clock in the morning. She fervently admonishes them, saying, for example, that they will have to pull their weight in the family. She lines them up against the wall, waves her finger at them, and states that she will "slap the black off" of one of them. She also states that she will knock their "teeth into tomorrow" and will "beat their brains out," although she does not. The children are marched downstairs to clean up the kitchen. The mother chastises the eldest son for not setting an example and for being immature. One sibling remarks he would "rather have a father than a mother any day." His siblings appear that they may agree with him, but Mother does not and she begins chasing the children around the kitchen. A change of scene to later that morning occurs, and apparently all but the mother are still asleep. The daughter has awakened and joins the mother in a tender conversation where the mother suggests that the daughter go to visit relatives for a couple of weeks during the summer. The daughter protests this idea.

3. For this chapter, the original version of the detailed description of the first fifteen minutes of *Crooklyn* was drafted by a woman of British ancestry who is in her forties, and was revised by an African American woman and an African American male, both in their thirties. Both females work in careers that involve children, and both have children of their own. The male is a clinical psychology Ph.D. candidate who does not yet have children. Any description provided for this chapter may be subject to the observers' own biases, though every effort was made to use neutral language in the detailed description of the first scenes of *Crooklyn*.

4. Because so many popular media depictions of African Americans are unduly negative and inaccurately stereotypical, the author was concerned about unwittingly presenting material for discussion that had no true resemblance whatsoever to African American life. To help gauge the appropriateness of *Crooklyn* as a material even remotely representative of African American life, a survey was conducted among thirty-three African Americans in higher education who were from a variety of socioeconomic backgrounds across the United States. *Crooklyn* was judged by them to be a moderately appropriate and representative stimulus. On a scale from one to nine, the mean score was six in favor of it being *positive* or favorable in its characterizations of African American life, and also six in favor of it being *accurate* in its characterizations.

5. This journal group was similar to the focus group in gender, age, and ethnicity. Almost all of the participants were first-time viewers. Both studies were approved by the appropriate college board, and students gave their written permission for their written comments to be published anonymously.

6. All of the comments presented were from European American participants unless otherwise noted. Of the thirty-three focus-group participants, twenty-seven were European American and six were of a variety of other backgrounds including African American, Hispanic/Latino, and Asian American. Of the fourteen focus-group participants, thirteen were European American and one was African American.

Works Cited

Allen, Brenda, and Lisa Butler. 1996. "The Effects Of Music and Movement Opportunity on the Analogical Reasoning Performance of African American and White School Children: A Preliminary Study. *The Journal of Black Psychology* 22(3): 316–28.

Allen, LaRue, and Shayda Majidi-Ahi. 1989. "Black American Children." In *Children of Color: Psychological Interventions with Minority Youth*, edited by Jewelle Taylor Gibbs and Larke Namhe Huang and Associates. San Francisco: Jossey-Bass.

Barnes, Esmeralda. 1992. "High Rates of Hospitalization for Blacks Seeking Psychiatric Help Point to Cultural Biases in Mental Health Care Profession, Experts Say." *Black Issues in Higher Education* 8 (October): 14–15, 46–47.

Berger, Kathleen, and Ross Thompson. 1995. *The Developing Person through Childhood and Adolescence.* New York: Worth Publishers.

Billingsley, Andrew. 1992. *Climbing Jacob's Ladder: The Enduring Legacy of African-American Families.* New York: Simon & Schuster.

Bowman, Barbara T., and Frances M. Stott. 1994. "Understanding Development in a Cultural Context." In *Diversity and Developmentally Appropriate Practice: Challenges for Early Childhood Education*, edited by Bruce Mallory and Rebecca New. New York: Teachers College Press.

Chideya, Farai. 1995. *Don't Believe the Hype: Fighting Cultural Misinformation about African-Americans.* New York: Plume.

Collins, Marva, and Civia Tamarkin. 1990. *Marva Collins' Way: Returning to Excellence in Education.* New York: Putnam.

Collins, Patricia H. 1990. *Black Feminist Thought: Knowledge, Consciousness, and the Politics of Empowerment.* Cambridge, MA: Unwin Hyman, Inc.

Community Council on Child Abuse and Neglect, Inc. 1982. *Role of the Educator in the Prevention and Treatment of Child Abuse and Neglect: Indicators of Child Abuse and Neglect.* Written and compiled by C.M. LeBoeuf, CSC, M.Ed. CCCAN, One Davis Boulevard, Suite 212, Tampa, FL 33606. (813) 251-8080.

Connecticut Advisory Council for Teacher Professional Standards. *A Proposal to Increase the Number of Minority Educators in Connecticut.* Presented to the Governor, State Board of Education, Education Committee of the Connecticut General Assembly. September 1995. Contact person: Cynthia L. Jorgensen, Education Consultant, Connecticut State Department of Education, Box 2219, Hartford, CT 06145.

Cooper, Pamela. 1996. "Thoughts on Communicating in Another Culture." In *Making Connections: Readings in Relational Communication,* edited by Kathleen Galvin and Pamela Cooper, 49–53. Los Angeles: Roxbury Publishing.

Deater-Deckard, Kirby, Kenneth A. Dodge, John E. Bates, and Gregory S. Pettit. 1996. "Physical Discipline among African American and European American Mothers: Links to Children's Externalizing Behaviors." *Developmental Psychology* 32(6): 1065–72.

Duncan, Birt L. 1976. "Differential Social Perception and Attribution of Intergroup Violence: Testing the Lower Limits of Stereotyping of Blacks." *Journal of Personality and Social Psychology* 34(4): 590–98.

Ebert, Roger. 1994. "Crooklyn." Review of *Crooklyn* (Universal Pictures Movie). *Chicago Sun-Times,* 13 May: 39.

Feagin, Joe, and Melvin Sikes. 1994. *Living with Racism: The Black Middle-Class Experience.* Boston: Beacon Press.

Fiske, Susan Taylor. 1993. "Controlling Other People: The Impact of Power on Stereotyping." *American Psychologist* 48(6): 621–28.

Foster, Herbert. 1986. *Ribbin', Jivin' and Playin' the Dozens: The Persistent Dilemma in Our Schools.* Cambridge, MA: Ballinger.

Foster, Michele. 1994. "Educating for Competence in Community and Culture: Exploring the Views of Exemplary African-American Teachers." In *Too Much Schooling, Too Little Education: A Paradox of Black Life in White Societies,* edited by M. Shujaa. Trenton, NJ: Africa World Press.

Gibbs, Jewelle Taylor, and Larke Nahme Huang. 1989. *Children of Color: Psychological Interventions with Minority Youth.* San Francisco: Jossey-Bass.

Hale-Benson, Janice. 1986. *Black Children: Their Roots, Culture and Learning Styles.* Baltimore, MD: Johns Hopkins University Press.

Hale, Janice. 1994. *Unbank the Fire: Visions for the Education of African American Children.* Baltimore, MD: Johns Hopkins University Press.

Hecht, Michael, Mary Jane Collier, and Sidney Ribeau. 1993. *African American Communication: Ethnic Identity and Cultural Interpretation.* Newbury Park, CA: Sage Publications.

Hill, Robert. 1972. *The Strengths of Black Families.* New York: Emerson Hall.

hooks, bell. 1993. *Sisters of the Yam: Black Women and Self-Recovery.* Boston: South End Press.

Kirchner, Joan. 1995. "Georgia School Superintendent Blows Whistle on Racial Tracking." *Associated Press/New London Day,* 13 June: A3.

Kunjufu, Jawanza. 1984. *Developing Positive Self-Images and Discipline in Black Children.* Chicago: African American Images.

———. 1986. *Countering the Conspiracy to Destroy Black Boys.* Vol. II. Chicago: African American Images.

Ladner, Joyce. 1971. *Tomorrow's Tomorrow: The Black Woman.* Garden City, NJ: Doubleday.

Ladson-Billings, Gloria. 1994. *The Dreamkeepers: Successful Teachers of African American Children.* San Francisco: Jossey-Bass.

Lassiter, Ruby F. 1987. "Child Rearing in Black Families: Child-Abusing Discipline?" In *Violence in the Black Family: Correlates and Consequences,* edited by Robert L. Hampton. Lexington, MA: Lexington Books.

Lee, Spike. 1994. *Crooklyn.* 114 min. Universal Pictures, 70 Universal City Plaza, Universal City, CA 91608. Videocassette. Available from MCA Universal Home Video (818) 777-4400.

Maccoby, Eleanor E. 1980. *Social Development: Psychological Growth and the Parent-Child Relationship.* New York: Harcourt Brace Jovanovich.

Pettigrew, Thomas, and Joanna Martin. 1987. "Shaping Organizational Context for Black American Inclusion." *Journal of Social Issues* 43(1): 41–78.

Richard, Harriette. 1996. "Filmed in Black and White: Teaching the Concept of Racial Identity at a Predominantly White University." *Teaching of Psychology* 23(3): 159–61.

Robertson, Judith P. 1997a. "Screenplay Pedagogy and the Interpretation of Unexamined Knowledge in Preservice Primary Teaching." *Taboo: The Journal of Culture and Education* 1 (Spring): 25–60.

———. 1997b. "Fantasy's Confines: Popular Culture and the Education of the Female Primary School Teacher." *Canadian Journal of Education* 22(2): 123–43.

Sagar, H. Andrew, and Janet Ward Schofield. 1980. "Racial and Behavioral Cues in Black and White Children's Perceptions of Ambiguously

Aggressive Acts." *Journal of Personality and Social Psychology* 39(4): 590–98.

Schofield, Janet Ward. 1986. "Causes and Consequences of the Colorblind Perspective." In *Prejudice, Discrimination, and Racism,* edited by John F. Dovidio and Samuel Gaertner. Orlando, FL: Academic Press.

Shade, Barbara. 1989. *Culture, Style and the Educative Process.* Springfield, IL: Charles C. Thomas.

Shaffer, David. 1994. *Social and Personality Development.* Pacific Grove, CA: Brooks/Cole Publishing Company.

Stephan, Walter G. 1985. "Intergroup Relations." In *The Handbook of Social Psychology,* 3rd ed. Vol. 2, edited by Gardner Lindzey and Elliot Aronson, 599–658. Hillsdale, NJ: Erlbaum.

Stephan, Walter G., and John C. Brigham. 1985. "Intergroup Contact: Introduction." *Journal of Social Issues* 41(3): 1–8.

Webster's Desk Dictionary. 1993. New York: Random House.

West, Carolyn. 1995. "Mammy, Sapphire, and Jezebel: Historical Images of Black Women and Their Implications for Psychotherapy." *Psychotherapy* 32(3): 158–66.

Willis, Winnie. 1992. "Families with African American Roots." In *Developing Cross-Cultural Competency: A Guide for Working with Young Children and Their Families,* edited by E. Lynch and M. Hanson, 121–50. Baltimore, MD: Paul Brookes.

Wilson, Melvin, et al. 1995a. "Promotion of African American Family Life: Families, Poverty, and Social Programs." In *New Directions for Child Development. African American Family Life: Its Structural and Ecological Aspects,* edited by M. Wilson, 68, 85–99. San Francisco: Jossey-Bass.

———. 1995b. "African American Family Life: The Dynamics of Interactions, Relationships, and Roles." In *New Directions for Child Development. African American Family Life: Its Structural and Ecological Aspects,* edited by M. Wilson, 68, 5–21. San Francisco: Jossey-Bass.

Educating beyond Tolerance: Reading Media Images of the *Hijab*

Sharon Todd
York University

Over the past few years, the *hijab* (that is, the head scarf and, often, loose-fitted clothing in the form of tunic or dress worn by some Muslim women) has attracted much Canadian media attention.[1] This attention galvanized around an incident involving the suspension of a student from a public high school in the Montreal area. On September 7, 1994, a twelve-year-old girl, Émilie Ouimet, a recent convert to Islam, was sent home for not complying with the request to remove her *hijab*. Her attire apparently was not within the bounds of the dress code established by the school, and the principal was reported as saying that "the wearing of a distinctive sign, like the *hijab* or neo-Nazi insignias, could polarize the aggressivity of students."[2] In all reports of the incident, the principal was supported fully by the parents' committee, which agreed that to allow the *hijab* to be worn in school would be to favor the rights of one individual—or group of individuals—over all other students who had to abide by the dress code in effect. The dress code was thus seen as a "leveling" device, a way to mete out equal status to all students. The pervasive sentiment reported was that to do otherwise would marginalize such students.

This incident raised a number of important concerns in all media reports of the incident. First, the right to public education was denied to a student on the basis of her religious dress; second, the question of what is to be "tolerated" in a multicultural society

Originally published as "Veiling the 'Other,' Unveiling Our 'Selves': Reading Media Images of the *Hijab* Psychoanalytically to Move beyond Tolerance" in the Fall 1998 issue of *Canadian Journal of Education/Revue canadienne de l'éducation* 23(4): 438–51. Reprinted with permission.

became a crucial issue. The discourse of individual rights, community responsibility, and the relation of religion to the state was foregrounded in Canadian reports of the Ouimet incident, and in these respects opened up a debate whose echoes may be heard in the biblical-creation-versus-evolution arguments presented in the United States. However, upon reading these reports, it became apparent to me that the issues had less to do with the specifics of the incident, and more to do with larger questions of social policy and definitions of community. The representations of *hijab*-wearing women were not the only troubling aspects of the reports; the differences among these representations also gave tremendous cause for concern. The arguments these representations served to legitimize had as much to do with the ongoing histories of Canadian and Quebec nationalisms as they did with representing the particular difficulties *hijab*-wearing women face in a multicultural society.

Both the French- and English-language local newspapers took this story to be exemplary of the issues multiculturalism poses to traditional expectations and behaviors of schooling practices. Indeed, going far beyond the bounds of the actual incident, articles and editorials discussed what the *hijab* means and why Muslim women wear it, all the while verging on, and sometimes tumbling into, a morass of the most blatant forms of stereotype and prejudice. Moreover, both presses constructed a public debate that spoke directly to their own views of what community and society are and should be. For this reason, it is not the stereotypical representations of the Ouimet incident per se that are so intriguing, but the way in which these stereotypes construct particular fantasies that serve the needs of two very different cultural groups in Montreal, and in Quebec more generally. I offer below first my rationale for reading these media accounts in a specific manner (that is, psychoanalytically), followed by my analysis of the reports. The essay concludes with some considerations of this type of reading for elementary school teachers.

Education, Stereotype, and "Tolerance"

Educators sensitive to issues of social discrimination work with the assumption that popular images have an effect upon children's attitudes and beliefs about themselves and others. The common feeling is that children are bombarded with stereotypes in toys, storybooks, and films, and that these images distort the truth about various social groups so depicted. Indeed, the stereotype is thought to be a relation of power, whereby privilege for one group is secured through the denigration and distortion of others. Thus educators often find themselves focusing their energies on redressing this distortion by encouraging students of all ages to think critically about what is represented to them and why, and by posing alternatives which better speak to the lived realities and aspirations of those who are most often subjected to stereotype. Often, multicultural education focuses on encouraging children to develop tolerant attitudes toward others, by not fearing difference, and by refusing to accept untruths about those differences as well.

While neither wanting to dismiss the need to work against discriminatory forms of representation, nor abandoning the hope that teaching can affect the way children interrelate with those whom they perceive as different from themselves, I nevertheless wish to challenge the logic which supports seeing representations in *either* negative *or* positive terms, and to problematize the assumption that tolerance should be the goal of our pedagogical practices. As Webster's *Dictionary* defines it, tolerance is "a fair and permissive attitude toward those whose race, religion, nationality, etc., differ from one's own." However, if one of our pedagogical goals is to encourage children to work for a more just future, then we are not talking about encouraging mere "tolerance" of others, but striving toward a new mode of understanding our selves *in relation* to others. Hence it is not just an attitudinal change *toward* an other—which still positions one individual vis-à-vis another individual—but a conceptual understanding that recognizes that no self is possible without an other, without an outside.

Following psychoanalytic insights, part of this understanding requires an acceptance that our interactions with images, insofar as they constitute our "outside," affect us unconsciously. They participate in our meaning-making activity and shape how we think about, dream about, and relate to all others around us. As Jacques Lacan (1977) puts it in his theory of the mirror stage, an infant begins to form a sense of itself as it "recognizes" that there is an other outside its own bodily limits. The image of the "other" in the mirror is not unlike the bodily presence of an other person (say, mother or father) with whom the infant identifies and forms an image of itself as being like that other, an "imago" (Lacan 1977, 2). In this way we establish a sense of self only in relation to, and not independent from, an other different from and external to our own bodily presence. Interestingly, educators often speak of how children "internalize" attitudes and beliefs (as do adults) from the society around them, seeming to suggest that images which populate children's culture do have unconscious effects. But, rarely do we address ourselves to how such images constitute a sense of self for ourselves and our children, and how they construct a vision or fantasy of society itself—that is, a social imaginary. How is it that we define ourselves as "selves" in relation to categories of otherness? Focusing on this profound connection between self and other enables us to think about how stereotypes in particular have a role in constituting who we think we are, and what society is. Moreover, in creating—and not merely being subjected to—specific images, what might this tell us about our "selves" in relation to the other that is conjured up for our own purposes of communication?

Homi Bhabha (1994), in rethinking the stereotype as being not only a relation of power but also a relation of desire, suggests that a sense of "usness" is at stake when stereotypes are produced: for whose desires are implicated when stereotypes are mobilized in popular media accounts of events? And how does a sharing of these desires create a sense of "us" in relation to "them?" It is to such questions that I turn in this essay, suggesting that their engagement may be helpful in dealing with the dynamic which structures and continues to make possible stereotypical forms of representation. To ignore this dynamic of desire and need may place us in the position of calling for mere tolerance, rather than struggling with the more difficult question of developing new social relations "beyond tolerance," ones which fully recognize the play of power and desire. Let me explain further what I mean by "beyond tolerance."

Moving beyond "Tolerance"

James Schwoch, Mimi White, and Susan Reilly (1992), in their call to teach critical media skills, propose that we understand that multiple meanings can be generated from any particular set of images. Understanding that there can be multiple levels of meaning moves us away from an overly simplified view of representations as being *either* positive *or* negative, and opens us up to questioning how images function differently, given their different social contexts and their different audiences. This suggests that anti-racist and multicultural education is about the *inquiry into* multiple meaning, and not merely about the *rectifying* of specific images. In inquiring into meanings of representations, educators may begin to address the ways in which images not only serve the needs of those who do the representing (such as the community group who puts out a particular newspaper), but also the ways in which they invite us (the readers, the consumers) to share a certain social imaginary, a certain fantasy of self and society. Taking this into consideration, anti-racist and multicultural education cannot be content in educating for tolerance, for the underlying fantasy or shared social imaginary is left unquestioned, unanalysed. Instead, I wish to make a distinction between educating *for* tolerance (with its implicit assumption that there is an "us" who tolerates "them") and educating *beyond* tolerance, with its emphasis on a consideration of the self-other relationship, where "usness" and "themness" are themselves open to question. Educating beyond tolerance requires an understanding that representations are not simply concerned with telling falsehoods or truths about groups, but are involved in constructing a sense of who "we" are, who "they" are, and how the society in which we live is understood. For instance, daily media representations of the black urban poor in the United States foster an image of poverty as being about blacks and about inner-city life. Not only do such representations fly in the face of statistics to the contrary, as most poor in the United States are white and rural (Books 1996), but they also are part of the raw material that shapes how we speak about, experience, and imagine the landscape of America (and this is particularly the case, perhaps, in the context of the Canadian imaginary). The point to be made here with respect to attending pedagogically to issues of representation is not whether an image correctly represents reality (is poverty primarily urban or rural, for example?), but how these images play into a fantastical understanding of what American society stands for. For instance, the Canadian media often rhetorically pose the question "Do we want our country to 'look like' the United States?" and in so doing invoke a social imaginary based, in part, on these media representations of poverty. That is, the portrayal of otherness (the United States in this case) constitutes a sense of self (a Canadian): by recognizing that "you" are other, I know who "I" am. Elisabeth Young-Bruehl in her study of prejudices states that inquiring into what needs or desires are being fulfilled through stereotypical representations is necessary in order to understand how social relationships come to look the way they do (1996, 20). Asking ourselves what needs and desires are fulfilled in media representations equally compels us to focus on how they function to sustain a particular psychical investment, one which encourages allegiance to a specific social group as it constructs an "outside" to that group. Thus, it is through recognizing who "them" is in the media that an "us" is formed.

In considering this self-other relation, rather than measuring whether the media represented *hijab*-wearing women "correctly," this essay itself performs what it asks critical educators to consider. That is, it offers a reading which focuses more on what needs and desires are served when an event is represented one way rather than another. The essay also argues, by way of comparative example, that such an inquiry can open up an alternative to reading media stories as neutral (as factual information), or negative (as stereotypical accounts), or positive (as getting the story "right"). Instead, I am interested in how the words on the page operate to define particular self-other relationships that constitute possibilities for moving beyond tolerance. While on the surface the Ouimet incident itself seems to be a flagrant demonstration of intolerance on the part of the school authorities, what I wish to emphasize here is that in the reporting of this incident other layers of meaning were being constructed, and that it is these meanings which, when made the subject of analysis, can lead to an inquiry into how selves and others are constituted, and not merely how they can be "correctly" represented. As we shall see, not only were the accounts reported in the press related to the political, cultural, and social climate in which they circulated, but they also constructed an imaginary ideal of what society is, and made an appeal to an "us" who shared this social imaginary, while simultaneously defining a "them" who clearly did not. The "us" and "them" contained in the reports do not only refer to mainstream, white Christian society versus Muslims who wear the *hijab,* but as well to the complicated Anglophone and Franco-phone tensions which set the context for the debate. As discussed below, to study media reports of this incident as evidence of intoler-ance does not unveil the full picture of what students, and readers generally, may be identifying with or denying in those reports. That is to say, by focusing on representations of the *hijab* as sustaining a sense of self for two different communities, perhaps we can begin to understand why media images play so powerfully into establishing a sense of self and community for the individual students we teach (as well as ourselves). Toward the end of the essay, I discuss how psychoanalyzing media representations in this manner may be a powerful device for teachers to move beyond mere tolerance in their classrooms.

Veiling the Other

Of course, the reporting of the Ouimet incident cannot be entirely isolated, its meanings never totally "free-floating" (Giroux 1994, 19). Rooted in what Homa Hoodfar (1993) calls the "making of the veil in Western minds," the media representations of the event—despite whether or not they supported Ouimet's presence in the public school—cannot be taken out of context. Both before and after the incident, a number of important factors played into how the *hijab* was represented, and how it shaped different senses of "self" and "other." First, the *hijab* has been the "object" of great debate in France in recent years, where it is now banned in all public schools in the name of secularism. Second, a few short months after the Ouimet incident, another Montreal girl was told to find a new school for the upcoming year should she wish to continue wearing the *hijab.* Third, the largest teacher's union in Quebec, Centrale de l'Enseignement du Québec (CEQ), voted on a resolution in the spring of 1995 banning the *hijab* from public schools—which does not carry any legal weight. Fourth, the Quebec Human Rights Commission and the Quebec Council on the Status of Women (1995) came out in support of those who choose to wear the *hijab,* the operative word here being "choose." Fifth, various Muslim, Arab, and Jewish communities have not been silent on the issue, hosting a number of conferences in the Montreal area and publicly condemning the attitudes expressed by the parents and teachers of Ouimet's former school. And last, the only Muslim school on the island of Montreal stopped requesting non-Muslim teachers to wear the *hijab* as a job requirement, following the directives issued by the Quebec Human Rights Commission.

It should be clear by now that the *hijab* is no innocent "signifier." It has come to symbolize everything from Islamic fundamentalism to freedom of religious expression to women's subordination as well as women's empowerment and equality.[3] To untangle this web of meaning is not my express purpose here. Indeed, as Shahrzad Mojab (1995) has pointed out, "to veil or not to veil: that is not the question," for there is no singular reason why women choose to wear the veil in Quebec or any other place for that matter. Instead, rather than seeking to find the ultimate meaning of why women wear the *hijab,* or giving a definitive statement as to its place in a multicultural society, or providing an account of how the *hijab* should be represented at all times, my focus here is on how representations of the *hijab as emblematic of specific ideals* are used to construct a social imaginary for two communities: that is, a shared fantasy of what "our" society is and should be. It is through an examination of the practice of "veiling the other," that we might learn something about "our" selves.

Unveiling "Our" Selves

I wish to turn now to a specific reading of the debate as it appeared in the local press and what the representations in the press yield in terms of defining a mythical identity called "our society." In reviewing the discourse over the few months following the Ouimet incident, it became increasingly evident that the press was by no means seamless in its orientation. Views ranged from acceptance of the *hijab*'s presence in Quebec schools to its outright banning. In terms of editorials, there was a general concern in all the presses about what the *hijab* means to Muslim women.[4] However, while there was considerable overlap in presentation of ideas on the *hijab,* there were noticeable differences between the French-language press and the English-language press. And, not surprisingly, there were also significant differences within the French-language press as well.[5] In general, there were two major motifs underlying reports of the incident. The French-language press, whether in favor or not of the presence of the *hijab* in schools, focused more on the *hijab* as a "symbol," and framed its concerns in terms of secular versus confessional (i.e., religious) education. On the other hand, the English-language daily, the *Gazette,* focused more on the human rights issue and the freedom of religious expression. I wish to sketch an outline of these views, following it up with an interrogation into the sense of self these texts position as center. The differences between the two views have to do with different attitudes toward the definition of public education which is tied to a history of a confessional education system in Quebec. A brief sketch of this background is necessary for understanding this relationship.

Except for a small minority, Francophones have traditionally been educated in French Catholic schools, as have English-speaking Catholics in their own schools (a minority within the Anglophone community). This left many non-Catholic immigrant populations along with the rest of the Quebec Anglophone population to be educated in Protestant schools. With the passing of the provincial Bill 101 in 1977, all immigrant children had to attend French-language schools unless they fell under certain criteria for exemption. The reasons for the passing of this law are extremely complex. For my purposes here I simply wish to highlight that, in part, its passing had to do with the sense of alienation and oppression French *Québecois* have felt at the hands of the monied ruling classes, which from 1763 to the 1960s largely tended to be English-speaking. And, coupled with declining numbers (low birthrate; not enough immigrants from Francophone countries) and the Francophones' minority status in North America, the *Parti Québecois* (a nationalist party which won office in 1976) acted "strategically" to ensure the preservation of the French language and culture through this bill.[6] The bill's effect, in the context of this discussion, is twofold. First, it plays an important role in the Anglophone community's response to the Ouimet incident, serving as the foil for its own emphasis on individual rights and freedoms. Secondly, the law changed the character of French-language Catholic schools on the island of Montreal, particularly in areas where many immigrants settled. In what were often relatively homogeneous schools, the new bill ushered in a multicultural dynamic within a relatively short period of time. The attitudes, therefore, of the French-language press reflect this profound struggle with the changing "Catholic" system. As well, with the Catholic Church's decreasing influence over the everyday lives of Québecois since the 1960s, there has been a push toward the secularization of the school system, and a desire to have school boards divided along linguistic rather than confessional lines.

On the other hand, the Anglophone population has continually championed the "right" of parents to choose in what language their children should be taught. Increasingly representing itself as an oppressed minority within Quebec, whose linguistic "rights" are continually being restricted, the Anglophone community (which is by no means homogeneous) has taken up the cause of education wholeheartedly. A political group, known as Alliance Québec, has been at the forefront of promoting this discourse of rights and has received a great deal of attention in the *Gazette*. In focusing on the linguistic character of education already, the move to secularism does not alleviate Anglophones' perception of the problem.

It is interesting to note briefly that while Québecois nationalism continually invokes the long history of French settlement (since the sixteenth century) and its ties to the land, the Anglophone community generally focuses on the relatively recent past to discredit nationalist ideology (e.g., its anti-Semitic elements in the 1930s, '40s, and '50s), and on the present, linking both periods to the liberal notions of individualism, rights, and responsibilities. Thus, it is against this backdrop of both of these communities and the complex ways their histories are invoked, that media representations of the *hijab* enact their roles in constructing a notion of "self" and "other."

The French Press

For the most part, the Ouimet incident sparked a flurry of editorials, letters, and op-ed features for the two main Montreal French-language dailies, *La Presse* and *Le Devoir*. Interestingly, however, the issue of what the *hijab* symbolizes became itself a "rallying symbol" for Quebec journalists. Repeatedly, journalist after journalist sought to assign a particular, singular meaning to the *hijab:* why women wear it, what messages it sends to others, and how it crystallizes an otherness which can be "fully" understood. In one extreme example of "putting oneself in the other shoes," a journalist at *La Presse* donned a headscarf for a day, claiming to want to know what it felt like to be treated as a Muslim woman. Of course, working under the assumption that she could fully identify with the other—and be seen to pass as the other—by simply wearing the *hijab* proved highly problematic. Smoking cigarettes and downing a beer at a local pub while working on her story (acts which are prohibited for strict observers of Muslim law) were perceived as disrespectful actions at best and "racist" ones at worst by many Muslims and non-Muslims alike. In the pursuit to assign a meaning to the *hijab,* the journalist omitted any connections the *hijab* has to cultural practices, understandings, and religious laws, a feature that appeared often, if in less extreme forms, in other articles in both the English- and French-language papers.

Taking into account the religious nature of the *hijab,* Pierre Bourgault in an opinion piece for *Le Devoir* (Sept. 20, 1994) saw the banning of the *hijab* as hypocritical within a confessional system that allows the crucifix to be displayed so prominently in Catholic schools. Indeed, for many who contributed to *Le Devoir* and *La Presse*, the *hijab* as a religious symbol has a doubtful presence in a school system which may be aspiring to secularism in the coming years.[7] Citing the situation in France as different, yet something from which to learn, commentators regularly agreed that the *hijab* posed problems in a context of secularism. The general idea is that if schools are to become secular, then no one shall wear any garb religious in nature, nor shall any school promote any particular religion through displays of religious iconography.[8] Indeed, J. Paré, the editor of the weekly magazine *L'Actualité*, pronounced his rather inflammatory views on the *hijab* as a religious symbol in the November 1, 1994, issue:

> The *hijab* is a rallying sign for Islamicists in their struggle against the "Western devil," in whose home some of them choose to live. In accepting this symbol, we are contributing to our own destruction, and that of our values of equality and tolerance, the very ones that Islamicists attack.

Putting aside the irony of tolerance which underlies this statement, no other editorial in the city even came close to such vitriolic prose. But what was not questioned in any criticsm of this piece was the idea that equality and tolerance were at stake in Émilie Ouimet's "decision" to wear the *hijab* to school. The hijab functioned as a threat to self-perceived notions of tolerance, and focused media attention around the issue of what tolerance means in schools and in society more generally. Pared down, the question essentially became "What do 'we' want?"

In several editorials in *La Presse*, Agnès Gruda recognized the *hijab* as "at once a religious and political symbol" (December 30, 1994). Likening the *hijab* to the cross at the time of the Inquisition, Gruda suggests that banning the *hijab* may in fact create martyrs which would fuel an Islamic fundamentalist movement here within "our" borders. Lysianne Gagnon, in comparing the Montreal banning of the *hijab* with the legislated banning in France in a two-part article for *La Presse* ("Le foulard Islamique" Nov. 5 and 12, 1994), draws what she considers to be an important distinction between teacher and student and their differing relationship to authority, religion, and the state. Arguing that the rights of religious expression should be enshrined for students (so long as they do not provoke harm to others), Gagnon asserts that these same rights be denied to teachers. She reasons that teachers represent the state, which is secular in orientation, and goes on to state that if any adult chooses to live an "ultra-religious" life, then that person has decided to live in the margins of society. As well, editorialists and commentators on the *hijab* issue often remark upon the fact that the Jewish kippa (or *yarmulke*) has never been an educational issue. The reason often given for this is that the *hijab* is a more potent symbol of gender, political, and social inequality. Thus, the French-language press, concerned as it is with secular versus confessional rights, regards the *hijab* as a problematic "symbol" which strains the impulse to secularism many of its contributors embrace.

There are two obvious criticisms to make in the line of argument presented thus far. First, the mark of a secular school system does not lie in whether or not students' or teachers' religious convictions are made evident through turbans, kippot, *hijab*s, or crucifixes, but whether religious ritual in the form of prayer, dietary laws, and insignias become institutionalized. Gagnon's piece constructs a myth of "our society's" secularism as a neutral stance. The assumption here is that "our society" does not really include those who wear religious garb such as the *hijab,* as is evidenced by how the phrase "our society" is continually invoked to call into question the acceptability of wearing such garb in the first place. Second, drawing attention to how "our society" is more accepting of the kippa in Quebec schools, for instance, fails to acknowledge that traditionally Jewish immigrants did not attend—by and large—Catholic schools, which is where most of the opposition to the *hijab*'s presence is now located. Thus, the discussion in the French-language press fails to engage the explicitly "Catholic" tradition of schooling in Quebec.

However, there is a more important line of analysis to pursue here, one which is perhaps helpful in moving beyond tolerance as the one and only issue at stake in discussions of multiculturalism. The continual linking and comparing of one religious symbol to another in many of these examples begs a few questions that cannot simply be defined in relation to the *hijab* alone. For instance, what is the dynamic that propels many authors to fixate on the *hijab* as symbol of something threatening (whether as a political, cultural, or religious symbol)? More important, perhaps, what does the association between the *hijab* and the crucifix or cross signify? The substitution of the *hijab* for symbols of political and religious power suggests that there is a process of projection taking place. In psychoanalytic theory, projection is not simply the act of imputing to the world one's own feelings, as everyday uses of the term often suggest; rather, it has specifically to do with feelings one cannot tolerate in one's self (Freud 1915). That is, projection occurs when the intolerable affect in the self is attributed to an other. It is a trick of the psyche which allows us to assign feelings onto an object—which is far "safer" than coming to terms with those emotions ourselves. Thus, what is tolerated or not tolerated in the social (intersubjective) sense is supported, but not determined, by what the ego can tolerate or not tolerate in psychical (intrasubjective) sense (Britzman 1998). But what is being projected onto the *hijab* in these discussions, and how does it constitute a sense of self and social imaginary in these reports?

Our first clue stems from the recurring connections made between the *hijab* and the crucifix or cross. In aligning these symbols as equal, as interpreting the *hijab* as though it functioned in the same way as the crucifix, the media reveal the underlying structure which fuels their fixation. The question of where the *hijab* fits in the public school echoes the profound aggressivity toward confessional education (marked by the cross) that supporters of secularism continually display. That is, the newly forming sense of social identity as secular, equal, and tolerant is still struggling with that old self-conception as religious, hierarchal, and homogeneous, the very qualities imputed to what the *hijab* symbolizes in contemporary Quebec society. Secondly, that the suspension of a student from school should lead to the continual reference to Islamic fundamentalism as a political threat to Quebec society seems a point worthy of analysis. That the *hijab* is considered a political symbol is nothing new. From the Algerian war of independence in the 1950s, to present-day Hamas in Palestine, the *hijab* can indeed carry enormous political weight as a symbol of defiance. In particular, however, the press alludes to political movements which "force" women to subject themselves to the laws of Islam, as has been the case in Iran and present-day Algeria, using these examples to further the representation of the *hijab* as a political threat to equality and tolerance. What is interesting to note here, of course, is the inability to distinguish the many different meanings the *hijab* has for women in the context of Western society (and other societies as well), and what instead is focused upon is the supposedly oppressive character of Islamic law in general and the *hijab* in particular, often revealing strong ties of identification with French attitudes toward Algeria. As that which links oppression and religion, the *hijab* crystallizes into an "other" that part of the "self" which contemporary Québecois are attempting to expel. The history of class and linguistic oppression, continually invoked in nationalist consciousness (particularly by the daily *Le Devoir*), and, therefore, continually lived in the present, coupled with the turn to secularism and the birth of new social identity (which is not only a nationalist issue), enables us to understand the highly charged and sometimes stereotypical representations of the *hijab* as involved in complex processes of establishing a sense of self, and appealing to an idealized version of the self in relation to an other. This does not mean, of course, that incendiary remarks or hateful proclamations should be swept aside; rather, they should serve as the raw material for delving into the dynamics that propel such commentary.

The English Press

The English press, while equally plagued by questions of what the *hijab* "really means," casts its discourse more in terms of individual rights, specifically that of freedom of religious expression. This discourse is perhaps more familiar to Anglo-American audiences, saturated as they are in liberal notions of rights, freedoms, and responsibilities, rather than the more semiotically oriented discussions which characterize the French-language media's response by and large. Hence, the former is concerned with deviations from an ideal of equality and tolerance, while the latter debate what equality and tolerance mean in the context of contemporary Quebec. This difference in emphasis is not without its impact. Aside from its misperceptions of the religious significance of the *hijab* (not unlike those made by the French-language press), the *Gazette* seized the apparently moral high ground and continually presented in all its articles dissenting views on the banning of the *hijab* from public school, and on the suspension of Émilie Ouimet. For instance, a report on remarks made by the president of the CEQ (Quebec's largest teacher's union) denouncing any ban was given full support by interviews with teachers who equally condemned it: the image which emerged was that of Francophone teachers across the province supporting the right for girls to wear the *hijab* in public educational institutions. The *Gazette*, in its desire to present the "wrongfulness" of the student's suspension, failed to give any indication that some teachers within the union indeed supported banning the *hijab* for a variety of reasons. Imagine the *Gazette*'s readership's surprise, therefore, when it learned of the CEQ resolution to ban the *hijab* a few days later—opposing the opinions of the president and her executive. In failing to report even a hint that the CEQ membership was not in full support of its president, the *Gazette* bent over backward to ensure itself as the holder of moral authority. In what may be characterized as its superego function, the paper was incapable of tolerating any dissensions to its own moral purpose.

Now, one might be seduced into claiming that if suspending a student from school for wearing the *hijab* is an act of intolerance, then the paper was fully correct in supporting a dissenting view which upheld tolerance. However, my point is that the paper in its zeal to champion religious freedoms failed to represent fully the complex arguments and debates happening in the teachers' union and in the French-language media at large, and in so doing revealed something about the nature of tolerance embraced by the *Gazette*. The reasons for this require some analysis.

The *Gazette*'s discourse must be situated within an anti-Quebec nationalist sentiment where individual rights and freedoms are invoked to call into question the possibility of a unified, sovereign, and "integrated" Quebec. Officially, Quebec has taken an "integrationist" stance toward its immigrant and minority populations. Its policies are designed to encourage the use of the French language in both private and public spheres, seeing the need less for immigrants to retain a strong sense of identity with their original communities, and more for them to develop a cultural identity consistent with the aspirations of promoting French language and culture within Quebec's borders. Thus, this policy, while distinguished from assimilation in that it does not favor the complete renunciation of one's "originary" culture, is quite distinct from Canada's "official" policy of multiculturalism which, at least in theory, promotes an understanding of smaller communities existing within larger ones. However, one must keep in mind the larger North American context with its prevalence of English in which Québecois experience themselves as a minority group, and who continually see Canada's multiculturalism policy as furthering English-language use in practice.

In line with this anti-Quebec nationalist perspective, then, the *Gazette*'s liberal position looks a little more problematic. For instance, a *Gazette* editorial of November 30, 1994, cautions the Quebec government not to follow in France's footsteps with regard to its stance on multiculturalism ("assimilation") and the banning of the *hijab*. You will recall that some Francophone journalists, in pursuit of a new secular identity for Quebec, did indeed align themselves with France and its policy of schooling devoid of religious symbolism. The *Gazette*'s disagreement with this type of alignment makes evident its assumption that issues of tolerance, religious freedom, and equality of the sexes are not topics dealt with by nationalists, and by Francophones more generally. That is, in posing as the bearer of the "right" questions (concerning freedom and rights), the *Gazette* did not simply champion the cause of equal access to public education, but used the incident to discredit what it perceived to be the nationalists' "rejection of multiculturalism" itself.

In another editorial entitled "*Hijab*ophobia in Quebec?" (November 24, 1994), the *Gazette* quotes the rather uninformed remarks made by the St. Jean Baptiste Society's then-new president François Lemieux. The Society's goal is to enhance the presence of French language and culture in Quebec, and thus it is emblematic of Quebec nationalism in the minds of many Anglophones, but not necessarily in the minds of all nationalists. (Indeed, many nationalists are far more supportive of minority rights than what is often represented in the leadership of this society and are definitely underrepresented in the pages of the *Gazette*.) In order to frame the *Gazette*'s support of the *hijab* question, the discussion led off with a statement made by Lemieux: "Wearing a *hijab* defies the values of the equality of men and women that we have here in Quebec." As well, the *Gazette* related Lemieux's comment that the *hijab* was not "compatible with our project." The *Gazette* read "our project" in a very particular manner, and while it correctly, I think, challenged Lemieux's arrogance in (and ignorance of) the issue, it nevertheless collapsed two meanings into one. Lemieux is referring in the first instance to values he perceives as entrenched *presently* in Quebec society at large—

legally and morally—and that somehow wearing the *hijab* defies those values(!). In the second instance, Lemieux appears to be referring to "our project" which is, as Peggy Curran put it in her *Gazette* column of November 24, the "pluralist sovereign Quebec of the *future*" (my emphasis). The *Gazette*, in collapsing these two meanings so that the values of Quebec society are simply read as the "values of preserving French language and culture," reveals its own self-understanding as a community under siege and places itself alongside Ouimet herself (and other Muslims) as being occluded from Quebec society. In other words, the *Gazette* primarily responds to the *hijab* issue through its own self-perception as victim.

Trying to gain political points through advocating religious freedoms, the *Gazette* puts forth the suggestion that acts of tolerance must guide government support for those who wear the *hijab*—implying of course that "our project" positioned nationalists as intolerant *tout court*. Another way of reading this statement might have been to launch into a debate about what the values of Quebec society are, who the major players are in devising these values, and what the relation of religious expression to education is. Instead, revealing a clearly obsessional character, the *Gazette*, even in a two-page special feature devoted to the *hijab* and school, saw its cause as countering Quebec nationalism, quoting a source who saw recent events in Montreal schools as evidence of "racism and xenophobia." In contrast, the Toronto *Globe and Mail* in its December 13, 1994, issue, offered a more detailed account of the reasons why the *hijab* has been perceived to be in conflict with a Quebec nationalist identity, attempting some kind of historical understanding of the relationship between the changing Québecois identity and the multicultural society that Quebec has become.

Indeed, the continual coverage of the *hijab* issue into the spring of 1995 revealed a commitment to responding to select Quebec nationalists' statements and failed to address adequately the subtleties of the debate as expressed in the French-language dailies. Yet, as mentioned above, one could also see present the concern to express indignation at Ouimet's expulsion, even by failing to report on the opinions of Francophone teacher members of the CEQ. Thus, on the one hand, the *Gazette* editorials scrutinized every "intolerant" statement made by nationalists (particularly those in official positions), while on the other, skewed those statements made by educators as well as others who did not fit the *Gazette*'s equation of Quebec nationalist = intolerant; Canadian nationalist = tolerant. Left out, of course, were the majority of opinions that could not fit into either camp. When examined closely, these two equations operated together, calling upon readers to identify with the same desire: to see Quebec nationalism as a threat to an enlightened, liberal sensibility.

As mentioned above, the *Gazette* very much enacted a super-ego role. According to Freud (1923), the superego is an agency which prohibits any transgression of the law (that is, the rules of conduct, behavior, and social organization which every society circumscribes). These rules are ideals against which an ego measures its own self value. The more severe the superego, the more the ego fails to live up to its demands (which are already pretty impossible). Thus, what gets created for the ego is an idealization that cannot bear its own consequences. The superego must continually exert its influence to the point where all are judged as harshly as is the self. What results, therefore, is a constant pressure to appear superior to others in order to protect the self from further humiliation and failure. In the case of the *Gazette*, this dynamic structures its discourse on the right to freedom of religious expression. In an important sense, of course, the law—insofar as it is institutionalized in the Canadian Charter of Rights and Freedoms and in the spirit (if not always the practice) of the judiciary—is socially sanctified, and it can, therefore, be understood that such laws inform a sense of self-definition for a particular society, and community. However, the *Gazette* failed to simply take up Ouimet's case as a contravention to the law, but sought instead to demonstrate how the "other" (in this case Quebec nationalism) failed to live up to its demands, trumpeting Canadian superiority along the way. Indeed, as discussed above, its editorials were primarily reactions to statements made about the *hijab* and multiculturalism more generally, the "right" to wear the *hijab* becoming virtually incidental and often tacked on at the end. Hence, the object of the *Gazette*'s zeal was not Ouimet's right to public education, but the failure of Quebec nationalism to live under the law of English Canada's discourse. The punitive language and its selection of topics for editorials construct a sense of "self" that argues for the respect of human rights at the expense of an "other" who purportedly does not. While I do not wish to suggest that individual rights and freedoms are not important issues, what the *Gazette*'s reactions demonstrate is that a concern to define "our society" in contradistinction to the *perceived* Québecois nationalist vision of "our society" continually propelled and framed the taking up of the *hijab* debate. That is, by continually reading any mention of "our society" by Francophones as always already xenophobic, the English-language press used the Ouimet incident to say "we" are not like "them." The finger-pointing in the English-language press, therefore, was directed primarily at Quebec nationalism in an attempt to distinguish itself as separate from—and better than—it. More important, then, the *hijab*, and the women who wear it, served as a foil to Quebec integrationist policies. Consequently, the English press missed the extent to which real girls were being denied access to a public education system that does not only have a legacy tied to Quebec national-ism, but to a wide-ranging Western legacy of portraying *hijab*-wearing women (and indeed Arabs and Muslims in general) as fundamentalists and/or terrorists (e.g., Ahmed 1992; Hoodfar 1993; Mojab 1995).

Conclusion: Thoughts on Teaching Language Arts beyond Tolerance

My goal in this essay has been to demonstrate (and not merely talk about) what a psychoanalytic reading of media reports looks like. It has also been to suggest that this kind of reading is helpful in uncov-ering the logic that frames the way we talk about issues of tolerance and intolerance, and enabling us to move beyond tolerance so that we may be able to look at how we construct images of ourselves through representing an other. In the case of the French-language media, the *hijab* stood as a symbol of struggle for an emerging new Québecois identity, while the English-language media utilized the *hijab* to proclaim the superiority of Canadian over Quebec national-ism. What I wish to do now is offer some concluding thoughts on how elementary school educators, particularly those concerned with the media, may develop strategies for thinking about what is left unwritten in conceiving of issues solely in terms of tolerance.

First, due to the fact that a psychoanalytic reading requires understanding texts as embodying histories of trauma and past experience, the historical contexts of media reportage are crucial to examine. In this sense, studying media representations is not only a matter for encouraging children to know more about "current events," but is a way in which students come to encounter and engage the past and therefore develop an understanding of their place and responsibility in a larger world. Thus, media studies take on enormous potential for integrating language arts with other subject domains such as social studies and history, and offer the potential for developing relevant links with the past—an issue which plagues many a teacher—and student—of history.

Second, in encountering the past in current newspaper reports, students and teachers also confront the pain and trauma of history. That is, teaching beyond tolerance places a demand on us to come to terms with the possible reasons why communities choose to repre-sent images in certain ways in order to cope with the difficulties of their own histories. Communities, like individuals, build up de-fenses—defenses which are shared and understood and have mean-ing for members in those communities. As we saw with both the French- and English-language media, the mechanisms of projection and an overly active superego respectively contributed to a com-munity's understanding of itself and its representations of otherness, and served to hide the painful coming-to-terms with a changing Quebec society. Indeed, through representing an "outside" to themselves, each of these communities (which are, of course, heterogeneous) attempted to position a "self" as center. Stereotypes therefore take on a role that surpasses the question of power relations. Instead, by inquiring into how they serve the needs and desires of those who represent them, we may learn a great deal about how we ourselves are caught up in forms of representation that build our egos.

Third, offering a comparison between two or more views of the present perhaps enables students to deal with the multiple layers of meaning a text has to offer. In this sense, examining media reports of a singular incident may also provide an awareness of the centrality of interpretation to our lives. That is, texts are not seen as purely authoritative, but as engagements with meaning which represent a combination of factual information with those desires, ideals, and struggles present in all forms of writing. Examining media representations psychoanalytically *with* students, and not *for* them, foregrounds the importance of interpretation for self-understanding. In this sense, it avoids the didacticism that often accompanies studies of stereotypes which students often either rebel against or develop strategies for accommodating (tolerating) in ways that accomplish little in challenging the conditions which make such forms of representation possible in the first place. If we as teachers continually present representations as either negative or positive, our students are left with few options for inquiring into their own prejudices.

Lastly, my call to read media representations psychoanalytically is central for recognizing that communities and identities are places where self and other are not mutually exclusive so much as they are mutually determining. This space of recognition enables us to acknowledge how "our" definitions of the other and how "our" invocation of the other contributes to producing the "our" in the process. As Bhabha asks, the question to face now is "how can the human world live its difference, how can a human being live Otherwise?" (1994, 64). It is not so much finding a singular answer to this question that is at stake in moving beyond tolerance, but finding a path of inquiry, of teaching and of learning, that keeps this question continually in sight.

Acknowledgment

I would like to thank Samia Costandi and her friends for sharing with me their experiences.

Notes

1. I acknowledge that not all veiling practices are Muslim practices. In talking about the *hijab*, however, I am focusing on that Muslim practice which has been featured in current media debates.

2. François Berger, "Élève expulsée de son école parce qu'elle portait le foulard islamique," *La Presse,* September 9, 1994, A1, and the *Gazette,* September 10, A13.

3. The various significations the *hijab* has had for women can be found in Ahmed (1992); Hoodfar (1993); Mernissi (1987). See also the Québec Conseil du Statut de la Femme (1995).

4. Mojab indicates that this preoccupation detracted from the "main issue, individual rights and freedom of religion" (1995, 7).

5. There were not obvious differences in the English press for the simple reason that there is only one English-language daily in Montreal, the *Gazette.* Another English paper, the *Mirror* (distributed freely on a weekly basis) basically agreed with the principles expressed in the *Gazette.*

6. An earlier bill (number 22) initiated by the Liberal provincial government in 1972 was a less extensive piece of legislation attempting to deal with similar issues.

7. As well, three months before the Ouimet incident, the CEQ voted for the complete absence of religious instruction in public schools.

8. A decade ago, there was also enormous controversy generated over the wearing of turbans in the Royal Canadian Mounted Police Force and more recently in the Royal Canadian Legions, where some veterans felt that any head-covering was flatly disrespectful, no matter what the meaning of it might be. It was quickly discovered, however, that Christian habits, for instance, did not carry the same weight as Sikh turbans, revealing of course how these veterans saw them"selves" in relation to "others."

Works Cited

Ahmed, Leila. 1992. *Women and Gender in Islam: Historical Roots of a Modern Debate.* New Haven: Yale University Press.

Bhabha, Homi. 1994. *The Location of Culture.* London: Routledge.

Books, Sue. 1996. "The Art of Seeing: Rural Poverty in the United States." Paper read at Canadian Critical Pedagogy Association Annual Conference, June 2–5, Brock University, St. Catherine's, Ontario.

Bourgault, Pierre. 1994. "Hijab et crucifix." *Le Devoir* (Sept. 20): A6.

Britzman, Deborah. 1998. *Lost Objects, Contested Subjects: Toward a Psychoanalytic Inquiry of Learning.* Albany, NY: SUNY Press.

Conseil du statut de la femme du Québec. 1995. *Réflexion sur la question du port du voile à l'école.* Quebec Human Rights Commission.

Curran, Peggy. 1994. "'Not compatible': Minorities feel excluded when values are attacked." Montreal *Gazette* (Nov. 24): A3.

Freud, Sigmund. 1915/1959. "Instincts and Their Vicissitudes." In *The Standard Edition of the Complete Psychological Works of Sigmund Freud,* edited by James Strachey. Vol. 14, 117–40. London: Hogarth Press.

———. 1923/1961. "The Ego and the Id." In *The Standard Edition of the Complete Psychological Works of Sigmund Freud,* edited by James Strachey. Vol. 19, 3–66. London: Hogarth Press.

Gagnon, Lysianne. 1994. "Le foulard Islamique." *La Press* (Nov. 5 & 12): B3.

Giroux, Henry. 1994. *Disturbing Pleasures: Learning Popular Culture.* New York: Routledge.

Gruda, Agnes. 1994. "L'école à voile." *La Press* (Sept. 19): B2.

"*Hijab*ophobia in Quebec." 1994. Montreal *Gazette* (Nov. 30): B2.

Hoodfar, Homa. 1993. "The Veil in Their Minds and on Our Heads: The Persistence of Colonial Images of Muslim Women." *Resources for Feminist Research/Documentation sur la recherche feministe* 22(3/4): 5–18.

Lacan, Jacques. 1977. *Écrits: A Selection.* Trans. Alan Sheridan. New York: Norton.

Mernissi, Fatima. 1987. *Beyond the Veil: Male-Female Dynamics in Modern Muslim Society.* Rev. edition. Bloomington: Indiana University Press.

Mojab, Shahrzad. 1995. "To Veil or Not to Veil: That Is Not the Question." *Between the Lines* 1: 7–8.

"Multiculturalism under attack." 1994. Montreal *Gazette* (Nov. 30): B2.

Nasrulla, A. 1994. "Educators outside Quebec mystified by hijab ban." Toronto *Globe and Mail* (Dec. 13): A1, A4.

Paré, J. 1994. "Quand l'habit Fait le moine." *l'Actualité* 19. 17: 12.

Schwoch, James, Mimi White, and Susan Reilly. 1992. *Media Knowledge: Readings in Popular Culture, Pedagogy, and Critical Citizenship.* Albany, NY: SUNY Press.

Young-Bruehl, Elisabeth. 1996. *The Anatomy of Prejudices.* Cambridge, MA: Harvard University Press.

9 Nightmare Issues: Children's Responses to Racism and Genocide in Literature

Vicki Zack
St. George's School, Montreal, Canada

Introduction

"I'm at part three of the book and I can barely read it! How can people live through that and I can barely read about it." Ten-year-old Mireille's comments, recorded in her reading log, are part of her response to Carol Matas's novel *Daniel's Story* (1993), a book of historical fiction dealing with the Holocaust. Set during a period of cataclysmic pre-war and wartime events, the novel traces one Jewish family as they are forced from their home in Frankfurt, Germany, to the Lodz ghetto in Poland and to the death camp in Auschwitz-Birkenau.

In our school, history and literature are vital and complementary components in the fifth-grade curriculum. While history provides the events, times, and locations, it is literature that reaches out and touches us. Through literature, history has a human face (Greenlaw 1984, 147). For example, after listening to parts of Mildred Taylor's *Roll of Thunder, Hear My Cry* (1976/1981), a novel that details the lived realities of a black family in segregationist Southern United States in the 1930s, ten-year-old Alyssa read the book herself, participated in discussions, and then placed on my desk the following note (reproduced below as she wrote it). Alyssa's language resonates with the emotional impact literature can have upon the reader:

> Vicki: I am so glad that you mentioned Roll of thunder, here my cry! If you hadn't I would never had read it! At the end I cryed, I cryed so

This essay is a slightly revised version of a 1996 essay published in *The New Advocate: For Those Involved With Young People and Their Literature* 9(4): 297–308. I join with the editor in gratefully acknowledging the permission given by *The New Advocate* to reprint the piece.

long and so hard, I don't think I—or anyone else for that matter—
will ever, NEVER cry so hard. I just LOVED it. Thanks so much
Vicki . . . Alyssa

In this chapter I will outline why I believe it is important for children
to learn about racism and genocide and will consider why literary
treatments of these topics constitute an important source of questions and discussions which speak to the heart as well as to the
mind. The focus will be on literature and history dealing with the
European Holocaust and the African American experience. Much of
the discussion will be illustrated by selected excerpts of children's
responses to literature and history as they explore shocking and
difficult issues. At the same time it will include my reflections on the
children's comments and questions, as well as my concerns pertaining to current educational practice. While this discussion does not
provide a prescriptive method of how to teach about intolerance and
genocide through literature, it does include an account of how my
values, beliefs, and experiences influence my classroom practice,
which in turn facilitates children's learning. The concluding section
contains an explicit rationale for this undertaking, as well as a brief
reflection on what it means for teachers and students to be political.

Learning about Racism and Genocide: Inquiry in a Fifth-Grade Classroom

The Classroom Context: "History That Hurts"

Every year for the past six years, my ten- and eleven-year-old students and I have engaged in discussions of racism against groups of
people all over the world and throughout history. Specifically, the
topics addressed include the African slave trade and its aftermath,
the nuclear attacks on the Japanese in Hiroshima and Nagasaki, and
the genocides carried out against the Armenians in Turkey and
against the Jews during the Second World War.

The classroom group in our bilingual (French/English) cosmo-
politan city (Montreal, Canada) is heterogeneous in regard to
achievement and is multiethnic, with a number of children from
India, China, Japan, and from Middle Eastern countries including
Lebanon, Iraq, and the United Arab Emirates. At times during those
years approximately a quarter of the twenty-five children in my
classroom have been Jewish. There have to date been only three
African Canadian/African American children in my class. All the
children in the class, however, have reacted with outrage when
reading literature about historical injustice. Even though the majority
cannot know firsthand what it is to suffer the racism endured by (for
example) African Americans, the responses to the study of the
history of slavery, of the civil rights movement, and of continuing
injustices, have been of shock, sadness, and anger.

The inquiries begin in part because they matter to me. I speak to the children of issues close to my heart. I introduce them to literature that I hope will touch them. The literature will teach them much of what they seek to know. This idea did not originate with me. Margaret Meek (1970/1988) has spoken eloquently about it.[1] I wait for the children to initiate inquiry and I go with them as far as they wish to go. We regularly discuss newspaper items that deal with war, family abuse, and homelessness, among other issues. The discussion of news events and our study of history brings us to the literature, and the literature returns us to the history, but on a different plane. Although it is usually I who introduce the books or the historical events that we discuss as a class, the children are at liberty to choose whether or not they wish to pursue the topic and readings. Each year the dynamics change. The learning resides in the interaction between particular children working together and reading particular texts. There are many and diverse routes of inquiry undertaken by individual children or small groups.[2]

Throughout the year the children decide what they want to read from a selection in our classroom library of more than four hundred titles, or from other sources, including our school library, municipal libraries, or home. I do not wish to give the impression that wrenching issues represent a major focus of our program. We read all kinds of books, many of which are joyful and mind-expanding in not so painful ways. But every year we do touch upon issues which shock. We pursue these topics as I read aloud to the children, as we write to each other via the reading log journals, and as we talk together. And always there are children who choose to think alone on the reading and not to discuss it with others.

Listening and Respecting

The children know their own minds and the extent to which they can cope with difficult knowledge. Lucy, for example, told me in her response log that she could not bear to read *The Devil's Arithmetic* (Yolen 1988) because it was about a concentration camp. She said:

> I don't even want to look at *The Devil's Arithmetic,* because *Number the Stars,* it just describes, like Anne Frank's diary, it describes what happens before you get to the concentration camp. . . . It doesn't tell you what's happening in the concentration camp.

Every year in my class there are children who shy away from stories of pain and suffering, as well as others who feel it is important to know. For example, Beth wrote recently, "Usually, I don't like to read or even like to hear books about the holocaust and stuff like that." And William commented after I read part of *Lisa* (Matas 1987) aloud to the class, "I wouldn't like to read [the rest of] it because it is not my kind of book. I don't like them if they're even the slightest bit scary." Lewis, on the other hand, said, "I think kids should learn about what happened in the past." In my teaching, I am guided by the principle that it is important to respect those who are not ready, or who are ready for some but not other works of literature.

The Children's Voices

I introduce a large variety of books, but invariably there are ones that I select repeatedly. In regard to teaching about the Holocaust, I provide *Lisa* (Matas 1987) and *The Man from the Other Side* (Orlev 1991). In relation to teaching about the African American experience of diaspora, enslavement, and resistance, I provide *Underground to Canada* (Smucker 1977), *Roll of Thunder, Hear My Cry* (Taylor 1976/ 1981), and the motion picture *The Long Walk Home* (Pearce 1990). Every year there are some comments and questions which always arise: How can people do those terrible things to other human beings? How can they say that people are inferior just because of their color, their religion? Won't they ever learn? What would I have done? Could it happen again?

The entry that follows is written by a child I have called Malka.[3] Written in 1992 in response to *The Man from the Other Side* (Orlev 1991), a book about the Warsaw Ghetto, the entry is stunning for its intensity. While I had forgotten much of the specifics, what I remembered was Malka's expression of fear. When I reread the entry and my response to it while preparing this essay, I realized that while her fear was dominant, the entry expressed much more, including her awareness of the presence of hatred and persecution in the world today. Following Malka's entry is my written response back.

> *The Man from the Other Side* scared me at one time. I forget when but I went to the back and read the last few sentences. That didn't help me at all. Then I went to the page before and started reading a paragraph. That just scared me more. It said the whole ghetto was on fire and whoever tried to escape, the Nazis shot. It also said there was this man with his two children. He blindfolded them and pushed them into the flames. Then he jumped after them. That was from the fifth floor balcony.
>
> One of the reasons why I took this book out is because it takes place in Warsaw where my grandpa lived in a ghetto till he was in his teens. Also because it takes place in W.W.II. Also because it is real and looks very interesting.
>
> Remember the conference on *Lisa* on Friday? I don't know why but I didn't feel comfortable. Maybe because I can't handle what actually happened and maybe I'm scared of all the dangers that can happen today with the Neo-Nazis and all the other anti-Semitism in this world. Vicki, I'm just very scared. Please don't tell anyone. Not a friend or my parents or my brother or your family.

Vicki's Response to Malka's Reading Log Entry:

Malka: This entry I'm writing is private, meant to be read only by you if that's the way you wish it. Malka, don't push yourself to read anything that you're not ready for. The whole experience during the Second World War was a nightmare for Jews. I felt as a child and teenager that it was monstrous. I needed to know, and yet couldn't bear to know. But I thought I owed it to my people to know about their anguish. Whatever I couldn't view or read I left alone. I knew there were other resources. Over the years I have gone through some periods where I've read a lot about the Holocaust. During other periods I've not read much at all. Actually, I wrote about some of what I struggled with in an article; the article deals with the time 3 children in my Grade 5 class (1989–1990) read *The Devil's Arithmetic*. Do you want to read the article? As I wrote the article I realized how much the Holocaust was part of my legacy, my heritage.

Please do not worry about the Neo-Nazis. I'll tell you that there are maniacs and terrorists and anti-Semites around in every decade. What happened during the Holocaust has made everyone more aware, more vigilant. It will never happen again because governments know what these riots can possibly lead to; they will not allow it. Good people everywhere are fighting. It is natural to be scared and awed and horrified. But please don't let it get to you. If you need to talk more, please tell me. Malka, I am writing an article about issues which are very tough for children to deal with (Holocaust, slavery, racism). You have helped me think. Thank you.

Vicki

As I reread the entry a number of years later, I appreciated even more why Malka's entry was so important to me. For one, it captured her position in time, in relation to her own personal odyssey to find readings which helped her learn about the experiences of her ancestors and of others who lived and died during those horrible times. She wrote her responses during a period when there were frequent reports in the media about racist attacks upon immigrants in Germany and France. This contributed to her fear of the possible recurrence of Nazi-type outbursts of racism and anti-Semitism. By that point in the year she had read a number of powerfully written books about the Holocaust and about World War II. Her log reading list included Sommerfelt's *Miriam* (1963), Matas's *Lisa* (1987) and *Jesper* (1989), Magorian's *Good Night, Mr. Tom* (1981), Reiss's *The Journey Back* (1976), and Orlev's *The Man from the Other Side* (1991). After the December break, she read Kerr's *When Hitler Stole Pink Rabbit* (1971) and Yolen's *The Devil's Arithmetic* (1988).

In rereading my response to Malka, I realized how much I had included about my personal history, recalling what it meant and means for me to deal with the Holocaust—as a Jew, as the daughter of Holocaust survivors, as a parent, as a teacher interacting with sensitive students, and as a writer struggling to communicate the reality of dealing with these issues in the classroom. I then thought of how various children felt—all connected, all taken aback by the events, but some, like Malka, exploring more deeply. However, it was writing this essay that caused me to consider more systematically the unspoken principles guiding my written response to Malka's anguish.

Judith Robertson, editor of this volume, asked me if I could step outside of my intimate personal connection to the response to Malka, and think about how and why I wrote to Malka as I did. Could I conceptualize my response, she asked, or suggest general principles for engaging with the literature of trauma? I struggled to delve more deeply, and was left feeling that what I do, I do implicitly. I could not summon to the surface the pedagogical reasons for why I answered Malka as I did. It was Judith herself, and a childhood friend, Joanne Rocklin, former teacher, former counseling psychologist and presently a children's book writer, who helped me to understand and frame the underpinnings. Judith suggested to me:

> You don't simply give language to Malka's worries, but also draw upon your own experience to do so. This gives your words a kind of authority, and also expresses your desire to make yourself known to the child as someone who has experienced a similar kind of pain. [Thus] . . . the breaches that happen when consciousness is wounded through difficult knowledge won't engulf and disintegrate the learner.[4]

Similarly emphasizing the adult teacher's difficult role as carrier of the wounds caused by narrative, Joanne Rocklin, responding to my query, wrote to me:

> I believe that ALL . . . good parenting, all good teaching, are based upon the same basic tenets inherent in the concept of a good relationship. And I personally think that this is your pedagogical "principle" that you have been asked to illuminate; it is already implanted in your essay. Your essay describes these aspects of the relationship without actually naming them:
>
> - the teacher (parent) acts as a role model of ego strength, revealing that she has felt similar strong feelings, that they have been painful, that she has learned and grown from them (and obviously has not been destroyed by them);
> - the teacher acts as a "container" for the student's feelings, allowing and encouraging an expression of them, showing that she is not shocked by them, which brings relief and understanding;
> - the teacher accepts the feelings shared by the student, allowing the student to feel that he or she can truly be a "real" self with her;

- while allowing the student to choose whether or not to share these feelings, implicit in the relationship is the knowledge that sharing and communicating and writing with a trusted "other" is a positive thing;
- the relationship is confidential;
- the student is not under an obligation to read these painful books or reveal feelings, but is made aware that the teacher is available if and when the student chooses to reveal them;
- the teacher offers hope, and/or enables the student to move forward from the trauma to possible positive, active response in the real world.[5]

In rethinking my actions with Malka, I now realize that in teaching the literature of trauma, the quality and expectations of the student-teacher relationship is critical. A real, human, trusting relationship, as in Buber's "I-Thou" relationship, is key.

Taylor's *Roll of Thunder, Hear My Cry* (1976/1981) is another book that, year after year, has had a marked impact upon the children. This award-winning novel describes the "coming of age" of Cassie Logan, the nine-year-old black protagonist. Cassie, and the young readers of the novel, learn about burnings, about the Ku Klux Klan, and about the unwritten, abominable "rules" of segregation that prevailed in Mississippi. Taylor conveys the solidarity of the Logan family and members of the black community, and tells of measures taken by the Logan family to preserve their dignity and to effect change.

In the 1991–92 school year the readings led to numerous literature study discussions. I began in 1991 in early December by reading the first five chapters aloud to the children. Following this introduction, a number of the children then completed the book on their own and we met to discuss various aspects. The children were appalled at the numerous ways in which the Logan children, indeed all the black children and adults, were made to feel inferior and powerless.

The reading log excerpts below reflect the children's anger, their sense of injustice, their confusion about certain aspects, especially about whether Miss Crocker, the teacher, was white or black, and most poignantly, the emotional involvement of the children who listened to and who read Taylor's book. It is apparent from the first excerpt (below) that my student, Alyssa, understands that Cassie is coming to realize that there are injustices she must accept, but Alyssa also faults Cassie's grandmother and mother for their meekness, and champions Uncle Hammer's daring:

Alyssa's Reading Log Entry on Roll of Thunder

Cassie Logan is a Black fourth grader, who doesn't know too much about the way Black and white people lived in 1933. In one part of the book, where Cassie and T. J. and Stacey and "Big Ma" have gone to Strawberry, when Cassie didn't know how the store owner went about waiting on people it really surprised me. Even more so when she made the big seen in the store. As I was reading . . . the part about when she bumped into Lillian Jean, I was thinking about how true those things were and what could be going through these peoples minds when they were so rude to Blacks like that! And the way Cassie felt so resentful to "Big Ma" for telling her to apologize. The way Cassie's uncle Hammer acts, I think is Really good. Like I mean he's standing up for his right's and I think that's really great! At first Mrs. Taylor does not (?give) enough description to what uncle Hammer is going to do when he goe's to the Simms. I understand how (?most) Black people would not act like uncle Hammer, as in when he quickly went through the bridge to make the Walaces think he was white, but I think that Cassie's mother went just a little overboard. It was almost like she was on the white peoples side.

Alyssa, and at times other readers, wondered why certain of the family members did not fight harder. What I appreciated (and what the children in my class to some extent could not comprehend) was the precarious life the Logan family led because they did dare to take a stand whenever they could. The Logan elders refused to be submissive, yet they had to refrain from actions that could put their lives in jeopardy.

In the novel, the black children inherit books that have been discarded by the whites, books that are in deplorable condition. In his reading log response, Mike writes about the listing of the condition of the books. Mike (and others) were confused about why Ms. Crocker, the teacher, did not get insulted by the list and the condition of the books. Indeed, some of the children—Anne and Glen, for example—thought at first that Ms. Crocker was white:

Mike's Reading Log Entry

I think that the list is discusting because they put a capital "W" for the white studends and a lower case "N" for the Black students. I(t) dosen't make sense why Ms. Crocker did not say any thing about the list. Wouldn't she be insulted too? Why did they keep the condition of the book? Was it to insult the Blacks? [Note that Mike independently identified the importance of the capital and lowercase letters]

Anne's Reading Log Entry

I was really upset that when the teacher had a look at the book she didn't care. If I were the teacher I would have been really hurt by what the two kids noticed, but I would not even thought of punishing them. It didn't make sence to me that the teacher didn't care, I wonder why. The white people in the book seem to be very predujust.

Glen's Reading Log Entry
I am furios . . . I do not blame Little Man for not wanting to pick the book up. Then the teacher said to be grateful. BAH! Is Miss Crocker Black or white? Now Little Man has to get whipped! I am so angry. Cassie just showed Miss Crocker the part with Nigra in it. Miss Crocker just said "That's what you are." I am furios over this matter and Whites give Black people books when they can not be used anymore!!!!!! I am glad that Mary Logan is not taking these books. What I mean is, she is putting a piece of paper over the offensive side. Good for her!

The children were appalled at the conditions and at the injustices. The entry excerpt by Rhona captures the coming of age of some of the readers in my class:

Before I started reading this book, I thought that books about war were the only books that could make you cry, or that could make you say, "how could anybody do something like that!?!" But I was wrong, because this book also makes me say "how could anybody do that!?!" Now I realize that war isn't the only bad thing that writers write about, there are also things like racism.

I treasure these instances of children's deeply felt responses to accounts of desperate times. It is important to note that they do not happen often. The reading log responses cited above are those which I found compelling. The children care very much about the people, about the issues, and about the world they live in. In addition, in thinking and writing and speaking about these events, the children are finding their voices, and in their reading response logs and in their discussions are expressing where they stand. As poet Seamus Heany has said, "Finding a voice means that you can get your own feeling into your own words and that your words have the feel of you about them" (cited by Hendry, Bicknell, and Wilson 1993, 71). It is the literature, often in conjunction with discussion, that evokes these responses.

Concerns in Teaching about Intolerance and Genocide

While I am deeply committed to the examination of these important issues in the school context, at the same time I have concerns about how issues of intolerance and genocide, and in particular the issue of the Holocaust, are dealt with in the school curriculum. These reservations dialogue with some of the concerns expressed by other researchers (Stotsky 1996) and historians (Dawidowicz 1990; Lipstadt 1995). In a recent article on the misrepresentation of the historical contribution of Rosa Parks to the black civil rights movement, Kohl (1995) shows how momentous events in history can be trivialized. I worry that a topic such as the Holocaust might become routinized, oversimplified, or even romanticized. In addition, it should not be used to serve other ends and agendas (Stotsky 1996; Dawidowicz 1990). There is also the danger of generalizing the Holocaust as a universal symbol of horror. As Dawidowicz and Lipstadt have suggested, it is important not only to document the commonalities in aggressions against peoples, but also to identify the uniqueness of these historical events. Finally, there is concern about the representativeness of the description. In a survey of the literature curricula in secondary school, Stotsky found that Holocaust literature constituted the only manifestation of Jewish life and culture, to the exclusion of almost any other work by Jewish writers. "What I am raising for discussion," Stotsky says, "is not dissimilar to the requests made by Black parents and others a decade or so ago who quite rightly felt that all children should see much more about the history and culture of Black Americans than simply their lives as slaves" (1996, 58).

A 1993 resolution passed at the National Council of Teachers of English Annual Convention in Pittsburgh affirmed that "students should read and discuss literature on genocide and intolerance within an historically accurate framework with special emphasis on primary source material" (NCTE 1994). Clearly, in teaching about instances of genocide the stress needs to be on the accuracy of historical representations and the uniqueness of particular contexts that give rise to mass human rights abuses. Even within that framework, however, there are multiple concerns. On the one hand, an experience which should consist of intense and meaningful exploration runs the risk of becoming a lock-step curriculum, production-driven and replete with worksheets. It is my belief that one would never elicit the kinds of reactions discussed throughout this paper by means of worksheets and comprehension questions. On the other hand, I have felt a visceral resistance to the suggestion presented in some curriculum sources and articles that students participate in role-playing as a means to arriving at a deepened understanding of concentration camp experience. I discovered recently that Dawidowicz (1990) articulated eloquently for me one reason for my opposition: The Jews who lived under Hitler's rule were confronted with cruel dilemmas, forced to make difficult, even impossible, choices about matters of life and death for which conscience could offer no direction and the past could give no guidance. Yet, many high school curricula frivolously suggest role-playing exercises in which students imagine how they would behave if confronted with such dilemmas. What kind of answers can come from American children who think of the Gestapo as the name of a game? (1990, 31).

At the same time, my concerns here are not meant as a blanket condemnation of all curriculum units on the Holocaust. I personally have not relied upon a published curriculum to frame the classroom engagement with sensitive topics, but rather have drawn on my own personal experiences and a lifetime of reading to deal with the text in response to the children's questions. Nevertheless, as Dawidowicz points out, there are some excellent curriculum materials at the secondary school level which allow for the subject to be taught with "integrity and without political exploitation" (1990, 31).

Parents as Partners

Parents play a vital role in the education of their children and need to be encouraged to be involved in their learning in school as well as out. They provide not only emotional support for their children but also additional perspectives on social issues. A number of years ago the parents of Howard, a child in my class, expressed concern about his intention to read Yolen's *The Devil's Arithmetic*, asking, "Why do they have to know about such horrors at such a young age?" While I explained that I had not assigned the book, that it had been recommended to him by a classmate, Elayne, I also pointed out that I could not advise him not to read it. The parents could have censored the book, but in the end they decided to let their son choose. Howard read, and then discussed, questioned, critiqued, and explored ideas in the book in depth, in collaboration with two other actively inquiring peers, Elayne and Audrey. Together these three students decided not to write in their logs. Instead, they participated in five extensive student-led discussions on aspects of the book that provided us all with new insights, and led to the writing of the article (Zack 1991) mentioned previously in this paper.

In discussing the above paragraph (published in *The New Advocate* (1996) version of this essay) with me recently, Howard's parents shed new and provocative light upon their concerns. Although one of the questions asked during that telephone conversation with Howard's mother in 1989 had had to do with "the horrors," the parents felt then and now that these are important issues, and they knew that I would deal with them sensitively in the classroom. They stressed that their apprehension was in relation to what they perceived as ambivalence on Howard's part in regard to the reading of *The Devil's Arithmetic*. Why was their son, an avid reader, not reading the book, for they saw that it remained long in his room, untouched? His mother suggested that it was Howard's affection for me and his feeling that I valued the book that pushed him to read it. This insightful reflection on the mother's part startled me and offered up a new dimension: Is there pressure previously unconsidered which moves children to read material which I have assumed they know they are free to choose not to read? I said earlier that the children know their own minds, and the extent to which they can cope. Is this perhaps something which needs closer and more explicit deliberation with the children? Although I would never not allow a child to read a book he or she chooses, I am resolved to speak more often with the children about staying in touch with their emotions, so that those children who feel a bit unsure will learn that they are free to, and should, put aside a work that is distressing to them.

The question the parents asked in regard to "the horrors," echoing other parents through the years, is an essential one. The children are indeed young, and bringing them face to face with evil involves risk. Thus I revisit my decision often, and each time I remain resolved that the acknowledgment of history, which includes evidence of the evil humans are capable of, must be put forward. Our concern about how harsh truths conveyed through literature affect children's sensibilities must be reflected against the wider reality that at this very moment children in some parts of the world are experiencing the very conditions the literature describes. Before significant change can take place, there must be a raising of awareness. Many adults grow up unaware of history, as was documented by Aurelia de Silva (1991), professor of children's literature, writing about her university-level students' reactions to Taylor's *Roll of Thunder, Hear My Cry* (see, too, Robertson 1997 for a citing of similar results). The findings of these researchers reveal that a number of university and preservice education students are ignorant of important historical events. Some research participants were shocked to learn that the events depicted in the novel actually had taken place, in their country, and not so long ago. By implication, in response to the question, "When is the right time to teach children about genocide?", I would suggest sooner rather than later, but always with care and understanding.

Reflections on Teaching about Intolerance and Genocide

The Rationale

Any pain is our pain: That's the root of tolerance.
Steven Spielberg, quoted in a *Montreal Gazette* article

Although dealing with instances of human rights violations has been an essential component of our fifth-grade curriculum, in the course of writing this essay I found I needed to make explicit both for myself and for others my rationale for teaching about these issues. It is my belief that each person on earth is both unique and equal to others, not "better" or "worse" than anyone else. While it sounds deceptively simple, Gloria Steinem (1996), in speaking recently about race, class, and gender issues in a presentation titled "Democracy and Self-Esteem," expressed the view that treating others with dignity must be made explicit as a principle for living: "The art of behaving morally is believing that [everyone] matters . . . and that there is something unique in each one of us." The belief that all people are equal is at times eloquently expressed by the children in my class, so it is not that I feel I have a mandate to teach morality because without me there would be none. Not so at all. However, I do feel the issue of the sanctity of life must be articulated, and that we must discuss instances in history in which this basic belief is not in evidence.

The children have spoken and written of racism as learned behavior. In responding to *Roll of Thunder*, Nora said, "When you are born you are not a racist . . . you are influenced," and Lewis asked, "Do you think the only thing that makes children prejudiced is adult influence?" In her written response, Liza wondered, "How come Jeremy and Lillian Jean are brother and sister and still feel so differently about Black people? I thought that if they were brought up together and their parents believe that Black people aren't really people, why does Jeremy not believe that?" Compassion, too, is learned behavior. I once jotted down these words by Susan Sarandon, who was reflecting on her family and her values in an interview: "Compassion isn't something that you get blindly through faith. It's hard work and it's something that you have to make a conscious decision to put into your life." Thus, if we are dealing with learned behavior, we—parents, teachers, and children—must engage in discussion about these behaviors. These discussions constitute an essential part of children's growth. My aim is to make children aware of ethnic and religious hatred, of inequities in regard to class and gender and other issues. My hope is that they will be inclined to speak out against injustice if they see it, acknowledge it, and confront it.

On Being Political

Caring takes many shapes.

Nel Noddings, *The Challenge to Care in Schools*

Joel Taxel once pointed out to me that very few educators speak explicitly about what it means to be political in the classroom, and he cited Carole Edelsky, Yetta Goodman, and Ken Goodman as notable exceptions (personal communication, September 1994). I remember thinking, "Am I political?" While I had thought and read, engaged in classroom discussions, and written about tolerance and multicultural issues, until this moment I considered these acts as socially and humanistically motivated. Then I realized that of course my actions were political, and I understood that I, who have never written a letter to the editor, and who have only attended one protest rally in my fifty-something years, am indeed committed politically. My commitment pertains to being actively involved both as a member of my immediate community and of the world community.

Some children in my class have been politically proactive. In cases where they have been moved by events in the media, they have written letters. One year six children wrote a letter to the editor of our local newspaper to protest a proposed rally of Neo-Nazis, which was to be held in the summer in Sorel, Quebec (see Blackman, Kaufman, Perri, Tritt, and Ulrich 1992). The children's position was championed by the National Director of the League for Human Rights. In a subsequent letter to the editor, she commended the students for speaking out, and said that "their actions can serve as a model for other students who are committed to making a difference" (Mock 1992).

In 1993 the children wrote to the federal government to urge that more active measures be taken by the Canadian government to help halt the killing in Bosnia. The reply from the government ministry was noncommittal. And, yet, even though they are frustrated at stalemates and oblique replies, at least these young people know something about the issues and about the importance of actively trying to shape society. Many of them have realized that it is important to determine where you stand, to know that you count, and that what you say and do may effect change.

When considering emotionally demanding subjects, one can lose heart in teaching. We all need hope, adults and young people alike. Of all the resources for teachers I have considered when dealing with these sensitive subjects (for example, Bat-Ami 1994; Marinak 1993), there is one that I have found particularly helpful. It is written by Gwenda Bond (1994), and entitled "Honesty and Hope: Presenting Human Rights Issues to Teenagers through Fiction." Bond deals with the weight of the task, both in terms of gravity and of responsibility. She also speaks of hope, and she addresses the challenge faced by those teachers and writers who present stories of suffering:

> They may . . . have to lead young readers into dark and disturbing areas of human experience, yet they have the responsibility to leave those readers at the end, not with a crushing burden of despair, but with a sense of hope. (42)

That is also our task as teachers and parents and caring adults. We must all learn to teach about intolerance and genocide. At the same time we must always remember that for children, it is their first encounter with man's inhumanity toward others. And it does not get easier.

Acknowledgments   I am deeply indebted to Barbara Graves for her involvement in discussions which helped shape this essay. I also sincerely appreciate the insightful comments and suggestions of Judith Robertson (editor of this volume), and Joel Taxel, Kathy Short, and Dana Fox, editors of *The New Advocate*, as well as those of the anonymous reviewers in response to previous drafts of this paper. A fortuitous meeting with Sandra Stotsky led me to several sources that proved invaluable to my thinking. My heartfelt thanks go, of course, as well to all the children in my fifth-grade classes who over the past seven years have delved with me into diverse issues, and who have affected my life profoundly.

Notes

1. The work to which I am referring is *How Texts Teach What Readers Learn* (Meek 1970/1988), but there are others in which she touches upon literature as well as literacy. Margaret Meek (also published as Margaret Meek Spencer) is one of a number of people (including Nancy Martin, James Britton, Yetta and Ken Goodman, and Shirley Brice Heath) whose work has been seminal to my understanding of children's literacy. Meek marvels at what learners can do, even as she speaks of "how complex a language function reading is, and how literate adults oversimplify it, or see no point in making conscious to themselves what they do when they read, or how children actually learn" (1992, 16). She deliberates upon reading in all its complexity of contexts, texts and purposes (1992, 25). Those readers interested in reading Meek's work should consult the Works Cited at the end of this essay (see, especially, Meek 1970/1988, 1983, 1991, and 1992; Meek, Aidan, and Barton 1977; Spencer and Mills, eds., 1988; and Maguire 1995).

2. Readers interested in a detailed examination of how one such inquiry unfolded may refer to an article I wrote a few years ago which describes three children discussing Yolen's *The Devil's Arithmetic* (see Zack 1991).

3. Pseudonyms have been used in all cases of the children's names. You will note that when she wrote the log, Malka asked that I not tell anyone—"not a friend or my parents or my brother or your family." In a subsequent conversation that occurred much later, Malka not only gave me permission to include her log entry, but felt strongly that it should be shared. She explained that it was during the time she was reading the book that she did not want her family to know that she was so scared.

4. Personal communication to the author from Judith Robertson, November 7, 1996.

5. Personal communication to the author from Joanne Rocklin, December 3, 1996.

Works Cited

Bat-Ami, Miriam. 1994. "War and Peace in the Early Elementary Class-room." *Children's Literature in Education* 25(2): 83–99.

Blackman, Gillian, David Kaufman, David Perri, Bryan Tritt, and Lindy Ulrich. 1992. "Stop the Rally by Neo-Nazis." (Letter to the Editor). The *Gazette*, Montreal, 18 June, B-2.

Bond, Gwenda. 1994. "Honesty and Hope: Presenting Human Rights Issues to Teenagers through Fiction." *Children's Literature in Education* 25(1): 41–53.

de Silva, Aurelia Davila. 1991. "Prospective Elementary Teachers Respond to *Roll of Thunder, Hear My Cry.*" *The Children's Literature Association Bulletin* 17(3): 10–17.

Dawidowicz, Lucy S. 1990. "How They Teach the Holocaust." *Commentary* 90(6): 25–32.

Greenlaw, M. Jean. 1984. "Book Review Sampler." *The New Advocate: For Those Involved with Young People and Their Literature* 7(2): 137–54.

Hendry, Diana, Stephen Bicknell, and Jennifer Wilson. 1993. "The *Signal* Poetry Award." *Signal* 71: 71–93.

Kerr, Judith. 1971. *When Hitler Stole Pink Rabbit.* London: Lions.

Kohl, Herbert. 1995. "The Politics of Children's Literature: Rosa Parks and the Story of the Montgomery Bus Boycott." In *Should We Burn Babar? Essays on Children's Literature and the Power of Stories*, edited by Herbert Kohl, 30–56. New York: The New Press.

Lewis, Anne. [Broadcaster]. 1994. "History That Hurts: The March of the Living." *News Report.* Canadian Television (Pulse News, Montreal), 15 August.

Lipstadt, Deborah E. 1995. "Not Facing History: How Not to Teach the Holocaust." *The New Republic* 212(10): 26–29.

Magorian, Michelle. 1981. *Good Night, Mr. Tom.* New York: Harper and Row.

Maguire, Mary. 1995. "Interview with Margaret Meek Spencer." In *Dialogue in a Major Key: Women Scholars Speak,* edited by Mary Maguire, 36–60. Urbana, IL: National Council of Teachers of English.

Marinak, Barbara. 1993. "Books in the Classroom: The Holocaust." *The Horn Book* 69(3): 368–75.

Matas, Carol. 1987. *Lisa.* Toronto: Lester & Orpen Dennys. [Published in USA as *Lisa's War.*]

———. 1989. *Jesper.* Toronto: Lester & Orpen Dennys. [Published in USA as *Codename Kris.*]

———. 1993. *Daniel's Story.* Richmond Hill, Ontario: Scholastic. [Published in conjunction with the United States Holocaust Memorial Museum.]

Meek, Margaret. 1970/1988. *How Texts Teach What Readers Learn.* Stroud, UK: Thimble Press.

———, ed. 1983. *Opening Moves: Work in Progress in the Study of Children's Language Development.* Bedford Way Papers 17. London, England: Institute of Education, University of London.

———. 1991. *On Being Literate.* London: The Bodley Head.

———. 1992. "Transitions: The Notions of Change in Writing for Children." *Signal* 67: 13–33.

Meek, Margaret, Aidan Warlow, and Griselda Barton, eds. 1977. *The Cool Web: The Pattern of Children's Reading.* London: The Bodley Head.

Mock, Karen. 1992. "Students Take Role in Fight against Spread of Racism." (Letter to the Editor.) The *Gazette,* Montreal, 29 June, B-2.

The Montreal *Gazette.* 1994. "Spielberg Urges Parents to Teach Children Tolerance." 30 June, D-3.

National Council of Teachers of English. 1994. "Latest NCTE Resolutions." *Council-Grams* 62(2) (April/May): 2–3. Urbana, IL: National Council of Teachers of English.

Noddings, Nel. 1992. *The Challenge to Care in Schools: An Alternative Approach to Education.* New York: Teachers College Press.

Orlev, Uri. 1991. *The Man from the Other Side.* Translated from the Hebrew by Hillel Halkin. Boston: Houghton Mifflin.

Pearce, Richard. (Director). 1990. *The Long Walk Home.* Videotape. Distributed by MCA Home Video Canada, 2450 Victoria Park Avenue, Willowdale, Ontario, Canada M2J 4A2. Phone 416-491-3000.

Reiss, Johanna. 1976. *The Journey Back.* New York: HarperCollins.

Robertson, Judith P. "Teaching about Worlds of Hurt through Encounters with Literature: Reflections on Pedagogy." *Language Arts* 74(6): 457–66. A slightly revised version appears in chapter 15 of this volume.

Smucker, Barbara. 1977. *Underground to Canada.* Toronto: Penguin.

Sommerfelt, Aimee. 1963. *Miriam.* Translated from the Norwegian by Pat S. Iversen. New York: Criterion Books.

Spencer, Margaret Meek, and Colin Mills, eds. 1988. *Language and Literacy in the Primary School.* New York: The Falmer Press.

Steinem, Gloria. 1996. "Equality and Self-Esteem." Unique Lives and Experiences Lecture Series. Place des Arts, Montreal, Quebec, April 22.

Stotsky, Sandra. 1996. "Is the Holocaust the Chief Contribution of the Jewish People to World Civilization and History? A Survey of Leading Literature Anthologies and Reading Instructional Textbooks." *English Journal* 85(2): 52–59.

Taylor, Mildred. 1976/1981. *Roll of Thunder, Hear My Cry.* New York: Bantam Books.

Yolen, Jane. 1988. *The Devil's Arithmetic.* New York: Viking Penguin.

Zack, Vicki. 1991. "'It Was the Worst of Times': Learning about the Holocaust through Literature." *Language Arts* 68(1): 42–48.

———. 1996. "Nightmare Issues: Children's Responses to Racism and Genocide in Literature." *The New Advocate: For Those Involved with Young People and Their Literature* 9(4): 297–308.

———. "Surviving the Holocaust: The Ordeal of the Hidden Child." Unpublished Paper.

10 Daniel Pinkwater's *Wingman:* Exploring Conflict-Resolution Strategies through Multiethnic Literature

Belinda Yun-Ying Louie
University of Washington, Tacoma

Douglas H. Louie
University of Washington, Tacoma

Intolerance takes many forms, one of which is condemning other people's ways of resolving conflicts. Anthropologists and sociologists have long argued that the way disputes are handled in a given society is strongly conditioned by cultural factors (Felstiner 1974; Gluckman 1969; Gulliver 1979; Nader 1969). Thus, for example, members of individualistic societies such as mainstream Americans tend to adopt a direct, active approach toward resolving conflict, such as confronting the target issue (Chiu and Kosinski 1994; Leung and Lind 1986; Ting-Toomey 1985). In contrast, people from Eastern societies expect that others should be able to infer unarticulated messages. Therefore, they tend to use nonverbal behavior and reciprocal sensitivity to resolve conflict (Bond and Wang 1983). Problematically, many ethnic minorities in North America encounter discrimination in cross-cultural conflict situations when people from the mainstream culture put down conflict-resolution approaches not conforming to the dominant (and frequently unquestioned) norm.

We argue that understanding the diversity of conflict-resolution approaches could prevent the wrongful labeling of behaviors and increase peoples' capacity to interact with others. In our multicultural society, students "need to learn how to interact with members of outside ethnic groups and how to resolve conflicts with them" (Banks 1991, 26). This essay presents a classroom unit in which a teacher guided his fourth-grade students to understand the diversity of conflict-resolution strategies using multiethnic literature portraying a Chinese American family.

Conflict-Resolution Process

The process of conflict emergence and resolution across cultures is studied by Victor Turner, an anthropologist. Turner (1974) contends that a conflict situation can serve as a guide for increased understanding of cultural values and norms: "Conflict seems to bring fundamental aspects of society, normally overlaid by the customs and habits of daily intercourse, into frightening prominence" (Turner 1974, 35). Turner (1980) identifies four phases in the evolution of a resolution in conflict situations across cultures:

1. Breach—There is a conflict between a person and other members in the community.
2. Crisis—The conflict worsens. People can neither ignore it nor deny it.
3. Redress—Action is taken to repair the conflict. (In cases where there is no redress, conflicts simply remain.)
4. Reintegration or Recognition of Schism—The offender is either reintegrated into the community or the community recognizes that there is a division.

Students can utilize Turner's model for conceptualizing the problem-solving behaviors of characters in multiethnic literature. After identifying character conflicts and Turner's four phases, students can analyze the motivation and action of story characters in each phase. Through processes of identification and reasoning, students may develop a greater awareness of their own reasoning and problem-solving behaviors. By using characters from other ethnic groups, students may gain perspectives by comparing characters' values and actions with their own (Norton 1990). Thus, literature may provide less risky ground for students to examine behaviors in times of conflict, without the emotional interference found in real-life situations. In addition, stories convey values, challenge assumptions, and engage readers in ways that speak not only to the intellect but also to the imagination (Duryea and Potts 1993). Finally, stories invite participation, encourage readers' reflection, and give a context for conversation and communication through which students may develop greater understanding of the conflict-related behaviors of literary characters and themselves.

A Brief Description of Our Project

A teacher's knowledge of an ethnic group is critical in creating a valid learning experience for students to understand the conflict resolution of the group. For the project outlined in this essay, there is a possibility of creating stereotypes if students simply identify the

"Chinese" ways of conflict resolution. Students need to understand both the ethnic-specific elements shaped by the Chinese culture and the universal elements shared by all groups in handling conflicts. In our project, we looked for a teacher who was knowledgeable about Chinese Americans and multicultural education. We planned the project with him, and one of us (B.Y.L.) observed the teacher throughout the week in teaching his fourth-grade class.

We assessed student learning in two sets of targets: knowledge targets and reasoning targets. Knowledge targets required students to demonstrate that they understood that people have different ways in resolving conflicts, and that discrimination may occur when people do not understand the diversity of possible conflict-resolution strategies. Reasoning targets required that students compare and contrast their own conflict-resolution strategies with those of literary (Chinese American) characters.

We emphasized the instruction-assessment link in our data collection. Thus, we taught students the above-named knowledge and reasoning targets, and we attempted to assess student learning through group discussion and student writing in small groups. Pedagogically, small-group instruction provides a nourishing context for students to explore issues and to articulate individual perspectives. During group discussion, a teacher is able to give immediate feedback to prevent students from relying on their existing frameworks to interpret ethnic story characters' emotion and action. Small-group discussion furnishes the teacher with evidence through which to assess developing knowledge.

For this unit we selected Daniel Pinkwater's short novel *Wingman* (1992) because of its authentic description of the tension and conflict-resolution strategies in a Chinese American family. Furthermore, the fictionalized school setting provided a familiar context for the fourth-grade students to examine their own thinking and behaviors in similar situations. In the novel, Donald Chan is teased at school because he is Chinese American and he is poor. His teacher gives him a Thanksgiving food basket in front of the whole class. The food basket hurts and humiliates Donald and his father tremendously. Subsequently, Donald begins to skip school. Later when a truant officer goes to their house early in the morning, Donald faces a crisis when his father learns about his action. As a backdrop to *Wingman,* many Chinese American fiction and nonfiction books were on display in the classroom. Students could select other books to read during voluntary reading time.

Classroom Application

The teacher modified Turner's conflict-resolution framework to guide student analysis of *Wingman* through a sequence of questions. He asked students to consider the following issues:

Step 1: Breach—Does Donald have any conflict with people around him?

Step 2: Crisis—Do Donald's conflicts with others worsen? Could Donald and the people around him ignore the conflict?

Step 3 and Step 4: Redress and Resolution—What do characters do about the conflicts? Were the conflicts resolved?

The conflict-resolution unit lasted for five days, using the one-hour language arts and social studies block each day. Although we planned lessons together with the teacher, the teacher alone addressed the questions and issues that emerged during classroom discussion. The following section provides a snapshot of the learning journey.

Day 1

Step 1: Breach—Does Donald have any conflict with people around him?

Since *Wingman* is a short chapter book that is easily read aloud, on the first day the teacher read the first chapter to the class. Students were eager to talk about what conflicts Donald faced in the story. Some students raised questions regarding Donald's conflict within himself. For example, the literary character has two names, a Chinese one at home and an English one at school. Students wondered why parents would confuse children by giving them two names. Although some students accepted Donald's name problem, they did not comprehend Donald's identity struggle associated with his two different names. The teacher clarified that many Chinese American families give Chinese names to their children to remind them of their family roots and heritage. He explained as well that these children also carry American names, because they are Americans living in English-speaking communities.

The teacher sought input from the Eurasian children in his class. These children all had Caucasian fathers and Chinese or Korean mothers. Admitting that, indeed, they had Chinese or Korean names, the students stated that they used only their American names at home and at school. Their friends were surprised to discover that their classmates had two names, just like Donald. However, when pressed to say their other names, the Eurasian students all shook their heads and refused to do so.

Day 2

Step 2: Crisis—Do Donald's conflicts with others worsen? Could Donald and the people around him ignore the conflict?

On Day 2, the teacher read more from the story. Students then worked in pairs to identify and to discuss whether and how Donald's conflicts with people deteriorated. Students recorded their observations to share with the class:

The problem gets worse because the teacher gives Donald a food basket in front of everybody. When Donald takes it home, his father jumps up and down on the stuff from the basket. His father even cries and throws everything into the garbage. Donald skips school.

Donald's problem gets worse and people cannot ignore it when a truant officer goes to Donald's house because he skips school for a long time.

Students easily identified the character's conflicts. They all recognized how severe the conflict felt to Donald because he skipped school to avoid going back to class. Moreover, students noted that Donald experienced a major conflict with his father when the truant officer visited Donald's house to expose his condition. The whole class agreed that Donald was in crisis because neither the school nor his father could ignore the issues. Students engaged in animated discussion about what their own parents would do if a truant officer went to their homes. The familiarity of the school setting and difficult predicament for the student helped readers to empathize with Donald.

Day 3

Step 3 and Step 4: Redress and Resolution—What do characters do about the conflicts? Were the conflicts resolved?

During the redressing and the resolution stages, a comparison of conflict-resolution strategies between cultural groups takes place. Students must first become aware of how they themselves think and act in conflict situations. Afterward, they need to reread the story to identify ways literary characters resolve the conflict. It is important for students to return to the literary text because readers' interpretations of narrative action are influenced by their pre-existing cultural beliefs.

Accordingly, on Day 3, the students worked in pairs to discuss ways in which they themselves would have handled the characters' conflicts. Students recorded their ideas on butcher paper, later posted on the board:

> When the truant officer comes to my house, I'll say I am sorry. I did it. I'll go back to school immediately. I'll never skip school again.

> I'll tell my father and the truant officer everything that happens to me at school. They should know that things are not good for me at school. They should not be mad at me. They should understand me.

> I'll tell them that nobody likes me at school. Everybody hates me. I am not learning anything at school anyway. I feel better when I read comics at the George Washington Bridge when I skip school. That's why I skip school.

> I will make up a story about a big bully at school. He calls me names. He tries to beat me up. I skip school because he scares me. When I go to the park every day to read comics, nobody bothers me there.

Furthermore, students imagined how they would resolve the conflict if they were Donald's father:

> I'll tell the truant officer that I'll talk to Donald. He'll be at school tomorrow. Thank you. I'll go to school with Donald to talk to the teacher.

> I think Donald's father should call the teacher. What happens at school? Why does Donald feel so bad about school?

> My father will call the teacher, the principal, the school board. If I skip school, he will get everybody to a meeting and talk.

> I'll talk to Donald. Don't do it again. It's not good to skip school. If you are not happy, you can go to another class. You can go to another school.

> I will tell Donald to go back to school. If he has problems with the teacher or other people, he should let them know. Donald should talk to people.

After the students posted and shared their written responses, the teacher asked them to identify what they felt to be the best way to resolve the conflict. This request was made in order to teach students *to question* the necessity of choosing the best way, thus leading them to the first knowledge target about the diversity of conflict-resolution strategies. In actuality, students were very hesitant to choose the best approach, and questioned the need to decide on the best way:

> Why can't we deal with the conflicts in different ways? It's hard to say which one is the best.

> It's okay if we do things differently as long as we deal with conflicts. We don't need to do things the way other people do.

> We are all different. By the way, there are so many ways to take care of conflicts. Why do we want to say which way is the best? I know that we are not supposed to get violent when we argue with people. Violence, guns, and all those stuff are not good. But everything here is okay because nobody talks about going out to kill people if they have a conflict.

Student reaction indicated that they realized and valued the diversity of conflict-resolution among themselves. The children's awareness would serve as a springboard later for helping them to accept the differences of conflict-resolution approaches between the Chinese American characters and themselves. Instead of lecturing students about the importance of such diversity, the teacher skillfully used the students' own words and ideas to help them reach this knowledge target on their own.

Day 4   Next, the teacher read three more chapters, and reread the compelling scene in which the truant officer visits Donald's family. Students then worked in pairs to identify character reactions in the face of conflicts. The instructional goal was to initiate a focused examination of character action. It was hoped that such knowledge could serve as a contrast or backdrop to help students better understand their own behaviors. Regarding Donald, students reported that:

> Donald cries because his father is ashamed of him.
>
> He is quiet. He doesn't say anything to his father and the truant officer.
>
> Donald feels very bad because he disappoints his father.
>
> He makes up his mind that he will never skip school again.

The teacher recorded student responses on butcher paper. He then initiated the same analysis with a focus on Donald's father. Students noted that:

> He does not say anything in front of the truant officer.
>
> He turns his back on Donald.
>
> He does not talk to anybody at school.
>
> When Donald comes home from school, his father fixes a very good dinner. He tells Donald that people may not be nice at school, But Donald still needs to go to school. When he gets older, he can punch them in the nose. I like that part.
>
> They sing a funny song together when they work in the laundry that night.

After students closely examined character action, they realized how their own conflict-resolution strategies differed from those of the storybook characters. The teacher then guided students to shift their attention to their own strategies as recorded on various pieces of butcher paper. He encouraged students to describe their approaches to conflict-resolution:

> We like to talk about things.
>
> We explain things. We talk to many people trying to find out what causes the problem.
>
> We are straightforward. We ask people what do you think? How do you feel?

Overall, students wanted verbally to explain, to rationalize, and to justify their habitual conflict-resolution actions. Their approach was forthright, explicit, and confrontational. They wanted others to understand what caused the conflict. There was an underlying assumption that each person related to the conflict should take responsibility to communicate his or her concerns.

Day 5   By this point, the teacher had finished reading the whole story to the class. He challenged the students to consider whether there were similarities between the Chinese American literary characters' ways of handling conflicts and their own. He also encouraged students to look for behaviors and reactions shared by many different people under similar situations. By focusing on "similarities across differences," the teacher tried to show the students some universal patterns in conflict situations. Student responses were as follows:

> I will hate school and skip school just like Donald if I know that people think that I am that poor.

> I will act sick and not go back to school just like Donald.

> Both the principal and the teacher are not nice to Donald. I hate to talk to people if I know they do not like me.

> Sometimes it is difficult for me to tell my parents what happens to me at school.

> I think Donald's father is so shocked that he doesn't know what to say. When my mom told me that my grandpa died of a heart attack in the middle of the night, I was so shocked that I didn't know what to say. My grandpa and I were very close. People thought that I didn't care because I didn't do or say anything.

Student responses indicated that they did have some understanding of why Donald avoided school, and why his father did not immediately confront the problems. Instead of focusing on emotions such as anger, discomfort, or avoidance, students were able to identify specific actions that they might follow in similar situations.

The teacher then guided students to examine the characters' ways of dealing with conflicts, looking for actions that the students would not select to do. At this point in the study, it became clear to us that the students possessed a limited understanding of some cultural practices of Chinese American people. We saw that if students were asked to identify Chinese American conflict-resolution strategies, in fact the learners would proceed according to their own pre-existing unquestioned frameworks. As a result, student responses would reinforce unconscious stereotypes. It is important to note that we hoped that we could slow the activation of stereotypes by guiding students to identify unfamiliar ways of behaving *before* bringing questions of ethnicity into the discussion.

Accordingly, students pinpointed some critical differences in conflict-resolution strategies between themselves and the characters:

> I still will not take insult this way. I'll tell people not to mess around with me.

> They feel bad. But they do not talk much.

He encourages Donald to hang in there without finding out what really happens at school.

Donald doesn't say he's sorry. His father doesn't force him to say sorry. His father seems to know that Donald feels bad. He doesn't say I forgive you or anything like that. He just fixes a good dinner and sings a funny song. He lets Donald know that things are O.K. He just doesn't say it out loud.

After students had compared and contrasted their own imagined problem-solving strategies with those of the Chinese American literary characters, the teacher asked students to think about what prompted the characters' actions. Although the teacher wanted students to articulate the values and motivations that shape social action, some students still passed judgment on the silence of the literary characters:

Donald didn't say anything. It's hard for me not to talk. I'll tell everybody what I feel. They need to know my story. But Donald may feel very bad because he hurts his father so bad that he doesn't care to talk about his story.

Donald and his dad look so timid. Why don't they speak for themselves? If they talked, the problems might go away faster.

It seemed to me that they ran away from the problems. Remaining silent would not do any good.

At this point, the teacher posed a critical question: Because some of us do not like the characters' ways in handling the conflicts, does it mean that their ways are bad? He paused to wait for student responses. The children offered the following insights:

They are different. It is not good or bad. It seems to me that they do not want to argue. Things are bad already. You don't need to keep on talking about it.

At the beginning, I find them very strange. Donald doesn't tell things to his father. His father doesn't yell at Donald. And then I read more, his father makes a good dinner and they sing a funny song together. Donald's father knows that Donald has made a mistake. Everybody knows about Donald skipping school. There is no need to talk about it. It is not a bad way to deal with the problem. I don't do things like that. But their way is pretty neat.

Just like the other day in class, we didn't need to choose which way was the best in all our answers. We are different, we can do things in different ways.

Many students argued that it is acceptable to have different ways to resolve conflicts. Many appeared to understand that differences exist across cultural groups, and that people can learn from one another.

This was a critical instructional target for this unit: students understood the diversity of conflict-resolution strategies.

The teacher reminded his students that it is easy to put down people who appear to be different, and that discrimination takes many forms. He asked students to name some examples of discriminatory behavior from *Wingman*. Some students mentioned that skin color, race, and poverty can serve as excuses to discriminate. One student suggested that people might discriminate against Donald because he did not speak much. This student felt that Donald might "look dumb" to others. During this discussion students were quick to indicate that Donald was a sharp boy who had developed excellent reading skills from reading comics! Students also argued that people should not be despised because they talk less. We view student support for the literary protagonist as a sign of their acceptance and ability to tolerate unfamiliar behaviors. The teacher concluded the unit by asking students to share their learning from the last few days. Students' reactions included the following:

> Different people have different ways to deal with conflicts. Some speak more. Some don't like to speak that much.

> Talking is not the only way to deal with conflicts. You can do nice things.

> It is not very easy for me to understand Donald's way. But it helps when we talk about how we are similar and how we are different. I can see why he may want to do things in his ways. It is okay.

Student responses revealed their understanding of the prevalence of explicit, verbal communication in their problem-solving approaches. At the same time, they accepted that Donald's family successfully resolved the conflict without any direct, confrontational talk about the problems.

Conclusion

Philipsen (1992) states that mainstream American culture is preoccupied with the importance of using verbal communication to resolve interpersonal conflicts. Informants in Philipsen's studies believe that "well-functioning individuals" are those who can talk about their personal concerns and perspectives. We argue that this prevalent and unquestioned cultural norm condemns those who do not communicate inner feelings as less competent members in the community. We feel that placing such a negative connotation on communication other than the verbal mode constitutes an act of intolerance.

This essay presents a classroom vignette about a project designed to help students understand the diversity of conflict-resolution strategies through multiethnic literature. Students in our study discovered how Donald Chan's Chinese American family preferred to use nonverbal communication to resolve conflicts. Victor Turner's conflict-resolution model provided the instructional framework through which to guide students to examine literary characters' thoughts and behaviors in conflict situations.

Through clearly focused discussions and small-group problem-solving activities, students were able to clarify the similarities and differences between the characters' approaches and their own. Students honestly admitted that they preferred the approach of open communication about conflict. However, at the end of the unit of study, they also accepted that open communication was not the only way to resolve conflicts. Donald Chan's family handled conflicts differently, yet the result was still satisfactory.

The purpose of this unit was to help students realize the potential intolerance people might have toward unfamiliar conflict-resolution strategies. Such understanding, hopefully, will prevent students from developing discrimination before they have an opportunity to learn about other people's actions and thoughts. Multiethnic literature provides a nourishing context for helping students to confront their own pre-existing mindsets, and to examine the motivations of others. Fighting intolerance is a long battle; as educators, we believe that teaching about conflict resolution through multiethnic literature constitutes a significant step toward this goal.

Acknowledgments

We want to express our heartfelt appreciation to the teacher and children who participated in this project.

Works Cited

Banks, James. 1991. *Teaching Strategies for Ethnic Studies.* 5th ed. Boston: Allyn & Bacon.

Bond, Michael H., and Sung Hsing Wang. 1983. "Aggressive Behavior in Chinese Society: The Problem of Maintaining Order and Harmony." In *Global Perspectives on Aggression.* New York: Pergamon.

Chiu, Randy K., and Frederick A. Kosinski, Jr. 1994. "Is Chinese Conflict-Handling Behavior Influenced by Chinese Values?" *Social Behavior and Personality* 22(1): 81–90.

Duryea, Michelle L., and Jim Potts. 1993. "Story and Legend: Powerful Tools for Conflict Resolution." *Mediation Quarterly* 10(4): 387–95.

Felstiner, William L. 1974. "Influences of Social Organization on Dispute Processing." *Law and Society Review* 9: 63–94.

Gluckman, Max. 1969. *Ideas and Procedures in African Customary Law.* London: Oxford University Press.

Gulliver, P. H. 1979. *Disputes and Negotiations: A Cross-Cultural Perspective.* New York: Academic Press.

Leung, Kwok, and E. Allen Lind. 1986. "Procedure and Culture: Effects of Culture, Gender, and Investigator Status on Procedural Preferences." *Journal of Personality and Social Psychology* 50: 1134–40.

Nader, Laura, ed. 1969. *Law in Culture and Society.* Chicago: Aldine.

Norton, Donna E. 1990. "Teaching Multicultural Literature in the Reading Curriculum." *The Reading Teacher* 44(1): 28–40.

Philipsen, Gerry. 1992. *Speaking Culturally: Explorations in Social Communication.* Albany, NY: State University of New York Press.

Pinkwater, Daniel. 1992. *Wingman.* New York: Bantam.

Ting-Toomey, Stella. 1985. "Toward a Theory of Conflict and Culture." In *International and Intercultural Communication Annual: Communication, Culture and Organizational Processes,* vol. 9. Thousand Oaks, CA: Sage.

Turner, Victor. 1974. *Dramas, Fields, and Metaphors: Symbolic Action in Human Society.* Ithaca, NY: Cornell University Press.

———. 1980. "Social Dramas and Stories about Them." *Critical Inquiry* 7: 141–68.

Rights, Respect, and Responsibility: Toward a Theory of Action in Two Bilingual (Spanish/English) Classrooms[1]

Beth Yeager
McKinley Elementary, Santa Barbara, California

Irene Pattenaude
McKinley Elementary, Santa Barbara, California

María E. Fránquiz
University of Colorado, Boulder

Louise B. Jennings
University of South Carolina

Introduction

To look is one thing.
To see what you look at is another.
To learn from what you understand is still something else.
But to act on what you learn is all that really matters.

The Talmud

This quote from the Talmud provides a snapshot of life in two fifth-grade bilingual (Spanish/English) classes in Southern California. In these classes, tolerant and intolerant actions are central for understanding how to construct and be responsible members of communities. In order to construct opportunities for differentiating between tolerant and intolerant actions, the two teachers, Beth and Irene, share a common view in which teacher and students are members of a community of learners (Glover 1986). In practices of inquiry that echo the quotation from the Talmud, these learners learn to see and make visible certain phenomena, to understand and learn from what is made visible, and to take action individually and collectively on what is learned. How these practices affect students' learning is reflected in a student essay:

In the beginning of the year we discussed responsibility. We all signed a piece of paper that said what our responsibilities were. Some of the things were respect for each other and to listen to each other. Most of us have tried really hard to follow what we signed. Some of the most common words in the community of Room 18 were why?, to observe, to be historians, to look for evidence, to think, to investigate, to interpret, and to make theories. Almost all of the time, whenever we do something, at least one of these words come up. . . .

Our community also studied the subject of tolerance. Most of the time we talked about the Holocaust, but we also talked about tolerance and intolerance. We talked about a lot of things that were tolerant and about things that were not. Some of the things we talked about . . . were helping each other, sharing with each other, respecting each other, being nice to each other, being cooperative with each other, working together, listening to each other, respecting all languages, all of us having rights, and finally, but not least being tolerant with each other. (Karen Ramirez 1996)[2]

Karen's essay captures many actions taken up in classroom life, including actions of tolerance (e.g., helping, sharing, respecting, listening to each other) and actions of inquiry (e.g., asking why, observing, looking for evidence, interpreting, making theories). In what follows we demonstrate how particular literate and inquiry processes provided opportunities for students living in these bilingual classes to make visible, understand, and take up responsible actions within multiple communities. Such actions across the academic year have potential for contributing to the growth of a generation "where learning is an outcome of inquiry, initiative, construction and responsible action toward justice and equity" (LeVesque and Prosser 1996, 332).

Our intention is to trace the journey Karen experienced in fifth grade that led to the text cited above. First, we describe the theoretical constructs that framed the fifth-grade journey. Then we introduce the ethnographic method and theory of action guiding the teacher's conceptualizations of inquiry[3] used for planning the tolerance focus that influenced student learning. Next, we describe the initiation of the journey during the first days of school when opportunities were made available for students to identify and integrate understandings about responsibility into a classroom "Bill of Rights." Then an illustrative case demonstrates how teacher and students take up particular literate and inquiry actions to examine a range of topics across content areas. Following the case is a description of how students bring literate and inquiry practices negotiated early in the year to a mid-year, literature-based, interdisciplinary study of the Holocaust.[4] This study focuses on expanding understandings of the constitutive nature of tolerant and intolerant actions for both individuals and groups. The study also makes visible how inquiry practices draw from intertextual[5] connections made available to classroom members throughout the year. These connections support students' growth in applying new understandings of tolerant actions to their own lives in the classroom, the school, and the neighborhood. Finally, we provide ideas for engaging students in writing for social action. The goal is to show how social action becomes a critical component of the tolerance focus. Examples of personal and community actions taken over the years by students living in and beyond these classrooms provide not a "one size fits all" prescription for bilingual writing process classrooms (Reyes 1992, 431), but snapshots of the journey undertaken by communities of inquirers.

Constructing Communities of Inquirers: A Historical Context

Many educators informed by a humanizing pedagogy (Bartolomé 1996) face constraints of time and a predefined curriculum. Yet, they struggle to find a place for teaching substantive issues such as tolerance and intolerance that offer potential for improving the quality of everyday life for all. Beth and Irene know this struggle well, and have worked and reworked the framework of their school year in order to integrate a focused study of tolerance within the ongoing literate and inquiry practices that support learning in their classrooms. Both initiated the tolerance focus in 1987. Six years ago, Irene joined the faculty at McKinley Elementary School and has worked with Beth in developing ways for linking inquiry processes and responsibility. They encouraged reflection from their students regarding individual and group understanding of tolerant and intolerant actions.

This particular school is a community school recognized by the district for redesigning the curriculum to fit the special linguistic needs of the majority of the school population. The ethic/racial designations for the school are 85 percent Latina/Latino, 11 percent White, 2 percent African American, 1.5 percent Native American, and 0.2 percent Pacific Islander (Santa Barbara School District 1995). Of the 520 students attending grades K–5, 63 percent are native speakers of Spanish predominantly representing immigrant and American-born Mexican families. By the fifth grade many students demonstrate some degree of competence in Spanish and in English even if bilingual fluency is not yet stable (Durán 1994).

Louise and María collected data in Irene and Beth's fifth-grade classrooms for three years. The data is a part of a series of linked ethnographic studies in K–12 classrooms conducted by the Santa Barbara Classroom Discourse Group, a collaboration of teacher-researchers and university researchers. The data is comprised of participant observations, videotapes, transcriptions, field notes, artifacts (e.g., student written work, student art work, family stories, and parent letters), structuration maps, slides, photos, and formal and informal interviews with the teacher and with small groups of students.[6] For this essay, the teacher-researcher team worked collaboratively to make visible the social construction of literacy (Cook-Gumperz 1986) through actions (literate, inquiry, and social) molded and taken up in Irene and Beth's fifth-grade classrooms that promote the ethical dimensions of learning.

During the six years in which Beth and Irene have collaborated, other researchers from the Santa Barbara Classroom Discourse Group have participated in the endeavor. This group uses the tools of the ethnographer (e.g., video camera and field notebook) to study how members construct classroom culture (Collins and Green 1992). The ethnographic method involves studying how members' actions and interactions shape and are shaped by particular classroom practices (Bloome and Bailey 1992), as well as by the language of the classroom (Lin 1993). The highly interactive methodology involves teacher-researchers, students, and university researchers in the collection, analysis, interpretation, presentation, and publication of classroom ethnographies. Fifth-grade students in the "Tower" community (Beth's classroom in the tower of the school) and in Room 18 (Irene's classroom) were able to take up the role of student ethnographers. Teachers expanded students' learning by teaching them to differentiate between notetaking (observing) and note-making (interpreting) in the study of their own classroom communities. These field methods helped members of the two bilingual classrooms to better understand how communities of inquirers are constructed from responsible actions (individual and collective) recorded across time.

Throughout their years of collaboration, Beth and Irene have worked to make visible and to articulate—for themselves, their students, and their students' families—the premises that underlie their vision for life in classrooms, a vision which bridges the gap between theory and practice. Following are the premises that underlie their pedagogical decisions for fifth grade:

- Classrooms are cultures (Collins and Green 1992).

- Communities of learners are co-constructed by members (Santa Barbara Classroom Discourse Group 1992a,b).

- As learners, students with the teacher and other adults co-construct ways of being students, including ways of being that are culturally responsible (Ladson-Billings 1995).

- The native languages of students are resources for co-constructing a common language of the classroom for learning (Fránquiz 1995; Lin 1993).

- Children need to be privy to the hidden curriculum (Aronowitz and Giroux 1985; Giroux and Purpel, 1983) as well as to their own knowledge-making processes and practices. "They should become the keepers of the windows of their souls," says Beth Yeager.

- Inquiry is a sound basis for instruction across the curriculum.

- Content is linked to a particular context (Rutherford and Ahlgren 1990) rather than to the performance of techniques; there is a discipline-based reflective way of knowing (Saxe 1988).

- These premises identify key principles, practices, and participatory actions (linguistic, academic, social) fundamental to learning in these fifth-grade classroom communities.

Rights, Respect, and Responsibility as a Foundation for the Academic Year

Now we describe how the fifth-grade journey initiated during the first days of school integrates the aforementioned premises. We show how particular opportunities assisted students in identifying and demonstrating their understandings about individual and collective rights, respect, and responsibility within a particular classroom community. If tolerance means taking responsibility to respect the rights of other community members, then to begin to understand and enact tolerance, students need multiple opportunities for understanding how responsibility relates to respect and rights. Opportunities for making these connections have become a year-long process in Beth and Irene's fifth-grade bilingual classrooms. The teachers take an explicit approach by helping students make visible what they think community and the 3R's (rights, respect, and responsibility) look and sound like. Students begin by explaining their understandings of the interrelatedness of these concepts. Then they take up opportunities for demonstrating responsible actions in order to improve the quality of life of the communities in which they are involved (i.e., classroom, school, and neighborhood).

Prior research shows that the first days of school are instrumental in shaping patterns of classroom life and defining what it means to be a student in this class in this year (Fernie, Davies, Kantor, and McMurry 1993; Fránquiz 1995; Jennings 1996; Lin 1993; Santa Barbara Classroom Discourse Group 1992a). Accordingly, we identify the particular social actions, inquiry actions, and literate actions that supported classroom members as they began their journey of learning and enacting tolerance.

In order to ground themselves in responsible actions, students and teachers begin on the first day of school to inquire into the range of meanings for community. First, students write their thoughts regarding the meaning of community. Students thus have an opportunity to reflect from prior experience before coming up with a shared classroom concept. After the first entry, students share their writing with others in a whole-class discussion, revising or adding to their own ideas. Thus, they learn to consider others' points of view. The list of shared ideas generated by classroom members is long and inclusive. It reflects family, school, neighborhood, and global understandings of what constitutes community. One list included "people, *barrio* (neighborhood), *familias* (families), together, same interests, helping each other, caring." What becomes evident is that once students have generated a "classroom" sense of what community means to them as individuals, they begin to see the cornerstone for understanding the responsibilities they each have for supporting the classroom community.

Next, students engage in a process to generate definitions of rights, respect, and responsibility. We feel it is important that students know, from the beginning, that the 3R's will be the foundation for all work accomplished together throughout the year. Additionally, the teachers create conditions for students to understand that each "R" cannot stand alone. We want students to understand that for every right there is a responsibility and that both are grounded in a basic notion of respect. In other words, the 3 R's are interdependent.

Students also write their definition of responsibility. These early definitions indicate that, at the beginning of the school year, they generally have an underdeveloped understanding of responsibility. Most students initially write that classroom responsibilities include "doing homework" and "listening to the teacher." These comments do not show students seeing themselves as having a responsibility to the classroom community. Instead, students see themselves as having an individual sense of what they need to do to be successful in the classroom. This finding across the years is surprising because the majority of students entering fifth grade at this school share a history of working with others in cooperative groups, relying on each other for their learning, and using conflict-resolution strategies to resolve problems.[7] It suggests that it is important to provide multiple opportunities to make explicit connections between these strategies and the concept of responsibility.

A similar process entails having students write personal definitions for each of the 3 R's. Group sharing then prompts students to revise personal definitions as influenced by others' points of view. Next, students interview parents for their understandings of the words *rights (derechos), respect (respeto),* and *responsibility (responsabilidad).* In this way, the journey toward a shared and comprehensive understanding of the 3R's becomes an inquiry process which involves parents.

After writing, sharing, discussing, and revising their under-standings of rights, respect, and responsibility, students engage in a lengthy process of small-group work and whole-class negotiation in order to develop a classroom Bill of Rights and Responsibilities, whose format aligns with the goals of the fifth-grade United States history curriculum. Large chart paper records this class-constructed Bill in both Spanish and English. All members of the classroom community, children and adults, sign the Bill before it is hung on the classroom wall. Students and parents sign individual copies, one of which is kept at home, the other at school. These rights and responsibilities become constant reference points throughout the year, mate-rial for discussion and reminders of the ways members of classroom communities expect to live and work together. The English version of the Tower's Bill of Rights in 1995–96 stated:

1. We have the right to feel safe in our classroom. We have the responsibility to walk and behave in a safe way without hurting anyone.

2. We have the right to study and to learn. We have the responsibil-ity to let others study without bothering anyone.

3. We have the right to be respected and to feel that we are equal in our class. We have the responsibility to help each other and to respect each other, without saying bad words and without laugh-ing at each other.

4. We have the right to be listened to by others. We have the respon-sibility to listen when others are speaking.

5. We have the right to have our own things and have the class respect our things. We have the responsibility to take care of the property of all.

As part of the construction of their understanding of responsi-bility, students also draw themselves demonstrating respect and taking action in the larger school setting. During the first week of school, then, two important events occur: the construction of a shared definition and the formation of a classroom text, the Bill of Rights and Responsibilities. Through these events, students not only examine personal definitions of what constitutes community, rights, respect, and responsibility, but they identify actions needed to carry them out. Students also experience the others' points of view, includ-ing their respective families, as they negotiate and construct a work-ing, viable set of guidelines from which their classroom community can evolve. Thus, the establishment of a Bill of Rights and Responsi-bilities can be seen as the first "action" step in the construction of individual and collective responsibility.

The processes of the first week also introduce students to particular actions of inquiry (observing, writing, interviewing, interpreting) that will support learning throughout all content areas. We believe that the action of constructing a common textual reference for classroom rights and responsibilities and the concomitant actions of inquiry required to produce an inclusive text are central to initiating particular ways of action that serve as a resource for present and future classroom communities.

Inquiry as Action

We ask students not only to take up the social actions they have defined in their Bill of Rights and Responsibilities, but also to understand and enact processes of inquiry that cross disciplines. The theory of action we propose examines the interrelatedness between social actions (3R's), actions of inquiry (e.g., observing, interviewing, interpreting from evidence), and literate actions (e.g., constructing and reconstructing texts). We now illustrate how a set of inquiry actions (observing, describing, interpreting, reflecting from multiple points of view), and a set of literate actions (notetaking and notemaking) accomplish the fifth-grade curriculum.

As seen previously, from the first day of school we teach observation defined as an ordinary practice. Besides observing overlap in each others' definitions of both community and the 3R's, during the first week of school students observe watermelons in order to solve a problem as mathematicians (for an analysis of this event, see Brilliant-Mills 1993). They also observe themselves as artists for painting self portraits. Thus, the action of observation becomes a common practice that crosses content areas, although the observational actions may look and feel different depending on the purpose for the observation—a purpose most often grounded in the actions particular to each discipline. Additionally, observation as a tool aids in the development of students' understanding of point of view, evidence, and interpretation. Understanding how evidence can be interpreted from different points of view becomes integral to Beth and Irene's goals for the development and understanding of empathy and tolerance and the construction of responsibility. Students in their classrooms learn to base their interpretations in evidence. This practice encourages critical thinking as students consider evidence, not just emotional reactions, to support their own point of view while, at the same time, considering others' perspectives.

The inquiry actions of observing, interpreting from evidence, and considering point of view occur over the year in and through a variety of literate actions. One of the literate actions used frequently is notetaking/notemaking, often called "double-entry journals" when used for other purposes. In this case, the left side is for notetaking—for recording what is observable. The right side, the notemaking side, is for interpretation of what has been observed and described. Students begin to understand observation and the gathering of data for different purposes across the disciplines early in the school year. They are introduced to notetaking as one of the actions of writers through "saturation observations" in a variety of school and community settings. The researchers then introduce the students to notetaking as an action of ethnographers. In this activity, the researchers encourage students to notice where they are physically positioned in relation to others, and to differentiate between their own descriptions and those of their peers. Students engage in these inquiry and literate actions in all of the disciplines at this time of the year in order to understand how these actions may differ depending on purpose and point of view.

It is critical for students to understand how evidence is interpreted from different points of view and for different purposes. It is at this point that teachers make explicit to students the relationship between notemaking and interpretation. Students observe and interpret a picture from the story of the "Three Little Pigs" from a particular character's point of view (e.g., that of the wolf, of the stick salesman) in the notetaking/notemaking format. Students then write or draw the history of this event using evidence from the witness whose perspective they took in the observation activity. They come to understand the actions of historians as well as the limitations of having only one point of view before drawing conclusions. In reflecting on the project, Jared shows his understanding of the actions of historians, the interpretation of data, and point of view:

> I learned that when you look at different points of view, they're all very different than each other. I think historians look at data the way it's shown and they interpret the data how they think it is. I also learned that there are different points of view even when you're looking at the same thing.

Students such as Jared continue to use the action of notetaking/notemaking as an inquiry tool for understanding ethnography (see Yeager, Floriani, and Green 1998), as well as in curricular areas such as literature and social science. Thus, notetaking/notemaking are literate actions which are made available for different purposes across the year. By mid-year, these literate actions and actions of inquiry become ordinary practices to classroom members. After winter break, this foundation of social actions (the 3 R's), literate actions (notetaking/notemaking), and inquiry actions (observing, describing, interpreting) are brought into a literature-based study of the constitutive nature of tolerance and intolerance.

The Tolerance Focus

The tolerance focus begins in January with a study of the Holocaust because it is an obvious example of atrocity in the twentieth century which continues to have an impact on our lives and decisions today.

The tolerance focus is carefully crafted and always evolving. This transformational character is due to the ongoing dialogue among Irene, Beth, and their colleagues. It is also affected by current events, local and global. Unfortunately, there are always new events which provide "teachable moments" within this focus of study. The cycle of activity[8] is interdisciplinary and literature-based and includes non-fiction. The tolerance focus also involves viewing videos, drawing and writing literature responses, and visiting museum displays.

We now describe events across the cycle of activity, where students critically assess actions of tolerance and intolerance from multiple points of view using the inquiry actions that have become ordinary practices within the classroom. The students learn from characters, plot, and setting in literature as well as from past and present interpretations of historical texts. They then use this information to examine the actions of individuals and groups in local and global contexts.

The context of the focus on the Holocaust is set with three introductory events. First, students read a picture book allegory of the Holocaust called *The Terrible Things* by Eve Bunting (1980). Teachers do not disclose in advance the historical context for the book, which shows the removal of specific groups by another strong, though invisible, group force. The setting is a forest and the characters are forest animals. The story allows students to speculate as to what the "terrible things" are that take away specific groups of animals from the forest and to think about why other groups of animals do not reach out to help. After listening to the story, students respond through pencil drawings that reflect their feelings and interpretations of the story. They then interpret their thoughts, questions, and concerns through a quickwrite format. The ensuing class discussion is grounded in what was happening in the allegory so that everyone has an opportunity to voice concerns about how the animals treated each other and to offer alternative endings or solutions to the problems the animals faced. In this way, students can consider a range of perspectives for comprehending the actions of characters in the story. This text becomes a referential point through-out the tolerance focus cycle of activity and after. Thus, inquiry actions (observing and interpreting events in the story) accom-plished through literate actions (drawing and writing responses in literature log) produce opportunities for students' refinement of what constitutes responsible social actions (providing concrete alternatives for dealing with the intolerant actions of the terrible things).

The second literate event in the tolerance focus is the reading and viewing of a photo essay representing Jewish children of the Holocaust, titled *The Children We Remember* (Abells 1983). Again, after a class reading of this text, students draw representations of their thoughts and feelings with black markers. Across the years students have drawn people crying, while others have expressed their feelings of anger through crossed out swastikas and Nazi soldiers being shot in retaliation. These visceral responses become important throughout the cycle of activity because we are constantly looking for ways to "touch" students and make the kind of intolerant actions addressed in texts real to them. This challenge is difficult in the face of the desensitization to pain and violence that is so prevalent among media references available to children today.

Next, students engage in actions of inquiry by interviewing family members for information about World War II and recording their points of view. After sharing and discussing the various points of view reflected in the family interviews, the students have an opportunity to learn about the broader historical context of the war by listening to a teacher or guest "lecture." Students take notes using the same literate action of notetaking/notemaking that has been used across the curriculum since the beginning of the school year. As a homework assignment, students read over the notetaking side of their "lecture" itself. At this point, students' interpretations often include dismay at how a person like Adolf Hitler could gain so much power over others. Many students also say they cannot understand how so many people could go along with Hitler and commit such intolerant acts against other groups of human beings. They also begin to see through this lecture that some people banded together to take responsible actions against intolerant acts (i.e., resistance movements, people who hid Jews, Catholics, Gypsies, and others).

In the following excerpt, Sergio, a student making the transition from Spanish reading and writing to English, describes (on the notemaking side) what he heard in the lecture. He writes in a shorthand, "listing" style that was recommended for taking lecture notes. On the notemaking side, Sergio draws on the literate and inquiry actions he has been developing during the first half of the year to interpret and draw conclusions from the information given. Thus, he uses the literate action of notetaking and the inquiry action of interpreting from evidence in order to declare the type of social actions he would take if he had been there.

Notetaking

There aren't that many jobs
they were worrying about WWII
and the countrys that want to change
how they live are Germany and Italy.

The Nazi party,
Adolf Hitler had the master race.

Notemaking

I think Adolf Hitler was a powerful man but at the same time he was a tyrant. I don't think he could have tooken over the world. There would have been a lot of people fight. If I were [there]

> Adolf Hitler wanted all races to be destroyed, except the Master race the German race.
>
> I would fought back. I wouldn't let him take over the world.
>
> Sergio (1995)

After working with the historical context, students share a second reading of *The Children We Remember* (Abells 1983). Since the students now have a broader understanding of social issues during World War II, they are able to demonstrate in their second quick-write a more profound understanding of why these events occurred. By this time students have also seen maps and tables of the locations of death camps and numbers of persons killed. They have also seen that some countries, such as Denmark, lost fewer Jews than other countries. Students begin to question why there is a difference.

Literature grounds the study of the Holocaust itself, although many other resources are used. In addition to the two picture books mentioned above, the central focus is a shared reading of a historical novel, *Number the Stars/¿Quién Cuenta las Estrellas?* (Lowry 1989a, 1989b). The novel is set in Denmark during World War II and relates one Danish family's efforts to help their Jewish neighbors escape to freedom in Sweden. Beth and Irene selected the text because it is appropriate for the ages and reading levels of fifth graders, is on the list of approved literature for California elementary schools, is available in Spanish and English, and has potential for expanding understandings of what the students have been talking about throughout the year (taking responsible social actions against actions of intolerance). During the shared reading of the novel, students also read excerpts from Anne Frank's *The Diary of a Young Girl* (1995), and *Zlata's Diary: A Child's Life in Sarajevo* (Filipovic 1994). Through the reading of personal narratives, students have an opportunity to compare past and present historical contexts and to increase understanding of the effects that actions of tolerance and intolerance can have on an individual child's life. This understanding can be further advanced when students have opportunities to make connections between excerpts from personal narratives and the novel they are studying in depth. Irene and Beth provide this opportunity by asking students to write diary entries from the four different main characters' points of view in *Number the Stars*. Through the juxtaposition of identities and through making entries in a diary, students try to imagine what it means to be walking in someone else's shoes.

The shared novel provides one perspective of the Holocaust, in essence a very positive one, in that people reach out to help others. The lecture that students received helps them begin to understand the competing political, economic, and philosophical circumstances that led to genocide. Students also view powerful videos, such as *Children Remember the Holocaust* (Gordon 1995), which does not have such a positive perspective. What touches many students in the video is the realization that they are viewing actual photographs and video footage of real people experiencing real cruelty and real intolerance. As mentioned earlier, the constant struggle for the teachers is making the past real and helping students believe that they can make a difference in addressing the intolerant actions which often are treated as normal, everyday, acceptable behavior in their lives.

Throughout the tolerance focus, students experience and respond to a wide variety of texts (lecture, literature, video, and picture books that extend their understanding of history as well as of current "ethnic cleansings"). Students also experience the personal stories of people around them, such as other teachers whose relatives were affected by intolerant actions of individuals, groups, and governments. One of the most significant events of the tolerance focus in 1995–96 was a visit from Judith Meisel, a Holocaust survivor, who brought the reality of her life into the students' lives. Thus, during the tolerance focus students are constantly asked to try to imagine being there, to reflect on what it feels like to be a victim of intolerance, to make intertextual connections between past and present actions of tolerance and intolerance by thinking in terms of "what if?" and "why?" In other words, there is a continuous focus on the implications of remaining silent and not taking action.

Significantly, the Holocaust is not taught in a vacuum, but is embedded in what has gone on before and what will come after the cycle of activity. The tolerance focus is grounded in practices of meaningful inquiry into the actions, interactions, and lack of intervention into the suffering of both real and fictionalized people. From the beginning of the academic year, students are provided with multiple opportunities for making meaningful connections within their own lives and for coming to understand their place within an ongoing and ever-changing history. As intertextual connections occur across the year, the students construct a referential system that helps them expand understanding of historical contexts, character actions, and mature responses to intolerance.

One location the teachers see for intertextual connections comes from the approved California social studies curriculum. Study of the Iroquois Confederacy is exemplary for teaching about nonviolent actions involved in the peacemaking process. For example, students explore the actions of the legendary Hiawatha and the Peacemaker. In this inquiry of actions toward peace, they make "peace belts" on which they superimpose the pine tree, the Iroquois symbol of peace, over conflicting points of view as experienced in their lives (two arguing parents, two gangs, two warring nations—whatever is important to them at the time). Throughout the study of

American Indians and other groups, students must make connections and investigate the actions of individuals living with conflict. Concurrently, students have opportunities to observe, describe, and interpret parallel actions of tolerance and intolerance toward individuals living during World War II (e.g., Holocaust victims or Japanese Americans in U.S. internment camps). In this way, intertextual connections are made available through the tolerance focus in the social studies curriculum.

Below is an excerpt from a student essay which demonstrates how he made intertextual links across the social science curriculum and tied these to inquiry practices that had become familiar within his classroom community:

> When we do our projects, like our newest one on the colonies, we don't just go too a book and write a report. We get information from a lot of different places and we use skills from other projects. . . . We always have to use evidence and we have to know the answer to the Tower's famous questions: So what? (What does it mean?), How do you know?, and Why? . . . All through our projects, we have to look at these points of view. When we did the colonies, we saw who was missing from some things, like Native Americans. Also when we share a book in class, we write letters and diaries from characters' points of view. When you're in the Tower, you have to look at different points of view. (Chris 1994)

Chris describes his classroom as one where students make meanings of a range of topics across disciplines through inquiry and literate actions and by considering different points of view. During the activity cycle focusing on tolerance, students brought practices of literate and inquiry actions into a study of the "whys" of acts of intolerance and genocide across time and in different settings. Students also examined and reflected upon responsible and tolerant responses. Thus, the nature of both intolerant and tolerant acts becomes more visible to students, who are able to make meaning of these acts through particular literate (notetaking/notemaking, making intertextual connections) and inquiry practices (observing, describing, interpreting from evidence, taking different "angles of vision"). Students, like Chris, then begin a process of acting upon these understandings through both individual and collective social action steps.

Up to this point, students have worked with some sights, sounds, words, and pictures that are evidence of humankind's capacity and potential for cruelty. At the same time, they have also uncovered individuals and movements that demonstrate human aptitude for strength, resistance, resilience, and care for others. Since some children begin to feel overwhelmed by all they have seen and heard, it becomes important to focus more explicitly on social actions for change. As we have demonstrated, in the beginning of the school year the fifth graders defined a particular set of social actions in terms of rights, respect, and responsibility within the classroom community. Toward the end of the tolerance cycle of activity, students broaden those understandings by addressing issues within their school, neighborhood, and world communities. Thus, students move into the action phase of the tolerance cycle by identifying particular social issues within the various communities that influence their lives.

Expanding the Meaning of the 3 R's: Responsibility to Act

Students begin the process of focusing upon tolerant and intolerant actions through four events. First, they draw upon their daily lives to develop a list of tolerant actions (e.g., talking through conflicts, helping classmates) and intolerant actions (e.g., name calling, fighting), which they later prioritize and graph according to degree of positive or negative impact. This literate action of graphing results in an effective visual display that develops deeper understandings of responsibility.

The second event is a field trip to the Museum of Tolerance in Los Angeles, California.[9] The museum comprises several parts, two of the largest being the Holocaust Museum and the Tolerance Center. The latter is an interactive center where visitors explore issues of stereotyping, prejudice, name calling, tolerance, and intolerance. Here, visitors can also view a brief but powerful movie on genocide. The museum visit is an overpowering experience that brings everything home. The key question asked in graphics throughout the museum is "Who is responsible?" We start asking that question ourselves early in the year at school, and it makes an impact on the children when they visit the museum. It becomes an important reference point.

Following this trip, students reflect on what they have seen and heard, personally and in terms of their own lives and community, as well as on what they have learned about tolerance and responsibility throughout the year. Their "tolerance essays" become a mechanism for moving students to an action focus, as demonstrated in this student essay:

> I think that it is all of our responsibility for what happened. The people who didn't speak up are also very responsible for what happened, because everything that people do, or what you do, in the past can affect what is happening today (right now) or in the future.

Irene and Beth seek the construction of responsibility alongside the construction of empathy. Oscar's essay reflects empathy while naming ways to deal with what has been learned (translated from Spanish):

Here in the Museum, we have engraved for us the bad things we do and this is always going to remind us, what it is to suffer. We have to change. We have to do tolerant things. It's our responsibility to change with respect to other people, because if we don't change, we can commit the same mistake as the Nazis and some day we will have to remember. That's why we will change (Oscar 1996).

Students then move to the fourth event, constructing a new definition of responsibility. Classes brainstorm and negotiate actions which reflect actions of community and personal responsibility. In the 1996 class, they were defined as:

1. Speaking up	Decir algo—Hablar en público
2. Having respect	Tener respeto
3. Taking action	Hacer algo—Tomar acción
4. Walking the talk	Siguiendo con lo que dice
5. Walking in someone else's shoes	Caminar en los zapatos de otra persona

Whereas students' early perceptions of responsibility centered on individual actions to be successful in the classroom, this list reflects how students' understandings broadened to include responsibility to act in order to maintain a just, respectful community. The important challenge is living up to the expanded definition.

Through events, students begin to take up individual and collective actions. The first opportunity for action involves the construction of a wall/mural outside of the school office. The inspiration for constructing the wall in the main entrance of the school community comes from the Wall of Remembrance in the United States Holocaust Memorial Museum in Washington, D.C. The wall is made up of individual inscriptions, each one sending a message from one child (or adult) to other children and adults. The messages convey what the sender considers important to remember and what the sender desires for the world.

Another opportunity for action occurs when each child is asked to draw a picture showing himself or herself taking a responsible action within the context of everyday life (usually at school). This action must be something that the student believes is realistically possible. Each student makes a public affirmation of action beginning with a positive "I will" statement. In this way, students take up the literate action of drawing in order to make a public statement of commitment toward responsible social action.

Finally, the students begin a process that involves them in collectively taking responsible action within the local community, action that reflects their understanding of tolerance and intolerance. Through a brainstorming process that involves parent interviews, individual writing, and small and large group conversations, students begin to define their concerns about their neighborhood and local community. Collectively, the class prioritizes problems to address. Each year, the students take a different set of actions.

In 1994–95, the issues of neighborhood safety and the pressure to join gangs were discussed throughout the year. Since these issues were very much a part of their lives, the students brainstormed actions that could be taken to spread the message of tolerance, respect for differences, and nonviolence toward others in the community. Students took action by writing pen pal letters to a school located in a so-called "rival territory"—the East Side. These individual letters attempted to explain a point of view regarding tolerance and respect for difference that reflected understandings from the tolerance cycle of activity. Collectively, the students wrote an open letter in Spanish and English that was sent to local newspapers, public agencies, local middle schools, and high schools. The letter expressed their desire for nonviolence and peace between Eastsiders and Westsiders. For the students this was a risky undertaking, for they feared that older students, including their siblings, would perceive that they had somehow "sold out." Thus, this letter involved both actions of commitment and actions of perceived risk taking. A nice turn of events occurred when a teacher in a nearby district (another "rival" area) shared the letter in the newspaper with her fifth-grade students. These students wrote to McKinley's fifth graders, expressing their admiration of their public act and asking for advice and support. Their responses validated the actions taken personally and collectively by fifth-grade students at McKinley.

The following year, four fifth-grade classes participated in taking up community actions. Because students were unable to narrow down the number of actions they wanted to take, four action committees emerged, composed of children from each fifth-grade class. These representatives planned the following actions, in which all students participated: (1) an open letter to the public about the need for positive action that was published in three newspapers, two English and one Spanish, (2) a campaign through skits to educate younger McKinley students about tolerant and intolerant actions, (3) a neighborhood campaign to distribute literature against drunk driving, and (4) a neighborhood cleanup held on the opening day of a new community park. Many of these actions encouraged participation from the larger community: local high school students responded to the open letter, and twelve community members joined in the neighborhood cleanup. Although positive action in the larger community often goes unsung, these students had the opportunity to learn that the actions of responsible human beings in a community can make a difference. Furthermore, these experiences provided a foundation for students to analyze, reflect, and broaden understandings regarding the actions necessary to realize the 3 R's (rights, respect, and responsibility) in the many contexts which influence their lives.

The Journey Continues

The journey that we have represented shows how students make the 3 R's meaningful by taking up a set of particular actions: literate actions, inquiry actions, and social actions. This theory of action offers teachers an approach to teaching that is multidimensional (integrating social and academic actions) and multidisciplinary (integrating concepts across content areas). This framework for action allows teachers and students to expand the selected school curricula in order to fit the needs of the local classroom community that is interested in engaging in a critical literacy as a form of ethical address (Giroux 1993). As the year advances, members learn to use literate actions (e.g., notetaking and notemaking, writing and drawing responses to literature) to discover and problematize a wide range of disciplinary knowledge. As these literate and inquiry actions become familiar in the fifth-grade classroom, students are directed into real-world situations that have an impact on their lives.

It is this "situatedness" that provides the context for taking up individual and/or collective social action. This evolving process has been referred to as the development of a critical social consciousness (Freire 1970, 1978), because students name, reflect critically, and act on their world (Wink 1997). The process of constructing responsibility can be seen as analogous with a definition of critical pedagogy, one that "challenges teachers and students to empower themselves for social change, to advance democracy and equality as they advance their literacy and knowledge" (Shor 1993, 25).

This essay demonstrates how literate actions and inquiry actions can create conditions for establishing critical consciousness. It suggests that learning to take tolerant and responsible actions requires the ability to observe, describe, pose questions, analyze, and interpret. Above all, this transformative process involves students moving from writing insightful literate responses to taking responsible actions. Thus, the dialogue between members of the classroom community and the wider community in which members live infuses a humanizing pedagogy (Bartolomé 1996) where actions for social justice become possible. The transformative power of this type of pedagogy rests on an understanding that all students are treated as knowers and active participants in learning for improvement of self and the world in which all selves live (Shor 1992).

For teachers like Beth and Irene who consciously use historical incidences of tolerance, intolerance, and genocide to help students produce work that demonstrates depth of feeling and imaginative visions of a more just world, the struggle is an enduring journey. This living, dynamic, and evolving curriculum is constantly constructed and revised to help students learn what it means to be a responsible member of a global community. For students in these classrooms, the theory of action realized in fifth grade becomes a point of departure rather than a destination.

Acknowledgments

The tolerance focus has evolved over the years so that it includes all fifth grades at McKinley School. We wish to acknowledge and extend our appreciation to our colleague Phoebe Hirsch-Dubin for her contributions to the Tolerance Project as a member of the fifth-grade team. We also want to thank María Rey and Nancy Morris for sharing in this effort during their year as fifth-grade teachers. Special thanks go to Judith Green and Carol Dixon, and members of the Santa Barbara Classroom Discourse Group for ongoing support. Additionally, we are grateful to Jules Zimmerman, Bob Ream, and contributors from the wider community toward the UCSB Tolerance Project. Finally, we thank several granting agencies who provided financial support for the study: The California Writing Project and South Coast Writing Projects (SCWriP), The American Educational Research Association Minority Program, the Inter-University Program for Latino Research and the Social Science Research Council, the University of California Institute for Mexico and the United States, and the Graduate Research Mentorship Program at UCSB.

Notes

1. Authorship of this essay reflects the equal contribution of all named authors. Beth Yeager and Irene Pattenaude are fifth-grade teachers. María Fránquiz and Louise Jennings were researchers in Beth and Irene's classrooms respectively. All four authors are members of the Santa Barbara Classroom Discourse Group, a group of teachers, administrators, doctoral students, and university faculty engaged in collaborative ethnographic studies of life in K–12 writing process classrooms. The authors are also fellows of the South Coast Writing Project and have presented from the data set represented in this essay at national conferences, including NCTE, AERA, and NABE.

2. Students whose voices have been included in this chapter assisted in writing this project into being. Permission has been obtained to use their real names as authors of their own work as cited in the chapter: Sergio Dueñas, Veronica Galvan, Jared Ingling, Oscar Morales, Chris Nordin, and Karen Ramirez.

3. Inquiry learning has been defined as an approach in which students are guided in their own learning in a stimulating environment that requires them to become examiners, questioning texts in and outside the classroom, and questioning the actions between each other as well as by themselves (see Farris 1997).

4. The authors acknowledge that there have been many holocausts in history which have resulted in the genocide of ethnic and indigenous groups. The capitalization of Holocaust in reference to the horrors inflicted during the Nazi regime indicates that the systematic extermination of European Jews and other groups during World War II was unique in the sense of incorporating methods of slaughter unseen in other genocides (i.e., the death camps). It does not indicate that any one group's victimization is qualitatively any more or less significant than another group's experience of inhumanity.

5. The construct of intertextuality has been discussed by Bloome and Egan-Robertson (1993) and Bloome and Bailey (1992) to mean that people propose intertextual links, and in interaction with each other they recognize, acknowledge, and assign social significance to these intertextual links. Over time, these intertextual processes establish particular ways of being a member of a classroom and contribute to establishing particular ways of engaging in literate action in the classroom (e.g., particular ways of problem solving, learning, and writing). These intertextual connections contribute to a referential system which is a resource for teacher and students across the year (Santa Barbara Classroom Discourse Group 1992b).

6. Informed consent from students, parents, teachers, and administrators was obtained for the three years of data represented in this essay.

7. The faculty members of this school have indicated that they value and use collaborative learning in a variety of ways. Additionally, the principal has arranged for conflict resolution to be introduced in all classes. A peer mediation system has been implemented on the playground as well.

8. A cycle of activity (Green and Meyer 1991) is composed of all events that were constructed by members of the classroom as they sought to accomplish a particular aspect of the academic curriculum. In this case, the fifth-grade teachers and students modified activities planned to meet the State of California Framework in both language arts and social studies.

9. One of the early action steps students take during the year is to earn money for this trip through a public dinner. The purpose of this month-long mathematical investigation is to understand how to coordinate estimating, purchasing, and organizing the dinner in order to make sufficient profit for classroom members to pay for transportation expenses to the Museum of Tolerance.

Works Cited   Abells, Chana B. 1983. *The Children We Remember.* New York: Greenwillow Books.

Aronwitz, Stanley, and Henry A. Giroux. 1985. *Education Under Seige: The Conservative, Liberal, and Radical Debate over Schooling.* South Hadley, MA: Bergin & Garvey.

Bartolomé, Lilia I. 1996. "Beyond the Methods Fetish: Toward a Humanizing Pedagogy." *Harvard Educational Review Reprint Series* 27: 229–52.

Bloome, David, and Frances Bailey. 1992. "Studying Language and Literacy through Events: Particularity and Intertextuality." In *Multidisciplinary Perspectives on Literacy Research,* edited by Richard Beach, Judith L. Green, Michael Kamil, and Timothy Shanahan, 181–210. Urbana, IL: National Council of Teachers for English.

Bloome, David, and Ann Egan-Robertson. 1993. "The Social Construction of Intertextuality in Classroom Reading and Writing Lessons." *Reading Research Quarterly* 28(4): 304–33.

Brilliant-Mills, Heidi. 1993. "Becoming a Mathematician: Building a Situated Definition of Mathematics." *Linguistics and Education* 5(3-4): 301–34.

Bunting, Eve. 1980. *The Terrible Things.* New York: Harper & Row.

Collins, Elaine, and Judith L. Green. 1992. "Learning in Classroom Settings: Making or Breaking a Culture." In *Redefining Student Learning: Roots of Educational Change,* edited by Hermine H. Marshall, 59–86. Norwood, NJ: Ablex.

Cook-Gumperz, Jenny. 1986. *The Social Construction of Literacy.* Cambridge, MA: Cambridge University Press.

Durán, Luisa. 1994. "Toward a Better Understanding of Code Switching and Interlanguage in Bilinguality: Implications for Bilingual Instruction." *The Journal of Educational Issues of Language Majority Students* 14: 69–88.

Farris, Pamela J. 1997. *Language Arts: Process, Product and Assessment,* 2nd ed. Iowa: Times Mirror Higher Education Group, Inc.

Fernie, David, Bronwyn Davies, Rebecca Kantor, and Paula McMurry. 1993. "Becoming a Person: Creating Integrated Gender, Peer and Student Positionings in a Preschool Classroom." *International Journal of Qualitative Research in Education* 6 (2): 95-110.

Filipovic, Zlata. 1994. *Zlata's Diary: A Child's Life in Sarajevo.* Translated with notes by Christina Pribicevic-Zoric. New York: Viking.

Frank, Anne. 1995. *The Diary of a Young Girl: The Definitive Edition.* Edited by Otto H. Frank and Mirjam Pressler. Translated by Susan Massotty. New York: Doubleday.

Fránquiz, María E. 1995. *Transformations in Bilingual Classrooms: Understanding Opportunity to Learn within the Change Process.* Ph.D. diss., University of California, Santa Barbara.

Freire, Paulo. 1970. *Pedagogy of the Oppressed.* Translated by Myra Bergman Ramos. New York: Seabury Press.

———. 1978. *Education for Critical Consciousness.* New York: Seabury Press.

Giroux, Henry. 1993. "Literacy and The Politics of Difference." In *Critical Literacy: Politics, Praxis, and the Postmodern,* edited by Colin Lankshear and Peter L. McLaren, 367–78. New York: State University of New York Press.

Giroux, Henry, and David Purpel. 1983. *The Hidden Curriculum and Moral Education: Deception or Discovery?* Berkeley, CA: McCutchan.

Glover, Mary Kenner. 1986. *A Community Of Learners: An Insider's View of Whole Language.* Tempe, AZ: Awakening Seed Press.

Gordon, Mark. 1995. *Children Remember the Holocaust.* Produced by Frank Doelger and Howard Meltzer. CBS Schoolbreak Special.

Green, Judith L., and Lois A. Meyer. 1991. "The Embeddedness of Reading in Classroom Life: Reading as a Situated Process." In *Towards a Critical Sociology of Reading Pedagogy,* edited by Carolyn Baker and Allan Luke, 141–46. Philadelphia, PA: John Benjamins.

Jennings, Louise. 1996. *Multiple Contexts for Learning Social Justice: An Ethnographic and Sociolinguistic Study of a Fifth Grade Bilingual Class.* Ph.D. diss., University of California, Santa Barbara.

Ladson-Billings, Gloria. 1995. "Toward a Theory of Cultural Relevant Pedagogy." *American Educational Research Journal* 32(3): 465–91.

LeVesque, J., and T. Prosser. 1996. "Service Learning Connection." *Journal of Teacher Education* 47(5): 325–34.

Lin, Lichu. 1993. "Language of and in the Classroom: Constructing the Patterns of Social Life." *Linguistics and Education* 5(3-4): 367–409.

Lowry, Lois. 1989a. *Number the Stars.* Boston: Houghton Mifflin Co.

———. 1989b. *¿Quien Cuenta las Estrellas?* Translated by Juan Lucke. Boston: Houghton Mufflin Co.

Reyes, María de la Luz. 1992. "Challenging Venerable Assumptions: Literacy Instruction for Linguistically Different Students." *Harvard Educational Review* 62(4): 427–46.

Rutherford, James, and Andrew Ahlgren. 1990. *Science for All Americans.* New York: Oxford University Press.

Santa Barbara Classroom Discourse Group (Green, Dixon, Lin, Floriani, and Bailey). 1992a. "Constructing Literacy in Classrooms: Literate Action as Social Accomplishment." In *Redefining Student Learning: Roots of Educational Change,* edited by Hermine H. Marshall, 119–50. Norwood, NJ: Ablex.

Santa Barbara Classroom Discourse Group (Dixon, de la Cruz, Green, Lin, and Brandts). 1992b. "Do You See What I See? The Referential and Intertextual Nature of Classroom Life." *Journal of Classroom Interaction* 27(2): 29–36.

Saxe, Geoffrey B. 1988. "Candy Selling and Math Learning." *Educational Researcher* 17(6): 14–21.

Shor, Ira. 1992. *Empowering Education: Critical Teaching for Social Change.* University of Chicago Press.

———. 1993. "Education Is Politics: Paulo Friere's Critical Pedagogy." In *Paulo Freire: A Critical Encounter,* edited by Peter McLaren and Peter Leonard, 25–35. New York: Routledge.

Wink, Joan. 1997. *Critical Pedagogy: Notes from the Real World.* New York: Longman.

Yeager, Beth, Ana Florriani, and Judith L. Green. (1998). "Learning to See Learning in the Classroom: Developing an Ethnographic Perspective." In *Students as Researchers of Culture and Community in Their Own Community,* edited by Ann Egan-Robertson and David Bloome, 115–39. Cresskill, NJ: Hampton Press.

12 Classroom Conversations: Young Children Discuss Fairness and Justice, Intolerance and Prejudice

Debbie Miller
Denver Public Schools

Anne K. Goudvis
Public Education and Business Coalition, Denver, Colorado

It is early January, and the snow falls silently outside the old wooden windows of the classroom. Five first graders sit expectantly around a cloth-covered table. A scented candle burns, pretzels await small hands in a china bowl. Writers' notebooks and individual copies of *Oliver Button Is a Sissy* (De Paola 1983) are open, yellow Post-it notes adorn the pages. Cathy, Jamal, Shawanda, Brandon, and Sarah are about the begin their first book club.

Cathy focuses the group with a question. "Well, guys, don't you think it's time to talk about the book?" Heads nod. Jamal looks at Cathy, opens his book to a page marked with a Post-it, and says, "Look here, I don't really understand why those bullies made so much fun of Oliver Button. Just because he likes to dance. It's mean and he was just doing what made him happy."

"Well, Jamal," says Sarah, "I'm thinking they don't understand that boys can be dancers. They probably think that only girls dance like that, you know?"

"Maybe," answers Jamal, "but they don't have to be so mean about it. It makes me think about how I feel when kids make fun of me for being so little. You should just ignore it."

"Oh, wait," says Alicia as she runs to get a copy of *William's Doll* (Zolotow 1972). She quickly finds the page she's looking for, smiles, and addresses the group. "You guys! Remember on this page in *William's Doll* when his father wanted him to have a basketball but not a doll, and his brother said 'Creepy' and the boy next door said 'Sissy, sissy'? It's the same thing. The bullies in *Oliver Button* and those guys in *William's Doll* just don't get it's okay for girls to do boy things and boys to do girl things."

"Yeah," says Jamal, "why are there boy things and girls things anyway? What's the difference?"

"Yeah," Brandon adds. "I think this is really important, we should tell someone."

"I'll write a note to Debbie [the teacher] at writing time," offers Shawanda.

These children are six years old, and as they meet together, they feel free to share their feelings, insights, and opinions about books. After four months of intensive instruction in thinking about and responding to books read aloud to them, they are able to make connections between texts, relate stories to their own personal lives, and carry on a discussion of issues important to children their age. The children in this integrated, south Denver classroom view characters like William and Oliver Button almost as if they were real people, living within their circle of friends. Using their imaginations, these young children created their own interpretations of characters' experiences and empathized with their predicaments. Debbie Miller reflects:

> The stories that truly engaged children were those that did not view childhood as idyllic and problem-free. The children connected with books that addressed serious topics, including unfairness, prejudice and loneliness, because they mirrored their own experiences and struggles. I wanted the literature we read together to challenge their ideas and stereotypes, and to provide a vehicle for discussing their own lives within a climate of tolerance and mutual respect.

A year and a half later, these same children, still together in second grade, listen with their classmates as Debbie reads *Promise of a New Spring* (Klein 1984), a book about the Holocaust. As participants in many literary conversations during their first- and second-grade years, these children moved from discussing issues close to their own lives to considering the experiences, predicaments, and emotions of people living in vastly different times and places. Creating a context for children's understanding by building their background knowledge of historical events and times enabled the children to grapple with the stories and personal narratives of people who had experienced discrimination and injustice.

> *Debbie:* The book we're going to read today, *Promise of a New Spring,* might remind you a little of *The Terrible Things* (Bunting 1989). Remember it was an allegory and the author told the story

through the animals. Listen carefully and I think you'll be able to make some connections to other books we've read. [Reading] "Those who suffered the most were the Jewish people. The Nazis took jobs away from the Jews and kept Jewish children from going to school. The Nazis forced the Jews to wear yellow badges. The Nazis decided to kill every Jew—young and old together. And to destroy every memory of the Jewish people, too." Are there any other people this has happened to?

Ellen: Anne Frank—in the book her family had to go into hiding and one day they were taken away.

Cathy: Other people were suffering, like in *Number the Stars* [Lowry 1989]. Then the Jewish family had to escape in the boat.

Leroy: In World War II there were survivors of the whole thing, there were some people who escaped from being under the Nazis.

Alicia: Where are the Nazis coming from?

Debbie: Remember how one person got to decide what's good and not good. Hitler wanted people to do what he thought was right, he wanted to eliminate the people who didn't agree with him.

Jamal: That's wrong. I don't know why the Jewish people didn't just take off their stars.

Jonathan: Maybe then they wouldn't have to be killed.

Leroy: How come? How come Hitler got rid of them?

Jamal: How did these wars start, anyway?

Alicia: It just isn't right to kill people. You don't have to be like the Nazis.

Jamal: Just because the Jewish people were different, everyone doesn't always act the same.

Lorie: And the German people aren't all the same, everybody's different.

Debbie: And we're all different in here.

Several aspects of these second graders' responses illustrate that they have learned to question and interpret literature and express their opinions by taking a moral stand. The children expressed outrage at the killings, wondering why Jews were killed ("How come Hitler got rid of them?"). Jamal questioned whether taking off their stars might have prevented the worst from happening. Alicia stated that killing is wrong. Questions such as "How did these wars start anyway?" illustrate that the children are engaged in "focused information seeking" (Busching and Slesinger 1995), trying to fill in gaps in their understanding of complex and disturbing historical events. As the children struggled to understand the plight of Jews during World War II, this was not the first time they had encountered themes of powerful people doing harm to others, or how prejudice and intolerance brought suffering to large numbers of people. While children would be expected to become engaged with stories such as *Oliver Button Is a Sissy* (De Paola 1983) or *Amazing Grace* (Hoffman 1991), confronting the grave circumstances in *Promise of a New Spring* (Klein 1984) is a different matter. Over a two-year period the children moved from discussing issues within their sphere of understanding, such as teasing or feeling different, to encountering issues of intolerance, prejudice, and injustice, first during the time of slavery in their own country, and later, within the context of World War II and the Holocaust. Although Debbie did not set out to teach young children about slavery, war, and genocide, these children's avid interest in and their ability to think critically about historical narratives and stories of people facing adversity and suffering because of their identity developed and changed over time. Indeed, it was the children's searching questions about the stories and historical vignettes of courageous people who did their best to stand up to injustice that fueled the class's two-year study of significant human issues through literature.

This essay describes the teaching and learning that occurred over a two-year period as an experienced teacher, beginning with her entering group of first graders and continuing through these children's second-grade year, brought thoughtful, compelling literature into her inner-city classroom. Together, the teacher (Debbie Miller) and a staff developer-researcher (Anne Goudvis) documented and reflected upon young children's developing capacity to interpret and understand literature. Debbie wanted her first graders to learn to read, but also to become thoughtful, critical, independent readers. She wanted to create a context for learning in which each child could develop his or her own voice, opinions, and ideas while at the same time honoring the thoughts, feelings, and perspectives of peers. With a racially and economically diverse classroom, Debbie knew it was imperative to build a community with twenty-five children who came from very different backgrounds:

> My classroom was wonderfully diverse, about half were middle-class neighborhood children. The other half were bussed in from one of Denver's most impoverished minority neighborhoods. I knew that establishing a sense of community where children value and respect each other as fellow learners and teachers was critical to the success of any instruction. Creating common ground was essential, especially in a classroom where children were encouraged to honestly share their thinking and respond to one another.

In Debbie's classroom were children who had never experienced racial prejudice and those who lived with racial tension, feeling alienated from the mainstream culture. The child who stopped at Dairy Queen every day after school and the child who lived in fear of drive-by shootings needed to learn to understand each other. Debbie knew that genuine compassion and respect for one another would have to develop over time. Only gradually could the children share their personal stories. A heavy-handed approach to addressing the differences in children's family circumstances would surely backfire. Responding to and discussing literature could help bridge the gap between children's vastly different experiences while at the same time building the common ground necessary to establishing a classroom community. With their new classmates, the children experienced characters who were being teased for apparent differences, or encountered the prejudices that many children face with respect to race and gender. As their ability to relate the texts to their own personal struggles and experiences grew, the characters in the stories became the focus for discussing serious issues, such as feeling left out or being teased or bullied—behaviors that surfaced in the normal course of classroom life. Debbie hoped that providing children the opportunity to learn about the world through the eyes of different characters would provide students with opportunities to discuss their own concerns, questions, and struggles with their classmates. Because Debbie wanted to encourage children's own powers of understanding and interpretation, she steered clear of discussions that moralized or assumed one correct interpretation of a story. Building upon her knowledge of the reading comprehension research (Pearson 1985) and an understanding of young children gained from fifteen years of teaching first grade, Debbie interwove literature discussions about the books she read aloud to the children with explicit instruction in reading comprehension strategies. Explicit instruction would enable children to think more carefully about their reading (Fielding and Pearson 1994). They would learn to draw their own conclusions from and develop an analytical stance toward literature. Without ways to teach the children to access, analyze, and think independently about what they were reading, Debbie knew she risked having the children mimic her ideas or respond on a superficial level to important issues.

Research in reading comprehension instruction indicates that there are several strategies central to an ability to think critically about texts (Pearson 1985). Debbie considered how best to teach the four strategies she felt were most appropriate for young readers. These included relating texts to their own experiences and background knowledge (accessing and using schema), making inferences, asking questions, and determining important ideas and themes in a text. If children could relate texts to their own knowledge and experience, they might be better able to understand the perspectives of different characters, situations, or problems in the stories they read. Learning to draw inferences would enable children to make predictions about, interpret, and think critically about characters' actions and story events. Asking questions could help children clarify what was going on in a story and lead them to focus on central issues and themes. Through questioning, children could learn to articulate what they were confused about and pose questions that would eventually result in a clearer understanding of the text. Finally, determining and focusing on central ideas and themes would enable children to develop their own conceptions of what was meaningful and important in their reading.

By demonstrating her own use of these strategies though modeling and thinking aloud, Debbie introduced each of these strategies to the children during their first-grade year. At the beginning of the year, Debbie modeled her own thinking for the children. She thought aloud about each book as she read it—asking questions, drawing inferences, and underscoring important ideas and central issues. The children observed Debbie as she asked questions and made connections between books and her own life. They soon began to chime in with their own thoughts, questions, and feelings. Their responses to stories were most often oral, but as the children became more confident readers and writers, they produced written and artistic responses. Debbie's initial questions illustrated that there were no clear guidelines for teaching reading comprehension strategies to six-year-olds:

> I was intrigued with the implications of trying to explicitly teach reading comprehension strategies, particularly for very young readers. All the research on reading comprehension instruction was based on studies with upper elementary or older children. Could primary-aged children engage in this kind of thinking? What would instruction in reading comprehension strategies look like in my classroom? Was it inappropriate to ask six- or seven-year-olds to ask questions about the text as they read, or to monitor their understanding of what they were reading? Weren't these strategies too sophisticated for children who were just learning to read?

This essay presents evidence of the ways in which children's developing knowledge of the reading comprehension strategies facilitated their literary understanding of stories and texts. Transcripts of children's discussions during read-aloud sessions, small-group discussions, and book club meetings, as well as a variety of children's written responses, were collected over the two-year period. Linking the children's oral and written responses with the teacher's lessons and reflections illustrates how and why the children became intensely interested in issues of fairness and justice, prejudice, and intolerance.

First Grade— Personal Experiences and Connections

At the beginning of the school year, Debbie selected literature to read aloud and discuss with the children that was within their own experience. Although she was in uncharted territory with respect to teaching reading comprehension strategies to children who were just learning to read, she believed that her classroom of children would thrive on thought-provoking literature. One of the original questions in Debbie's journal, "What would reading comprehension instruction look and sound like in my classroom, with my children?", guided her decision to introduce the strategies by talking about her own learning:

> At the beginning of the year, I teach the children about schema. I always begin by naming the strategy and telling the children why it's important. I tell them we can think about schema as what we already know or have experienced and that we can connect this knowledge and experience to our reading. I model the strategy with a text that I clearly connect to—such as *The Two of Them* (Aliki 1987). As I read, I stop and think out loud about how the book we're reading connects to my own life. I talk about my own background and experiences in relation to specific things that happen in the text.

To model her own use of a strategy, Debbie first asked the children to watch carefully as she alternately read the book out loud and stopped to share her thinking about it. She continued to share her own thoughts and questions as she moved into the "guided practice" phase of her instruction (Fielding and Pearson 1994). At this instructional point, the children offered their own thoughts, making connections between the characters and events in the book and their own lives. Debbie continued to guide, or scaffold, the children's thoughts to ensure they understood how to link their experiences with the text:

> The children begin to contribute to the discussion as they make connections to their own lives and experiences. We work hard on framing their responses. They are encouraged to say, "When I read these words," or "When I saw this picture . . ." to link the text with their thinking.

As children tried out the strategies during independent reading time, Debbie devised ways to help children keep track of their thinking and remember what they wanted to contribute to the share session. With the children's help, she developed a code to identify when and where they used their schema during reading. They would put a Post-it with an "R" next to the place where the text reminded them of their own life or experiences, or a "?" to mark the place where they asked a question. As the children added other strategies to their repertoire, Debbie wrote a brief definition of each strategy on a big chart. This was a constant reminder of their collective thinking and guided children as they worked independently.

Debbie's journal illustrates how the group learned to connect literature to their own experiences:

> We experienced what it was like to feel teased when Oliver Button wanted to learn to dance, or sensed the prejudice Grace felt when told by other children she couldn't be Peter Pan because she was a girl and she was black. As we shared our own experiences with similar situations and feelings, we learned the language of readers and writers, classmates and friends.

Despite children's enthusiastic responses to the read-aloud discussions, by October Debbie wondered if the children were really beginning to think independently about the books they were reading. She had a nagging concern that they were simply mimicking her thoughts and comments, rather than bringing in their own ideas and interpretations. Did they ask meaningful questions of the text and each other? Could they focus on important ideas and information, rather than trivial incidents and details? Debbie wanted to see if the children were able to use the comprehension strategies she had demonstrated on a daily basis to construct meaning and think originally, either on their own or with the support of their peers. Transcripts of the children's small-group conversations were examined to see if explicit reading comprehension instruction was indeed helping the children to draw inferences, ask questions, and determine important ideas and themes in the stories they were reading. A small-group discussion of *Oliver Button Is a Sissy* (De Paola 1983) illustrates how the children used their growing knowledge of these strategies in conversations about books:

> *Lorie:* When those boys say "Oliver Button is a sissy!", I think that's wrong. I think Oliver Button is sad. What do you think, Ellen?
>
> *Ellen:* I think he's sad and maybe mad.
>
> *Lorie:* They should have said "Oliver Button is a hero." They shouldn't write that he's a sissy.
>
> *Joshua:* And Oliver Button should say, "Please don't call me names."

The children, who were by this time familiar with the story, strongly identified with Oliver's feelings. They were able to view the situation from Oliver's perspective and explain how they might feel in similar circumstances. The children appear to be "taking part" in the story, going so far as to rewrite the characters' words, saying, "They should have said 'Oliver Button is a hero'."

> *Ellen:* Maybe what happened to Oliver Button happened to him when he was a little boy. If Oliver played with me and Anna (another child in the class), we wouldn't call him a sissy.

Lorie: I wonder what will happen to him the next day at school? What do you think, Ben?

Ben: I think those boys—the bullies—might be his friends.

Jonathan: But I still wonder why they called him a sissy?

The children drew inferences about what might have happened to Oliver "the next day"—inferences that took them beyond the actual ending of the story. They also asked each other questions and solicited others' opinions, directing the conversation and keeping it going. The child who imagined herself and her friend in the story described how they would accept Oliver as a playmate ("If Oliver played with me and Ann, we wouldn't call him a sissy."). Likewise, Joshua wanted to be there to offer advice to Oliver about what to say to the bullies. The children's understanding of how to read strategically, in particular, the ability to draw inferences and ask questions, enabled them to take a critical stance with respect to familiar stories. They developed individual responses to stories and moved beyond previous discussions. Using the familiar and well-loved texts as an anchor, the children built up enough confidence in their own opinions to see themselves as readers who could think independently about books.

As the children gained more experience with additional strategies and the book club format, they would sometimes articulate specific strategies as they used these during the course of discussions. Sarah reread *The Two of Them* (Aliki 1987) with her book club, a story about a child and grandfather that portrays their close, loving relationship which eventually ends with the grandfather's death. As Sarah spoke, she announced her strategy of choice:

Sarah: I would like to synthesize: This is a love story. They loved each other always. They did things for each other.

Ellen: Once upon a time, there lived a little old man and his granddaughter. He sang her songs and told her stories. She liked that and they loved each other for always. They always remembered each other for always.

Sarah: Good synthesis, Ellen.

The transcripts provided evidence that the children had internalized the reading comprehension strategies. They asked questions involving literary imagination (Busching and Slesinger 1995) when they wondered about what would happen to Oliver "the next day at school." They used their schema to connect the childhood predicaments they read about to their own lives. When Sarah and Ellen talked about synthesizing, they knew it meant pulling together the most important ideas and events in the story in a way that made sense. Evidence from the children's conversations about books also illustrated they were aware of how to conduct small-group discussions. For instance, some children frequently asked other children, "What do you think?", soliciting each others' ideas and opinions. At one point, Brandon suggested to his group that it was time to ask Joshua and Marie what they thought. As he put it, "It's time for them to have a turn. They've been listening and listening." Although Debbie had used whole-class discussions to model these behaviors, she was surprised that many of the children so easily integrated these practices into their conversations.

There appear to be several explanations for why these children were able to engage in productive discussions. First, their knowledge of the comprehension strategies fostered their engagement with stories and provided a scaffold for their thinking and questioning. They knew how to ask a thoughtful question or use information about the characters and story events to draw inferences about what might happen. Their ability to focus on important ideas and themes in books meant that they avoided the obvious, as well as trivial details, pitfalls of typical conversations with young children.

The children's engagement with literature was also encouraged because they had developed a common language for discussion. When they asked a question, it meant that they were really wondering about something or wanted to clarify a part of the story that was confusing. They were willing to work hard at understanding that which wasn't apparent or actions taken by characters that troubled them. Rather than racing to finish a book, the children seemed to relish their conversations and developed a genuine interest in their classmates' thoughts.

Finally, an understanding of group dynamics and etiquette enabled the children to work together to construct meaning. Children engaged in collaborative conversations, where they tried out new ideas, listened to the opinions of others, and "revisited ideas that disturbed or intrigued them" (Levstik 1993, 74). They were willing to offer opinions and ideas without fear of criticism and could articulate their confusions and questions knowing that they were part of a supportive community of learners. Their openness to sharing their thinking with others would prove important as the children encountered more sophisticated literature in the coming year.

Second Grade— Real-World Connections

Having created some conditions for mutual regard and understanding in the classroom, Debbie now focused on ways to bring literature into the classroom that would expand children's knowledge of and perspective on the world. She knew the children were ready to expand their understanding of some of the issues they had encountered as first graders—personal struggles with feeling different and encountering unfairness and prejudice. Now Debbie faced a new challenge: how to address the diversity of experiences children brought to the classroom. She comments,

> I had worked so hard to create a classroom learning community that I had not really stopped to think about how diverse our group really was. I had not addressed the differences within the class—and hadn't thought about how my diverse group of children presented a golden opportunity to learn about each others' backgrounds and perspectives. Because we had one year together and felt safe with each other, I knew it would be possible to build on themes we had begun to discuss already: injustice, intolerance, and prejudice. Although I was a little uncomfortable with these issues, as most of us are, I felt it would be possible to promote understanding between children of different neighborhoods, races, and backgrounds. Once again, literature provided the vehicle for tackling potentially difficult but important issues and themes together.

Debbie started out by introducing the book *We Are Alike, We Are Different* (Ruiz 1992). She used this book because it addressed similarities and differences, with a matter-of-fact approach to "surface" differences. As children brought in pictures of their families and friends, they discussed how much they valued their own individual family experiences and traditions. Being "different" now had a new connotation: it meant respecting each person's individuality and uniqueness. Emphasizing the ways in which children in the classroom respected and liked one another despite outward differences was an important theme that preceded tackling themes about racial and gender differences. These young children were outspoken about how unfair it was that the main character, Grace, in *Amazing Grace* (Hoffman 1991) is told by her classmates that she cannot play the role of Peter Pan because she is a girl and she is black. This provided an entrance into a discussion of more serious issues of prejudice and intolerance that began the day that Alicia brought in a book to share: *If You Traveled on the Underground Railroad* (Levine 1989).

As Debbie read the book aloud, some of the children could not conceive of enslavement and others had knowledge and views that came from discussions at home. The children noticed immediately that the book was organized around questions, and were especially interested in questions about the meaning of slavery and if and how slaves tried to escape their fate ("What did it mean to be a slave?" "Why did slaves run away?" "How would you trick the slave hunters?"). Because they lacked background knowledge and information about the topic, their own questions focused on seeking out specific information: "If they caught a slave who ran away, what happened to him or her?" and "How did people get to be slaves anyway?" One question the children came back to again and again, as they expressed disbelief at the treatment of the slaves, was "Is this really true?"

> I took the lead from the children's questions as well as their outrage. I knew I needed to build their background knowledge so that they could understand the historical context of slavery—that it had happened a long time ago and that it was part of a very different way of viewing the world. Now the concerns I had about tackling issues of race and prejudice were real. I worried that the discussions would create tension between the children and between the children and myself, and put our respectful, cohesive community at risk.

The children's questions were so searching and their desire to understand issues of slavery and prejudice so strong that Debbie decided it was important to provide more information, not cut off the discussion. As children learned more about people such as Harriet Tubman, who worked to free the slaves, and read about Rosa Parks and other contemporary heroes and heroines of the civil rights movement, they came to admire individuals who stood up for what they believed and fought against intolerance and injustice. Debbie found that complicated historical issues involving prejudice, intolerance, and cruelty—originally assumed to be beyond the children's grasp—were opened up through historical and personal narratives, which described the actions and feelings of individuals caught in difficult and emotionally charged situations.

Levstik (1993) points out that well-written narratives which are "historically sound" also support "informed and disciplined imaginative entry into events" (71). Unlike historical information that is foreign and abstract to children, or texts that provide a "correct" interpretation of historical events or issues, narratives give children an opportunity to interpret for themselves important and disturbing moral and ethical issues. The power of this experience helps to explain children's intense interest and engagement. In Debbie's class, the children became caught up in the lives and problems of the people they read about. Getting to the heart of the human and moral issues presented by the narratives helped them to cross boundaries of place and time.

As the children learned more about slavery during the 1800s and moved into more recent narratives of people who fought for racial equality and civil rights, the class reached a turning point in its study of prejudice and injustice. Jamal, an African American child, looked Debbie straight in the eye one day and asked, "Why are we always the ones with the troubles? Why is it always us?" In an effort to help the children understand that other groups had experienced massive injustice and cruelty, Debbie read them *Number the Stars* (Lowry 1989). This is a chapter book about a Jewish family in Denmark during World War II, who, when the Nazis invaded, were hidden by friends and helped to escape to Sweden.

> I anticipated that this book would illustrate to all the children that people other than African Americans had been the object of extreme mistreatment and cruelty. At the same time, the heroic efforts of the Danish people to rescue and help almost all of the Danish Jews escape was ultimately a positive and life-affirming story. I thought that this book would be the culmination of our investigation of prejudice, injustice, and intolerance, and that we could end with hope, not despair.

Debbie's "culminating activity," however, proved to be a springboard for further difficult questioning and debate. As the children listened to the story, they became engaged with the main characters, Anne Marie and Ellen, children who are caught up in events beyond themselves. They used their prior knowledge, gained from the readings on slavery and the underground railroad, to begin to make connections between groups caught in extreme situations of human cruelty.

As Debbie moved from reading and discussing books about familiar circumstances and predicaments to social events that involved mass suffering, pain, cruelty, and death, she wondered about her decision to introduce literature dealing with difficult and traumatic historical events. Could the children come to understand difficult concepts of prejudice, intolerance, and injustice if they were not presented within their own frame of reference? Why introduce stories of the plight of Jewish children during World War II—narratives of unthinkable pain and suffering—to such young children? Wouldn't one run the risk of trivializing issues such as the genocide of European Jewry and the traumatic cruelty and death experienced by so many people when children didn't have the background information and understanding that at least provides a context for these events? Why even bring up a topic—genocide—that may well be impossible for a seven-year-old to fathom? Venturing once again into unknown territory, Debbie realized that it was crucial to allow the children's questions and responses—not a predetermined agenda —to drive the discussion.

Children's responses to *Number the Stars* (Lowry 1989) included connections to and comparisons with books read previously, as well as many searching questions. These questions illustrated how little background they had with respect to World War II, and suggested that the children felt compelled to ask why this was happening to innocent people.

> *Alicia:* Debbie, this is exactly like Harriet Tubman and the underground railroad. They were hiding slaves, and now in this book, they were hiding the Jews.

Leroy: Well, are the Jews black?

Cathy: I'm wondering if Ellen (the Jewish girl in the story) will get to freedom.

Alicia: Where are these people, anyway?

The children understood that the Jews were being persecuted and that brave people took considerable risks to help them escape, just like Harriet Tubman risked her life to help slaves navigate the underground railroad. Children's interpretations of the predicament that Ellen and her family found themselves in connected to their previous learning about Harriet Tubman and her role in helping slaves escape. The children grasped the central idea—Will Ellen get to freedom?—but Debbie spent a considerable amount of time explaining what was happening in Denmark during World War II to provide some background for the story. The children's lack of historical context and background information about Europe and the events of the war, however, resulted in continuing confusion and myriads of questions. When the children wondered who "these people" were and whether or not Jews were black, their struggles to understand the most basic facts about the Jews' predicament were apparent. Debbie expressed her reservations about going forward with the study:

> I never intended to pursue a study of the Holocaust with such young children because I thought it would be too distressing. I knew it was important to respond to Jamal's questions, because all the books we had read only considered prejudice and intolerance in the context of race. However, children's continuing questions and concerns about World War II and the plight of the Jews needed to be discussed. Instead of addressing issues of genocide and atrocities head-on, it seemed more appropriate to think through some of these themes with stories. I knew that our common language for thinking about literature had helped us explore complicated human events (such as slavery and prejudice) before; I had to trust that this approach would serve us well once again.

Debbie tried to respond to the children's questions with information about World War II. Their lack of background knowledge in geography, politics, and history made it difficult for them to understand where the war was taking place, who was fighting, and why they were fighting. The children's journal responses, written after Debbie's attempt to build some geographical and cultural background, illustrated that providing more information only fueled their questions.

In the journals, the children, despite their young age, "understood the universal need to cry out in question, as a protest against dehumanizing circumstances" (Busching and Slesinger 1995, 349).

Leroy wondered, "Why is there so much anger from one man to another? Why is there so much violence in one country to another?" Shawanda wondered, "Why did the Second World War begin? Why did they hate the children?" Jonathan asked searching questions about Hitler's hatred for Jews: "Why did he kill the Jews? Why did he blame the Jews? Why did he hate the Jews?" Ben succinctly wrote about what he and his classmates were learning, saying "What kids in Room 203 know about wars is that people die and a lot of killing goes on a lot."

Despite their riveting questions, Debbie still wondered if these children were indeed constructing their own interpretations and explanations for difficult and complex human issues. Did their knowledge of the reading comprehension strategies they had used with more familiar texts serve them well as they tried to understand unimaginable events and situations? Did the children have the tools to articulate their confusions and pursue answers to disturbing questions? Were they really understanding characters such as Harriet Tubman and the fictional Anne Marie and Ellen in *Number the Stars,* people caught in situations of social injustice and prejudice so grave that they were difficult for anyone, much less seven-year-olds, to understand?

As the children listened to *Number the Stars* (Lowry 1989), *The Promise of a New Spring* (Klein 1984), and other stories about the Holocaust, it was clear that their lack of background knowledge did not interfere with their understanding of the basic human issues at stake for the Jewish people. It was the book *Rose Blanche* (Innocenti 1985), however, that provoked the children's most passionate feelings. As Debbie read the story of a little girl in a German town who discovers hungry children behind the barbed wire of a concentration camp in the woods near her house, the children tried to interpret what is going on:

> *Joshua:* I wonder why she's on the Nazi side.
>
> *Lorie:* She's not!
>
> *Cathy:* When she hears they're going to kill them, she'll go back to town and tell them, like Harriet Tubman.
>
> *Jonathan:* If she were German, she would have tried to find out what happened to the little boy [in the story a little boy tried to escape from a truck that was driving him to the concentration camp—Rose Blanche witnessed his attempted escape].
>
> *Lorie:* But she did—she followed that truck, and found those children.

The children viewed Rose Blanche as a heroine, linking her willingness to try to save the Jewish children behind the barbed wire to the character of Harriet Tubman. They realized right away that Rose Blanche was no ordinary child, as she followed the truck when she noticed the little boy trying to escape.

> *Debbie:* [reading] "Rose Blanche was getting thinner. In town, only the Mayor was staying fat. Everyone watched everyone else. Rose Blanche hid her food in her school bag and sneaked out of school early." Do you understand what's going on?
>
> *Ellen:* She's trying to give food to the children.
>
> *Brandon:* I have a prediction—one day she's doing that and the mayor catches her.
>
> *Alicia:* That little girl—she's standing up for what is right.
>
> *Marie:* She's letting the other children eat her food. They don't have enough food!

Using their powers of inference, the children realized that Rose Blanche was taking considerable risks to give food to the children. Some children worried that the mayor would catch her.

> *Debbie* [reading]: "By now she [Rose Blanche] knew the road by heart. There were more children by the wooden houses—they were getting thinner behind the barbed wire fence. Some of them had a star pinned on their shirts. It was bright yellow."
>
> *Children:* Look! That's the Star of David! In that book!
>
> *Abbie:* Something's going to happen!
>
> *Jonathan:* They're going to catch her! They're going to catch her because she's giving food to the children.

There was considerable tension in the room as Debbie read this part of the story. The children were intensely interested in finding out what happened. Some were obviously anxious, given the ominous tone of the last part of the book.

> *Debbie* [reading]: "Rose Blanche disappeared that day. She had walked into the forest alone. Fog had erased the road. In the middle of the woods, the clearing had changed. It was empty. Rose Blanche dropped her school bag full of food. She stood still. Shadows were moving between the trees. It was hard to see them. Soldiers saw the enemy everywhere. There was a shot. Rose Blanche's mother waited a long time for her little girl."
>
> *Ellen:* Maybe she died . . .
>
> *Jonathan:* I think she got caught by the Germans, they caught her giving food to the children.
>
> *Leroy:* She's dead.
>
> *Alicia:* It doesn't tell you what happened.
>
> *Leroy:* She got shot, I know she's dead.

[Children are all talking at once]

Brandon: They thought she was a German, they are running in the other direction.

Leroy: They thought she was one of the Jewish people.

Lorie: She's not shot, I think she escaped.

Jamal: I think she was not shot . . . but I wonder if her mother ever found her.

Debbie: [trying to keep things under control] We won't learn as much if we can't listen. It's going to be really important to reread. We'll need to reread it to make it clear.

The children blurted out their outrage and frustration at Rose Blanche's killing. A few children refused to believe that a child doing such good could die. "She escaped . . . I just know she escaped," Jamal repeated over and over again. Some children argued about whether or not Rose Blanche had been shot accidentally. Others stated that she had been shot on purpose by the Nazis, inferring that the children behind the barbed wire fence had met the same fate. What the children did not realize because of their lack of background knowledge was that the camp was being liberated by the Allies, and that it was difficult if not impossible to determine who was responsible for Rose Blanche's death. The ambiguous ending made attributing the responsibility for this one, final act of violence a difficult, if not futile, effort. This did not satisfy the children, however, who sought a clear resolution to the story.

During lunchtime, they continued to argue heatedly for their own interpretations of the story. After lunch, Debbie brought the group back together and asked the children to take turns and try to listen to each other. Lorie, who had been one of the most outspoken and found herself in heated arguments with the other children, raised her hand:

Lorie: Can I get a piece of paper and write? I'm trying to understand the book.

Debbie: Lorie is a really good thinker. She's learning to solve her problems through writing. Why don't we all get our journals and try writing about the things you want to talk out loud about. Let's go to our seats and try to write about something that's important, or something that's hard to understand.

As the children shared their journal entries, many of them stuck with their original interpretations of the story, despite discussion to the contrary. It was apparent that some children simply could not accept the killing of a child, particularly one who has risked her life to save the Jewish children in the concentration camp. Many children mentioned Rose Blanche's mother and their mutual loss;

others (like Jamal) were resistant to the horrible truth and injustice of such a story, hoping against all evidence that Rose Blanche somehow survived. The children wrote:

Jamal: I think she's not shot because the Nazis were going the other way. Maybe she was in a cabin with plenty of food and clothes and never died. Question: Did her mother ever find her?

Charlie: I think that Rose Blanche was a sweet little girl who was not a Jewish. I think she got shot because they thought she was an enemy. Nazis surrounded it and one shot her because it was so foggy to see and because she would still be holding the flower but the flower was on the barbed wire half of the fence and she was died because she was shot in the head.

Cathy: I think that she was German, so she rooted for the German. But she didn't know what the German were doing so when she followed the truck she found out. And they thought she was Jewish and shot her.

Leroy: I don't understand when the soldiers is moving and also I don't understand because they said she disappeared. I am thinking she disappeared for life.

Through their written responses, these children illustrate concerns typical of young children: explaining in detail their own version of what happened to Rose Blanche and an overriding concern about whether her mother ever found her. Leroy, realizing that while it was not exactly clear what had happened to Rose Blanche, felt she did not come back. His solution to the puzzle was to conclude the following: "I am thinking that she disappeared for life."

These personal and thoughtful responses to a tragic story that defied understanding are clear evidence that these children are engaged with the "risky stories" some other writers in this text describe (see, for example, Britzman; Robertson; Shawn; Simon & Armitage Simon; and Zack). What, then, happens when young children are confronted with literary examples of disturbing human behaviors such as prejudice, intolerance, injustice, and cruelty? How did children's interest in significant human issues develop and change over time? What made them so intent on understanding these difficult texts and experiences? Reflecting on children's learning with the most troublesome of topics provides some unexpected conclusions.

Children's growing understanding of ways to question and collaborate on meaning making through talk and writing enabled them more clearly to articulate humane and searching responses to literature, even with stories that were originally assumed to be beyond them. While it may be the case that North American children in the 1990s cannot truly understand the predicaments of a Harriet

Tubman or a Rose Blanche, if engagement, tolerance, empathy, and outrage indicate some level of understanding, these children certainly were on a path to possible learning of value. These children's thoughtful and disarming questions, voiced in discussions and written responses, seldom had easy answers. Their spontaneous insights and willingness to speak up about unfairness and injustice whenever they discerned it made for difficult and troubling discussions. Although their understanding of the facts and details of World War II was sketchy, and in some cases, quite confused, this did not prevent them from being willing to think and learn more about the significant human issues central to the events and times.

In this chapter we argue that careful nurturing of young children's powers of interpretation and analysis through comprehension instruction can facilitate their active engagement with literature in several ways. These children developed strong connections with characters (both real and fictional) and their predicaments, making unfamiliar situations and difficult circumstances more real and immediate. Other children seemed to listen, but were resistant to delving further into disturbing events. Debbie respected their reticence. Most of the children in the classroom refused to accept simple answers or pat responses to their questions. They seldom agreed on one interpretation of a story. The classroom climate that encouraged respect for ideas and opinions helped to strengthen children's confidence as they collaborated to make meaning with respect to difficult and disturbing topics. Some children evidenced a desire to continue to ask questions and talk about events in books that they found troublesome, resulting in discussions that linked dilemmas and problems from their own lives. After reading *The Promise of a New Spring*, one small-group conversation diverged into a discussion of conflict between the gangs in one child's neighborhood. The other children listened wide-eyed as Leroy described seeing gang members on his street and how afraid he was of them. "Before I went home, there was a car on the corner. They be asking me to join," he commented. "What did you say to them?" asked Joshua. "I didn't just run away. I went up to them and I said, 'No, I want to live to be older. No, thank you. I don't want to die so fast,'" replied Leroy.

Whether Leroy truly "stood up to" the teenagers in his neighborhood is hardly the point. Leroy's clear understanding of the implications of joining a gang ("No, I want to live to be older.") were quite insightful for a seven-year-old. By telling his story, Leroy illustrated that he knew what to say in a difficult situation, a lesson he might have learned from reading about Harriet Tubman or Rose Blanche. Perhaps telling his friends about this strengthened his own resolve with respect to a problem that he confronted on a daily basis in his neighborhood. This conversation sparked a larger one about gangs and violence in Denver, with one child pointing out "There's a war right here in Denver." That day, the children from the middle-class neighborhoods learned a great deal from their peers who lived in the midst of uncertainty and potential danger.

In thinking about what encouraged children's interest, the thematically related and carefully selected literature not only helped to create a classroom environment of tolerance and understanding, but resulted in a shared frame of reference over time. With their teacher and each other, these children constructed shared interpretations and explanations of difficult human issues and situations. Had they not participated in a classroom community where mutual respect and caring prevailed, the children might not have been so open to discussing prejudice, intolerance, and finally, genocide, in such an honest and heartfelt manner.

The changes observed in these children's learning suggest that it is important to explore further the power of historical narratives and stories to teach children about important issues. While they may not have understood prejudice, intolerance, and injustice in a historical or political context, these children came away with a clear sense of how each of these affects the lives of people, either past or present. Children's attempts to understand and make sense of history—and perhaps contemporary events as well—are best illustrated by their willingness to take a moral stand, whether it meant expressing indignation to real or perceived gang members or trying to raise money to help stop wars elsewhere. What better history lesson could they have learned than that each of us is responsible for ensuring that there is some justice and fairness in the world? And that continued engagement in reading the stories of others is—even for young children—one step in the right direction.

Works Cited

Busching, Beverly, and Betty Ann Slesinger. 1995. "Authentic Questions: What Do They Look Like? Where Do They Lead?" *Language Arts* 72(5): 341–51.

Fielding, L., and P. D. Pearson. 1994. "Reading Comprehension: What Works." *Educational Leadership* 51: 62–68.

Levstik, Linda. 1993. "I Wanted to Be There: The Impact of Narrative on Children's Historical Thinking." In *The Story of Ourselves: Teaching History through Children's Literature*, edited by Michael O. Tunnell and Richard Ammon. Portsmouth, NH: Heinemann.

Pearson, P. David. 1985. "The Changing Face of Reading Comprehension Instruction." *The Reading Teacher* 38: 724–38.

Literature and Nonfiction Resources Cited throughout the Chapter

Aliki. 1987. *The Two of Them*. New York: Harcourt Brace.

Bunting, Eve. 1989. *The Terrible Things*. New York: Harper & Row.

De Paola, Tomie. 1983. *Oliver Button Is a Sissy*. New York: Harcourt Brace.

Hoffman, Mary. 1991. *Amazing Grace*. New York: Dial.

Innocenti, Roberto. 1985. *Rose Blanche*. New York: Stewart, Tabori and Chang.

Klein, Gerda. 1984. *Promise of a New Spring*. New York: Rossel Publishing.

Levine, Ellen. 1989. *If You Traveled on the Underground Railroad*. New York: Scholastic.

Lowry, Lois. 1989. *Number the Stars*. New York: Dell Yearling.

Ruiz, W. 1992. *We Are Alike, We Are Different*. New York: Penguin.

Zolotow, Charlotte. 1972. *William's Doll*. New York: Scholastic.

Additional Recommended Readings

Keene, Ellin. 1997. *Mosaic of Thought: Teaching Comprehension in the Reader's Workshop*. Portsmouth, NH: Heinemann.

Pearson, P. David, and J. Dole. 1987. "Explicit Comprehension Instruction: A Review of Research and a New Conceptualization of Instruction." *Elementary School Journal* 88: 151–65.

Tierney, R., and M. Gee. 1990. "Reading Comprehension: Readers, Authors and the World of Text." In *Beyond Communication: Reading Comprehension and Criticism*, edited by D. Bogdan and S. Straw. Portsmouth, NH: Boynton/Cook.

Waggoner, M., C. Chinn, H. Yi, and R. Anderson. 1995. "Collaborative Reasoning about Stories." *Language Arts* 72: 582–89.

III On Facing Uncertainty in Teaching

13 South African Teachers' and Students' Resiliency in Combating Apartheid Violence

P. J. Nomathemba Seme
Old Dominion University

This essay describes how teachers and students struggled to survive the violent learning environments in selected African schools. It explores what intolerance means in the racially segregated and unequally funded schools in South Africa under the apartheid system. The essay further illuminates some survival strategies of selected teachers, including their reliance on prayer, building community support and networks, and cooperating and sharing. Finally, it draws some conclusions and implications for teachers in other war-torn settings, or for those experiencing inequalities rooted in past racial histories.

General Context

After scores of decades, South Africa has finally dismantled violent apartheid laws which affected communities in a variety of ways. For example, families were disrupted by mass removals and the migrant labor system (Marks and Andersson 1990). Blacks[1] (Africans, Coloreds, and Indians) had no say in the political, economic, and educational policies governing their lives. In fact, there was an inequality in the distribution of educational resources among different racial groups. For example, the per capita education expenditure on school pupils in 1989–90 was R3,739.00 for whites and R930.00 for Africans (Cooper et al. 1992; at this time, a South African rand was worth about forty cents). From inception, the architects of the apartheid design, such as Verwoed, explicitly stated that blacks deserved unequal and less quality education than whites. This intolerant language in the education policies and conditions led to the discontent that has been expressed over the years through a variety of means, including demonstrations, riots, and boycotts. Since 1976 schools, businesses, and political organizations within and outside the country exerted pressure on the regime to relinquish power. By the mid-1980s violence escalated as the pressure mounted. This led to the release of political leaders from prison early in 1990 and the beginning of talks about a negotiated transition of power (Sommer 1996). This transition period was marked with heightened violence and intolerance among members from different political organizations. For example, in the province of Natal alone, over a thousand people were killed, and some people were forced to flee their areas of residence while those in the war-torn areas were completely displaced (Sithole 1996).

When sociopolitical violence erupted, schools were not immune, yet teachers were expected to teach and children to learn. For example, I witnessed how schools were affected in the spring and the winter of 1991 when I was collecting data for my doctoral thesis on teachers' perspectives on approaches for teaching beginning reading in first-grade classrooms in African schools. These elementary schools were located in the African townships which had experienced the worst violence in 1990, in the Natal region.

Although my research did not ostensibly set out to examine the challenges of teaching under violent conditions, the interviews with teachers revealed that teaching and learning were intricately intertwined with the sociopolitical environments educators worked and lived under. Within this context, I heard and witnessed ways in which teachers struggled to make teaching and learning possible. For example, some schools had buildings without teaching-learning materials; others had dilapidated walls with teachers and children shivering in the winter cold and simmering in the summer heat; others were without walls altogether. However, there was hope and determination in the voices of the teachers and a sparkle in the eyes of the five- and six-year-old children, despite the violence that was raging in the sociopolitical arena and spilling into the school buildings through vandalism and destruction. The daily living conditions were extremely difficult, but learning was going on.

Under these pressures, how did teachers and students struggle to survive the violent learning environments? How did they teach tolerance in a society that was inherently violent by design? The following discussion attempts to address these questions from the perspectives of the selected teachers.

Violence Defined

In South Africa one cannot discuss teaching and learning without examining the political, social, and economic violence that people have endured over the years. In this essay, the term *violence* takes both a descriptive and a normative sense (Degenaar 1990; Hoffmann and McKendrick 1990; Marks and Andersson 1990). In Degenaar's view, the descriptive sense of the term *violence* connotes the infliction of harm or use of force on someone. Such harm could be emotional and/or mental in nature. On the other hand, the normative use of *violence* "is linked with violation" and thereby evokes the "notion of illegitimacy" (73). Furthermore, normative violence

> reflects the realization that force language is not adequate and that in using the word *violence* one is relating to some value ascribed to someone/something against whom/which force is used. (Degenaar 1990, 73)

Hoffmann and McKendrick (1990) go on to categorize willful acts of violence into legitimate and illegitimate types. For example, the legimate forms of violence might include sports and law enforcement, while illegitimate forms might include violence inflicted on persons or property.

The literature identifies various forms of violence, ranging from physical violence and violence of poverty to structural violence. Within this range, the meanings of what is violent might depend on the community's construction. For example, the burning of the school buildings could be interpreted by some people as a crime while others might see it as an expression of resistance against the apartheid structures, thus making the violence a political type of act and not necessarily a crime punishable under the criminal law. Probably it is for this reason that Degenaar (1990) argues that *violence* is a metaphorical term because it deals with morality, which essentially focuses on what is *just or unjust,* and not merely on what is *legal or illegal.* According to Degenaar (1990, 82), citing Johan Galtung, violence is built into the institutional structures which are set out "to deprive other communities of equal power and chances to a quality life" and conditions. In South Africa, the apartheid system was purposefully designed to keep blacks in an inferior status in all spheres of human life.

The work of teachers in black schools was then complicated. Teachers had to teach a curriculum which they did not support and which they did not help to develop, while they were contemporaneously placed in unconducive teaching-learning environments. These teachers needed to employ teaching techniques that would meet their students' needs, as well as to develop survival strategies in order to endure those teaching conditions. How does one teach tolerance in such conditions? Heller and Hawkins (1994), quoting the *American Heritage Dictionary,* define tolerance as "the capacity for or the practice of recognizing and respecting the beliefs or practices of others" (344). If teachers were tolerant, according to this definition, would this mean that they would have to endure and respect the practices and beliefs that others (those in charge in the apartheid system) imposed on them? What would tolerance in the apartheid conditions mean?

Vogt (1994) offers three definitions of tolerance. For purposes of this paper, the one of interest to me offers the following description that is relevant to sociopolitical contexts:

> Tolerance is intentional self-restraint in the face of something one dislikes, objects to, finds threatening, or otherwise has a negative attitude toward—usually in order to maintain a social or political group or to promote harmony in a group. (Vogt 1994, 280)

Within the context of this definition, Vogt maintains that in sociopolitical contexts, tolerance can only be a viable option when three ingredients are simultaneously present. These are diversity, equality, and peace among the people involved. However, in a South African context, there was no equality and peace among races and political groups in the early 1990s. Violence was at its peak while a negotiated transition from minority rule to a democracy was under way. The country was filled with a hope for transformation and change while fear of escalating violence also mounted. Schools mirrored in microcosm the events that were taking place in the larger sociopolitical arena of the times.

Why Focus on Teachers and Students under Intolerable Conditions?

While a reasonable number of studies and writings have described the impact of such violence on communities and individuals in South Africa, there are few studies that reported experiences from the students' and teachers' perspectives, in particular. For example, Nzimande (1993) echoed a similar observation in the introduction of his study that reported the effects of violence on high school students in major industrial areas in Natal in 1991. Nzimande's study used a survey questionnaire and focused interviews with selected students.

Most studies analyzed the classroom conditions and context from the writer's point of view rather than from the teachers' or students'. For example, such studies reported on the lack of educational facilities and teacher training, high repetition and drop-out rates in early grades, and the use of traditional teaching approaches and curriculum issues (Johnson 1991; Mdluli 1980). However, they tended to avoid examining "the processes, struggles, and ambiguities that teachers experienced in teaching under various contexts in classrooms" (Seme 1993, 53). Kallaway (1984) and Robertson (1969) attributed this lack of analytic studies that are grounded on descriptive data to the politics and oppressive nature of the apartheid era which had no interest in raising issues and potential questions that the system was not prepared to handle. Even some of the frequently quoted analytic works on "the struggle of education in South Africa," such as that of Pam Christie (1985), offer a general overview of issues and experiences of teachers and students without grounding them on a particular context, time, and place.

There is a need, therefore, for teachers' perspectives to be heard and understood in context because teachers are the ones who work with children daily. Moreover, while the institutions that created apartheid are gone, their effects will be felt for a long time as the new government wrestles with ways to redress the past wrongs. It is for this reason that, below, I will share the stories of struggle, hope, and survival from selected African teachers.

Targeted Schools

As part of my research study, I observed and interviewed sixteen first-grade teachers and administrators in eight primary schools (grades 1–7) in the African townships of Region A and Region B, in the Natal province (Seme 1993). Since first graders in these schools were introduced to literacy in their first language and then to English, gradually, I conducted and transcribed the interviews in a Zulu language and later translated the analyzed transcripts into English for presentation purposes.

The selected schools had gained a reputation in their respective communities for having effective teachers. Parents fought hard to get their children admitted to these schools. Teachers in these schools felt that they were "trying very hard" to develop a good foundation for children to succeed. Some shared the joy and pride they experienced when high school teachers in the area commended them for providing a good foundation to students. They were proud to see their "products" go to higher education institutions and become successful in the community. Teachers noted that these were indications that meant something was working, although they never knew what it was as they tried different things to get children moving forward.

While the focus on the teachers and schools with strong programs and good reputations might give an impression that all was well in education under apartheid, Swartz and Levett (1990) warn that this might not necessarily indicate that people are coping well and "violence is not serious" (275). On the other hand, the fact that violence engulfed teachers' and students' learning environment does not mean that they in turn were "hapless and helpless victims" (Mark and Andersson 1990, 61–62). In fact, Brook, Field, and Labbo (1995) describe township schools as "good examples of [schools] that continue to function despite prevailing violence and unrest in the surrounding communities" (82).

Of course, as in any battle, some children were never successful in these schools and sometimes teachers wondered as to what happened to those fallen and unsung "heroes." They would remember certain children who either had reading problems or who left a mark in the teachers' minds for whatever reasons. For example, one teacher wondered aloud about one student who had a reading problem and had repeated the first grade four times. This girl could not write a sentence and forgot how to write words she had learned previously. Educators finally promoted her to the next grade because of her age, which did not help either. They had tried all the techniques they had within their repertoire. None of them had any training in helping children with reading needs, and they did not know where to refer struggling readers for help. No agencies existed in these communities, nor was training available in black colleges or most black universities to deal with such issues.

The following section provides a narrative description and analysis of the effects of different forms of violence on selected teachers and students. I chose to tell the story from the perspective of one principal, Mam Sithole, and her colleagues at Khwezi Lower Primary (L. P.). As a case study, it will offer a lens through which to understand how a particular school community experienced violence. The information from this study might not necessarily be generalized, but could offer a window for what is possible in such conditions.

Mam Sithole regarded herself more as a teacher than a "principal." Why? She persuasively argued that she was simply appointed to lead and manage the school without any qualifications that distinguished her from teacher colleagues. She stated, "Any of the teachers here could take this position and do a much better job than I do." Consequently, Mam Sithole never separated her "new" duties from the duties of the teachers she worked with. She continued to be involved in teaching and practice issues in the classroom.

In addition, I selected Mam Sithole because she articulated the possibilities of what happened when violence occurred in her school, how she and her colleagues handled such violence, and how she as a "leader" could make intolerable conditions tolerable for both children and teachers. Using one school as the major focus provides a context and particularity in the discussion of violence which becomes complex and interwoven with other factors in the school and community (Scharfstein 1989). For purposes of comparison and contrast, I will also draw from the perspectives of teachers and students in other schools. Although the information is true, the names of the districts, schools, and teachers have been changed to protect the individuals involved.

Effects of Violence on Teachers and Students at Khwezi L. P.

Khwezi Lower Primary (L. P.) School (Grades 1–4) was under the Department of Education and Training[2], which was directly controlled by the central government. Khezi L. P. was located in one of the townships in Region A that had experienced the worst violence in 1990. Families had fled their homes, and houses were destroyed. The school windows were broken, walls vandalized, and books and other materials burned.

Most members of the community, including teachers, administrators, and parents, referred me to Khwezi L. P., citing the facts that teachers were "active" and their principal "gives them freedom to do things they want to do." I wondered what kind of freedom these people referred to in the context of administrative bureaucracy and sociopolitical violence.

When I came to observe and interview teachers in February at the beginning of the academic year in 1991, the principal and teachers individually told me stories of violence and its effects on them and students. For example, Mam Sithole (the principal) laid the background on what I would expect to find in the classrooms. She first apologized that the classrooms were not at the standard they had hoped to have reached then. She then clarified further the reasons for this situation:

> We cannot say that we are doing wonders, we are not a project school. But we are trying very hard. Our school has been vandalized twice and more than any school here. At one stage, I called to inform the circuit [area] inspector, and he thought I was just talking about the burglary that you usually find in schools. He came, and when he saw the damage, he went back to the office to get the assistant director of education. When the assistant director saw the damage, he went back to call the director from the regional office. This is the extent to which the damage was done. During that time, it was as if the tornado has gone passed over this township.

In the above story, Mam Sithole evoked images of high level education administration officials becoming speechless after witnessing the damage done to the school buildings. This reaction highlighted the seriousness of the damage because, generally, vandalism and burglary are routinely experienced in schools. Principals with their meager resources try to repair such damage, but this extensive destruction went beyond the capacity of Mam Sithole's school to handle. The education department had to be significantly involved. In this situation, seeing would mean believing, which would then make it easier to plead for money for major school repairs.

The scenario described in Mam Sithole's case was not an anomaly. For example, in her study of teacher survival in the primary schools in the townships in Pretoria, Motala (1995) also observed that vandalism and burglary were common phenomena. At face value, the vandalism and destruction of school property could be characterized as a crime, an "illegimate" form of violence. However, close scrutiny reveals that such violence was partly socio-political and structural in nature. For example, when the members of one political organization were attacking their opponents, everything in their way, including schools, was destroyed or burned down. Such violence is spiral in nature in that schools are seen as a negative symbol by youth who resent the racist and oppressive views of the education officials. Moreover, the intolerance of views among members of different political organizations (e.g., Inkatha Freedom Party and the African National Congress)[3] which led to conflict in areas such as Pietermaritzburg in the 1990s was covertly sponsored by the government itself for its own purposes (Cooper et al. 1992; Nzimande 1993).

Mam Sithole explained the psychological and emotional effect that vandalism had on teachers at Khwezi L. P.:

> On the day the school had been vandalized, we were all wrecked up. You know, I would see that the teachers' spirit was low, low, and you could see that it bleeds deep down inside. I personally cried—tears came dropping one by one. I asked, "But Lord, what has really happened after so much work has been done. We are trying. Why should Satan come in such a way?" . . . When I came here in 1987, this office was burned down. So there were no records, there was nothing, I had to start from scratch. But if the Lord keeps me starting from scratch all the time, I will end up being discouraged and not being able to work.

The above story highlights the feelings of hurt that teachers experienced when the work they had accumulated over months and years was destroyed in an instant. It is important to note that black schools received next to nothing for school supplies, materials, and books during the apartheid years. This meant that teachers and principals had to be ingenious and creative in developing ways of supporting their teaching. This was a crucial factor since most families could not afford to buy, on their own, the materials, supplies, and books that children needed. Consequently, active teachers collected, among other things, newspapers, magazines, empty shoe boxes, rolls of paper towels and toilet paper, soap and cereal boxes, rice or flour bags, and egg trays. As part of the collection drive, they also solicited support from the children and businesses in the local area. These materials were used to create and store literacy and numeracy tasks for children in the classroom. Such work demanded the teacher's time, interest, patience, and enthusiasm. It is therefore not surprising that teacher morale was affected by the violence that befell Khwezi L. P.

As noted earlier, the teachers at Khezi L. P. had spent time pulling together the meager resources, creating learning materials, and collecting books on their own. The first-grade teachers in particular were using the Breakthrough to Literacy approach[4] to reading. They also had classes for helping young children bridge the gap between home and school. Breakthrough to Literacy encourages teachers to provide varied opportunities for students to create their own texts as part of the construction of meaning. Given the large class sizes of forty or more pupils per teacher, teachers needed to create various occupational tasks that would engage children in learning while the teachers worked intensively with another group in the teaching corner.

When the classroom buildings had been burned and vandalized, all that work was gone. They would have to start from scratch again, without any funding and support. For example, Mam Dlamini, a first-grade teacher, told me that all the work I was seeing in April was new because "they spoiled all our good teaching aids. You could have seen the stains on the walls, it was terrible." From observing the class, it was obvious that the teachers were actively rebuilding their supplies and creating literate classroom environments, as depicted in the children's work on the classroom walls, activities on the boxes along the classroom walls, and materials displayed on the window seats.

Teachers were collecting the local newspapers and magazines for the classroom and library. Children used pictures from these materials to create their own books and stories. Interestingly, the local newspapers and magazines dealt with issues affecting the community more than the books that were designated for first graders. It is important to note that, at least while I was observing, the issues relating to gross violence such as death, riots, and such were never discussed explicitly in class. Given that these were five- and six-year-olds, teachers were more focused on the technical aspects of helping children learn to read and understand what they were reading and writing. Teachers used familiar family, religious, and household topics without engaging in a critical discussion about them. For example, when introducing the sound "b" as in "ubaba" (father), the teacher would begin with some discussion about what the father sees when he arrives home. The "anticipated" answer would be that he would see the mother. As children gave alternative responses, the teacher would go on pointing at them until she heard a sentence: *"Ubaba ubona umama."* ("The father sees the mother.") She would then latch on to this meaningful sentence, which is in the teachers' manual, to develop the lesson. She focused children on the words in the sentence and then their respective sounds and letters.

The discussion about the alternative responses children gave about what happens when father comes home fell by the wayside. Such discussions did not even take into consideration the possibilities that some homes might not have fathers and why this was so.

It is not surprising to me that the texts that both teachers and children used and created during reading took a neutral tone rather than being taken as social acts to be pondered and deliberated upon at opportune moments. Such actions should be viewed in light of the political climate of the time since people who held different political views in the community were unpredictable and the situation was still volatile. Teachers might not have preferred to open the topics that would lead children to believe they belonged to a particular side. Even some young children were actively involved and sometimes used by adults during the political struggle. Teachers and students were not safe either in or out of school (Seme 1988). As Brook, Field, and Labbo (1995) also reported, even during the April 1994 first democratic elections in the country, some teachers, principals, and students in some KwaZulu-Natal areas feared teaching and talking about the major current event. Teachers in the Brook, Field, and Labbo study avoided teaching election-related lessons, fearing that these lessons might "incit[e] or inflame factionalism and tension among their students. Thus, emotional involvement and the possibility of political repercussions were strong inhibitors" (84). Such fears were well founded because the political climate was still clouded with the effects of apartheid violence. The ingredients for tolerance as an option were inadequate, for, as Vogt (1994) noted, tolerance requires diversity, equality, and peace.

Since the scars of violence were still fresh in the community, many homes were deserted. Even families who remained behind were still afraid to send their children to schools at the beginning of 1991, fearing that violence might erupt again. The enrollment at Khwezi L. P. had dropped so dramatically that some teachers were sent to other schools where the enrollment had increased. Even when the peace accord was signed among the rival groups in the community, fear was still high. Teachers and parents, noted Mam Sithole, "could not realize how genuine peace was and how long it would last. Is it really true?"; other teachers echoed these thoughts. Uncertainty in the community led to uncertainty in the classroom. For example, how long would it take before these teachers came back? While it seemed that teachers had regained their poise and gone back to work, one could ask, what did it take to build teacher morale in violent conditions at Khwezi L. P.? What did intolerance mean to them? What strategies did they use? These questions will be addressed in the following pages.

Teaching in Conditions of Violence: Teachers' Strategies of Resistance

Unlike Khwezi L. P., whose enrollment had dropped, other schools like Nobel Higher Primary (H. P.) School in Region B were dealing with other forms of violence, such as inadequate classroom space. For example, the township in which Nobel H. P. was located had been expanding and the population had been growing over the years, but the number of schools had not increased to match the demand. In 1990, the township had further been flooded with more people who had settled the vacant lots in the township after the government had repealed the Group Areas Act which restricted movement to locate to different parts of the country based on race. This population growth created challenges for schools which were already underresourced and understaffed. As described by Seme (1993), parents wanted their children admitted in the first grade, regardless of whether space and resources were available. Some parents even sent underaged children in order to allow for the possibility of failure and to give the child a chance to repeat the grade while still young.

Some parents threatened teachers' lives if they did not admit their children. For example, the teacher at Nobel H. P. recounted an incident wherein she was told she would be physically harmed if she did not accept the child. Teachers were aware of cases where teachers had been killed. For this reason, threats were taken seriously since according to several teachers, "teachers have no security inside and outside the school premises." On several occasions, teachers had written memoranda to the respective Education Departments "demanding the provision of security and sufficient facilities" (Sithole 1996, 4).

On the other hand, the school policy required teachers to take only a certain number of students depending on the space available. This created a conflict for teachers. Should they take children when there was no physical space to keep them nor adequate support for them? Should they chase children away and let them languish in the violent streets in the township without education? Or should they face the rage of parents, some of whom might have threatened physical harm if their children were not admitted? Since the administrative policies were to be adhered to while at the same time the parents' needs and demands had to be met, teachers had to figure out ways of coping with these conflicting demands.

Teachers at Nobel H. P. decided to break the department rules by admitting more children than they could handle, but they did not record the surplus in the school register. The unregistered children were called *floats* (Seme 1993, 143). Everybody in the school, including the principal, knew about the scheme. Teachers told me it was a *secret* because the administrators beyond the school buildings, at the higher levels, did not know about it. Teachers acknowledged that they were working under pressure and were not happy about different things they were told to do by the department. The education department had not listened to their concerns as expressed in a variety of formal and "informal" channels. So these floats sat around the edges and squeezed themselves in. As they participated in lessons, some of them caught up and were promoted to the second grade. When those children who had been officially enrolled failed at the end of the year, the floats took over the registered children's admission numbers to the second grade. The administrators in the department did not have a clue as to what was going on because they received "clean" statistical data about children's enrollment, but not the true classroom realities. In a study of Soweto primary schools, Motala (1995, 169–170) made similar and additional observations: it was also clear that principals, teachers, and parents "subvert the system" in order to "survive the system." In some instances principals deliberately kept numbers high in their schools in order to get higher subsidies, and included preschool children in their numbers, parents falsified addresses and ages in order to gain access for their children to schools; and teachers engaged in highly unreliable record keeping in order to get the job done in the shortest time possible. All of these were silent but salient forms of resistance against intolerable teaching-learning conditions.

Teacher Morale and Coping Strategies

At Khwezi L. P., Mam Sithole described how she and her colleagues confronted the damage that had been caused in their school. She elaborated:

> The tears would come down. But all of a sudden, I said, if I cry, as a mother in the house, children would then scream and be hysterical and I would not know what to do. So, I had to take myself out of that feeling of being morose. I just had to motivate them.

She further described how she then addressed the teachers:

> Now, children are here to learn. We should put behind us all that has happened as if it never occurred. Like God, when you repent, She or He forgives your old sins. So let's bury everything that happened in 1990 and start 1991 with a fresh look. Let us begin and work because if we sit down to mourn and cry to God, after all, it will not help us.

Mam Sithole took a lead in rekindling the spirit and enthusiasm, to face the challenge rather than to be despondent. As Straker (1992) notes, people are affected differently by violence. Some gain power and energy and find a purpose for living, while others feel disempowered and helpless. As was the case at Khwezi L. P., the presence of children in school became the driving power and realization that "the work cannot stop" because children are here and are our future.

As seen above, Mam Sithole drew her strength from her belief in God in order to energize her colleagues. Since most teachers in the school shared a common faith, it thus became the unifying force. The Human Sciences Research Council (1987, 38) also notes that five out of every six people in the urban areas claim church membership, and Christianity predominates among Africans. Even the inspectors "came and joined in the morning prayers every day" after the major disaster. As all the segments of the school community banded together, the pain of violence became bearable and thus resiliency and resolve strengthened. In fact, this is a strategy prevalent in the African community wherein "people turn to family, friends and church to sustain themselves in times of trouble" (Marks and Andersson 1990, 62). Such a support system becomes a survival strategy by itself, as Hirschowitz, Milner, and Everatt (1994) explain: "Resiliency against the effects of violence is facilitated by an individual's personality, by supportive family networks and a supportive external social system. A supportive environment can, of itself, be healing" (90).

When officials in the educational administration office joined forces with teachers experiencing a difficult time as noted earlier, they were thus strengthening the support system and family network. It is interesting to note that the top administrators were also living under intolerable conditions because they had to enforce the unequal education policies, policies in whose formulation they had no input. These administrators frequently received complaints and demonstrations from teachers in their local district. The black administrators, in particular, had their own survival strategies against violence of different kinds. When these top administrators could find opportunities to connect in tangible ways with the communities they served, both the teachers and administrators found "a supportive environment" which was truly "healing" and helping them continue to work and survive. This incident highlights the complicatedness of the various forms in which violence manifested itself in people's lives and work and what specific ways they dealt with them.

Marks and Andersson (1990) note that it is difficult to research and pin down scientifically the various forms of apartheid violence in everyday lives of the people. The ways in which people defensively or offensively respond to situations may be interpreted as mundane or simply traditional, and not viewed as forms of resistance to the conditions in which they live. So, by receiving different kinds of community support, Mam Sithole was also energized to build teacher morale. In building teacher morale, Mam Sithole was thus setting the framework upon which teachers could focus on children's learning in spite of adversities. Her action by itself was then a form of silent but salient resistance to violence. The success of this strategy could be noticed as Mam Sithole's face filled with a smile when she said, "We started the year with a great spirit, enthusiasm and wonderful cooperation. We are not a project school, but with the help from God, we will continue to go forward, we are not going to stop!" Sommer (1996, 55), drawing from Sharp's theory, would characterize this strategy as a nonviolent action against the oppressive state because it makes people realize their potential and power.

The spirit of determination and enthusiasm reverberated in the first-grade classes I observed. For example, Mam Dlamini's class had a lot of energetic early-emergent readers. Sometimes she expressed that she was overwhelmed with the demand to keep them engaged in meaningful learning activities given the minimal resources. She admitted that sometimes when she felt she no longer knew how else to help the learner, she would "pray every day before we begin the lessons. As the time goes on, you see the light bulb turns on and she or he progresses. That's when you realize that prayer works."

Mam Dlamini was struggling with theoretical questions about what happens when the child finally understands, which Duckworth (1987) might refer to as "the having of wonderful ideas." However, she did not have the structural support to realize how such questions actually helped to build knowledge in her context. Thus, she resorted to a survival strategy of enlisting God's help for things she could not explain. Meanwhile she tried all she could within her limited resources.

One strategy used at Khwezi L. P. involved sharing classes. That meant that a teacher who was regarded as good at introducing children to letter sounds and words would first take the children for a couple of days. Once they got a feel for which direction to go, the other teachers would then take over to reinforce and extend the learning during reading. This strategy was particularly useful since not all teachers were trained in the Breakthrough to Literacy approach which they felt was effective in getting children to learn to read and write less stressfully and faster compared to the traditional approaches (Seme 1993). As I observed the sharing of classes in this school, I began to see why several people recommended Khwezi L. P. to be part of the schools I should include in my sample, and why they described teachers at this school as having "freedom." I realized the "freedom" I had heard about meant that teachers had the ability and opportunity to do things they wanted to do. Moving children from one class to another or switching a teacher from one class to the other was based on the teachers' and students' needs and did not require the principal's approval each time they did it. Nor did these actions need to be "approved" by the administration officials. There was cooperation among teachers in the first grade. I noticed a variation of such sharing among teachers in other schools I visited.

Khwezi L. P. galvanized both teachers and students to work toward a common theme of *unity*. From the principal's office to the classrooms, there were motivational posters on the walls. During the morning devotions, the theme was emphasized. In the classrooms teachers would draw students' attention to the theme, emphasizing that they should work together and help each other. Such a spirit was readily apparent as I witnessed children freely moving around and enlisting help on their work from other students. When the teacher left the room, students continued to find work to do. Some volunteered to give each other spelling tests and graded them, while others read to themselves or with peers. In the process, there was a lot of cooperation and discussion. The teacher emphasized that children knew the importance of working together in harmony in her class. At one time during the recess, two boys got into a quarrel and came to the teacher to report, but the teacher said, "Go back and resolve the problem. Come back and tell me how you have solved the problem. You know we do not tolerate fighting here." I observed a similar trend at Cape Higher Primary (Grades 1–7), when the theme for the week during the morning devotion was *being thankful*. This theme set the tone for the lessons for the week, as teachers would informally reinforce certain values, attitudes, and character traits among students. From these observations, it seemed that the teachers taught tolerance in and through informal processes and means of socialization, rather than through formal teaching (Vogt 1994). Formal teaching might have been more focused, for example, exploring in detail written texts by using thematic units, teaching specific tolerance strategies (Gehrig 1991) and multimedia computer software (Williams and Johnson 1995). In this case, informal teaching of tolerance used the daily life experiences of the children and teachers as text for learning.

The spirit of cooperation and openness was also inculcated among teachers at Khwezi L. P. For example, Mam Sithole did not conduct teacher evaluations alone. Instead, a teacher evaluation was a forum in which teachers began to learn from and listen to each other in a professional manner. Times were set during which all teachers in a grade level would visit the class in progress taught by another colleague. They would take notes, ask questions, and discuss what they saw. Teachers used these sessions as an opportunity to challenge each other's assumptions and draw upon each other's strengths to grow. When such cooperation was built, it became "easier" to work with a positive attitude under adverse but supportive conditions. In fact, on one occasion, the inspectors came unannounced for teacher evaluations. Coincidentally, they found all teachers of the same grade observing other teachers and holding discussions about what they noticed. The inspectors were astounded and wished other schools could emulate Khwezi L. P. When the inspectors had requests from some important visitors or guests who wanted to visit schools in the district, the inspectors referred them to Khwezi L. P.

While this was a positive recognition, teachers began to feel that they were put on the spot. It could have been misperceived by other schools that the teachers at Khwezi L. P. were the administration's "pets." Because of the apartheid system's history and what it represented in the eyes of most teachers and students, it was not always a prestigious honor to be recognized or aligned with the administration. In order to circumvent the development of envy or mistrust among other schools, teachers at Khwezi began to develop networks with neighboring schools wherein they could meet, without the top administrators' presence, and discuss issues that affected them and ways they were handling these issues. These networks were at their infancy stage while I was in the field.

Teachers capitalized on the transition period by doing what they felt was helpful to the advancement of their learners and themselves. For example, teachers at Khwezi L. P. ignored the bureaucratic chain when they learned about workshops or conferences in a particular location. As they shared in the interviews, they secretly attended these professional meetings without seeking or waiting for approval from the administration. The belief was that when you build a teacher, you build learners. In fact, Mam Sithole defiantly and sarcastically said, "I would like to be fired for having attended a professional meeting." These professional workshops were sponsored by nongovernmental organizations and groups in the country and within some universities. Some courses were offered during the school days.

Since these professional workshops were outside the jurisdiction of the district or regional educational administration, if teachers wanted to attend they would have to get permission in advance. However, during this particular transition period in South African political history in 1991, teachers like Mam Sithole felt they could no longer wait for approval to receive education to help them improve their teaching practices. They had been deprived exposure to various education opportunities long enough, so that when such opportunities arose, they were willing to risk their careers. Since this was the just course—the course toward advancement of the black child—being fired for such a course would likely evoke community sympathy. This might lead to a direct challenge of the government structures by the people. The process of political change and optimism in the face of violence created confidence among teachers, particularly at Khezi L. P. Teachers felt that the time for receiving mandates without having input was over, and time for "consultation" had arrived.

Summary

Stories from the principal and teachers at Khezi L. P. illustrate the following themes. Despite violent conditions, teachers were inspired by the presence of innocent children, thus fueling their commitment and determination to strive for a better future. The strong spiritual belief in the power of God in their lives helped sustain them in times of trouble. The sense of community after disaster was a galvanizing force in the school and community. The prospects for political change built a positive attitude toward life and work. Teachers became creative and resourceful during times of adversity. The story at Khwezi L. P. illustrates that one strong person with a vision and dedication can motivate teachers to survive and work under intolerable conditions. As seen in these stories, teachers at Khwezi L. P. were not only followers. They contributed and became "leaders" in a variety of ways that were reflected in the cooperative ventures and teacher networks they developed. When more teachers are involved as "leaders," their networks have a greater likelihood of being sustained compared to a situation in which leadership is entrusted to only one person. If that one "leader" leaves the district, everything might crumble, but at Khwezi there were indications that this was circumvented.

Conclusion

The apartheid structures have been destroyed, but the scars of violence they inflicted provide a clear reminder about the past. African schools are still largely overcrowded, underresourced, and understaffed. Parents who can afford to take their children to better resourced schools can now freely do so, but for the poor who cannot freely move because of financial constraints, the same schools remain the only hope for their children. Teachers in these schools can make or break the realization of children's dreams. The stories from Khwezi L. P. and other schools can serve as an anchor and support for teachers. The stories show that with leadership and support among their own, teachers can inspire each other. With a moral and political vision, determination, and an energizing and positive attitude, teachers can look toward the present and the future with optimism. Upgrading programs for teachers might help, but teachers do not always find the knowledge transferable into the classroom. For this reason, teachers also need to realize the power and resourcefulness they possess when committed to teaching, particularly under intolerable conditions.

While the lessons from the above stories could resonate with teachers in similar conditions in South Africa, the elements in these stories depict some universal characteristics inherent in humans and demonstrate their potential to survive and transform their situations. Violence as a universal phenomenon occurs in various places and forms. For example, in the United States, Jonathan Kozol (1991) still observes the "savage inequalities" in schools, long after integration and equality have been institutionalized. Who can better stand up for children in those schools than teachers? As Heller and Hawkins (1994) point out, there are various forms of violence; therefore, different kinds of tolerance need to be taught. Other lessons can be learned implicitly from the teachers' stories, including how children can be helped to prosper under a teacher's care.

Acknowledgments

Part of the data presented in this chapter was initially collected in 1991 for the doctoral thesis study entitled *South African Teachers' Perspectives on Teaching Beginning Reading* which was submitted to the Harvard Graduate School of Education, Cambridge, Massachusetts, in 1993. That study was partially funded by the Harvard Institute of International Development, Cambridge, Massachusetts. I therefore thank my doctoral committee, Joseph Maxwell, Courtney Cazden, and Israel Scheffler, whose support inspired the analytic work I pursued in this essay. I also appreciate the Education and Training Department and the KwaZulu Education and Culture Department in South Africa for allowing me to conduct the research in schools. In particular, I am indebted to the principals, teachers, and students, whose names are protected, for their cooperation. I also owe gratitude for helpful comments on the previous drafts I received from Nomsa Geleta of Chadron State College in Chadron, Nebraska; Katherine Bucher of Old Dominion University in Norfolk, Virginia; and the editor of this book, Judith Robertson. I take full responsibility for the content and the views expressed in this essay.

Notes

1. Throughout this chapter, the term *black* is used to refer to all people other than whites in South Africa. *African* refers to the indigenous people of South Africa.

2. Under the apartheid system, the education of different racial groups (whites, coloreds, Indians, and Africans) was administered under separate education departments. African areas were demarcated on "ethnic" lines, called "homelands." Education for Africans who lived in areas designated as "white areas" was controlled by the government under the Department of Education and Training.

3. The Inkatha Freedom Party started as a cultural movement in 1975 and changed into a political party in 1990. Political differences and strategies led to different conflicts with other political organizations, such

as the African National Congress (ANC) which was founded in 1912 and was banned for decades. The ANC operated underground inside the country while some leaders were in jail and others in exile. It was unbanned in 1990, led the negotiated settlement toward a political transition, and won the first democratic election in 1994.

4. The Breakthrough to Literacy approach was initially developed and became successful in Britain. In the 1970s, the Molteno Project, under the auspices of the Institute for the Study of English in Africa at Rhodes University, adopted the approach in teaching beginning readers using different African languages.

Works Cited

Brook, D. L., S. L. Field, and L. D. Labbo. 1995. "South Africa's Transformation as Seen at School." *Social Education* 59(2): 82–86.

Christie, Pam. 1985. *The Right to Learn: The Struggle for Education in South Africa.* Johannesburg: Ravan Press.

Cooper, Carole, et al. 1992. *Race Relations Survey 1991/92.* Johannesburg: South African Institute of Race Relations.

Degenaar, Johan. 1990. "The Concept of Violence." In *Political Violence and the Struggle in South Africa,* edited by N. Chabani Manganyi and André du Toit, 70–86. New York: St. Martin's.

Duckworth, Eleanor. 1987. *"The Having of Wonderful Ideas" and Other Essays on Teaching and Learning.* New York: Teachers College Press.

Gehrig, Gail. 1991. "Strategies for Teaching Greater Tolerance of Cultural Diversity." *Teaching Sociology* 19 (January): 62–65.

Heller, Carol, and Joseph A. Hawkins. 1994. "Teaching Tolerance: Notes from the Front Line." *Teachers College Record* 95(3): 337–67.

Hirschowitz, R., S. Milner, and D. Everatt. 1994. "Growing Up in a Violent Society." In *Creating a Future Youth Policy for South Africa,* edited by David Everatt, 67–96. Johannesburg: Ravan Press.

Hoffmann, Wilma, and Brian McKendrick. 1990. "The Nature of Violence." In *People and Violence in South Africa,* edited by Brian McKendrick and Wilma Hoffmann, 1–35. Cape Town: Oxford University Press.

Human Sciences Research Council. 1987. *The South African Society: Realities and Future Prospects.* New York: Greenwood Press.

Johnson, David. 1991. "People's Education and the Politics of Writing: Issues, Perspectives and Possibilities for a Future South Africa." In *Apartheid Education and Popular Struggles.* Edited by Elaine Unterhalter, Harold Wolpe, Thozamile Botha, Saleem Badaat, Thulisile Dlamini, and Benito Ksotsengs, 172–84. London: Zed Books.

Kallaway, Peter. 1984. *Apartheid and Education: The Education of Black South Africans.* Johannesburg: Ravan Press.

Kozol, Jonathan. 1991. *Savage Inequalities: Children in America's Schools.* New York: HarperPerennial.

Marks, Shula, and Neil Andersson. 1990. "The Epidemiology and Culture of Violence." *Political Violence and the Struggle in South Africa,* edited by N. Chabani Manganyi and André du Toit, 29–69. New York: St. Martin's.

Mdluli, S. B. 1980. *A Description of the Educational System of KwaZulu with Emphasis on Pupil Repetition.* Bloemfontein: University of the Orange Free State.

Motala, Shireen. 1995. "Surviving the System—A Critical Appraisal of Some Conventional Wisdom in Primary Education in South Africa." *Comparative Education* 31(2): 161–79.

Nzimande, Blade. 1993. *Schooling in the Context of Violence.* EPU Working Paper, No. 3. Durban, South Africa: University of Natal.

Robertson, Ian. 1969. *Education with Political Purpose: The South African System.* Qualifying Paper, Harvard Graduate School of Education.

Scharfstein, Ben-Ami. 1989. *The Dilemma of Context.* New York University Press.

Seme, P. J. Nomathemba. 1988. "A Black South African Perspective on Dialogue Journals in a Mother Tongue Language." *Dialogue* 5(1): 5–7.

———. 1993. *South African Teachers' Perspectives on Teaching Beginning Reading.* Ed.D. diss., Graduate School of Education, Harvard University.

Sithole, Jabu. 1996. "KZN War Affected Education Heavily." *Witness Echo* (Pietermaritzburg)(November): 4.

Sommer, Henrik. 1996. "From Apartheid to Democracy: Patterns of Violent and Nonviolent Direct Action in South Africa, 1984–1994." *Africa Today* 43(1): 53–76.

Straker, Gill. 1992. *Faces in the Revolution: The Psychological Effects of Violence on Township Youth in South Africa.* Cape Town: David Philip.

Swartz, Leslie, and Ann Levett. 1990. "Political Oppression and Children in South Africa: The Social Construction of Damaging Effects." In *Political Violence and the Struggle in South Africa,* edited by N. Chabani Manganyi and André du Toit, 265–86. New York: St. Martin's.

Vogt, W. Paul. 1994. "Introduction: Six Questions about Tolerance and Education." *The Review of Education/Pedagogy/Cultural Studies* 16(3–4): 273–76.

Williams, May M., and Richard J. Johnson. 1995. "Teaching Tolerance with Multimedia." *The Executive Educator* (June): 16–17, 44.

Teaching Risky Stories: Remembering Mass Destruction through Children's Literature

Roger I. Simon
Ontario Institute for Studies in Education, University of Toronto

Wendy Armitage Simon
Dundas Public School, Toronto Board of Education

In the introduction to the English translation of Yukio Tsuchiya's classic antiwar story *Faithful Elephants: A True Story of Animals, People and War* (1988), Chieko Akiyama states:

> the biggest gift adults can give to children is to make public the complete history of . . . war, and to help them consider how we can realize the human ideal. I hope this book will be read throughout the world and that seeds of peace and war prevention will be sown.

Yet, after reading *Faithful Elephants* neither of us thought it suitable for classroom use. This picture book left us deeply disturbed and angered by its detailed portrayal of sustained cruelty. Despite its heroic intent, for us (in the educational situations we could anticipate for ourselves), Tsuchiya went too far for his story to be used in productive conversation with children about historical realities and the possibility of a more just and peaceful future. For this reason we were astonished by the promotional text on the book's cover which reported that *Faithful Elephants* has been extremely popular in Japan, where it has been reprinted seventy times since its publication in 1951 and, for decades, read on Japanese radio on the yearly anniversary of Japan's surrender in World War II. In recent years in North America, there has been an increase in the availability of literature written for children that attempts to convey the realities and human

Grateful acknowledgment is made to *English Quarterly* for permission to reprint this essay, which appeared in an earlier version under the same title in 1995 in *English Quarterly* 28(1): 27–31.

experiences of war and genocide. A central question that any teacher or parent has to confront when deciding whether to encourage and support the reading of these texts is whether or not they are too graphic, too emotionally manipulative, and/or too focused on scenes of violence, cruelty, destructiveness, and suffering. As indicated by the disjunction between our response to *Faithful Elephants* and its widespread acceptance in Japan, how one judges whether or not a text has gone "too far" is not straightforward. More is at stake than questions of age-appropriate subject matter. Such judgments also evoke questions as to how our ethnocultural and national histories as well as ongoing communal relations are implicated in what we define as the value and dangers of encouraging children to engage historical narratives that may be deeply disturbing.

The following thoughts are a culturally and historically contingent attempt to wrestle with the question of how teachers might understand and respond to the risk in specific historical narratives. Our focus is on picture books and novels intended to help children remember, understand, and confront the implications of the Nazi genocide of European Jewry (the Holocaust) and the use of nuclear weapons on the people of Hiroshima and Nagasaki. While we will not systematically consider the question of the substance, sequence, and scope of curriculum units which might contextualize the reading of such materials, we will be concerned with what the "risky" aspects of such texts require in the way of a curricular response.

What is at stake in these texts is not just the provision of information and the humanization of impersonal historical accounts and statistics. In addition, the hope is that stories of persecution and suffering will become part of a remembrance which will have some progressive, moral force. This is based on the familiar assumption that literature has the power to facilitate an ethical sense within, which enhances a concern for others, responsibility to the values of diversity and human rights, and a sense of hope which, while developing the capacity to look life in the face, maintains a vigilance against injustice.

Risky Stories

It is no surprise that narratives which express experiences of people during the Holocaust or in the aftermath of the bombing of Hiroshima might be disturbing. Obviously, stories that graphically deal with degradation, pain, and death can be emotionally invasive. Not only may students reasonably respond to overly graphic texts with psychic defenses which drastically limit what might be learned from such stories, but reading such texts may initiate depression and nightmares and/or reactivate trauma memories. Furthermore, rather than encouraging students to learn more about the events portrayed, scenes that are emotionally invasive may actually deter students from seeking more information.

Emphasizing the importance of maintaining a "safe classroom environment," guidelines for teaching the Holocaust often suggest that teachers avoid using images and texts that exploit students' emotional vulnerability (Parsons and Totten 1993). Such concerns, in part, explain the heavy emphasis in Holocaust children's literature on themes of hiding, rescue, and resistance. Typically, these texts offer plotlines written to elicit reader identification with heroic characters who, while confronting dangerous situations and challenging tasks, pull the narrative through to a form of redemptive conclusion. While set in a historical context which includes the horrors of deportation, degradation, and extermination, rescue and resistance stories tend to avoid vivid descriptions of events that convey the extent to which people can inflict suffering and death on others. While something of a shattering tragedy has to be conveyed, the emphasis is usually on the tenacity of the human spirit and people's extraordinary efforts to preserve human dignity and life.

There are, however, texts that are widely available and stocked in school libraries that do depict experiences of deportation, incarceration, and mass extermination of Jews. Texts also exist which vividly portray the immediate and long-term effects of the bombing of Hiroshima on individual children and adults who struggled to survive the aftermath. To provide a clearer image of why these texts evoke risks for their readers, consider the following examples. In our view, scenes from these texts radically disrupt beliefs which provide a measure of stability and predictability about life, rupturing assumptions about what it means to be human and what is beyond the bounds of possibility.

Daniel's Story (Matas 1993) is a novel published in conjunction with an exhibit at the United States Holocaust Memorial Museum. It is commonly used in grades 7 and 8 but has been used in junior school grades as well. Daniel, (a fictitious character) narrates his experiences as a Jewish child living through the Nazi persecution and genocide of European Jewry. The story begins with Daniel's prewar experiences in Frankfurt. In this setting he witnesses growing persecution of Jews in Germany. Eventually, he and his family are deported to the Lodz Ghetto, where they live for a period of time. They are then transported to and incarcerated in Auschwitz, where his mother is killed. Subsequently, Daniel and his father are moved to Buchenwald where, as the war ends, they are liberated. His sister, who also survived Auschwitz, dies in a displaced persons' camp. We are not here concerned with the literary or historical merits of this novel, but with exemplifying text which, rather than avoiding emotionally difficult scenes, does depict events such as the deportation to and arrival at Auschwitz, the practice of extermination, the burning of bodies, and the processing of huge quantities of appropriated clothes, cut hair, eyeglasses, and other personal effects. Here is a brief excerpt during which Daniel describes his experience soon after his arrival at Auschwitz:

> We are taken into a barracks, where we are forced to undress. We have to leave our things. I tuck my pictures deep into my boots. Then we are hustled into a long room that has two benches running down the center, and prisoners with razors standing along the benches. The guards are constantly screaming at us and pushing us, so we don't have time to think or react. Our heads are shaved, and then our entire bodies. The barbers cut as they shave us. Then the guards push us into another room, where prisoners pour disinfectant over us. I can't help but scream. It is terribly painful, because I am bleeding from the cuts the barbers gave me. (75–76)

Such text stands in marked contrast to that found in such well-used and highly regarded books as *Number the Stars* (a story set in the context of the rescue of Danish Jews), *Jacob's Rescue*, (the story of Polish Christian Alex Roslan and the three Jewish children he hides from the Nazis and Polish informants) and, of course, *Anne Frank: The Diary of a Young Girl*. In the two rescue stories, though the reader is confronted with individual death and suffering, there are no scenes directly dealing with the Nazi practices of systematic degradation and genocide. In *Anne Frank*, the focus is on Anne's sensitivity, intelligence, and hopeful outlook, without any direct confrontation with the realities of genocide that lead to her death.

Similar comparisons can be found in the literature related to the bombing of Hiroshima; specifically in picture books that could be used in the junior grades. The following story not only graphically depicts young children being subjected to human-initiated pain and death, but calls into question assumptions about a parent's ability to keep children safe under any circumstances. Originally published in Japan in 1992 and just recently translated, *Shin's Tricycle* (Kodama, 1995) is a true story (underscored by photographs of Shin and his partially destroyed tricycle on the last page). Narrated by Shin's father, it tells the story of a three-year-old (Shin) who desperately wanted a tricycle for his birthday but couldn't have one because of the metal shortages in wartime Japan. His uncle finds a tricycle and brings it to Shin. Shin and his best friend Kimi are depicted laughing and playing with the tricycle, while Shin's sisters (Michiko and Yoko) are in the house. At this point in the narrative, the reader turns the page to be visually jolted by an illustration of the blinding bright blast of the atomic bomb. From this point on, the book pictorially and verbally conveys the effects of the atomic bomb on the children in the story. The following excerpt occurs after sequences of images and text that relate how Shin has been badly hurt (he dies soon after) and Kimi "was gone, lost somewhere under the house." Shin's two sisters are pinned under the roof beams when a "wall of fire" races toward the house. The text accompanies a visual illustration of Shin's father attempting to rescue his daughters.

> "Michiko! Yoko!" I screamed. "I'm coming!"
> With all my strength I tried to lift the roof beams, but couldn't. The fire was very close now, and it was so hot I feared my clothes would start burning. Suddenly, the beam on top of Michiko and Yoko burst into flames.
> "Michiko! Yoko!" I cried in horror. I was helpless to save my girls. There was nothing I could do. But Shin still had a chance, so Mother and I rushed him away from the raging fire to the river.

In a similar vein, *Hiroshima No Pika* (*The Flash of Hiroshima*) is a detailed and visually compelling depiction of the effects of the atomic bomb on people, their lives, and their city, as told through the story of a little girl, Mii, and her parents. After three pages setting up Mii's family life and a depiction of the city prior to the blast, the next twenty-two pages of the book provide a detailed account of the efforts of this little family to survive during their (and the reader's) encounter with the devastating effects of the dropping of the bomb. It should be noted that while in *Shin's Tricycle* the atomic bomb simply occurs, *Hiroshima No Pika* is quite explicit in naming the "United States Air Force bomber Enola Gay" as the plane that dropped the bomb, thus making it clear that the suffering of the people of Hiroshima was a result of human action (however, the text offers no explanation for this action). These two texts stand in marked contrast to Eleanor Coerr's now famous and familiar *Sadako and the Thousand Paper Cranes* (1977). This is a poignant story of a twelve-year-old girl who develops the "A-Bomb disease" (leukemia) and her struggle to maintain hope and survive. She folds 650 paper cranes before she dies, trying to live out the legend that one might be cured by folding one thousand cranes. The story begins in 1951, hence avoiding all the details of the dropping of the bomb and its immediate aftermath. Very much like *Anne Frank, Sadako* is a story through which children can celebrate human courage and optimism while keeping the realities of mass destruction contained in the abstractions of "war" or "the bomb."

What would warrant encouraging and supporting children to engage risky texts like *Daniel's Story, Shin's Tricycle,* and *Hiroshima No Pika*? The authors of such books commonly have two basic intentions: (1) to memorialize victims of mass death and destruction through the production of texts that may serve as a lasting memory to those who suffered and were killed, and (2) to present a warning that may instill caution and protect against future evil and indifference. Providing images of the tremendous suffering inflicted on innocent people as a consequence of deliberate human actions, the authors hope to create memories of things past that inform aspirations, plans, and actions that would prevent any recurrence of such unwarranted violence and cruelty. This is consistent with contemporary assumptions as to what education must be accountable to: developing a moral sensibility that would not be indifferent to suffering and the infringement of the rights of others; a critical understanding of stereotyping and prejudice and how these are integral to racism, sexism, and anti-Semitism; and a sense of responsibility and ability to take action in support of those democratic institutions which protect a tolerance for diversity and human rights. Such accountability criteria are rooted in a belief that things can be better and that education can participate in this betterment. In this view, even though it poses some risk, one is required to disclose and expose what happened in order to prevent its recurrence.

However, memory is not straightforwardly redemptive. In the face of contemporary events such as the war in Bosnia and the genocide which recently occurred in Rwanda, the wish that risky stories will straightforwardly serve as a warning which will sensitize individuals to injustice and serve as a goad to action seems just that, merely a wish. While we do not discount the possibility that engaging risky stories set in the context of the Holocaust or Hiroshima might serve as a form of inoculation against the horrors of human indifference and will to power, the prospects of such seem a weak basis on which to risk confronting children with the radical disruptiveness of stories which depict the destructive capabilities of our species.

Shadow Texts

How might we think about this in another way? To start with, the injunction "listen and remember" is insufficient. As educators, we need to be sensitive to the fact that remembrance of events is conditioned by the terms on which, individually and collectively, people are able to admit disruptive and disturbing images and narratives into historical memory. What is needed is a better understanding of what it means to listen to or read stories of cruelty and suffering set in contexts like the Holocaust or the bombing of Hiroshima. How do people engage narratives of events whose content is disturbing; events which unhinge us; which seem deeply out of joint with our grasp of reality?

This is an important question for teachers helping children to mediate risky stories. At the very least, it expands a teacher's responsibility to not only help in comprehension of narrative, but as well, to help students acknowledge and articulate what they need or want to know. At stake is a teaching practice which proceeds from the recognition that stories of genocide and mass destruction evoke questions (sometimes barely stated) rooted in the need to assimilate these stories into some communal framework of interpretation which makes intelligible the regularities and possibilities of daily life. This is why the following questions are so commonly asked: Did this story really happen or is it made up? If it was real, could it happen again? Could it happen to me? Why did people let these events happen? Why did people in the story respond as they did? How could anyone do this to innocent people?

Initiated by the basic disturbances set in motion by narratives of extreme cruelty and suffering, these are hard questions, and children recognize them as important. It is not just emotional threat that accounts for the silence that comes over a classroom when children are read stories of cruelty and mass destruction. Such stories tap into issues quite different from those raised by conventional schooling activities like doing math, practicing handwriting, and listening to light-hearted stories read by a teacher. It is our contention that risky stories, well told, make present a testimony—an owning of the truth of an experience—whose call to witness breaks the boundaries of what children normally experience of schooling. What is initiated actually ruptures everyday routines, transforming a group or class engagement with certain stories into something serious and significant beyond conventional classroom concerns.

It is in response to such concerns and the difficult questions they pose that stories of genocide and mass destruction foster the writing of what we call "shadow texts," secondary narratives constructed in response to the unresolved questions a primary narrative elicits. Shadow texts are written as people attempt to mediate the questions that accompany and move in time with the hearing of an account (Mitchell 1994, 190). As an example, consider our own reading of the previously mentioned *Faithful Elephants*.[1] It is a story set in Japan during the Second World War. Because of the bombing of Tokyo, it is decided that all the animals in the Tokyo Zoo are to be killed to prevent them running loose in the city if the zoo is hit by bombs. The zookeepers are able to poison all the animals except three well-loved performing elephants. They try to poison the elephants' food and inject them with a serum, but all this fails. It is ordered they be starved to death. Over half the pages in the text are devoted to visual and textual depiction of the elephants starving and begging for food in front of the zookeepers by attempting tricks for which they have previously been rewarded. The zookeepers are upset, but most of them persist in this action until finally the elephants die.

Not surprisingly, we found ourselves asking how the zoo-keepers could persist in this torture of animals that they had previously nurtured. At the very least, could they not have found some other way to kill the animals? Could they not have found a way to move the animals away from being hit by bombs? The text does not provide answers to these questions which strike at the heart of our preferred beliefs about the viability of sustained human cruelty. To alleviate this disruption, we assumed that with Japan rapidly being defeated and with the existence of many shortages of materials, the zookeepers could not obtain bullets or guns (which would have at least eliminated the elephants' suffering). This is the shadow text we have written. It is not based on factual evidence but is rather a presumption (founded on what we previously learned about material shortages during wartime) that allows us to maintain the belief that the human zookeepers had no choice, unwilling as we are to seriously entertain the possibility that they were indifferent to the elephants' suffering or simply stupid. It is a shadow text we prefer, although we remain unconvinced by it and critical of the humanist desires which seem to drive our interpretive preferences. Our point, of course, is that all such disturbing stories will elicit attempts to write shadow texts. Whether or not a teacher participates in a conversation which helps construct these shadow texts, it is important to emphasize that there will likely be an attempt to construct them on whatever terms (factual or not) are ready at hand to a child.

What we are edging toward is turning the potential damage of risky stories on its head and asking of the positive consequences to helping children to develop frameworks within which to accept stories that are fundamentally disturbing. Thus recognizing that risky stories evoke shadow texts, the task would be for students and teachers to find ways to uncover those questions which structure the shadow texts any given story produces and collectively explore how to respond to these questions. Anticipating this task, it then follows that the stories a teacher chooses to use, the preparation students have before hearing stories, and the accountability teachers demand of students' engagements will affect how students mediate the disruptions posed by a text.

Whatever the basis on which a group of students might claim the memory of a story, it is important to be sensitive to the fact that such practices will define the limit of a collective understanding of stories of events such as the Holocaust or the bombing of Hiroshima. The boundaries of this limit cannot be simply the responsibility of a group of student readers. Teachers have a responsibility to participate in this discussion and must be able, to a degree, to anticipate the kinds of questions a text will elicit as well as provide an expanded set of resources students might use to write alternative shadow texts.

It is crucial that teachers be prepared to enact this responsibility, considering that students may not be able to work through the difficulties and irresolvability of questions elicited by risky stories. Students may either write the shadow texts that serve their own (at times racist or sexist) preconceptions or repress, dismiss, or become indifferent to the stories.

Thus teachers need to face up to their own preparedness to teach such stories. If teachers have little background information about a historical event and its context and have not either resolved the questions such stories elicit or found a way to live with the unknowability of many of the questions they raise, perhaps they should not incorporate these stories in their curricula. Teachers must also be prepared to recognize the pedagogical limits of using or discussing risky stories in the inability of students to successfully write shadow texts which resolve the threats such stories elicit.

The Classroom as a Community of Memory

The basic educational purpose of attempting to integrate stories of genocide and mass destruction into a compilation of narratives that express the range of human possibilities is so that new codes of behavior might be based on this information. While a specific story may individually touch any given student, we conceive of the educational project behind placing such stories on the curriculum in more social terms. Thus teaching risky stories is not simply a matter of helping individual students mediate such stories themselves. Rather, it is a matter of structuring a practice among a group of children in which readers (or listeners) can claim a story as their own so that as they remember this story, it becomes part of their repertoire of living memories; a way in which history can come truly alive.

This is why, in our view, a fundamental part of any unit or theme that includes risky stories would be the opportunity for a group of students to work through (from the stock of beliefs and conventions they find workable/plausible/acceptable) how to respond to any given story. Such opportunities are enabled by the fostering of a reading community or, preferably, a *community of memory*. This community is one created in the process of (and thereby contributes to) comprehending risky stories *and* taking on the obligations that hearing or reading these stories requires.

This means teaching risky stories must address a double agenda. First, there needs to be time during which the teacher and children share written or oral responses to stories. This sharing must be structured so as to address the basis on which stories are comprehended and shadow texts are written. Second, and equally important, each story needs to be understood as a call to readers to witness an account of what happened to a particular population of people at a certain time in history. This means readers of risky stories are being called to take on the responsibilities and obligations of what it means to witness an account. It is crucial that teachers are clear what these obligations are and what they mean for planning classroom activities.

Witnessing requires making judgments as to the substance and significance of what is to be remembered about a story. These judgments are cognitive and ethical, and imply the acceptance of particular responsibilities. First, it is required that one bear (support and endure) the weight or psychic burden of that history, acknowledging that memories of violence and injustice do press down on one's personal and collective sense of humanity and moral equilibrium. Second, it is required that one bear (carry) or transport/translate stories of past injustices beyond their moment of hearing (or being read) by taking these stories to another time and space where they become available to be heard or seen again. Third, it is required that one bear the responsibility of showing or telling what one has witnessed in the reading or hearing of a story in a way that makes clear why a reader or group of readers thinks it is an important story to remember (Simon and Eppert 1997).

By retelling a story or stories, students initiate their own testimonial address to others. Pedagogically, retelling is anything but an abstract or arbitrary exercise. It must be accomplished concretely as students consider if, why, to whom, (and crucially) how, when, and where a testimony would be retold. Thus students would have to decide what aspects of a testimony must be emphasized and what could be left out. In the context of these deliberations, they would need to explain why they have chosen to re-present (and remember) the testimony on the specific terms decided on; clarifying, as well, how precisely this re-presentation is to be communicated (via words, images, gesture, song, etc.). In such considerations, students would have to make clear in what way (if any) their re-presentations take into account the persons to whom they address their witness. In addition, consideration needs also to be given as to whether there are particular times that seem most appropriate to re-present a given testimony and whether there are particular spaces or spatial arrangements most appropriate to their re-presentation.

In preparing a group of students for this task of witnessing, there are obviously specific language skills that must be developed. Clearly students must be able to reconstruct an experience by reflecting on the key elements of a story, select and organize information, choose appropriate vocabulary to use in retelling, determine their audience and the needs of the audience, and sequence events in a logical order. However, in addition to preparatory skill development, what is needed to work through the task of witnessing is a communal (be it a group or class) sense of why it is important to remember particular stories by passing them on to others. Any attempt to implement a community of memory in a teaching situation requires a framing and sustained conversation about the practices of public memory. In focusing on why passing on stories is important, what can be opened for exploration is the power of storytelling as a social practice.

Conclusion

Teaching from within a community of memory requires discussing and wrestling with the significance of the *social act of retelling* stories. Terrence Des Pres (1988) views words as weapons against oppression even though a story, memoir, or poem will not in itself change the world. He asserts that memory transmitted through literature or poetry can make something happen: "It allows me to know what I fear, to understand (by standing under) the burden of my humanness. It also makes possible the essential decency of compassion, of suffering with—a symbolic action, to be sure, but one without which the spirit withers, the self shuts down" (23). If we take this view seriously, at stake in the practice of witnessing risky stories within communities of memory is the sustained and very conscious performance of remembrance. This performance (via the concrete practice of retelling) is a communicative act with the potential to enact historical consciousness as a moral and pedagogical force. Thus, if one begins with the assumption that remembrance through retelling has at least the potential to contribute to the lessening of systemic violence in the world, this requires that a community begin to consider and devise the storytelling practices needed to place the burden of our humanness under the demands of compassion and justice.

Felman and Laub (1992) suggest "Memory is conjured . . . in order to address another, to impress upon a listener, to appeal to a community. . . . To testify is thus not merely to narrate but to commit oneself, and to commit the narrative, to others: to take responsibility—in speech—for history or for the truth of an occurrence . . ." (204). Deciding which stories should be retold to whom and in what way requires that students take on this responsibility through the speech acts which (1) name a story as important to pass on; and (2) re-present that story in concrete form to others. In this context the classroom becomes a site in which a nuanced vocabulary of witnessing can be built, enacted, and borne out in the practice of living memory. It is through such practices of "re-memory" (Morrison 1987) that people are able to hold on to an affirmation of life in the face of death and to be vigilant to the requirements of building a just future. These are not easy tasks, nor can they be accomplished alone.

Concretely they define pedagogic grounds for a community which remembers.

Note   1. For a positive judgment on the productive use of *Faithful Elephants* in North American classrooms, readers should see Crowell (1993) and Whitmore and Crowell (1993).

Works Cited

Coerr, Eleanor. 1977. *Sadako and the Thousand Paper Cranes.* New York: Putnam.

Crowell, Caryl G. 1993. "Living through War Vicariously with Literature." In *Teachers Are Researchers: Reflection and Action,* edited by L. Patterson, K. Smith, C. Santa, and K. Short. Newark, DE: International Reading Association.

Des Pres, Terrence. 1988. *Praises and Dispraises: Poetry and Politics in the Twentieth Century.* New York: Viking.

Felman, Shoshana, and Dori Laub. 1992. *Testimony: Crises of Witnessing in Literature, Psychoanalysis, and History.* New York: Routledge.

Kodama, Tatsuharu. 1995. *Shin's Tricycle.* Translated by Kazuko Houmen-Jones. New York: Walker and Company.

Matas, Carol. 1993. *Daniel's Story.* New York: Scholastic.

Morrison, Toni. 1987. *Beloved.* London: Chatto & Windus.

Parsons, William, and Samuel Totten. 1993. *Guidelines for Teaching about the Holocaust.* Washington, DC: United States Holocaust Memorial Museum.

Simon, Roger I., and Claudia Eppert. 1997. "Remembering Obligation: Pedagogy and the Witnessing of Testimony of Historical Trauma." *Canadian Journal of Education* 22(2): 175–91.

Tsuchiya, Yukio. 1988. *Faithful Elephants: A True Story of Animals, People, and War.* Translated by Tomoko Dykes Tsuchiya. Boston: Houghton Mifflin.

Whitmore, Kathryn, and Caryl G. Crowell. 1993. "What Makes a Question Good Is. . . ." *The New Advocate* (December).

15 Teaching about Worlds of Hurt through Encounters with Literature: Reflections on Pedagogy

Judith P. Robertson
University of Ottawa

L ate he come walking and it be Nightjohn and he bringing us the way to know." Presented in the beautifully cadenced language of Black English, these images bring to a close the novel *Nightjohn*. Authored by Gary Paulsen (1993), the narrative is an explicit account of white cruelty, the experience of black African American resistance to slavery, and the passionate struggle for life and literacy that enable the telling of a story. The lyrically unflinching first-person voice of the preadolescent protagonist, Sarney, relates how life is lived in the American South in the 1850s on a plantation owned by "old Clel Waller": "He wants that we should call him 'master,' and they's some do when he can hear but we call him dog droppings and pig slop and worse things yet when he ain't listening nor close" (14). The text makes intelligible some very disturbing aspects of the human condition. It gives considerable measure to dimensions of human barbarism. It reveals how savagery operates socially in explicitly gendered and racialized ways. It raises important questions about how the elements of history determine how a story shapes itself. It sheds light on the materiality of language and the potential for social analysis and enablement through words. At the same time, the narrative remains attentive to the risks of hope by refusing a happily-ever-after ending that imagines human communities living together in loving solidarity.

Language arts teachers face a formidable task when they attempt to teach children lessons about the sanctity of life through literary encounters with worlds of pain. This essay explores three issues. First, what knowledge are we trying to teach when we ask children to read stories about incidences of horror? Second, how do preservice elementary teachers experience the dangers and possibilities of using such literature? And third, what concepts and strategies can literary practitioners call upon to assist child readers and teachers in working through the psychic dangers that attend literary learning about loss through human cruelty?

History in the Real

As any beginning teacher will attest, standard texts and curricula produced to facilitate classroom practices in language arts education for the most part remain silent about the significant pedagogical challenges of genres like children's historical fiction or autobiographical life stories. In a quick shelf survey of publisher samples of current language arts texts for beginning teachers marketed for use in my Canadian faculty of education, I discovered none that included index entries for discussions of "trauma" or "risk" in literary learning. I did find many, however, that proposed guidance for teaching about "historical literacy" or "historical fiction." The information provided under these entries is illuminating both for what it does and does not say about the genres. Here is one example:

> Based on facts and set in the past, historical fiction is realistic, true to the time period depicted, but is not restricted by it. It contains convincing dialogue between characters and accurate descriptions of setting and happenings, furthering children's knowledge of other times and places. When integrated into subject areas this literature not only supports learning the facts of history but it makes history more real and relevant (Cullinan 1989). If children understand the past, they will have a better understanding of the future. Historical fiction can make the past come alive for students. It can make content area learning more interesting by providing related knowledge about people, places, and events in history. It also can help students become aware of their own heritage. (Bromley 1992, 51–53)

The passage comes across as invitational, authoritative, natural, and instructive. Teachers are invited to view historical fiction as a form of expressive realism, in which verisimilitude, authentic voice, the capacity for provoking empathy through identification with characters, and a one-to-one correspondence between story and history serve as a defense for the moral inviolateness of the text and hope for the future (Bogdan 1987).

While such exhortations are well intentioned, they are problematic. There are significant unthought areas in the above claims that need to be examined if pedagogical encounters with worlds of hurt are to be anything other than hurtful. First, the passage nullifies by virtue of omission the possibility that encounters with the characters, themes, and events narrated in historical fiction and autobiographical life stories will produce disturbing effects in readers (see Davis 1997; Mier 1985). Second, it marks the value of historical fiction as one that emanates from the "truth," "based on facts . . . true to the time period depicted . . . accurate." The discussion provides no space for discussing the relations between story and history, where questions of historical truth and the devices of rhetoric and narrative that make life experiences both intelligible and open to interpretation need to figure (Bristow 1991; Simon and Armitage Simon 1995). Third, the presentation of literature as a reflection of life (through "convincing dialogue . . . and accurate descriptions of setting and happening") grounds its logic on assumptions about the transparency of language. The suggestion is that learning about extreme suffering can occur somehow straightforwardly through narrative accounts that provide for certainty, clarity, and understanding. This conclusion is naive because it fails to anticipate and then to prepare for the doubt, messiness, and risks involved in witnessing the mute materiality of suffering itself.

Like the text cited above (i.e., Bromley 1992), similar instructional texts for novice teachers (e.g., Block 1993, Booth 1994, Jacobs and Tunnell 1996, Tompkins and Hoskisson 1995) are unequivocal in their advocacy of novels and picture books like *Nightjohn, Sadako and the Thousand Paper Cranes* (Coerr 1977), *Hiroshima No Pika* (Maruki 1982) or *Faithful Elephants* (Tsuchiya 1951) in elementary grades. However, they provide little explicit guidance to help teachers work through complex psychological issues pertaining to how life stories about trauma might relate to effects in children's learning. Typically, the value dimension of historical genre study is addressed implicitly through taken-for-granted discourses about the transparency of language, literature as a reflection of life, historical narratives as "real," and the moral inviolateness of particular (usually termed "quality") texts. Not addressed are the real issues of struggle involved in experiencing (through language) pain.

Preservice Teachers Reading *Nightjohn*

At the faculty of education where I teach, I have observed that preservice elementary language arts teachers are acutely aware of the gaps in textbook discussions surrounding the use of risky stories in teaching. Moreover, they are in need of instructional guidance on how to think about and teach in the face of literature's disturbing affects. In what follows I describe my experience as a teacher in a university setting, in which preservice teachers were asked to read

Nightjohn, and to think about whether, how, and why they would teach such a text in upper elementary classrooms. The study I draw from involved 135 preservice teachers in their certification year. My observations derive from their journal entries and classroom discussions following the reading of the text. Informed, written consent was provided by the research participants prior to the research, and pseudonyms are used throughout my discussion to present their struggles around teaching *Nightjohn.*

The question arises as to why I (as a language arts instructor) would want to subject education students to such a learning experience, and the ethics of so doing. *Nightjohn* is a novel read by large numbers of local preadolescent elementary students. Because preservice students are called upon to teach this text (and other historical narratives) in practice teaching, I wanted them to think through the grounds of defense for using "risky stories" in language arts education.

The concept of "risky stories" is developed by Simon and Armitage Simon (1995; see also their essay in this volume). The term refers to stories that graphically deal with degradation, pain, and death whose emotional invasiveness for child readers requires a pedagogical response that enables a progressive moral force in the lives of individuals. I will return to the implications of this argument in a few moments. For now, suffice it to say that the study I describe was motivated by my conviction that teachers are obligated to study the processes of their own learning before unmindfully projecting unacknowledged and unrecognized fantasies and desires on students. Given the repressive effects of institutional and textbook discourses that help to structure preservice teacher learning within faculties of education (traced throughout this essay), I see the obligation of the teacher educator as particularly pressing in this regard: not to act with the messianic desire to correct insight in novice teachers, but rather to enable the conditions whereby educational insight itself may be self-examined in a way that allows it to recognize the limitations and possibilities of its own framings, boundaries, and containing devices (see, for example, Bogdan, Davis, and Robertson, 1997).

In journal entries following our examination of *Nightjohn,* Alicia wrote that "the incidences were overwhelming." Jane described her reading experience as "compelling and jarring." Shawn said, "The book was one of the most riveting I've ever read . . . I had knots in my stomach." Despite their feelings of somehow being better off for having read the book ("I honestly believe that I learned a lot from the experience," wrote Jane), they expressed concern about the generative impact both on themselves and on children of asking them to bear witness to historical and psychological realities of a profoundly disturbing kind.

The preservice teachers seemed to anticipate that literature enables a kind of projective identification in learners that other kinds of classroom experiences (e.g., doing sums or learning spelling by rote) do not so easily allow. Implicit here is an unconscious recognition of how education, as it is often managed, acts as an instrument of bourgeois repression (Foucault 1970; Freud 1930). In his reflection on *Nightjohn,* one preservice teacher, Michael, worried that students may actually model the negative behaviors and attitudes (including whipping and namecalling) that structure the grim relations between dominant and persecuted characters in the text. Given that a common discourse used for the defense for literature is the value it offers for vicariously inhabiting other lives, Michael's anxiety about what reading *Nightjohn* may actually produce in terms of regressive classroom relations appears reasonable. At the same time, it is problematic in that such reasoning can result in the justification for a sanitized literature curriculum, purged of problematic characters and messy, threatening situations. A "model curriculum" seen from this vantage promises to heal by removing problematic representations and replacing them with bearable fictions. This stand is recognizable in the claims of political conservatives, who worry that students will be negatively influenced by painful stories.

In the research, another preservice teacher, Alana, also worried about the impact on children's learning of explicit depictions of torture. She wrote:

> I realize that as educators we cannot gloss over the truth or ignore the past because we find it unpleasant. However, I'm not sure I would feel comfortable with the responsibility of planting these images in the heads of eleven-year-old children.

Alana's concern centers on questions of accountability and unpredictability in learning and teaching. She expresses uncertainty about her ability to anticipate or even answer to the erratic effects of "planting" particular images (which go unnamed by her) into children's systems of meaning making.

Daria, too, expressed anxiety about the threat of psychic wear and tear (for both students and teachers) that reading historical fiction provokes. She imagined that she should be in possession of certain knowledges in order to face *Nightjohn*'s disturbances:

> I may be forced to deal with some strong emotions that I may not have encountered before . . . the children would need a lot of background on the subject and they would require a lot of opportunities for expression.

As I worked through the responses to *Nightjohn,* I realized that the preservice teachers' expressions of gravity in reading signal a key component for literary pedagogy. That is, that language arts teachers have a responsibility to prepare actively for dealing with the "erratic effects of planting particular images." The preservice teachers present articulate reminders about the categorical dangers (including paralyzing emotionalism, regression, the need for knowledge, and the desire for safety in the classroom) that need to be considered before risky stories are called upon to educate. It is not, I believe, that they do not recognize the potential value of teaching a book like *Nightjohn.* Indeed, their anxieties remind me of a point made in more complex terms by Shoshana Felman in her eloquent defense of the analytic potential of literature: "[L]iterature . . . *knows it knows but does not know the meaning of its knowledge,* does not know *what* it knows" (1987, Felman's italics).

Accordingly, I would paraphrase the worries of the preservice teachers in the following way. If literatures of trauma engage readers and threaten to disturb the pleasures of denial by representing reminders (images, stories, representations) of the repressed elements of human experience (i.e., the capacity and will of humans to kill, mutilate, and dominate life itself), then how should pedagogy proceed? The readers of *Nightjohn* appear vigorous in their assent that the story possesses the ability to "break the sea frozen within us . . . unleashing currents of pain and doubt" (Tritt 1987, 26–31). But given that such hammering can have deeply subjective and emotional impact, what strategies and practices can teachers employ to reduce the risk of breach in student learning?

Psychoanalysis and Literature

Before addressing strategies for assisting literary learning, it is necessary to think about what painful literary learning puts at risk in readers. If we view the above statements by preservice teachers as symptoms of distress, what is causing the symptomatic distress signals? What "contents" come knocking at the door of collective classroom consciousness following the highly emotional experience of reading *Nightjohn,* in ways that appear blanketed under the guise of wish-fulfillment (i.e., the desire to protect children, to hide—both children and themselves—from less-than-ideal divisions and disorders of reality)?

Psychoanalysis brings to literary understanding a dynamic theory of mind that reminds us that individuals possess more knowledge than they can bear to recognize. In the words of Shoshana Felman, readers possess "a knowledge that does not know what it knows and is thus *not in possession of itself*" (1987, 92, Felman's italics). Knowledge resists its own insight by relegating difficult aspects to a realm defined by Freud as a dynamic part of the psychical system—namely, the unconscious. According to Freud, mental life is "full of active yet unconscious ideas" and "symptoms proceed from such ideas" (1912, 262). The contents of the unconscious, for Freud, are ideational representatives of instincts. Because an instinct can never become an object of consciousness, it presents in the unconscious through ideas, fantasies, or imaginary scenarios (Laplanche and Pontalis 1973, 474–76). *"The unconscious speaks,"* writes Felman, through individuals' structures of response in dialogue with others, *including other texts* (1987, 123).

Freud's theory of repression, and Felman's elaboration of how reading experiences force a confrontation with difficult knowledge about the self, assist in the interpretation of the preservice teachers' responses to *Nightjohn*. Literatures of trauma engage "sleeping" readers and threaten to disturb the pleasures of forgetful being. Risky stories present unequivocal reminders (semiotic provocations) of the repressed (untamed and unacknowledged) elements of human nature and experience—including the will to dominate. Arguably, then, reading the experience of Sarney and her community provoked for the preservice teachers (who anticipated the same provocation of distress in their students) the fragility of the psychic structure possessed by all readers. In psychoanalytic terms, the ego encounters violent repressed aspects of its other in literary representations, and this meeting provokes the threat of ego disintegration. The demonic "other" (symbolized by the brute, the slave-owner) intrudes on the reader's comfortable and illusory image of benign selfhood. The confrontation initiates a frightful remembering. In *Nightjohn* this dynamic is provoked by symbolization of the "maggoty-faced" plantation owner and his acts of elemental cruelty, which include acts of rape, hunting and murdering black people with dogs, and dismemberment.

A concrete example of the disintegrating effects of this kind of reading experience can be witnessed in the following preservice teacher's journal entry. Mara expresses her dynamic literary encounter with otherness, a psychic event fraught with pain:

> I must admit that I never knew the extent to which slave owners went in terms of punishment. Getting eaten alive by dogs is absolutely abhorrent. All the things that were done to slaves were utterly inhumane and cruel. Nobody should have to live such a life of pain and misery. To not be able to have light, pray, read and write is completely unjust. Having to eat the same thing day in and day out from a trough like animals is utterly despicable. While reading this story, I found myself in the quarters among the slaves. I was there. I felt the horrible pain and suffering they endured.

The structures of feeling in Mara's response are those of psychological snapping communicated through the language of shock and dismay. Her journal entry isn't simply emotional. Rather, something breaks for Mara in her writing: her forgetfulness of what it is like to "be a slave." Something snaps: her desire to keep the problems of remembering at bay, in a way that protects her image of herself in the present, and her connectedness to others over time. The experience haunts her. Again and again I witnessed in the preservice teachers' journals explicit examples of this painful predicament in learning.

Psychoanalytic theory helps us understand such dynamics in literary response. According to Freud, human subjectivity is founded on helplessness, and repression is one of the ego's mechanisms of defense for the disavowal of helplessness.[1] In reading, as in dreaming, representations that cut too deep cause us to wake up, or to remember what we would willingly forget: namely, notions of ourselves as separate from others, and benign. Arguably, Mara's painful encounter with *Nightjohn* caused her to "wake up" to forgetful aspects of being. The book intruded forcibly on her ego-consciousness, and exposed her sadness, shame, and reproach in its aftermath. I imagine that *Nightjohn* instigated panic in her, springing from something like a fragmentation or disintegration of her illusory (ego) knowledge.

Mara's panic is defensive. It is intensified because she studies and wants to succeed within an eight-month professional certification program which requires her to demonstrate a competitive mastery of the skills and knowledges of teaching. To complicate matters, she must formulate a language of pedagogical mastery within the terms of educational discourses that would have teachers "relinquish their claims on special knowledge" by leaving the "students to be their own best teachers" (Willinsky 1990, 195–96). These tendencies act on Mara unrelentingly in practice teaching sites, where her professional competence is measured in direct relation to her success in arranging "child-centered," "active," and "motivating" learning activities. I imagine that the thought of having to design "discovery" methods for teaching *Nightjohn* terrifies this beginning teacher.

Her writing charts her reproach, where her shield against professional de-composure is heard in the pulsing tenacity of her language. Mara represents her struggle through a language of "absolution": "absolutely abhorrent, utterly inhuman, cruel, pain, misery, completely unjust, utterly despicable." Absolution suggests three things for me, here: the preservice teacher's cry that there should be some "absolutes" to guide one's journey through the primordial disarray of teaching and learning; the appeal for "absolution" (or exoneration) from what feels like sullied confusion in her anticipated future as a teacher; and the avowal that she has "absolutely . . . utterly" witnessed enough in reading *Nightjohn*, and now deserves some thoughtful guidance about how to carry what she has learned into productive classroom practice. Literature that provokes such contest for students and teachers alike is risky, indeed.

Pedagogy and the Psychic Wear and Tear of Risky Stories

I want to move on to questions of how to support preservice teacher learning about the teaching of traumatic stories. By implication, I am arguing that by providing the conditions for insight in novice elementary teachers about how to use stories to teach about worlds of hurt, there is greater likelihood of effecting positive change in the literary learning experiences of children.

Is it possible for pedagogy to anticipate a method that can assist itself in working through psychic peril in literary learning? In the conceptual terms of psychoanalysis, such a praxis would require teachers to assist students (and themselves) in binding the split parts of the ego in such a way as to repair the fraying and possibly irremediably damaging aspects (including denial or paralysis) of encounters with pain. At the same time, it is necessary to ask how pedagogy can proceed in a way that avoids fostering redemptive or salvation fantasies in readers who encounter extreme suffering.

One of the risks involved in using stories like *Nightjohn* is that readers may seek refuge from discomfort by imagining that mass suffering is confined to a "safe" or "finished" past that does not possess continuing implications for human relations in the present. Some theorists refer to these defensive impulses as "salvation" or "redemption" fantasies. Linenthal (1995), for example, speaks of the "lure of redemption" in connection with the creation of the Holocaust Museum in Washington, D.C. Some groups felt that the museum should emphasize resistance and rescue. Others believed that the museum should enable insight into the "predicament of the aftermath" (251). In the end, museum creators settled on the educative value of "unresolved closure," arguing that, "No survivor of the Holocaust could ever be completely liberated" (254).

In a similar vein, Britzman (1998) addresses the conflicts involved when autobiographical life stories are used in elementary classrooms. She argues, for example, that for teachers and children to use *The Diary of Anne Frank* as an unproblematized object upon which to project idealized desires for innocence, salvation, and hope ignores important historical and psychological realities. It ignores, first, the unequivocal fact of the abuse, starvation, and murder of a twelve-year-old female Jewish child at the death camp of Bergen-

Belsen, by a community intent on demonizing Jews in law, through betrayal, and otherwise. By implication, then, for classroom learning experiences to focus on Anne Frank as a heroine of innocence, hope, and survival (i.e., she lives on to inspire us through her story) ignores the reality of her slaughter, and knowledge of the historical conditions of the Third Reich that organized it.

By implication, in teaching stories of loss (including *Nightjohn*), careful thought needs to be given to identifying the social and structural conditions that led to the violations depicted in the story. Furthermore, these conditions must be seen to be still productive for living in the present. The intent of such teaching is not to deny children the resources of hope, nor is it to equate stories of mass suffering. Rather, the idea is to help students begin to identify the varying conditions present in paradigms of destruction, and to produce vigilance in learners about the ongoing implications and effects of loss in the world today. Britzman calls on the teachings of Anna Freud to draw attention to the fact that what readers notice in the world is, in essence, what lives within the self. The difficult question, she argues, is how to address *both* the inner world of the educator *and* that of the learner. The psychological reality of literary encounters with stories of pain is that processes of repression set in to defend readers from recognizing unbearable truths of the self, the human condition, and the implication of self in relations of domination. Britzman's interpretation of Meyer Levin's response to Anne Frank's diary serves as an exemplary reminder of the compulsion human beings share to imagine the self as rescuer (see also Britzman's essay in this volume).

Indeed, the lure of redemption played out in the journal entries of some preservice teachers reading *Nightjohn*. Several respondents imagined that Canadians are somehow exempt from the haunting legacy of ideologies of racism, the forced confinement or deportation of ethnic "others," or the partial annihilation of indigenous territorial groups. The fantasy enacted itself in recognizable scripts, including nationalist articulations of racist denial (i.e., "we were and are 'different' from the American racist 'other'"), or reproachful and escapist rationalizations such as, "All slave owners were not like that." The painful observation Britzman makes from her study (above) is that the rescue fantasy is not to rescue the other, but the self from the difficult acknowledgment of one's own narcissism, aggression, and capacity to hate. The history of Anne Frank's diary, she argues, implicates education in its own failings. A key element in teaching risky stories must then be to assist readers in recognizing the connection that exists between an impossible past and one's own ongoing implication in it. Risky stories ask readers to remember what is most willingly forgotten.

What are the pedagogical alternatives to the fostering of utopian dreams through risky stories, especially given what we know about the need for the ego to defend itself against difficult knowledge? Simon and Armitage Simon (1995; see also their essay in this volume) have developed the concept of the "shadow text" in an effort to offer a corrective to the abandonment, illusionment, or neglect of children who read stories of risk. The shadow text is a story the ego tells itself in an attempt to guide its own confusions or dismay in the face of difficult knowledge. In telling itself a story about how something could have been allowed to happen, the ego involves itself in a recapturing or reparation of its own frayed edges. (I will provide some concrete examples in a moment.) The notion of the shadow text embraces both the reader's urgent need to symbolize in response to a textual provocation, and the disciplining effects of this language production on consciousness. The process of constructing a shadow text helps the conscious self work through those questions provoked by the story that exasperate cognitive or moral bearability. Simon and Armitage Simon offer the concept as a way of drawing the attention of educators to issues of teacher responsibility and student safety in learning (see also Simon and Eppert 1987).

In practice, however, shadow texts are slippery to work with in the classroom, as I discovered through the experience of teaching *Nightjohn*. For while shadow text production can indeed help readers to "order" or work through knowledge of historical loss, at the same time traumatic stories can produce shadow texts that are symptomatic of the truly radical questions that narratives of hurt invoke. In the words of Roger Simon, "sometimes they are written easily, sometimes unconvincingly, and sometimes no adequate text can be written, although the compulsion to write one may still exist."[3] In terms of strategies for fostering shadow text production in elementary classrooms, teachers must ensure that students are given structured opportunities to regard both their own and others' shadow texts. Teachers need to help students evaluate different shadow texts and develop new ones. Discussions need to grapple with why some shadow texts may be inadequate, or even dangerous. The goal here is not to correct insight, but rather to teach children that ambiguity and the revision of opinion or perception is a necessary part of understanding the lives of others. Shadow text production thus requires the following specific classroom conditions: dialogue among writers, active listening, rewriting, critical reflection, and an unending return to difficult texts. The strategy requires vigilance on the part of the teacher who needs to be able to anticipate and work with the kinds of dilemmas that life stories of trauma might provoke in readers. Teachers need to imagine, in advance of teaching risky stories, possible shadow texts that could make reply to such difficult knowledge.

In the instance of the preservice teachers reading *Nightjohn*, the shadow text production occurred through private reflection in journals (to which I responded) and in frank classroom exchanges, including small and large group work. The book provoked such difficult existential questions in adult readers as, "How can such cruelty exist?", "How could some slave owners have acted with such life-denying bias toward blacks?", "How can it be that the law supported such action?", and "Why didn't anyone do anything to help Sarney and her people?" In creative visualizations of how they would use *Nightjohn* in teaching, some preservice teachers imagined that they would emphasize to children that not all whites and not all Southern plantation owners acted with such elementary cruelty toward black people. Some imagined that they would focus on the men and women who challenged oppressive conditions. Others imagined that they would help children to examine the time when black people were free in their home countries, or the role of some Canadians in assisting runaway slaves to freedom. In reviewing these texts, we discussed collectively why it is necessary and difficult not to succumb to illusions and idealizations. The discussion focused in part on the identification of contemporary acts of language and event that bear the marks of racist and other hatred in Canada today, and education's responsibility to carry such matters into literary learning.

One preservice teacher imagined a shadow text that I found remarkable (yet troublesome) for its quality of anticipatory hope in teaching. Danny's shadow text alerted me to just how interminable is the process of "binding up the wounds of narrative," and that "the narrative texture of this metaphoric bandaging is always insufficient, leaving gaps and openings" (Schweizer 1997, 4). In his writing, Danny grappled with how it is that Nightjohn, a teacher who endures monumental suffering, finds the desire to continue to teach Sarney to read. In his efforts to work through what he projects as Nightjohn's cruel dilemma, Danny crafted a shadow text in which he imagined that "being a teacher imposes moral obligations of a large order, including the passion to endure, integrity, courage, and risk in the 'pitschool' of life." (In *Nightjohn*, the enslaved blacks escape nightly, in order to learn to read, to an unsheltered and hazardous site off the plantation called the "pitschool.") For me, Danny's shadow text exemplifies the impulse to treat suffering through the creation of fiction—both a jeopardy and a possibility in shadow text creation. Danny's fantasy enacts his desire to survive in the "pitschool" of teaching, at the same time as it reveals the poignant limitations of picturing the "pitschool" of teaching as a remedy for extreme suffering.

In addition to Britzman, who counsels against fostering redemption fantasies in reading, and Simon and Armitage Simon, who argue that children's collective understanding and vigilance can be strengthened through the pedagogy of shadow texts, Lucy Dawidowicz (1990) focuses on the importance of forethought and precision in developing historical literacy. She provides some reassuring guidelines for teaching about the Holocaust. I believe that the principles she presents are relevant to the teaching of subjugated knowledges in general through historical narratives.

Dawidowicz argues, first, that the elementary lessons of history must not be aimlessly presented or overgeneralized. An example of this would be for a teacher to articulate her goal for working with a Holocaust narrative as, "We're learning about this event so that it will not happen again." Dawidowicz's impatience with this line of thinking is that it fails to identify *the precise information* that will help children form principled judgments about the past. Dawidowicz reminds educators that in order to help children make meaning from historical narratives, teachers must first educate themselves, through taking the time to read and learn about those organized acts whose sole intention was to mark and (ultimately) kill targeted groups of people throughout history. In the instance of the Holocaust, she teaches that an important instructional component of the lesson is the denial of human rights of the Jewish people by laws enacted by a totalitarian regime that then exacted obedience on nations through penalties of death. Dawidowicz reminds us that by omitting such knowledge of the relations between totalitarianism, law, and compliance, educators produce magical forms of thinking in students about the conditions that organize genocide. Such magical thinking is tantamount to polishing a mirror: it results in the comforting illusion that exposure to images can inoculate readers against the contagions of history.

Dawidowicz argues that historical insight is also diminished through classroom discussions that unmindfully resort to languages of abstraction to talk about the events of mass murder. For example, the use of words like *extermination, elimination,* and even *genocide* obviate the insight of the "Final Solution": that an entire group of people was targeted to be killed systematically on the basis of perceived and practiced difference. According to Dawidowicz, moral lessons that focus on teaching children "individual responsibility," "care," "prejudice," and "respect for democratic values" also hinder specific understandings about the explicitly anti-Semitic character of the Nazi dictatorship and its refusal to honor the principle of the sanctity of human life. In connection with arguments about abstruse language, Dawidowicz explains why having children role-play the parts of historical subjects (e.g., Gestapo and concentration camp inhabitant) is indefensible. She writes,

> These exercises have been known to produce unprecedented emotional tensions in the classroom, among some students arousing fear, panic, and overidentification with Jewish victims and, among others, releasing sado-masochistic urges, violent responses, and overidentification with the murderer. (27)

Dawidowicz exhorts against mistakes of curricular aimlessness, overgeneralization, and imprecision, which result in missed opportunities for educating children about how the denial of the rights of others is constructed along a continuum of discursive and juridical events that are humanly organized and, hence, potentially amenable to human understanding and collective will to change.

Taking a cue from Dawidowicz, teacher educators must be mindful of the contradictory conditions that structure the learning of new teachers. For example, it is worth pointing out that in the Canadian province of Ontario, language arts teachers are taught to create learning experiences in which children can "retell and enact real and imaginary events in sequence" and "express feelings . . . and experiences through role-play and presentation" (Ontario Ministry of Education and Training 1995, 53). In the context of teacher education, then, it is necessary to devote instructional time to problematizing this learning outcome against the grain of particular kinds of narratives. When I asked preservice students to "explain why it is never defensible to have children act out the roles of murderers, victims, or judges from historical literature," preservice teachers were able to reason in connection to *Nightjohn* that "perspective taking has its place, but roles can become reality" (Lynn), and "by exposing children to this book, we want to teach that slavery was wrong, morally and humanly. Having them act it out would not be sending that message at all" (Peter). Some others resisted these explanations, rationalizing their desires to have children enact historical narratives as an example of ensuring "active engagement in learning."

Another variable that affects learning to teach risky stories is signaled by the work of Pajek and Blase (1984), who discuss the novice teacher's evolving sense of self in teaching. These researchers help to explain why uncertainty in learning to teach is so difficult to tolerate, a point that has clear implications for teaching narratives of hurt. The researchers observe that beginning teachers identify deeply with students, who serve psychically as "self objects" by "mirroring . . . grandiosity or by representing an idealized figure of perfection, thus, regulating and maintaining . . . self-esteem" (13). In terms of language arts instruction, Pajek and Blase alert us to the psychic and social desires that imperil the beginning teacher's ability to withstand uncertainty in teaching narratives. Similar findings are reported by Robertson's (1997) study of the rescuing impulses of beginning white female teachers, and Britzman and Pitt (1995) in their analysis of the unconscious dynamics of desire that play out in classroom discussions of stories between teachers and students.

In the research, a third point of concern in forging an adequate literary pedagogy for *Nightjohn* had to do with the preservice teachers' knowledge of history. My work with *Nightjohn* occurred with fourth- and fifth-year university students. I was frequently reminded by them that they felt themselves to be ignorant of historical knowledge. This ignorance was made startlingly apparent to me in one preservice teacher's word-for-word interpretation that the setting for *Nightjohn* was the White House (in the story, Clel Waller's white house is meant to register metaphorically). Many others were unable to identify understandings relating to the social, political, and cultural conditions that resulted in the forced deportations and enslavement of black African peoples. In general, the preservice teachers attributed their lack of historical knowledge to uninspired teaching in high school.

I have another theory. Today's preservice students are for the most part products of the development of the "New Literacy" in classrooms across North America throughout the '70s and the '80s. As Willinsky (1990) points out, new trends in language teaching over the past few decades have made possible a level of vibrant engagement with literature, unattainable under previous "top down" and didactic approaches to skill instruction. But education's gains must also consider its losses, in terms of the insights new teachers (nourished in the conditions of the New Literacy) are able to import into classrooms. For example, Willinsky traces the trends of the New Literacy back to Romanticism, and he finds disturbing echoes in some educators' suspiciousness of the authority of texts, anti-intellectualism, and "resistance to a certain bookishness" (1990, 176). These behaviors replay in some preservice teachers' impatience (or hostility) toward time spent on theory in teacher education. The condition is worsened by tendencies within faculties of education today to remove the study of history from required foundations courses. These are not signs that bode well for the making of significance in learning. Preservice students must wage difficult battle against the limitations of their own schooling: that history teachers seem to have failed to make history a place where one can recognize oneself, and that literature teachers have not always assisted understanding about the narrative devices that help structure the ways in which we are able to imagine ourselves. That faculties of education hesitate to engage with troubled truths about knowledge only adds gunpowder to the mix.

Pedagogy as Support Material—and the Limits of This Space

If teachers do embark on the use of risky stories in the classroom, then language arts teaching must be able to meet the sense of homelessness that attends transitions and break-aways in learning. By homelessness I refer to the experience of feeling in exile from a text or one's experience of the text, traced throughout this essay. Language arts educators can draw on psychoanalytic knowledge to understand better how to assist learning in these conditions. I have argued that the structure of feeling haunted by a text prevails when the reader is forced to abandon an emotional place that he or she believed to be comfortable or secure. Feeling outcast in reading needs to be anticipated as a structure of response in student and teacher engagements with historical narratives. I have tried to provide some classroom guides to support the itinerant during this difficult time of learning.

The ability of the teacher to imagine the classroom as a canvas or holding place upon which disturbed readers can project fragmented colors of the mind, through vigilance against redemptive fantasies (Britzman 1998), through the creation of reparative shadow texts (Simon and Armitage Simon 1995), and through thoughtful curricular aim, background research, concrete language, and sharp focus (Dawidowicz 1990) may make children's historical learning possible. English Studies in teacher education must make space for helping new language arts teachers anticipate the need for these principles of care in teaching risky stories. Reading literature must be comprehended as a potentially disturbing psychic event. The openness of texts, and the interminable ambiguity of making meaning around them needs to be accepted as part of the terrain of teaching literature. At the same time, history's stories must be taught in ways that make their meanings apparent for the present.

The warrant for such methods is that support material is provided for helping readers to negotiate the slippery psychological spaces of history and story. The reader may find strength in the realization that selfhood is a condition continually in the making, and that living honorably commits oneself—with all of the ambiguities and difficulties entailed—to vigilance and possibility. Such insight creates the conditions whereby symptoms in reading may not simply return to haunt the ego in a persecutory or disintegrating way. Readers achieve insight within a frame that provides a safety net for both witnessing and working through knowledge of pain.

At the same time, the framework suggested here can never be anything but simply that—a framework that describes the limits of a place of learning and insight. This is not a joyful space. It is not playful. And it is decidedly not in mastery of itself in terms of the knowledge it generates. The framework simply provides some modest insurance against the dangers of engulfment, in which the ability of children and teachers to rise to the challenge of creating meaning of value from reading risky stories will always involve hard work and hurt, because the process involves projecting the parts of the ego and objects not assimilated by the ego onto a framework for learning. Such a classroom assumes special significance for learners because it provides the transitional figures (ideas, words, representations, other learners, and a morally wide-awake teacher) that can support the difficult passage out of childhood.

Acknowledgments   Funding for research was provided by the Ontario Women's Directorate, the Ontario Deans of Education, and the University of Ottawa. I gratefully acknowledge their support. Thanks also to the preservice teachers who agreed to participate in the study, and whose thoughtful engagements allowed for the generation of insight about the risks and possibilities of teaching about worlds of hurt through encounters with literature. A special thanks to Deborah Britzman, Roger Simon, and Timothy Stanley, who responded to earlier drafts of this paper.

Notes   1. I am grateful to Deborah Britzman, who pushed my understanding of Freud's concepts of repression and helplessness in this section of the paper.

2. This analysis was assisted by Timothy Stanley, whose e-mail communication to me (March 13, 1997) caused me to tighten earlier ideas: "Isn't the radical connection to these impossible pasts recognition of one's self within them? This recognition of one's self both within victims and abusers (and bystanders) is necessarily painful and transformative."

3. This explanation was provided in an e-mail communication from Roger Simon to the author, January 2, 1997.

Works Cited   Block, Cathy Collins. 1993. *Teaching the Language Arts: Expanding Thinking through Student-Centered Instruction.* Boston: Allyn & Bacon.

Bogdan, Deanne. 1987. "Literature, Values, and Truth: Why We Could Lose the Censorship Debate." *English Quarterly* 20: 273–83.

Bogdan, Deanne, Hilary E. Davis, and Judith P. Robertson. 1997. "Sweet Surrender and Trespassing Desires in Reading: Jane Campion's *The Piano* and the Struggle for a Responsible Pedagogy. *Changing English* 4(1): 81–103.

Booth, David. 1994. *Classroom Voices: Language-Based Learning in the Elementary School.* Toronto: Harcourt Brace Canada.

Bristow, Joseph. 1991. "Life Stories: Carolyn Steedman's History Writing." *New Formations* 13 (Spring): 113–31.

Britzman, Deborah P. 1998. *Lost Subjects, Contested Objects: Toward a Psychoanalytic Inquiry of Learning.* Albany, NY: SUNY Press.

Britzman, Deborah P., and Alice Pitt. 1995. "Pedagogy and Transference: Casting the Past of Learning into the Presence of Teaching." *Theory Into Practice* 35(2): 117–23.

Bromley, Karen D. 1992. *Language Arts: Exploring Connections.* 2nd ed. Boston: Allyn & Bacon.

Coerr, Eleanor. 1977. *Sadako and the Thousand Paper Cranes.* New York: Dell.

Davis, Marie. 1997. "Editorial: Recollection, Recontextualization, and Rereading: Part 1." *Canadian Children's Literature/Littérature Canadienne pour la Jeunesse* 22(3): 3–4.

Dawidowicz, Lucy. 1990. "How They Teach the Holocaust." *Commentary* 90(6): 25–32.

Felman, Shoshana. 1987. *Jacques Lacan and the Adventure of Insight.* Cambridge, MA: Harvard University Press.

Foucault, Michel. 1970. *The Order of Things: An Archaeology of the Human Sciences.* New York: Random House.

Freud, Sigmund. 1953/1973. "A Note on the Unconscious in Psychoanalysis." In *The Standard Edition of the Complete Psychological Works of Sigmund Freud,* edited by James Strachey. Vol. 12, 262. (Original work published 1912). London: The Hogarth Press.

Freud, Sigmund. 1930. *Civilization and Its Discontents.* London: The Hogarth Press.

Jacobs, James, and Michael Tunnell. 1996. *Children's Literature, Briefly.* Englewood Cliffs, NJ: Merrill.

Laplanche, Jean, and J. B. Pontalis. 1973. *The Language of Psycho-analysis.* Translated by Donald Nicholson-Smith. New York: Norton.

Linenthal, Edward. 1995. *Preserving Memory: The Struggle to Create America's Holocaust Museum.* New York: Viking Penguin.

Maruki, Toshi. 1982. *Hiroshima No Pika.* New York: Lothrop, Lee & Shepard.

Mier, Margaret. 1985. "The New Realism in Children's Literature." *English Quarterly* (Spring): 42–48.

Ontario Ministry of Education and Training. 1995. *The Common Curriculum: Provincial Standards, Language, Grades 1-9.* Toronto: Queen's Printer.

Pajek, Edward F., and J. J. Blase. 1985. "Teaching, the Loss of Innocence, and the Psychological Development of a Professional Self." In Garrod, Bartell, Rampaul and Seifert, 10–24.

Paulsen, Gary. 1993. *Nightjohn.* New York: Bantam Doubleday Dell.

Robertson, Judith P. 1997. "Fantasy's Confines: Popular Culture and the Education of the Female Primary School Teacher." *The Canadian Journal of Education/Revue canadienne de l'éducation* 22(2): 123–43.

Schweizer, Harold. 1997. *Suffering and the Remedy of Art.* Albany, NY: SUNY Press.

Simon, Roger I., and Wendy Armitage Simon. 1995. "Teaching Risky Stories: Remembering Mass Destruction through Children's Literature." *English Quarterly* (Fall): 27–31.

Simon, Roger I., and Claudia Eppert. 1997. "Remembering Obligation: Pedagogy and the Witnessing of Testimonies of Historical Trauma." *The Canadian Journal of Education/Revue canadienne de l'éducation* 22(2): 175–91.

Tompkins, Gail E., and Kenneth Hoskisson. 1995. *Language Arts Content and Teaching Strategies.* 3rd ed. Englewood Cliffs, NJ: Merrill.

Tritt, Michael. 1987. "Teaching Holocaust Literature: Methods and Strategies." *English Quarterly* (Fall): 26–33.

Tsuchiya, Yukio. 1951. *Faithful Elephants: A True Story of Animals, People, and War.* Translated by T. T. Dykes, 1988. Boston: Houghton Mifflin.

Willinsky, John. 1990. *The New Literacy: Redefining Reading and Writing in the Schools.* Routledge: New York.

"Dimensions of a Lonely Discovery": Anne Frank and the Question of Pedagogy[1]

16

Deborah P. Britzman
York University

In the last year of entries to her diary, a fifteen-year-old Anne Frank responded to a London radio broadcast calling for diaries that documented for future generations the experiences of war. "Of course," writes Anne Frank on March 29, 1944,

> [E]veryone pounced on my diary. Just imagine how interesting it would be if I were to publish a novel about the Secret Annex. . . . Seriously, though, ten years after the war people would find it very amusing to read how we lived, what we ate, and what we talked about as Jews in hiding. Although I tell you a great deal about our lives, you still know very little about us (243–44).

Anne Frank names the pedagogical mystery that is her diary: as a place of secrets, how can we be told a great deal and still know very little? As for its pedagogical purposes, this mystery becomes crystallized in two of its haunting qualities: the painful context of its writing as one document of the European Jewish destruction and Anne Frank's hopeful knowledge that while addressing "Kitty" her diary, she was also writing a diary to and for the world.

Not without argument, versions of *The Diary of Anne Frank* have been translated into fifty-five languages[2]. The North American school curriculum largely preserves the 1950s representations of the *Diary*, or what Judith Doneson (1987, 150) paradoxically terms, "an Americanized universal symbol." Over the course of the postwar years, the *Diary* has been the subject of plays, films, musical compositions, and commemorative sculpture and art. Throughout Europe, streets have been named in memory of Anne Frank, educational foundations and youth organizations have been formed, and in Amsterdam, the "Secret Annex" has become a historic site of pilgrimage. There is even an Anne Frank Web site on the Internet. The young girl called Anne Frank haunts not just the writings about the Jewish European genocide, where one must pass through Anne Frank on the way to the impossible thought of the sheer numbers of those murdered. With so much to consider, we are also faced with far more complex pictures[3] that lend pathos to the daily conditions of the diary's writing and then the painful death of Anne Frank in the Bergen-Belsen camp. All at once, the figure of Anne Frank has been bordered with too much history, too much affect.

And yet, with the recent publication of a new translation and the more complete *Diary* known as the Definitive Edition, and with the Dutch government's 1986 authorization of the historical authenticity of the *Diary* as an answer to the revisionist attempts to deny the event of the Holocaust, the document must serve as one proof of the Jewish European genocide and of the existence of the particular experience of one Jewish adolescent. In pedagogical efforts, these two purposes however, point to a very large problem. The *Diary* is often approached as giving voice to the one and a half million Jewish children who were murdered in Europe during World War II[4]. But even as it serves the popular imaginary, providing "part of the vernacular of tragedy" (Doneson 1987, 151) in pedagogy, the *Diary* is also used to consolidate an idealized figure for adolescent and adult identification. This fragile pedagogy, as we shall see, is not outside of other debates over the history of the *Diary*'s popularity and reception.

Within the questions of how the *Diary* is represented and the detours of its encounters, of being told too much and knowing too little, three very different senses of time occupy the same space: the time of the writing, the time of the finding and publishing of the *Diary*, and our own time of pedagogical engagement. These dimensions of time coarsen the fault lines of the arguments over the *Diary*'s readings and suggest something about the more general stakes of what has become known as Holocaust education in public schooling. For if, as Alvin Rosenfeld (1993, 80) argues, we know that the Holocaust happened, "what we lack is not an adequate written record but the means to assimilate it to the conceptual norms of interpretation." What is it then, to explore the pedagogical limits of "the conceptual norms of interpretation"? How might these competing histories—the history recounted in the *Diary* and the historicity of engaging in a reading of the *Diary*—shape our pedagogical efforts? And why complicate what seems to be the curricular efforts at preservation?

Even these sorts of questions are insufficient when we stop to consider the skeletal facts of the Frank family and the story of education they force us to confront. In 1933, the year that Freud's books were publicly burned in Vienna and the year Hitler was popularly elected as Chancellor of Germany, the Frank family fled Frankfurt for Amsterdam. Anne Frank was four years old, and upon the family's arrival in this new country, her parents enrolled her in a Montessori school. In Jon Blair's documentary *Anne Frank Remembered,* we can listen to Otto Frank recall why the family moved to Amsterdam: "I didn't want to raise my children in German education." In 1942, when Anne Frank was thirteen years old and received as a birthday gift a diary, the Dutch government surrendered to the German Army and the Netherlands came under German law. As with all Jewish children, Anne Frank was forbidden to attend Dutch schools. On July 5, 1942, Anne Frank's sister, Margo, was required to report to the Gestapo for her transport orders. The next day, the Frank family along with one other family went into hiding. Later they were joined by an eighth member. For over a year, Otto Frank had been preparing the attic of his pectin factory, located two and a half miles from their home.

The family lived in hiding for about two years. Their connections to the outside world were facilitated by four of Otto Frank's Christian employees, books smuggled in, and a radio. An anonymous phone caller to the Dutch police reported on the Franks, and on August 4, 1944, the Frank family, the Van Damm family, and Mr. Dussel were arrested. Of the 25,000 Jews in hiding in Amsterdam, approximately 9,000 were betrayed. Of the 60,000 Dutch Jews deported and interned in concentration camps between 1942 and 1945, only 6,000 people survived. And, of the eight people who lived in the Secret Annex, only Otto Frank survived the war. Miep Gies entered the Annex the day after the arrest and gathered from the floor the scattered pages of Anne's diary. She returned the diary to Otto Frank a few months after he was liberated from Auschwitz. The first printing of the Dutch *Diary* in 1947 was modest; the publisher worried whether there would be an interested public to receive it.

These are the skeletal facts of the *Diary*'s writing and finding. One must pass through the overwhelming numbers to reach the singularity of the event. Our understanding must be burdened by the weight of implication, what Cathy Caruth (1996) calls history, where the past as reconstructed, "is no longer straightforwardly referential (that is, no longer based on simple models of experience and reference)" (11). One must take these facts on a detour and confront the failings of an educational system and its teachers, democracy and its public, the publishing industry and its readers, civil law and its exclusions, indeed the social imaginary of pedagogy itself. And within these failings, each of us might ask, what is at stake for the learner and teacher when the time of learning and the time of history itself, is, in the words of Shoshana Felman, *"dissonant, and not just congruent,* with everything . . . learned beforehand" (Felman and Laub 1992, 53, Felman's italics)?

My approach to the historicity of the *Diary*'s reception is inspired by what Erik Erikson (1964) called, in his explorations of the ethics of psychoanalytic inquiry, "that lonely discovery." This is the question of responsibility, implication, and the haunting reach of a history that cannot be put to rest. We might extend the reach of this affect to the *Diary* itself. As Anne Frank sorted through her own conflictive understandings of self and other and grappled with the otherness of the self, she, too, was involved in her own lonely discovery. Then, the finding of the diary is a second time of "that lonely discovery." And now, perhaps, that lonely discovery can be made from our present reading.

The Curious Time of Learning

In our own time, which after all is never just our own time, how can we grapple with the stakes of the learning when the learning attempts to be made from identifications with what can only be called "difficult knowledge"? Can the terms of learning acknowledge that studying the experiences and their traumatic residuals of genocide, ethnic hatred, aggression, and forms of state-sanctioned and hence legal social violence requires educators to think carefully about their own theories of learning and how the stuff of such difficult knowledge becomes pedagogical? How shall each of us confront the difficulties of learning from another's painful confrontation with victimness, aggression, and the desire to live on one's own terms? The sorts of questions I am raising cannot be settled by the slogan, "We are all Anne Frank" (Rosenfeld 1993; Lester 1989). This slogan hopes for an easy identification. But if we are honest, the *Diary* actually provokes what Felman and Laub (1992) call "the crisis of witnessing." When we are asked to listen to another's pain, we are incapable of responding adequately because the knowledge offered is dissonant, in the order of trauma, and also because our response already comes too late. The response is belated and can be only a working through of belated knowledge (Felman and Laub 1992; Friedlander 1992; LaCapra 1994; Moses 1993; Stern 1995/1996).

Educators across the spectrum of education are aware of the idea that knowledge of human cruelty can be depressing, debilitating, and defensively engaged. Indeed, this very worry is an implicit tension in discussions of Holocaust education (Felman and Laub 1992; Linenthal 1995) and in the teaching of the *Diary* (Doneson 1987). Can the study of genocide avoid a painful encounter? Is the amount of pain the thing that provokes disengagement? But para-doxically, these anxieties may be an effect of the educator's dis-avowal of her or his own difficulties of engagement. Then, the educator's worries transfer into an ambivalent pedagogy that wishes to protect adolescents from—even as it introduces adolescents to—these representations. The disavowal, or the refusal to engage a traumatic perception of helplessness and loss, often pushes educators to the opposite spectrum of affect: the focus on hope and courage as the adequate lesson to be made from difficult knowledge. However, hope is a very complex affect that may actually take the form of a defense. Michael Silberfeld (1988, 47) argues that hope is neither a static concept, nor "a token that can be given or taken away. . . . The dynamic concept of hope is related to the feelings of loss and in turn, to the sense of entitlement." This is so because hope is a fragile bridge to continuity and expectation. Precisely because hope speaks to the wish for attachment, it is also quite vulnerable to the very conditions that constitute its founding moments: times where one must also come to terms with discontinuity and loss.

But in a pedagogy that insists upon hope as a strategy to slide over the pain of loss, and when its dynamic qualities are ignored, hope works as idealization. Idealization involves efforts "to place some aspect of oneself or the group on a pedestal to then derive faith, hope and sustenance from this idealized part" (Moses 1993, 193). Paradoxically, idealization may well be a symptom of the "crisis in witnessing." How is this so?

The problem with the desire to idealize is that its strategies are also an attempt to find an ultimate truth in a context that, to return to Alvin Rosenfeld's point, defies any of our personal means "to assimilate [the event with] the conceptual norms of interpretation." When the vicissitudes of life and death cannot conform to the idealization, it becomes very difficult to live with or in loss. While the recourse to hope and courage may serve as an ego-ideal, the injunction for hope and courage can be felt as tyrannical to the ego and hence may inhibit any understanding or allowance for experiences where hope and courage cannot be mustered, or where these desires can only be considered in the belated time of mourning. Moreover, in bypassing altogether the conditions of helplessness, loss, and conflict, the vicissitudes and profundity of even the smallest amounts of hope and courage cannot be worked through. As we will see, however, the various placings of the *Diary* on a pedestal of affirmation as a means to dissipate the dissonance and loss of its context is not outside of the traumatic histories of the *Diary*'s reception. Indeed, the histories of the *Diary*'s reception may well mark our pedagogical unconscious.

The Times of the Finding

In our pedagogical efforts, the *Diary of a Young Girl* becomes unhinged from its own contentious historicity. The time of Anne Frank becomes static, as if there was only the ethnographic present of Anne endlessly making her entries. And while this quality may be implicit in the genre of diary and sustained by the 1950s play and Hollywood film, the figure of Anne Frank placed only at her desk seems to preserve the wish to keep her safe in hiding. This observation is not meant to imply that the Holocaust is somehow left unmentioned either in the *Diary* or in pedagogy. Indeed, while the wish to keep Anne Frank safe from harm may well be a rescue fantasy provoked by the knowledge of what happened, it is also impossible to read this diary and not consider the painful conditions of its writing and its finding. The ethnographic present, however, itself an ambivalent sense of time, works as a wish for preservation and as a defense against loss.

But the *Diary*'s history did not end in its writing or with its finding. Its history begins with postwar Jewish ambivalence over our status in European and North American societies after World War II. And this history is tangled in an exponential Jewish sense of loss and an ongoing mourning marked partly by an anxiety about the general public's anti-Semitism and despondency toward the magnitude and traumatic residues of the destruction. When Anne Frank's diary was first considered for publication, the question raised—albeit differently by Otto Frank and the Dutch publisher—was, how could postwar Christians read the diary as relevant to them? The question haunted how the diary was to be promoted, and then returned to structure the rewriting of the diary for the 1955 play and 1959 film.

Otto Frank believed the reception might best be facilitated by framing the publicity around the diary's publication as having universal appeal. For Otto Frank, the *Diary* should represent a story of adolescence, not a Jewish story. Before the war, the Frank's were a highly assimilated middle-class Jewish family of Enlightenment. Indeed, Otto Frank served in the German army in World War I. The family considered themselves German citizens, and, in the prevailing anti-Semitic definitions of their time, racially Jewish (Graver 1995). By 1947, Otto Frank and the Dutch publishers understood that Jewish particularity would not sell well to the general public who had grown weary of the sheer magnitude of the Jewish genocide. The ambivalence was whether a Jewish child could or even should be a universal figure capable of standing in for every child. At the same time, Otto Frank hoped that the publication of the diary could be a means to educate Christian readers as to the humanity of the loss[5].

Both the Dutch and English version of the *Diary* were marketed originally as an extraordinary statement about a young girl's hope for humanity in spite of war. Recall one of the most famous extrapolated sentences from one of the last entries to the diary that now works as synecdoche: "I still believe, in spite of everything, that people are truly good at heart" (332)[6]. In Anne Frank's wish for a normal life and for a magical healing (where "people would find it very amusing"), parts of the *Diary* do wonder about the capacity of humans to move beyond hatred and despair. But what tends to be lost in this idealization of belief is that Anne Frank's hope for continuity and expectation was betrayed. And, much of the diary is a meditation on Jewish suffering and on the melancholic condition of being, for the simple fact of her Jewishness, an outcast.

Here is what Anne Frank wrote near the end of her April 11, 1944, entry, after a break-in and police examination of the first floor of the pectin factory:

> We've been strongly reminded to the fact that we're Jews in chains, chained to one spot, without any rights, but with a thousand obligations. We must put our feelings aside; we must be brave and strong, bear discomfort without complaint. . . . The time will come when we'll be people again and not just Jews! Who has inflicted this on us? Who has set us apart from all the rest? Who has put us through such suffering? . . . In the eyes of the world, we're doomed, but if, after all this suffering, there are still Jews left, the Jewish people will be held up as example. . . . We can never be just Dutch, or just English, or whatever, we will always be Jews as well. And we'll have to keep on being Jews, but then, we'll want to be. (261)

Unlike the Hollywood film that rewrites this entry into a universal declaration that all people and nations have suffered, the passage is complex, conditional, and ambivalent. It sets in conflict Anne's experience of the world's need for Jewish denial with the Jewish demand to choose Jewishness. One of the "thousand obligations" that emerged from this antagonism was the injunction to idealize bravery in a context where bravery could not surmount, repair, or even make sense of Anne's knowledge of deportation and her thoughts on impending death. Paradoxically, the only proof of bravery becomes silence, the prohibition against narrating one's doom. Within this prohibition lies still another obligation: being forced into a confrontation with an anti-Semitic definition of Jewishness that renders irrelevant the ambivalent longing both to belong without distinction and to be seen as distinct. The *Diary* becomes a space for working through such obligations. In its meditation on the persistent struggle against claustrophobia, Anne Frank can also refuse these impositions by inventing a fantasy of life in the past, present, and future. Then, the *Diary* defies any obligation, specifically in those entries that examine her inner world and that craft small pleasures from listening to Mozart on a radio broadcast, commenting on her collection of pictures of Hollywood film stars, and exploring the mysteries of love and sexuality. But even these passions are haunted by her terror of and incredulity toward the cruel actions of those who complied with the Nazi occupation.

With the publication of the Definitive Edition, we now know that Otto Frank edited entries where Anne candidly discusses sexuality and her stormy relationship with her mother. This might be the second finding, one that concerns Otto Frank's ambivalence about publishing his daughter's diary, and his worries over how those depicted in the diary would be remembered. But a parallel history of the diary's reception co-exists in the crafting by postwar Jewish communities in North America, Europe, and Israel (Gilman 1986; Graver 1995; Rosenfeld 1991). Part of this other history crystallizes in the author Meyer Levin's bitterly epic and unsuccessful thirty-year battle with Otto Frank over the rights to publish his play about the diary[7]. For Meyer Levin, while the diary could come to represent a story of Jewish suffering that only a Jew could tell, there would always be the question of those who would not listen and acknowledge—even within Jewish communities—the particularities of Jewish suffering. Whereas Otto Frank desired Anne Frank to be universalized as adolescent in her capacity to hope, Meyer Levin desired Anne Frank to be a monument, indeed, what Volkan (1981) terms in his work on complicated mourning, "a linking object" to the memory of six million. And while both responses may have in common the desire to memorialize, the directions each took are not outside the traumas of loss and the ways the vulnerable work of mourning becomes interrupted, even as it must proceed bit by bit with the knowledge that comes too late.

Meyer Levin first came to the French version of the *Diary* in 1950 while living in Europe. Prior to the war, Levin had published many novels of Jewish life, but always felt fame had eluded him because the publishing industry viewed his work as "too ethnic" and "too Jewish" for mass appeal. In 1945, he was an eyewitness reporter to the liberation of Auschwitz. When Levin first encountered the *Diary*, he became convinced that this document *along with his efforts to make it known*, would radically reshape how the Holocaust could be understood. When the *Diary* was published in English and carried a preface signed by Eleanor Roosevelt, its popularization and reprinting were largely due to Levin's 1952 essay review first published in the *New York Times*. In that review, one sentence continues to stand out in terms of contemporary pedagogical efforts: "Anne Frank's voice becomes the voice of six million Jewish souls" (cited in Graver 1995, 26).

Meyer Levin then wanted to write a play based on the *Diary*. Otto Frank agreed that he try. But while, for Levin, only a Jew was capable of identifying with and writing about the suffering of Anne Frank, Otto Frank desired a play that would focus on the indelibility of the human spirit and the power to dramatize just that. Otto Frank viewed the identity of the author as irrelevant and eventually selected the play by the Christian team of Frances Goodrich and Albert Hackett[8] over Levin's play. For Levin, this choice was an affront to Jewish memory, and what Levin would come to see as "the second death" of Anne Frank. This betrayal, from Levin's perspective, inspired his thirty-year public struggle against Otto Frank.

By 1974, still hoping for vindication and sympathetic acceptance, Levin would write his own story of what he felt had gone terribly wrong. After all, Levin had sued Otto Frank for the rights to publish a play based on the *Diary*, and this legal action was scandalous. Running over three hundred pages long, Levin's near-epic account is aptly titled *The Obsession*. And much of this text is a struggle to understand his three engagements in psychoanalysis, where he tried to confront his own compulsion to control the reception of the *Diary*. His second analyst asks, "The enemies you tell of are undoubtedly real. The question is, are they worth all the trouble you give yourself over them?" (19). The question does not stun him, for a larger struggle preoccupies this text. Levin cannot decide whether some obsessions are worthy, even as the cost in his life is misery.

The first paragraph of *The Obsession* tells the whole story in miniature:

> In the middle of life I fell into a trouble that was to grip, occupy, haunt, and all but devour me these twenty years. I've used the word "fall." It implies something accidental, a stumbling, but we also use the word in speaking of "falling in love" in which there is a sense of elevation, and where a fatedness is implied, a feeling of being inevitably bound in through all the mysterious components of character to this expression of the life process, whether in the end beautifully gratifying or predominantly painful. (7)

Levin's fall into trouble repeated and reversed the mystery of the *Diary*. For Anne Frank, "Although I tell you a great deal about our lives, you still know very little about us." For Meyer Levin, the sentence might read, "Although I tell myself all, I understand little." For pedagogy, the sentence might repeat Levin's poetic insight into the fall, for educators cannot know "whether in the end [their efforts with the *Diary* will be] beautifully gratifying or predominantly painful." Both Otto Frank and Meyer Levin desired Anne Frank's *Diary* to be an inspiration and an education. This, too, is the present pedagogical hope. But no one can agree, to return to Levin's poetic insight (189), "whether in the end [reading the *Diary* would be] beautifully gratifying or predominantly painful." Nor would there be agreement on whether the *Diary* would represent the particularities of Jewish suffering or the universal condition of adolescents. This, too, becomes our pedagogical dilemma if we think of adolescents as in need of protection from suffering or as incapable of engaging the suffering of another. In both directions, the strained hope for the *Diary* is symptomatic of significant anxieties that begin with how it should be encountered and what it might take for readers to identify with it. This is part of its pedagogical history where the time of Anne Frank continues to reside in an ethnographic present that works to preserve its status as a cultural icon and sustain the wish to rescue and hence not betray, again, the family in hiding.

We are left with difficult pedagogical questions. How do the contentious receptions of the *Diary* unconsciously live in our pedagogy? How is it possible that histories of which we may have no knowledge return, but now as a symptom called education? Can the *Diary* serve as both a universal coming of age and a voice for the vast numbers of murdered Jewish children? Does the appeal to universalism actually work as a disavowal of the psychic events that might be made from the reading of the *Diary*? How do these unresolvable tensions structure the fault lines of our own unconscious pedagogical efforts?

We might risk a few observations about how the haunting historicity of Anne Frank's *Diary* structures our pedagogical unconscious. It seems as though in our rush to make Anne Frank an object of adulation that can then serve as a means for identification, we have ignored the complex conditions of any hope. And these conditions are what Freud (1968a) called "the work of mourning." For remember, if hope is to be complex and dynamic, one must be willing to acknowledge the difficult conditions that invoke hope in the first place, namely the vicissitudes of loss and losing. My sense is that our pedagogy still resides in the fault lines of mourning and melancholia: we desire to remain loyal to the dead (by keeping Anne Frank at her desk and ignoring the conflicts made from the last fifty years of the *Diary*'s reception), and we desire to make from the *Diary* an insight into our selves (by offering young readers Anne Frank's daily observations). Perhaps these contradictory desires, however differently lived, were also those of Meyer Levin and Otto Frank. But what seems to be in need of attention is how this demand to remain loyal shuts out insight into the conflicts, ambivalences, and desolations that are a part of the work of mourning. The attempt to be loyal is not the same thing as identifying with the fate and positions of another. And the idealization of hope which seems to be a compromise formation that ignores this difficult difference actually only covers the pain of loss. What seems most crucial is a way to consider, then, what the risk of learning has to do with the work of mourning. And perhaps the greatest risk of learning is that lonely recognition that knowledge of loss and our own insufficient response can only be made in a belated time.

The Time of Pedagogy

At the heart of psychoanalytic work is an ethical call to consider the complexity, conflicts, and plays of both psyche and history. It is these conflicts—Eros and Thanatos, love and aggression—that education seems to place elsewhere. And then these forces seem to come back at education as interruptions, as unruly students, as irrelevant questions, and as controversial knowledge in need of containment. These are felt as aggressive returns when education conducts itself as if the separation of good and bad was not a dilemma for the learner and the teacher, and as if stories and their conflicts somehow end on the last page and do not reach elsewhere. And yet, as Sigmund Freud (1968b) observed, these conflicts return in the symptom of the difficult knowledge held in curriculum, where we ask children and adolescents to engage with difficult knowledge of life and death while we ourselves barely acknowledge how our own anxieties weigh heavily upon pedagogical efforts.

The individual anxieties we bring to the study of difficult knowledge also belong to the history we study. And so, part of our work is to tolerate the study of the difficult reception of the *Diary* and the ways this reception inadvertently repeats in the form of pedagogy. For perhaps what the historicity of the *Diary* offers is not the voices of millions, but the ways millions have tried to engage the voice of one. We cannot predict whether this engagement "falls into trouble" like Meyer Levin, or whether the engagement can become one of exploring the vicissitudes of loss and attachment and the woeful insufficiency of the belated response. In the study of difficult knowledge, we are offered too little and too much, too early and too late. To tolerate this time of otherness is, I think, the challenge of pedagogy.

This challenge of pedagogy is also the challenge to the pedagogue. Learning, it turns out, is crafted from a curious set of intimacies: the self's relations to its own otherness and the self's relation to the other's otherness. This is forgotten when the adult's desire for a stable truth found in the insistence upon courage and hope shuts out the reverberations of losing and being lost. Now, we reach our last lonely discovery: teaching, it turns out, is also a psychic event for the teacher. If the pedagogy of the *Diary* enacts the educator's desire for a rescue fantasy, stable truth, and the splitting of good and evil through the idealization of the good object, we lose the chance to work through the ambivalences that are also a part of the crisis of witnessing.

A few years ago, a group of international analysts met in Israel for a conference titled "Persistent Shadows of the Holocaust: The Meaning to Those Not Directly Affected" (Moses 1993). In a curious way, this conference lived the tensions that come from engagement with and hopes for Anne Frank's *Diary*. The learning in this conference, like any learning, could only be approached by way of a detour. The detour began over disagreement as to the title of the conference. Participants could not agree on what being "not directly affected" meant, even as they could acknowledge the indirection of affect. While they could acknowledge that the Holocaust does not affect everyone the same way and those who identify as affected do so very differently, many could not tolerate a conversation between a Jewish analyst and a Christian German analyst. And they worried over the ways the Holocaust has entered "part of the vernacular of tragedy" (Doneson 1987) as they transformed the question of who is affected into one of "what affects for whom?"

Then, the analysts could not come to a common definition of mourning. One suggested that when it came to the event known as the Holocaust, the work of mourning is interminable, because the loss is inconceivable even as it demands an addressee. Curiously, what brought them together was a hesitation. And it had to do with the question that returns us to education. If individuals do the work of mourning, can we also say that such work can be attempted by nations? How does a nation come to terms with its internal violences, and how do these internal violences return in the form of a curriculum? How does a nation mourn its history? And what place does education have in such a project?

The figure of Anne Frank also haunted this conference. She returned in the form of a symptom known as the "Anne Frank Syndrome." The term is given over to children of survivors who try to rescue their parents from what the parents have already been through. The child or adult wishes to preserve a happiness that could not have occurred. And this designation raises the question of how the Anne Frank Syndrome might haunt our own pedagogical attempts, our own crisis of witnessing.

If education is to become a working through, a learning, then we might work within the words of Anne Frank when she began reformulating her diary for others: "Although I tell you a great deal about our lives, you still know very little about us." And although we say a great deal about the *Diary*, we still know little about how we read it through ourselves. The curious time of pedagogy is the time of knowing too much and learning too little, of being too early and too late.

But what can allow this time to be counted is the interest in provoking new conditions of learning that can tolerate the time when the contentious history of the *Diary* meets that other contention, each of our selves.

1. This paper, given as a keynote address at the National Council of Teachers of English Annual Convention, November 1996, draws from a much larger consideration of learning from "difficult knowledge." See Chapter 6, "That Lonely Discovery: Anne Frank, Anna Freud and the Question of Pedagogy," in Britzman (1998), *Lost Subjects, Contested Objects: Toward a Psychoanalytic Inquiry of Learning* (Albany: SUNY Press).

2. For a critical discussion of the stakes in different translations of the diary, see Rosenfeld (1991). While translation always means a transfiguration of meaning from one language to another, and thus poses a question of loss of meaning, Rosenfeld studied how the Schultz German translation of the *Diary* changed Anne Frank's discussion of German responsibility for the Jewish genocide into a much vaguer condemnation of war. The Schultz translation leaves out specific references to German responsibility. Rosenfeld makes the argument that two contradictory understandings result from censoring the *Diary.* On the one hand, Anne Frank, who was born in Frankfurt, cannot be viewed as a German who lost her citizenship. On the other hand, the fact that Germans persecuted German Jews is also forgotten. In the censorship of the *Diary,* Rosenfeld notes, "Some of the most telling features of Anne Frank's story have never been told to German readers, who for some four decades now have been reading a bowdlerized version of the diary" (268).

3. The recent exhibit at the Jewish Museum in New York titled "The Illegal Camera: Photography in the Netherlands during the German Occupation, 1940–1945" offers a sense of a country under German law. The photographs were taken secretly because with the imposition of German civil law, the taking of photographs was restricted. The photographs offer chilling documentation of the utter normalcy of life in Amsterdam during the Nazi Occupation and gradual social breakdown of that very normalcy.

4. Deborah Dwork (1991) discusses the difficulties of studying the experience of Jewish European children and their lives under the Nazi regime. Dwork argues that, depending upon location, Jewish children under the age of ten were not required to wear a Jewish star sewn on the clothing. Children under the age of ten, deported to camps, were murdered quickly, as were their mothers. Dwork notes that only 11 percent of Jewish children alive before the war survived the war.

For those who were able to go into hiding, few administrative records were kept, due to the danger of these documents becoming found. And except for the documentation preserved from the Theresienstadt ghetto, the vast majority of children could not document their lives. The documentation that does exist, in spite of state-sanctioned efforts to erase the genocide, offers, as Dwork argues, threads of specific lives woven in difficult conditions. In Dwork's words:

At a much younger age than their elders, and with far less maturity and a less developed sense of identity, children also had to cope with the Nazi (and their Fascist allies') process of differentiation (wearing a star), separation (segregation from their erstwhile "Aryan" companions), isolation (banishment from their former physical world of school, park, playground, library, cinema, ice cream parlor), and finally, deportation and extermination. (xxxii)

These were the conditions, as well, for Anne Frank. However, Anne Frank also represents some unusual conditions. Her family stayed together in hiding and attempted to live life normally. Despite their hiding, Anne Frank had, for two years, the conditions to write her diary entries. Dwork notes that the diary written by Anne Frank is exceptional in this regard. With the recent translation and English publication of Binjamin Wilkomirski's (1996) childhood in camps, more difficulty is posed. Wilkomirski's fractured recollections raise the question of the chaos of retrospection, when memory attempts to narrate chaos, pain, and inconceivable cruelty from the vantage of an adult possessed by a childhood that remains caught in woeful disregard. Readers of this text must grapple with their capacity to understand a child's trauma.

5. Otto Frank was ambivalent about how the *Diary* was to be represented and introduced. In a letter to Meyer Levin, Frank writes:

I always said, that Anne's book is not a warbook. War is the background. It is not a Jewish book either, though Jewish sphere, sentiment and surrounding is the background. I never wanted a Jew writing an introduction for it. It is (at least) read and understood more by gentiles than in Jewish circles . . . (cited in Graver 1995, 54).

6. The sentences that grapple with this often-quoted declaration bring us to the central conflict Anne was caught in:

It's utterly impossible for me to build my life on a foundation of chaos, suffering and death. I see the world being slowly transformed into a wilderness, I hear the approaching thunder that, one day, will destroy us too. I feel the suffering of millions. And yet, when I look up at the sky, I somehow feel that everything will change for the better, that this cruelty too shall end, that peace and tranquillity will return once more. In the meantime, I must hold on to my ideals (332).

7. Graver's (1995) book is a richly detailed account of Meyer Levin's thirty-year struggle to craft the meaning and reception of the *Diary*. In documenting the very contentious Jewish response to the standing of the *Diary*, Graver makes the insightful argument that rather than a footnote in the history of Jewish secular arts, the episode of Meyer Levin's "obsession" with the *Diary* is emblematic of the trauma of the Shoah, Jewish response to North American anti-Semitism, and the conflicts with Jewish generations. The sum of these debates within Jewish communities over the past fifty years can be seen as a precursor to contemporary tensions in identity

politics that center the question of who can know an event, the problems of epistemic privilege, and the rendering into a hierarchy social suffering with the assertion of experience and the myth of direct apprehension of history. And while Meyer Levin's struggle focused on the reception of the *Diary*, a different argument is offered by Bettelheim (1980). Bettelheim, himself a survivor of the camps, argued that the *Diary*'s acceptance in North America was an enactment of the general public's denial of the magnitude of the Holocaust. This idea emerges from what Bettelheim saw as the Frank family's refusal to understand the Nazi policy of Jewish destruction. Bettelheim writes: "By eulogizing how they lived in their hiding place while neglecting to examine first whether it was a reasonable or an effective choice, we are able to ignore the crucial lesson of their story—that such an attitude can be fatal in extreme circumstance" (247).

8. Frances Goodrich and Albert Hackett were best known for being part of a script rewriting team for the MGM Frank Capra film, *It's a Wonderful Life*. They were also part of a writing team for the script of the play version of Anne Frank's *Diary*. While each succeeding draft lessened the writers' attempts to highlight humor, Goodrich and Hackett continued to soften the dimension of the diary's Jewish tragedy, and emphasized, instead, a human spirit capable of rising above tragedy. But the Jewish references in the play seem to assume a non-Jewish audience, and the play becomes awkward when, for example, during the Chanukah scene, Otto Frank pauses to explain the holiday to the Jewish dentist. Much later, Mr. Dussell's surviving son attempted to correct the misperception of his father as being ignorant of Jewish learning (See Graver, 85–87; 125–31).

Works Cited

Bettelheim, Bruno. 1980. *Surviving and Other Essays*. New York: Vintage Books.

Blair, Jon, in association with the British Broadcasting Corporation and the Disney Channel. 1996. *Anne Frank Remembered*. 117 min. Culver City, CA: Columbia TriStar Video, videocassette.

Caruth, Cathy. 1996. *Unclaimed Experience: Trauma, Narrative, and History*. Baltimore: The Johns Hopkins University Press.

Doneson, Judith. 1987. "The American History of Anne Frank's Diary." *Holocaust and Genocide Studies* 2(1): 149–60.

Dwork, Deborah. 1991. *Children with a Star: Jewish Youth in Nazi Europe*. New Haven: Yale University Press.

Erikson, Erik. 1964. *Insight and Responsibility: Lectures on the Ethical Implications of Psychoanalytic Insight*. New York: Norton.

Felman, Shoshana, and Dori Laub. 1992. *Testimony: Crises of Witnessing in Literature, Psychoanalysis, and History*. New York: Routledge.

Frank, Anne. 1995. *The Diary of a Young Girl: The Definitive Edition*. Edited by Otto Frank and Mirjam Pressler. Translated by Susan Massotty. New York: Doubleday.

Freud, Sigmund. 1968a. *Mourning and Melancholia* (1917[1915]). *The Standard Edition of the Complete Psychological Works of Sigmund Freud*, Vol. 4, edited by James Strachey, 243–58. London: Hogarth Press.

Freud, Sigmund (1968b). *New Introductory Lectures on Psycho-Analysis and Other Works* (1932–1936). *The Standard Edition of the Complete Psychological Works of Sigmund Freud*, Vol. 22, edited by James Strachey. London: Hogarth Press.

Friedlander, Saul, ed. 1992. *Probing the Limits of Representation: Nazism and the "Final Solution."* Cambridge, MA: Harvard University Press.

Gilman, Sander. 1986. *Jewish Self-Hatred: Anti-Semitism and the Hidden Language of the Jews.* Baltimore: The Johns Hopkins University Press.

Graver, Lawrence. 1995. *An Obsession with Anne Frank: Meyer Levin and the Diary.* Berkeley: University of California Press.

La Capra, Dominick. 1994. *Representing the Holocaust: History, Theory, Trauma.* Ithaca: Cornell University Press.

Lester, Julius. 1989. "The Stone That Weeps." In *Testimony: Contemporary Writers Make the Holocaust Personal*, edited by David Rosenberg, 192–210. New York: Random House.

Levin, Meyer. 1974. *The Obsession.* New York: Simon & Schuster.

Linenthal, Edward. 1995. *Preserving Memory: The Struggle to Create America's Holocaust Museum.* New York: Viking.

Moses, Rafael, ed. 1993. *Persistent Shadows of the Holocaust: The Meaning to Those Not Directly Affected.* Madison, CT: International Universities Press.

Rosenfeld, Alvin. 1991. "Popularization and Memory: The Case of Anne Frank." In *Lessons and Legacies: The Meaning of the Holocaust in a Changing World*, edited by Peter Hayes, 243–78. Evanston: Northwestern University Press.

Rosenfeld, Alvin. 1993. "Anne Frank—And Us: Finding the Right Words." *Reconstruction* 2(2): 86–92.

Silberfeld, Michel. 1988. "The Psychology of Hope and the Modification of Entitlement Near the End of Life." In *Attitudes of Entitlement: Theoretical and Clinical Issues*, edited by V. Volkan and T. Rodgers, 41–52. Charlottesville: University Press of Virginia.

Stern, Anne-Lise. 1995/1996. "Mending Auschwitz, through Psychoanalysis?" *Strategies: A Journal of Theory, Culture and Politics* 8: 41–52.

Volkan, Vamik. 1981. *Linking Objects and Linking Phenomena: A Study of the Forms, Symptoms, Metapsychology, and Therapy of Complicated Mourning.* New York: International Universities Press.

Wilkomirski, Binjamin. 1996. *Fragments: Memories of a Wartime Childhood.* Translated by Carol Brown Janeway. New York: Schocken Press.

IV Additional Resources

17 Uncloseting the Classroom Library: An Annotated Bibliography of Teacher Resources

Sarah-Hope Parmeter
University of California, Santa Cruz

Teaching about genocide and intolerance is the opposite side of a coin whose face is teaching about diversity and celebration. Truly appreciating difference demands that we confront our failures: the times when difference has been seen as a cause for violence, for injustice, for eradication, rather than for celebration. Lesbians, gay men, and bisexuals comprise a community that has historically faced waves of destruction, from the witch hunts of the middle ages (the label "witch" could easily be applied to any woman living without the benefit or protection of men; gay men were, at this time, literally "faggots," material for burning, a label which has outlived its historical origins in the public consciousness), to the repeated anti-gay purges in the modern military, to court rulings ripping children away from their gay parents, to pervasive sodomy laws, which may be used only rarely, but which remain a potential source of prosecution. To be or to become lesbian, gay, or bisexual is to experience the risk of being the subject of one of these purges, whether it takes the form of a literal holocaust or the form of less visible, daily erasures and unkindnesses.

To be lesbian, gay, or bisexual is also to be a member of a culture. While gay folk come from every conceivable background, we also hold much in common: partnerships, households, families, neighborhoods, community groups, business and professional associations, athletic events, religious organizations, holidays, political movements, historical landmarks, publishing houses, theater, art, and films. However, while we are members of this community by "birthright," we are almost never raised within this community. Gay children are almost always the offspring of straight parents who, even if they are accepting, are in no position to pass on the historical and cultural knowledge that might be used as a form of proactive self-defense against bigotry and violence. Instead, we go through a years-long process, often beginning in childhood, of gradual identification both of our own sexual/affectional orientation and of the community of which we are members.

Children of lesbian, gay, and bisexual parents are similarly challenged by the lack of general recognition of gay culture. While most of these children are themselves heterosexual, they face many of the same battles faced by gay youth, including difficult decisions about coming out. However, when these children come out they are revealing a family, rather than an individual, identity. They may feel deeply torn between love for their parents and resentment for the difficulties their parents' sexual/affectional identities create for them. These children may need to define themselves apart from the gay community, but they also need the support that community can offer them as a place of familial identity.

It was with the needs of these two groups of children in mind that I began compiling this bibliography of classroom resources. The following pages discuss books that will allow lesbian, gay, and bisexual children a chance to meet themselves on the page, to picture the rich unfolding of their lives, to see their sexual/affectional identity as a source of possibilities, rather than limitations. These are books that will offer children from lesbian, gay, and bisexual families affirmation, that will validate their parents' ways of loving, while setting them free to choose their own paths. These are the books that give teachers—lesbian, gay, bisexual, and straight—the historical and cultural knowledge they will need to serve as guides to these children on their journeys.

Guidelines for Material Selection

The body of lesbian and gay-inclusive literature for children and adolescents is actually fairly large, but unfortunately quite uneven in terms of both focus and quality. This bibliography is not intended to offer a complete listing of all materials published on the topic, but rather a well-developed presentation of the materials most useful— in terms of literary quality, inclusiveness, age-appropriateness, and ethical framework—for classroom teachers. While the topic of lesbian/gay/bisexual identity has become increasingly visible in recent years, much of what is published either reflects the worst aspects of the teen "problem novel" or is poorly written. Teachers looking to expand their classroom libraries or to broaden their own understanding of the lives of gay/lesbian/bisexual families and youth need to pay attention to the issues described below in choosing reading materials if they hope to create genuinely inclusive classrooms that reflect a full range of individual identities and family structures.

The Gay "Problem"

All too often a character's gay identity is treated as the central "crisis" of a book, rather than as just one aspect of that character's identity. Such books frequently focus on homophobia and gay-bashing, painting a bleak future for youth who are wrestling with lesbian, gay, or bisexual identity. One such title is Frank Mosca's *All American Boys* (1995). The level of violence the book's main characters face—one is beaten so badly he requires hospitalization, the other's pet carrier pigeons are brutally slaughtered—would be apt to push youth questioning their own sexual/affectional identities further into the closet. In contrast, Norma Klein's *My Life as a Body* (1987), while inappropriate for younger readers because of its sexual content, is refreshing for its inclusion of a lesbian secondary character whose sexual orientation is never the subject of controversy.

A related problem is presented by books like Lesléa Newman's *Heather Has Two Mommies* (1991), a book ostensibly for primary-grade children. This story explains Heather's dual-mommy situation by providing, among other things, a detailed explanation of the process of artificial insemination. Because this was one of the very first children's books published on the topic, it is included in many bibliographies and is often cited as an exemplar in the literature. However, lesbian parents in this book come across as something of a medical oddity, as is not the case in another of Newman's books, *Gloria Goes to Gay Pride* (1991), which presents a lesbian family as part of a larger, supportive community.

Diversity

In general, literature dealing with gay, lesbian, and bisexual characters and stories is Anglo-dominated, although the books for younger children are somewhat more ethnically diverse than those for adolescents. *Asha's Mums* (1990) and *How Would You Feel If Your Dad Was Gay?* (1991) are two of the better children's books in terms of reflecting an ethnically diverse cast of characters. Diversity in books for older readers is essentially nonexistent. Only two titles, *Big Man and the Burn-Out* (1985) and *S. P. Likes A. D.* (1989) include significant characters who are not Anglo. This issue of diversity is particularly important, given stereotypes within the gay community and society as a whole that tend to depict the gay community as exclusively white. Oftentimes, coming out is particularly difficult for youth of color because they feel they are being forced to choose between their ethnicity and their sexual/affectional orientation. Gay youth need to see that they can live productive lives, reflecting their full identities, within the gay community.

Setting   Many books for older readers are set in exclusive, private (often boarding) schools, which distances them from most teens' realities. While such books might provide escape reading for lesbian/gay/bisexual youth, they do not model real-life strategies for survival and affirmation. These books also tend to include a problematic "seductress" character, who often manipulates or abuses a more naive central character who is attracted to her. Typical of these titles are Janet Futcher's *Crush* (1995), Deborah Hautzig's *Hey, Dollface* (1978), and Janice Kesselman's *Flick* (Harper and Row). Books with public-school settings, like *Unlived Affections* (1995) and *Big Man and the Burn-Out* (1985), are much more likely to offer lesbian/gay/bisexual youth an opportunity to rehearse major undertakings such as coming out to families and friends or responding to anti-gay harassment.

The Invisible   With the exception of one of the nonfiction "handbooks" for older
Bisexual   readers, *The Journey Out* (1995), none of the books currently available deal with bisexuality as a valid sexual/affectional identity: characters are depicted as either gay or straight or as in the process of deciding which of these two categories they fit into. This lack of diverse symbolic types mirrors the popular culture's inability to view bisexuality as anything other than a transitional identity, representing either experimentation, which will soon be abandoned, or internalized homophobia, which has not yet been overcome.

Despite these problems, there is a solid group of books that do offer constructive, accepting, and useful depictions of lesbian and gay lives. While these books are not enough—more good literature in this field is desperately needed—they do offer children and adolescents opportunities to learn comfortably about lesbian and gay experience and to see their own experiences and the experiences of their families reflected in literature.

Children's   Elwin, Rosamund, and Michele Paulse. 1990. *Asha's Mums*. Toronto:
Books about   Women's Press.
Contemporary
Lesbian/Gay/   This book focuses on a teacher's refusal to believe that her
Bisexual Life   student, Asha, lives with two mothers. It includes a
                    multiethnic cast of characters and features lovely illustrations.
                    An excellent story for introducing or acknowledging the
                    concept of gay families.

Heron, Ann, and Meredith Maran. 1991. *How Would You Feel If Your Dad Was Gay?* Boston: Alyson Publications.

While gayness is the central "problem" in this book, it's handled well, showing the "coming out" decisions children of gay parents have to make. Multiethnic cast. Black and white drawings.

Jordan, MaryKate. 1989. *Losing Uncle Tim*. Niles, IL: Whitman.

While Uncle Tim—who has died of AIDS—is never identified as gay, it's easy to infer this, and his character is lovingly and sympathetically drawn. A particularly good book for younger children dealing with HIV-related illness or with a death of any kind. Beautiful illustrations.

Newman, Lesléa. 1991. *Gloria Goes to Gay Pride*. Boston: Alyson Publications.

This book offers a celebratory depiction of the full range of members in a gay community and their straight supporters, making it useful for teaching about the concept of "allies."

Willhoite, Michael. 1991. *Families: A Coloring Book*. Boston: Alyson Publications.

This book isn't groundbreaking, but it does reflect a variety of family structures and features a multiethnic cast of characters. The illustrations might be useful for a variety of classroom purposes.

Adolescent Books about Contemporary Lesbian/Gay/Bisexual Life

Bess, Clayton. 1985. *Big Man and the Burn-Out*. New York: Houghton Mifflin.

This novel offers an ethnically diverse cast and includes two gay adults whose identity is never a source of controversy. It treats adolescents' questioning of their sexuality as normal, while avoiding "it's only a phase" reasoning.

Brett, Catherine. 1989. *S. P. Likes A. D.* Toronto: The Women's Press.

The central character of this novel, S. P., sees her lesbianism as an "issue," but she has friends who accept it comfortably. All women characters in the book are strong, independent innovators and represent a diversity of ages.

Garden, Nancy. 1991. *Lark in the Morning*. New York: Farrar, Straus & Giroux.

In this novel, by the author of the better known *Annie on My Mind*, the young lesbian characters are secure in their identities and have a loving, stable relationship—though they have yet to come out to their families. The central plot deals with a pair of abused, runaway children whom the lesbian protagonist tries to help.

Heron, Ann, ed. 1983. *One Teenager in Ten: Writings by Gay and Lesbian Youth.* Boston: Alyson Publications.

This book tells the stories of gay and lesbian youth in their own words, and, as a result, the quality of writing varies. Not all teens' experiences have been good, and the book is frank about topics like teen sexual activity that may be uncomfortable for some adults to deal with, but the truthful, first-person voices in this book make it an important resource.

Heron, Ann, ed. 1994. *Two Teenagers in Twenty: Writings by Gay and Lesbian Youth.* Boston: Alyson Publications.

This is an update of *One Teenager in Ten* which includes some material from the original book, plus new pieces. Again, all the pieces included are written by lesbian/gay/bisexual youth. This book also offers useful information on resources available, as well as a gay pen-pal service for teenagers, sponsored by Alyson Publications.

Homes, A. M. 1990. *Jack.* New York: Vintage.

Although an adult novel, this book could be easily read and appreciated by a much younger audience. The central plot follows a young man's discovery that his father is gay, but the book is rich in subplots and avoids a "problem novel" format. The gay community is sensitively portrayed, and the author captures well the turmoil of adolescence.

Koertge, Ronald. 1989. *The Arizona Kid.* New York: Avon.

This novel features a straight teen who spends the summer living with his gay uncle and working at a race track. While the uncle is somewhat stereotypical (very attentive to fashion, a host of elegant parties), his character is dealt with affectionately. The book also illustrates the impact of AIDS on the gay male community. This book deftly balances difficult social issues with good-natured humor and allows us to feel genuine affection for all its characters.

Shannon, George. 1989. *Unlived Affections.* New York: Harper & Row.

After the death of the grandmother who raised him, a young man discovers while reading family correspondence that his father was gay. All the characters in this book are richly and lovingly portrayed, and both gay and straight relationships are treated respectfully.

Velez, Ivan. 1987–1990. *Tales of the Closet*. New York: Hetrick-Martin Institute for the Protection of Lesbian and Gay Youth (2 Aster Place, Third Floor, New York, NY 10003).

This is actually a series of comic books which follows the lives of a group of ethnically and sexually diverse lesbian and gay New York teens. These books are satisfying in their depiction of the ways teens can build their own support networks, but also present very brutal depictions of anti-gay violence and homophobia. The stories are explicit and include good information on safer sex for heterosexuals and gay men, but nothing on lesbian safer sex. Their format may make them engaging and accessible for students who are less interested in novels.

Teachers' Books about Lesbian/ Gay/Bisexual Culture, History, and Experience

Alyson, Sasha, and Lynne Y. Fletcher, eds. 1991. *Young, Gay, and Proud*. Boston: Alyson Publications.

This is an updated edition of a "coming out handbook" for lesbian and gay youth. It includes useful information on a range of topics, such as support services, education, religion, and sexuality. Because of unevenness in its content, this book will probably be more useful for young gay men than it is for young lesbians.

Amnesty International. 1994. *Breaking the Silence: Human Rights Violations Based on Sexual Orientation*. New York: Amnesty International Publications (322 Eighth Avenue, New York, NY 10001).

This book provides a survey of conditions affecting lesbians, gay men, and bisexuals worldwide. While its focus on human rights abuses makes much of the information it presents disheartening, it would provide teachers with an introduction to the global struggle for gay human rights.

Bauer, Marion Dane, ed. 1995. *Am I Blue? Coming Out from the Silence*. New York: Harper Trophy.

This collection of fiction written for and about lesbian, gay, and bisexual youth is delightful in its variety. The title story, which centers on a young man's wish to turn all gay people blue, making them instantly recognizable, would work quite well for opening classroom discussions on issues of intolerance and stereotyping.

Clyde, Laurel A., and Marjorie Lobban. 1992. *Out of the Closet and Into the Classroom: Homosexuality in Books for Young People.* Deakin, Australia: ALIA Thorpe (c/o The Australian Library and Information Association, 9-11 Napier Close, Deakin, ACT 2600, Australia).

This bibliography offers a comprehensive listing of books for children and youth that include lesbian/gay/bisexual identity in some way. The usefulness of the titles included varies: some are listed simply because of the use of gay-related insults or name-calling, while others treat sexual/affectional identity more extensively.

Jennings, Kevin, ed. 1994. *Becoming Visible: A Reader in Gay and Lesbian History for High School and College Students.* Boston: Alyson Publications.

While this book is written for older readers and would not be useful for most grade-school students, it can provide teachers with excellent source material regarding lesbian and gay history. It includes chapters on homosexuality in a variety of cultures, the emergence of the modern gay rights movement, and contemporary struggles. Because it is formatted like a textbook, with reading questions and suggested discussion and writing activities, creative teachers may find ways of integrating this material into their own, age-appropriate units.

Manasse, Geoff, and Jean Swallow. 1995. *Making Love Visible: In Celebration of Gay and Lesbian Families.* Freedom, CA: Crossing Press.

This book, written for adults, offers portraits of a wide variety of lesbian and gay families. Elementary school teachers may find it most useful for the many family photographic portraits it includes, which could be used as part of a classroom "family collage" or as discussion starters.

Pollack, Rachel, and Cheryl Schwartz. 1995. *The Journey Out: A Guide for and about Lesbian, Gay, and Bisexual Teens.* New York: Puffin Books.

Like *Young, Gay, and Proud,* this is a "coming-out handbook for youth." It is the better of the two books, offering specific definitions of terminology, self-assessments to help teens prepare to come out, and an extensive, national listing of resources. This is an excellent book for teachers who want to serve as advocates or allies. In addition to being useful for lesbian/gay/bisexual youth, this book could also be helpful for a boy or girl with a sibling in the process of coming out.

Pollack, Sandra, and Jeanne Vaughn, eds. 1987. *Politics of the Heart: A Lesbian Parenting Anthology.* Ithaca, NY: Firebrand Books.
This book offers teachers insights into the day-to-day concerns and experiences of lesbian parents and their children. It includes chapters on deciding to raise children, coparenting, resolving family conflicts, and community.

Rafkin, Louise, ed. 1990. *Different Mothers: Sons and Daughters of Lesbians Talk about Their Lives.* Pittsburgh: Cleis Press.

Like the previous title, this book offers insights into lesbian families. The children included in this collection of oral histories and interviews vary in age and background, and reflect very different degrees of comfort with their parents' sexual/affectional identities.

Whitlock, Katherine. 1989. *Bridges of Respect: Creating Support for Lesbian and Gay Youth.* Philadelphia: American Friends Service Committee (American Friends Service Committee, 1501 Cherry Street, Philadelphia, PA 19102).

One of the first publications ever targeted at adults working with lesbian and gay youth, this book offers a valuable introduction to many topics of concern, including the costs of homophobia, providing safe and equitable educational environments, health and sexuality education, social services, and legal concerns.

Acknowledgments

I would like to acknowledge the editor of this volume, Judith Robertson, for recognizing the appropriateness of including lesbian/gay/bisexual concerns in this volume that teaches about genocide and intolerance. I would also like to acknowledge the work of my colleague Ellen Louise Hart, who has worked tirelessly with me over the years to encourage our profession to recognize and address the specific needs of lesbian/gay/bisexual students. Readers are encouraged to consult Caroline Heller's "Gay and Lesbian Resources" (in Carol Danks and Leatrice B. Rabinsky, eds., *Teaching for a Tolerant World, Grades 9–12*, 344–55. Urbana, IL: NCTE, 1998) for additional resources to help teachers better understand gay and lesbian issues.

18 Mirror, Mirror on the Wall, Who Is the Fairest One of All? Using Children's Literature to Teach about Aging

Dona J. Helmer
Montana State University, Billings

A geism is a significant social issue in Western society. Numerous studies have found consistent stereotyping of elderly characters in children's literature. In addition to promoting negative attitudes toward the elderly, stereotyping can create fear and dread of aging, and may also enhance intergenerational conflict. These issues may become even more important in the coming years with the increasing numbers and proportions of aging populations. This essay creates an awareness of images and negative stereotypes of older persons and offers a method of using children's picture books to develop a positive understanding of aging and the elderly. An intensive annotated bibliography of materials is included.

Every hour of every day, the percentage of the population defined as old increases. Pfiser, a leading global health-care company, recently predicted that by 2050 there may be 30 million Americans over the age of 84, as compared to only 3.3 million in 1997 (Pfizer 1997).

While some cultures revere and cherish older members for their wisdom, other cultures idolize youth and denigrate the elderly. "Ageism," defined by Robert Butler as "the process of systematic stereotyping and of discrimination against people because they are old" (1975, 11), is a widespread problem in these cultures. The books and media, the folktales and the fairy tales, the funny stories all carry embedded messages about aging (McGuire 1993). Pervasive societal perceptions and messages about the elderly are readily internalized by children. Studies have found that children as young as three years old internalize accepted stereotypes, and these attitudes toward the elderly remain a stable and enduring part of the child's life and adulthood (Jantz 1977).

These stereotypes remain for several reasons. First, modern children have little sustained contact with older persons and therefore do not challenge their preconceptions about older persons (Gutknecht 1991). Second, many teachers and parents unwittingly continue to foster ageism by using stereotypical, traditional fairy tales like "Snow White" in which the stepmother is obsessed with her fading beauty and covets the beauty and youth of her stepdaughter. In addition to folktales, negative images of older characters also permeate the entire body of children's literature. Even books like Wanda Gag's perennial favorite *Millions of Cats* (1928) has a "very old man and very old woman" who are unhappy because they are living alone. Since the classics of children's literature have a tendency to be passed down from one generation to the next, longer works like Frances Hodgson Burnett's *Little Lord Fauntleroy* (1886) which depict grandfathers who are white haired and crotchety continue to remain in print and contribute to the problem. This is because well-intentioned teachers choose these materials for read-alouds even though there have been many books with positive images printed during the past two decades (Kazemek and Rigg 1988). In fact, the increase in the number of books for children about the elderly has been so dramatic that Paulin has called the 1980s the decade of the grandparents (Paulin 1992).

Since books with more positive images are readily available, teachers should help children find these materials and should choose and use materials in their classrooms which foster positive attitudes toward aging and the aged. Children should study the aging process in elementary school. Martha John noted several reasons why children should study the elderly. First, it is important for children to learn that positive intergenerational relationships are possible. Second, children need to understand that aging is a natural part of the life process. Third, children need to learn about aging so that they can deal with it realistically. Finally, children need to learn that older persons can and do make significant contributions to society. Children who learn about the elderly have a better understanding of the changes that will take place during their own life span (John 1977).

The need for curricular units and materials to develop children's positive attitudes and understandings of the elderly was driven home to me in a big way when I was working as a librarian in a K–6 school on Adak, an island in the Alaskan Aleutian chain. Adak was a secured military installation and the home of approximately 6,000 people, mainly naval personnel and their families who rotated off-island every four years. The oldest people on the island were teachers in the public school system. The average age for those "old people" was forty-five. Since Adak was 1,500 air miles from Anchorage, Alaska, most children had little or no contact with their older grandparents.

This created an unusual situation. Everyone had to pass a rigorous physical exam. The teachers were all essentially healthy and active physically and mentally. The children on Adak had little contact with the elderly. No one on the island was caring for older relatives because the elderly were simply not allowed on the island. In a world in which most children do not live close to their grandparents or see their grandparents on a regular basis, this was an extreme case. The children on Adak did not see their grandparents live active, productive lives. They only had prolonged contact with oldsters when there was a family health crisis.

Into this existence there arrived three families whose older relatives had medical problems during the school year. One grandmother was diagnosed as having Alzheimer's, one grandfather had cancer, and another had a stroke. The teachers and librarian were faced with the task of explaining these conditions to the children of the elementary school and also of helping the children understand that these difficult events would not necessarily happen to everyone's parent or grandparent.

Since we had no vibrant seniors on the island with whom students could form intergenerational linkages, we, of necessity, turned to children's picture books as a platform for discussions. We began by doing a quick review of literature. We were looking for positive images that we could use in a variety of situations. We were looking for books for storytime, for literature circles, and for sustained read-aloud.

We started to look critically at all the books and tales we were using in K–6. We looked at the portrayal of oldsters. We found that certain words—for example, *poor, alone, small, sad, sick, very old, crooked*—were used almost routinely in folktales and fairy tales. Some of the standard classics of children's literature conveyed very subtle secondary messages that contributed to an overall negative and lasting feeling toward aging. Using Dodson and Hause's *Ageism in Literature: An Analysis Kit for Teachers and Librarians* (1981) we proceeded to develop the following ten-item checklist to help us look more thoughtfully at the literature we were using.

Ten Quick Ways to Judge a Book for Ageism

1. Is the older character the main character or a secondary stock character?

2. Is the older character infirm or ill?

3. Does the author use stock terms like *little* to describe the older character?

4. Is the older character active, productive, and/or successful? Is he or she involved in life?

5. Do the older characters just look backward in time, or do they look forward to the future?

6. Does the character exhibit a positive life force, through such qualities as sense of humor, skill, problem-solving ability, creativity, or insight?

7. Does the book present aging as a natural and lifelong process?

8. Is the older character an individual in his or her own right, or merely someone's grandparent or relative?

9. Are the illustrations evocative, visually interesting, and humane?

10. Is the older character portrayed with dignity?

We also used standard reviewing tools to find additional titles to add to our library collection. We used sources like the *Horn Book Magazine, Sensitive Issues: An Annotated Guide to Children's Literature, K–6; The Bookfinder; More Creative Uses of Children's Literature;* and *Books to Help Children Cope with Separation and Loss.*

Next we created lessons that looked critically at books and used children's picture books to teach about aging. For example, we examined common words often used to describe older persons, and we discussed the negative associations of such words. On another occasion, we investigated the sadness that people feel when they have to leave a home that holds special memories. We developed different activities that can be used to create a viable curriculum that includes units on aging. For example, students can speculate what it would be like to be old and living with other family members. Children can write other endings for the stories listed in the annotated bibliography. Students can interview old people and create oral histories (Hickey 1991). Students can start their own "memory box" and collect memories. They can invite senior citizens into classrooms to share their experiences. We found that by making small changes in our current curriculum, by taking the time and effort to discuss the images of older persons contained in traditional literature, we were able to counteract some of the negative effects of representations of ageism.

Once we started looking for materials, we found there were many excellent books available with older characters. The following annotated bibliography is a list of the works we found that gave children a broader perspective on aging and increased their understanding of the elderly. The bibliography is arranged under broad topics and is not definitive or exhaustive.

Children's Books Portraying the Elderly

Picture Books with Positive Intergenerational Relationships

Although not all older people are grandparents, it is sometimes difficult to find books with older characters who are not "simply grandparents." This list attempts to provide a sampling of the best picture books about intergenerational relationships.

Ackerman, Karen. 1988. *Song and Dance Man*. New York: Knopf.

> In this Caldecott Award-winning book, a grandpa who is used to being on the stage shares his past and his zest for life with his grandchildren. This book presents a positive look at an older family member who retains his interest in life while building on past experiences and memories.

———. 1994. *By the Dawn's Early Light*. New York: Atheneum.

> A young girl and her brother stay with their grandmother while their mother works at night. This book shows an older person helping and making a contribution to the family unit.

Anderson, Lena. 1989. *Stina*. New York: Greenwillow.

> Stina spends summers with her grandpa by the seashore. They each pursue their own interests, but Stina learns a great deal about living with her grandpa. This book shows intergenerational respect.

Booth, Barbara. 1991. *Mandy*. New York: Lothrop, Lee & Shepard.

> Mandy and her grandmother have a special relationship based upon mutual love. Mandy is deaf, and her grandmother communicates with her using sign language. When Grandmother loses her favorite pin during one of their walks, Mandy is determined to find it for her. This book portrays intergenerational caring and respect.

Buckley, Helen Elizabeth. 1994. *Grandfather and I*. New York: Lothrop, Lee & Shepard.

> This simple text with accompanying large color illustrations portrays a young boy who thinks his grandfather is the perfect person to spend time with because he is never in a hurry. The book presents a positive warm relationship between the boy and his grandfather.

———. 1994. *Grandmother and I*. New York: Lothrop, Lee & Shepard.

> In this work a young girl finds her grandmother's lap is just the right place when she needs something (or someone)

soothing. Large, soft illustrations and short text make this a good choice for storytime and discussion for grades K–1.

Bunting, Eve. 1989. *The Wednesday Surprise.* New York: Clarion Books.

When she comes to visit, Grandmother always brings a bag of books to share with seven-year-old Anna. This book shows mutual caring and intergenerational sharing of interest in new things.

———. 1994. *A Day's Work.* New York: Clarion Books.

When Francisco tries to help his grandfather find work, he discovers that even though the old man cannot speak English, he is still a productive and knowledgeable human being.

Caseley, Judith. 1991. *Dear Annie.* New York: Greenwillow.

Annie has always corresponded with her grandpa and has saved all his answers. She now has over one hundred notes from him to share with her class for show-and-tell. This story could be used as a basis for a pen-pal club with older adults or grandparents.

Crews, Donald. 1991. *Bigmama's.* New York: Greenwillow.

Caldecott medalist Donald Crews tells about summer visits to see the relatives in the country. This is a warm, inviting picture book that portrays a close family with respected grandparents.

Dorros, Arthur. 1991. *Abuela.* New York: Dutton.

While she is riding on the bus with her *abuela* (grandmother), a young girl imagines that they are flying over New York City. This bright, bold picture book joyfully depicts old and young people enjoying each other on an imaginative journey.

Douglas, Barbara. 1982. *Good as New.* New York: Lothrop.

When a favorite teddy bear gets threatened with destruction, Grandpa fixes it by restuffing the bear. This book presents old people as creative problem solvers.

Greenfield, Eloise. 1988. *Grandpa's Face.* New York: Philomel Books.

When Tamika sees Grandfather rehearsing for a part, she is frightened by his face, but he reassures her that he will never look like that. The picture book depicts a grandfather as a productive, active, and creative person who understands the fears of his granddaughter.

Henkes, Kevin. 1986. *Grandpa & Bo*. New York: Greenwillow.

> When Bo visits his grandpa in the summer, they play ball, garden, listen to records, and genuinely enjoy each other's company.

Hest, Amy. 1986. *The Purple Coat*. New York: Dial.

> When Gabrielle insists that she wants a purple coat instead of the blue one her mother wants her to have, Grandpa comes up with the creative solution of making her a reversible coat.

Hoffman, Mary. 1991. *Amazing Grace*. New York: Dial.

> Grace, a young African American girl, wants to try out for the part of Peter Pan. Her Nana tells her she can do anything she wants and be anyone she wants. This grandmother is a strong, supportive individual.

Howard, Elizabeth. 1991. *Aunt Flossie's Hats (and Crab Cakes Later)*. New York: Clarion.

> Sarah and her sister love to visit their great-great aunt who has a house filled with fun and excitement. Aunt Flossie shares stories about her hats. The picture book depicts an older female who is not a grandmother but still an important, integral part of the family.

Johnson, Angela. 1990. *When I Am Old With You*. New York: Orchard.

> A young boy and his grandfather spend the day on the porch and the boy promises, "When I am old with you, Grandaddy, we'll do all our favorite things." This book can help children speculate about growing old and what they will do when they are older.

Lasky, Kathryn. 1976. *I Have Four Names for My Grandfather*. Boston: Little, Brown.

> Poppy, Pop, Grandpa, and Pops are all different names used by the young narrator for his grandfather. Stunning black-and-white photographs accompany the text.

Lloyd, David. 1988. *Duck*. New York: Lippincott.

> Tim calls all his animals "duck" until Grand teaches him the right names. This simple story portrays a loving, caring older person who takes time to teach the younger character.

MacLachlan, Patricia. 1980. *Through Grandpa's Eyes*. New York: HarperCollins.

A young boy learns a different way of seeing the world from his blind grandfather. Illustrations by Deborah Kogan Ray combine with Patricia MacLachlan's sensitive text to present a positive portrait of John's grandfather who has adjusted to his blindness.

———. 1991. *Three Names*. New York: HarperCollins.

Great-grandfather looks back over his life and tells about his youth. He remembers a special dog who had three names—each one bestowed by a different member of the family.

———. 1994. *All the Places to Love*. New York: HarperCollins.

A young boy describes all the favorite places he shares with his family on his grandparents' farm.

Mathis, Sharon Bell. 1975. *The Hundred Penny Box*. New York: Viking.

Aunt Dew, Michael's 100-year-old great-great-aunt comes to live with him and his family. She has a box that contains one hundred pennies—one for each year of her life. Michael loves to count the pennies and listen to stories about her life.

McPhail, David. 1979. *Grandfather's Cake*. New York: Scribner.

Grandmother asks the boys to take a piece of cake to Grandpa, who is tending his sheep on the mountain. The boys manage to keep the cake away from all different kinds of potential cake thieves, and when they give it to Grandpa they find a surprise—Grandmother has included cake for all of them! This is a twist on *Little Red Ridinghood*.

Polacco, Patricia. 1990. *Thunder Cake*. New York: Philomel.

An understanding grandmother helps her granddaughter lose her fear of thunderstorms.

Rice, Eve. 1988. *Aren't You Coming Too?* New York: Greenwillow.

Amy is the only one in her family who has nowhere special to go until her grandfather takes her to see the animals in the park. This book depicts a thoughtful and caring grandfather.

Rodowsky, Colby. 1992. *Jenny and the Grand Old Great-Aunts*. New York: Bradbury.

Before she goes to visit her great-aunts, Jenny's daddy tells her how much he used to enjoy visiting his aunts. When Jenny arrives, Aunt Abby shows her the attic and together they find all kinds of memorabilia.

Rylant, Cynthia. 1982. *When I Was Young in the Mountains.* New York: Dutton.

Although the grandparents are really secondary characters in this Caldecott Honor Book, it is still useful. A young girl tells how her grandparents were a part of her life in the mountains.

———. 1984. *This Year's Garden.* New York: Aladdin Books.

All the members of this large family contribute to the garden, including an active grandmother who cans its produce. Strong intergenerational text.

Schecter, Ben. 1989. *Grandma Remembers.* New York: Harper & Row.

A grandmother and her grandson walk through the empty rooms of the house where grandma and grandpa lived for many years. The house holds many memories, but at the end of the book grandmother is ready to move to her new place.

Scott, Ann. 1990. *Grandmother's Chair.* New York: Clarion Books.

While visiting her grandmother, Katie asks her about a special chair. The grandmother shows Katie pictures of her great-grandmother, her grandmother, and even her mother when they used the chair as children. Before Katie leaves, Grandmother gives Katie the chair.

Shelby, Anne. 1995. *Homeplace.* New York: Orchard Books.
A grandmother and her grandchild trace their family tree.

Sisulu, Elinor. 1996. *The Day Gogo Went to Vote: South Africa, April 1994.* Boston: Little, Brown.

Thembi and her great-grandmother, who has not left the house for many years, go together to vote on the momentous day when black South Africans are allowed to vote for the first time.

Smucker, Barbara C. 1996. *Selina and the Bear Paw Quilt.* New York: Crown.

When her Mennonite family moves to Upper Canada to avoid involvement in the Civil War, young Selina is given a special quilt to remember the grandmother she left behind.

Torres, Leyla. 1995. *Saturday Sancocho*. New York: Farrar, Straus & Giroux.

> Maria Lili and her grandmother barter a dozen eggs at the market in order to get the ingredients to cook their traditional Saturday chicken sancocho. Warm multicultural intergenerational story.

Ziefert, Harriet. 1989. *With Love from Grandma*. New York: Viking.

> Sarah's grandmother decides to make a special afghan for her. Together they go shopping for the yarn, and when Grandma arrives in the fall for a visit, she has knit all the strips but not sewn them together. All the family helps put the afghan together.

Zolotow, Charlotte. 1972. *William's Doll*. New York: Harper & Row.

> William wants a doll but his father gives him a train. His grandmother, who understands him, gives William the doll so that when he grows up he will know how to be a father. Grandmother is portrayed as a wise, caring individual.

———. 1984. *I Know a Lady*. New York: Puffin.

> This classic by Zolotow tells a story of an older woman who makes everyone feel special. She is cheerful, takes long walks with her dog, bakes cookies, and waves to all the children who pass her house. Sally meets this special woman and grows to love her.

Books about Illness and Death

Illness and death have difficult effects upon families. These picture books make an attempt to portray the changes realistically.

Ackerman, Karen. 1990. *Just Like Max*. New York: Knopf.

> Aaron is fond of his Uncle Max and enjoys going up to his apartment to visit him. One day when Max suffers a stroke, Aaron sees him being taken away in an ambulance. When Max comes home from the hospital, he must be cared for by Aaron's mother. This book can lead to a discussion of older relatives and the changes that occur when they suffer a stroke.

Bahr, Mary. 1992. *The Memory Box*. Niles, IL: Whitman.

> At the beginning of this book, Gramps explains that there is a special box in which people can store their memories. The child and his grandparents talk about their memories and create new ones to put in the box. Later, Gramps begins to lose

his memory, and Grandmother explains that he has Alzheimer's disease. This book provides information about Alzheimer's, and also helps readers concentrate on remembering the "good times."

De Paola, Tomie. 1991. *Now One Foot, Now the Other.* New York: Putnam.

Bobbie and his grandfather are friends. When his grandfather has a stroke, Bobbie helps him on his road to recovery by helping him relearn all kinds of things. Although sentimental, this is a useful book for discussion of changing roles and illness.

Delton, Judy. 1986. *My Grandma's in a Nursing Home.* Niles, IL: Whitman.

When Jason visits her in the nursing home, Grandmother doesn't remember his name, and he finds it very difficult to adjust to her Alzheimer's disease. Eventually, he learns to accept her condition, and he learns what a difference his visits make to his grandmother and the other patients. This book is useful as the basis for a discussion about social and institutional care for dependent elderly persons.

Fox, Mem. 1985. *Wilfrid Gordon McDonald Partridge.* Brooklyn: Kane/Miller.

When a small boy with four names goes next door to an old folks' home, he meets a woman who also has four names but she can't remember things. He tries to discover the meaning of "memory" so that he can help her. He shares his treasures and his memories, and Miss Cooper remembers and shares some stories of her own. This is a warm intergenerational story about two characters who like and enjoy each other.

Gould, Deborah. 1987. *Grandpa's Slide Show.* New York: Lothrop, Lee & Shepard.

When the grandkids come to visit, Grandpa gets out the slides and he, Grandma, and the grandchildren enjoy the show. However, one weekend when the boys come to visit their grandparents, there is no slide show. Their mother stays with them because Grandpa is in the hospital. The next day, they learn Grandpa has died. Each of the boys reacts to the death in a different way. At the end of the story one of the boys asks if they can have a slide show. The entire family learns that they can still remember Grandpa through the slides and their memories.

Greenfield, Eloise. 1993. *William and the Good Old Days.* New York: HarperCollins.

A little boy remembers his grandmother before she became ill. During her long recovery he tries to imagine how things will be when she comes home from the hospital.

Guthrie, Donna. 1986. *Grandpa Doesn't Know It's Me: A Family Adjusts to Alzheimer's Disease.* New York: Human Sciences Press.

When Elizabeth is in first grade, her grandfather starts forgetting things. Eventually he moves from an independent living situation to living with relatives because he is diagnosed with Alzheimer's disease. This sensitive book is sponsored by the Alzheimer's Disease and Related Disorders Association in an attempt to answer children's questions about Alzheimer's disease.

Hamm, Diane J. 1987. *Grandma Drives a Motor Bed.* Niles, IL: Whitman.

Although Josh's grandmother is paralyzed from the waist down and confined to her electric bed, she is still mentally alert. Grandpa is the primary caregiver. This picture book presents a realistic look at what it means to a family when an older grandparent needs long-term care.

Henriod, Lorraine. 1982. *Grandma's Wheelchair.* Niles, IL: Whitman.

Four-year-old Thomas helps his independent grandmother who uses a wheelchair. This picture book shows that the elderly can still contribute to the family even though they may have a handicap.

Kibbey, Marsha. 1988. *My Grammy.* New York: Carolrhoda.

When Amy's grandmother comes to live with the family, Amy doesn't understand why she acts the way she does. Finally her dad explains that Grandmother has Alzheimer's disease. This story helps children understand the need for compassion for people who are ill.

Sakai, Kimiko. 1990. *Sachiko Means Happiness.* Toronto: Children's Book Press.

Sachiko's grandmother, who is also named Sachiko, has Alzheimer's disease and does not know her family any more. When young Sachiko is sent to entertain grandmother and to help run errands for her, she learns to accept her grandmother's disease.

Thomas, Jane. 1988. *Saying Good-bye to Grandma*. New York: Clarion.

When her grandmother dies, seven-year-old Suzie is curious and fearful about Grandma's funeral. This book describes what happens from a child's viewpoint from the time the family hears the news until after the funeral.

Stories Dealing with the Natural Continuity of Life

Aliki. 1987. *The Two of Them*. New York: Mulberry Books.

After her grandfather dies, a young granddaughter sits in the orchard he loved and remembers him. She also realizes that the blossoms on the trees will come year after year. This sensitive book illustrated by the author is a useful way to begin a discussion on the different seasons of life.

Cech, John. 1991. *My Grandmother's Journey*. New York: Bradbury.

Feodosia Belevstov, the real-life protagonist of this book, survived the Russian Revolution and World War II before emigrating to the United States. This book details the events in her life, and as her life progresses readers come to understand the natural process of aging and growing old.

Coats, Laura Jane. 1989. *Mr. Jordan in the Park*. New York: Macmillan.

The happiest moments of Mr. Jordan's life were spent in the park. This story tells about all the different stages of his life from childhood through youth and on to old age and how he spent them in the park. The changes in the park underscore the fact that his life had different seasons.

Cooney, Barbara. 1982. *Miss Rumphius*. New York: Puffin.

As a young girl Alice helped her grandfather who was an artist. When she told him that she wanted to travel and eventually live by the sea, he told her that she must "do something to make the world more beautiful." And when she grew up she did travel and live by the sea, but as an old woman she also left the world a more beautiful place. This picture book portrays aging in a positive, vital way. Beautiful illustrations make this a good choice for storytime.

———. 1988. *Island Boy*. New York: Viking Kestrel.

This beautifully illustrated picture book by Caldecott medalist Barbara Cooney traces the life story of Matthais as he grows from a little boy to a grandfather on a small island off the coast of New England.

Hines, Anna. 1991. *Remember the Butterflies.* New York: Dutton.

> When a girl and her brother find a dead butterfly in the garden, they take it to their grandfather because he can fix anything. As the grandfather patiently explains that he cannot make dead things come back to life, he also explains the life cycle. During the summer the children and their grandfather observe and enjoy the other butterflies, but when winter comes the grandfather dies. Their mother explains that his death is part of the human life cycle.

Elders as Wise Mentors and Teachers

Bauman, Hans. 1985. *Chip Has Many Brothers.* New York: Philomel Books.

> Chip, a young boy who lives with his siblings and his grandmother in the midst of the forest, must go on a dangerous quest to help his sister who is sick. His grandmother, who is his mentor, is portrayed as a wise, caring individual who is a respected member of her Native American community.

Blos, Joan. 1989. *The Grandpa Days.* New York: Simon & Schuster.

> When he learns that his grandfather built a tree house as a young boy, Phillip resolves to build something too. He tries to build rocket ships and cars but fails until he finds something that he and his grandfather can do together. This book portrays the grandfather as an intelligent and helpful character.

Caseley, Judith. 1990. *Grandpa's Garden Lunch.* New York: Greenwillow.

> Grandpa loves to work in his garden and teaches Sarah to help. When the vegetables are ripe, Grandma invites Sarah to lunch. Both grandparents are depicted as active, robust individuals.

Castanda, Omar. 1993. *Abuela's Weave.* New York: Lee & Low Books.

> A young Guatemalan girl and her grandmother grow closer as they weave some special creations and then make a trip to the market in hopes of selling them. Bold, bright illustrations accompany this sensitive text which portrays the grandmother as knowledgeable and wise.

French, Vivian. 1993. *Caterpillar, Caterpillar.* Cambridge, MA: Candlewick Press.

> A young girl's grandfather grows caterpillars and butterflies in his garden, and the girl learns about the natural process of life from him. The older character is portrayed as knowledgeable.

James, Simon. 1993. *The Wild Woods.* Cambridge, MA: Candlewick Press.

As they walk in the woods and see a squirrel, Grandfather explains why Jess can not keep the squirrel as a pet. This book portrays an older character as a wise teacher.

Merriam, Eve. 1991. *The Wise Woman and Her Secret.* New York: Simon & Schuster.

Everyone in the village wants to know the secret source of the Wise Old Woman's wisdom but no one can uncover it until little Jenny asks her questions and finds out that being curious is the source of wisdom. This book depicts an older character as a wise mentor.

Polacco, Patricia. 1993. *The Bee Tree.* New York: Philomel.

In this warm and beautifully illustrated picture book, a wise grandfather teaches his granddaughter about the value of books.

Stolz, Mary. 1988. *Storm in the Night.* New York: Harper & Row.

When a thunderstorm occurs, Thomas's grandfather tells him about his youth.

Nontraditional

These picture books depict older characters who are independent, self-reliant, and sometimes quite unusual.

Bogart, Jo Ellen. 1994. *Gifts.* New York: Scholastic.

A nontraditional grandmother travels around the world and brings back gifts for her granddaughter.

Caines, Jeanette. 1980. *Wisdom Wishing.* New York: Harper & Row.

Two children spend their vacation with their unusual grandmother who wears tennis shoes and can make kites fly. Grandmother is portrayed as active, enjoyable, and funny.

Hedderwick, Mairi. 1985. *Katie Morag and the Two Grandmothers.* London: Bodley Head.

Katie has two special grandmothers. She has Island grandmother, who is a farmer, and Mainland gramma, who wears frilly clothes and cosmetics and dislikes large animals. Each of the grandmothers has her own distinct personality and Katie Morag obviously loves them both.

Hoffman, Mary. 1988. *My Grandma Has Black Hair.* New York: Dial.

This grandmother is as striking as her hair, and she wants to be called Sylvia. She tells wonderful stories about when she was a kid in the circus where her parents were trapeze artists.

Kesselman, Wendy. 1985. *Emma.* New York: Doubleday.

Emma is 72 years old and begins to paint. The illustrations in this picture book are by award-winning artist Barbara Cooney, who skillfully depicts Emma's joyous, creative spirit.

Lasky, Kathryn. 1988. *Sea Swan.* New York: Macmillan.

Elizabeth Swan has a very full life, but when the grandchildren are away it seems boring. On her 75th birthday, she decides to learn to swim. She finds that she likes it so much that she designs a new house by the seashore. This story depicts an active, involved older person.

McCully, Emily Arnold. 1991. *Grandma Mix-Up.* New York: Harper Trophy.

In this easy-to-read book, young readers will meet grandma Nan, who is neat and orderly and has white hair and glasses, and grandma Sal, who is more nontraditional. The stories about these two vastly different grandmothers are just plain fun to read.

———. *Grandmas at Bat.* New York: HarperCollins.

Pip's two grandmothers simply cannot agree on anything, but they do agree to take over the coaching of Pip's baseball team. This creates hilarious chaos in an easy-to-read format.

Olson, Arielle North. 1990. *Hurry Home, Grandma!* New York: Dutton.

While Timothy and Melinda prepare for another traditional Christmas, their grandma is busy having wild adventures in the jungle. Just in time, Grandma flies her own plane to join them for the celebration.

Swartz, David. 1991. *Supergrandpa.* New York: Lothrop, Lee & Shepard.

A sixty-six-year-old grandfather who is barred from entering the 1000-mile Tour of Sweden race because of his age, "unofficially" joins anyway and through sheer determination finishes victoriously.

Walter, Mildred Pitts. 1991. *Justin and the Best Biscuits in the World*. New York: Random House.

> A nontraditional grandpa teaches Justin how to make beds, clean, and cook. When Justin's special grandpa enters a biscuit baking contest, he wins!

Ward, Sally. 1991. *What Goes Around Comes Around*. New York: Doubleday.

> Tap dancing Grandma Rose makes and delivers soup to people. When Isabel's mother is sick, Grandma Rose takes Isabel on a soup run.

Wild, Margaret. 1993. *Our Granny*. New York: Tichnor & Fields.

> Bright, bold illustrations accompany a text that clearly demonstrates that grannies come in all shapes and sizes, but "our granny" is the best.

Williams, Barbara. 1975. *Kevin's Grandmother*. New York: Dutton.

> Kevin and his friends discover that they have two different types of grandmothers. Kevin's grandmother likes peanut butter soup, MAD magazine, motorscooters, yoga and skydiving. His friend's grandmother likes checkers, ice cream, and teaching piano. Both women are interesting, lively individuals.

Family History

These picture books deal with elderly characters who are repositories of family lore.

Bunting, Eve. 1990. *The Wall*. New York: Clarion Books.

> A young boy and his father come to Washington, D.C., to find the name of the boy's grandfather on the Vietnam War Memorial. This is a good story about family history and a long-deceased grandfather.

Flournoy, Valerie. 1985. *The Patchwork Quilt*. New York: Dial.

> Grandmother is making a quilt with the scraps from the family's favorite old clothes. When she does not feel well, Tanya offers to help with the quilt. Eventually everyone in the family helps with the project and they all realize that Grandma is an important source of family history.

———. 1995. *Tanya's Reunion*. New York: Dial.

> In this sequel to *The Patchwork Quilt*, Tanya and her grandmother help with the preparations for a big family reunion. As

they work, grandmother tells Tanya about the farm in Virginia where she grew up. This beautiful picture book illustrated by Jerry Pickney shows the importance of family history in which grandmother figures as a warm, knowledgeable person.

Moss, Marissa. 1994. *In America.* New York: Dutton.

> While Walter and his grandfather walk to the post office, his grandfather recounts how he decided to come to America while his brother Herschel stayed in Lithuania. This book portrays an older character as source of family history.

Adjustments and Family Problems

These picture books deal realistically with misunderstandings and family adjustments to aging and old persons.

Caseley, Judith. 1986. *Grandpa Came to Stay.* New York: Greenwillow.

> After Grandma dies and Grandpa has a stroke, he comes to live with Benny's family. Benny adjusts to the situation, and he and Grandpa sing songs and do things together. However, there are difficult times, and Benny sometimes gets angry at his grandpa. When Grandpa tells Benny that he misses Grandma, they both go to her grave and plant flowers. In this sensitive book, Benny learns about his grandfather and eventually comes to understand his moodiness.

Hines, Anna. 1988. *Grandma Gets Grumpy.* New York: Clarion Books.

> While spending the night at Grandma's house, Lassen and her four cousins get out of hand. Grandma, who is normally a fun person, gets grumpy. This book helps children understand how their behavior can affect others.

Knox-Wagner, Elaine. 1982. *My Grandpa Retired Today.* Niles, IL: Whitman.

> There are relatively few books on the topic of retiring. Grandpa retires as a barber and a party is given for him, but he doesn't seem to have adjusted to the idea of retirement until Margery helps him understand that there will now be more time for both of them to enjoy each other.

Komaiko, Leah. 1989. *I Like the Music.* New York: Harper Trophy.

> When a grandmother and her granddaughter find out that they have very different musical tastes, they learn to respect those differences.

Malone, Nola Langner. 1979. *Freddy My Grandfather.* New York: Four Winds.

When you live in a multigenerational household, there are sometimes problems. In this book a little girl shares her thoughts about the things that are good and also the things that are irritating about her grandfather who lives with her and her parents.

Stock, Catherine. 1984. *Emma's Dragon Hunt.* New York: Lothrop.

Emma Wong's grandfather has just arrived from China and she must learn about him.

Vigna, Judith. 1984. *Grandma without Me.* Niles, IL: Whitman.

A young boy is upset because he can't spend Thanksgiving with his grandmother because of his parents' divorce. The boy and his grandmother write to each other, and his mother helps him make a picture of himself to send to his grandmother. This is a realistic story about how a family deals with a difficult situation.

Poetry and Other Books of Interest

Livingston, Myra Cohn. 1990. *Poems for Grandmothers.* New York: Holiday House.

This is an excellent anthology of poems about all different kinds of grandmothers.

Raynor, Dorka. 1977. *Grandparents around the World.* Chicago: Whitman.

Although a bit dated, this book contains forty-six full-page photographs of grandparents and children from twenty-five countries. Each photograph is accompanied by a brief text.

Longer Read-Aloud Chapter Books

Lowry, Lois. 1979. *Anastasia Krupnik.* Boston: Houghton Mifflin.

When she is ten years old Anastasia manages to know her grandmother as a real person.

MacLachlan, Patricia. 1991. *Journey.* New York: Delacorte Press.

When they are left by their mother with their grandparents, two children feel their lives are destroyed until sensitive Grandfather finds a way to restore their past to them.

Slote, Alfred. 1990. *The Trading Game.* New York: Lippincott.

> During a summer filled with baseball and baseball card trading, Andy learns about his father and his grandfather who played professional baseball. Good read-aloud for grades 4–5.

Stolz, Mary. 1991. *Go Fish.* New York: HarperCollins.

> After spending the day fishing in the Gulf of Mexico with his grandfather, eight-year-old Thomas spends the evening listening to tales of his African heritage.

Other Sources of Information

The following are excellent resources for curriculum materials, bibliographies, and research:

Generations Together
121 University Place, Suite 300
Pittsburgh, PA 15260
Librarian: Jonquil Feldman
Phone: 412-648-7150.

National Academy for Teaching and Learning about Aging (NATLA)
200 Executive Blvd., Suite 201
P. O. Box 246
Southington, CT 06489-0246
Contact Person: Donna Cooper
Phone: 860-621-2079

Works Cited

Butler, Robert. 1975. *Why Survive? Being Old in America.* New York: Harper & Row.

Dodson, Anita, and Judith Hause. 1981. *Ageism in Literature: An Analysis Kit for Teachers and Librarians.* Acton, MA: Acton-Boxborough Regional School.

Gutknecht, Bruce. 1991. "Mitigating the Effects of Negative Stereotyping of Aging and the Elderly in Primary Grade Reading Instruction." *Reading Improvement* 28 (Winter): 44–51.

Hickey, Gail. 1991. "And Then What Happened, Grandpa? Oral History Projects in the Elementary Classroom." *Social Education* 44 (April/May): 216–17.

Jantz, Richard, and Carole Seefeldt, et al. 1997. "Children's Attitudes toward the Elderly." *Social Education* 41 (October): 518–23.

John, Martha. 1977. "Teaching Children about Older Family Members." *Social Education* 41 (October): 524–27.

Kazemek, Francis, and Pat Rigg. 1988. "There's More to an Old Person Than Appears." *Joys* 1 (Summer): 396–404.

McGuire, Sandra. 1993. "Promoting Positive Attitudes toward Aging: Literature for Young Children." *Childhood Education* 69 (Summer): 204–210.

Paulin, Mary. 1992. *More Creative Uses of Children's Literature.* Hamden, CT: Library Professional Publications.

Pfizer Perspectives. 1997. "Forget about an Old Age Spent Sitting on the Sidelines." *The Atlantic Monthly* 280 (July): 55–57.

Additional Recommended Resources

Dryer, Sharon. 1989. *The Bookfinder: A Guide to Children's Literature About the Needs and Problems of Youth Aged 2 and Up.* Circle Pines, MN: American Guidance Service.

Rasinski, Timothy, and Cindy Gillespie. 1992. *Sensitive Issues: An Annotated Guide to Children's Literature, K–6.* Phoenix: Oryx.

Rudman, Masha, et al. 1993. *Books to Help Children Cope with Separation and Loss.* New York: Bowker.

19 African American Resources

Joseph A. Hawkins Jr.
Montgomery County Public Schools, Maryland

Glenda K. Valentine
Teaching Tolerance Magazine

With the exception of the Harlem Renaissance (1919–1940), it is extremely difficult to find another time in U.S. history when the depth and breadth of African American resources is greater than it is today.[1] While the choices of quality books and literature, software, and films seem endless, the growing number of outstanding Internet and online electronic resources available to educators may make attempts to keep up appear impossible.

The choices we offer center around three issues. First, since this book is about teaching tolerance, we thought it critical that readers read a few pieces on tolerance. We believe our specific resource recommendations on African Americans are framed within the concept of teaching tolerance.[2] Second, there are many organizations prepared to help educators teach tolerance, and we encourage educators to seek out the advice of experts when necessary. Others have gone before us, and it would be foolish not to take the marked trail. Finally, we leave readers with our "best of the best" list of resources covering curriculum guides, organizations, journals and magazines, software and Internet resources, films, and literature. This list comes out of our professional relationship with the Teaching Tolerance Project in Montgomery, Alabama.

Readings on Tolerance for Teachers

Finding provocative, well-thought-out articles, essays, and books on tolerance is easier than it used to be. In fact, it is not uncommon for such books to climb the bestseller lists and stay there, as the recent success of books such as Hillary Rodham Clinton's *It Takes a Village* or William Bennett's *The Book of Virtues*[3] indicates. At the same time, teaching about genocide and intolerance is an extremely difficult moral undertaking. We believe the readings recommended here do an outstanding job of grounding educators in the meanings of tolerance. We implore readers not to skip over these readings. Teaching about genocide and intolerance cannot occur in an intellectual or social vacuum. Educators must understand the moral implications and consequences of bringing such lessons into their classrooms and school buildings.

Ayers, William, and Patricia Ford, eds. 1996. *City Kids, City Teachers: Reports From the Front Row.* New York: The New Press.

A marvelous collection of essays written by frontline educators who dare us to see urban kids, especially children of color, from a perspective that honors their humanity and possibility.

Banks, James, and Cherry McGee Banks, eds. 1995. *Handbook of Research on Multicultural Education.* New York: Macmillan.

According to the authors, "The main purpose of this *Handbook* is to assemble in one volume the major research and scholarship related to multicultural education that has developed since the field emerged in the 1960s and 1970s." The *Handbook* does a remarkable job of relating theory to research, and research to practice.

Beauboeuf-Lafontant, Tamara, and Augustine D. Smith, eds. 1995. *Facing Racism in Education.* Cambridge: Harvard Educational Review.

This reprint of a series of previously published articles offers educators suggestions and tools for battling racism. The role of racism in education is examined through scholarly research papers, poetry, music, and personal accounts.

Boyd, Dwight. 1996. "Dominance Concealed through Diversity: Implications of Inadequate Perspectives on Cultural Pluralism." *Harvard Educational Review* 66: 609–630.

Boyd discusses the issue of "groundless tolerance" and argues that a commitment to tolerance cannot be a mindless or casual decision.

Bullard, Sara. 1996. *Teaching Tolerance: Raising Open-Minded, Empathetic Children.* New York: Doubleday.

This book helps all adults who care for children understand how children learn prejudice and how they can be guided toward tolerance. Written by the founding editor of *Teaching Tolerance* magazine, it balances theory and reflection with practical advice and a long list of resources.

Cohen, Joshua, ed. 1996. *For Love of Country: Debating the Limits of Patriotism*. Boston: Beacon Press.

This collection of essays written by some of the world's most prominent intellectuals challenges our thinking about what it means to be a citizen of the world. Elaine Scarry's essay, "The Difficulty of Imagining Other People," makes the reader face some incredibly difficult questions about how we judge the worth of other humans.

Delpit, Lisa. 1995. *Other People's Children: Cultural Conflict in the Classroom*. New York: The New Press.

This book courageously confronts the dilemmas caused by changing cultural demographics in our classrooms. Lisa Delpit uses evocative essays to discuss how preconceived stereo-types, assumptions, and expectations continue to build educational barriers between white teachers and students of color.

Fine, Michelle, et al., eds. 1997. *Off White: Readings on Race, Power, and Society*. New York: Routledge.

Off White is a collection of scholarly essays that approaches multicultural issues from a "white racialization process." Every white teacher teaching in America should read this book.

Franklin, John Hope. 1993. *The Color Line: Legacy For the Twenty-First Century*. Columbia: University of Missouri Press.

One of America's most distinguished historians takes an uncompromising look at racism in America today and, at the same time, gives each of us new hope and direction.

Gates, Henry Louis, and Cornel West. 1996. *The Future of Race*. New York: Knopf.

As we head into the twenty-first century, Gates and West, two of the country's best-known African American scholars, offer a sobering assessment of what it means to be an African American in America.

Gioseffi, Daniela, ed. 1993. *On Prejudice: A Global Perspective*. New York: Doubleday.

It is hard to find another collection of writings on prejudice and intolerance more complete than this volume.

Harding, Vincent. 1990. *Hope and History: Why We Must Share the Story of the Movement.* Maryknoll, NY: Orbis Books.

This marvelous book sets the civil rights movement in its proper context—a struggle to expand American democracy.

Heller, Carol, and Joseph A. Hawkins. 1994. "Teaching Tolerance: Notes from the Front Line." *Teachers College Record* 95: 337–68.

This article surveys school and community-based programs teaching tolerance and discusses various definitions of tolerance for school settings.

Kohl, Herbert. 1995. *Should We Burn Babar? Essays on Children's Literature and the Power of Stories.* New York: The New Press.

Teachers planning to teach the story of Rosa Parks must read Kohl's essay, "The Story of Rosa Parks and the Montgomery Bus Boycott Revisited." Kohl offers brilliant suggestions on how to teach this important history.

Kohn, Alfie. 1997. "How Not to Teach Values: A Critical Look at Character Education." *Phi Delta Kappan* 78: 428–39.

Teaching tolerance is part of the larger effort to teach character development in school children. Kohn takes a critical look at what not to do when designing such programs for young children.

Kushner, Tony. 1995. *Thinking about the Longstanding Problems of Virtue and Happiness.* New York: Theatre Communications Group.

Best known for his award-winning Broadway play *Angels in America,* playwright Tony Kushner shows off his writing diversity in this book of thought-provoking essays. "Some Questions about Tolerance" is a must-read for any person about to embark on an understanding of tolerance.

Wolff, Robert Paul, Barrington Moore, and Herbert Marcuse. 1965. *A Critique of Pure Tolerance.* Boston: Beacon Press.

This simple collection of three essays explores the philosophical foundations of tolerance.

Organizations

Those seeking information about African Americans have a variety of organizations (listed below) to which to turn for assistance. Many organizations produce specific teaching materials on African Americans, and some are prepared to go further by actually producing tailor-made reading lists or providing teachers and other educators with hands-on training opportunities through specially designed institutes or annual conferences. In addition, some organizations such as NAME and The National Conference have state affiliates prepared to assist educators locally with their special needs.

National Association for the Education of Young Children
1834 Connecticut Avenue NW
Washington, DC 20009
(800) 424-2460

> NAEYC offers a wealth of information about anti-bias education for young children, and publishes *Anti-Bias Curriculum: Tools for Empowering Young Children* (1991), one of the most widely used anti-bias books in North America.

National Association for Multicultural Education (NAME)
1511 K Street NW, Suite 430
Washington, DC 20005
(202) 628-NAME

> Offers a wealth of information about African Americans and other racial and ethnic groups, and publishes a regular journal, *Multicultural Education,* which features a regular resource column for teachers.

National Black Child Development Institute
1023 15th Street NW, Suite 600
Washington, DC 20005
(800) 556-2234

> NBCDI publishes a variety of pamphlets and magazines full of useful information on a variety of topics, including parenting and child health care.

National Coalition of Education Activists
P. O. Box 405
Rosendale, NY 12472
(914) 658-8115

> NCEA provides information and referrals on a wide range of issues such as tracking, and multicultural and anti-racist education.

Network of Educators on the Americas
1118 22nd Street NW
Washington, DC 20037
(202) 429-0137

> Produces a regular catalog of K–12 resources on multicultural education. Many of its teaching guides, especially the Caribbean series, are extremely low-cost.

Poverty & Race Research Action Council
1711 Connecticut Avenue NW, Suite 207
Washington, DC 20009
(202) 387-9887

> Regularly published newsletter *Poverty and Race* is full of timely discussions that have an impact on African Americans and other racial minorities.

Rethinking Schools
1001 E. Keefe Avenue
Milwaukee, WI 53212
(414) 964-9646

> Best known for its publication *Rethinking Schools,* this organization also acts as clearinghouse and hot line for teachers seeking information on minority youngsters.

State 4-H Office
114 Ag Hall
University of Nebraska
Lincoln, NE 68583-0700
(402) 472-9009

> The 4-H curriculum *Many Faces, One People* presents detailed lesson plans and activities that explore stereotyping, cross-cultural problem-solving, and "building differences."

Teaching Tolerance
The Southern Poverty Law Center
400 Washington Avenue
Montgomery, AL 36104
(334) 264-0286

> Publishes twice-yearly magazine of educational resources and ideas for promoting respect for diversity, free to teachers. Free teaching kits, *The Shadow of Hate* and *America's Civil Rights Movement,* cover significant African American historical events.

The National Conference
71 Fifth Avenue, Suite 1100
New York, NY 10003
(212) 206-0006

> Founded in 1927 as The National Conference of Christians and Jews, this organization dedicates itself to fighting bias, bigotry, and racism in America. Teaching guides (e.g., *Actions Speak Louder: A Skills-Based Curriculum for Building Inclusion*) are used in schools throughout the country.

Journals and Magazines

There are a considerable number of scholarly journals and magazines to which educators should turn for assistance in identifying resources and materials on African Americans. Many of the periodicals listed below focus exclusively on African Americans.

Black Issues in Higher Education
Cox, Matthews & Associates
(703) 385-2981

The Black Scholar (also known as *The Journal of Black Studies and Research*)
Black World Foundation
(510) 547-6633

The Journal of Black Psychology
Association of Black Psychologists—Sage Periodical Press
(805) 499-0721

The Journal of Negro Education
Howard University Press
(202) 806-8120

Multicultural Education
National Association for Multicultural Education—Caddo Gap Press
(805) 750-9978

Multicultural Review
Greenwood Publishing Group
(203) 226-3571

Race, Gender, & Class: An Interdisciplinary & Multicultural Journal
Queens College—CUNY
(718) 997-3070

Rethinking Schools: An Urban Educational Journal
Rethinking Schools
(414) 964-7220

Skipping Stones: A Multicultural Children's Quarterly
Skipping Stones
(503) 342-4956

Teaching Tolerance
Southern Poverty Law Center
(334) 264-0286

Worthy Web Sites

Between June 1996 and January 1997, the number of Internet Web sites worldwide nearly tripled in number, moving from 230,000 sites to nearly 700,000 sites.[4] With this kind of growth it is impossible to cover all the possibilities here, and no attempt is made to do so. Educators should use the Internet to search for relevant resources and materials on African Americans. Most of the sites are loaded with relevant links and bookmarks to other African American Web sites.

African American History and Culture
http://www.scils.rutgers.edu/special/kay/afro.html

African American Historic Texts On-line
http://curry.edschool.Virginia.EDU/go/multicultural/sites/
    aframdocs.html

African American Newspapers
http://www.afroam.org/

Afronet
http://www.afronet.com/

American Slave Narratives
http://xroads.virginia.edu/~HYPER/wpa/wpahome.html/

Black Entertainment Television
http://www.betnetworks.com/newhome.html

Black History—Bonanza of Bookmarks for Classroom Teachers
http://www.mcps.k12.md.us/curriculum/socialstd/
African_Am_bookmarks.html

Black World Today
http://www.tbwt.com/index2.htm

Britannica Online—Guide to Black History http:// blackhistory.eb.com/

Ethnic Studies at the University of Southern California http://www.usc.edu/Library/Ref/Ethnic/index.html

Harvard University—W. E. B. Du Bois Institute for Afro-American Research http://web-dubois.fas.harvard.edu/

Library of Congress Resource Guide for the Study of Black History and Culture http://www.loc.gov/exhibits/african/intro.html

Martin Luther King Jr. Papers Project at Stanford University http://www.stanford.edu/group/King/

NAACP Online http://www.naacp.org/

National Black Child Development Institute http://www.nbcdi.org/

NetNoir—The Soul of Cyberspace http://www.netnoir.com/index.html

Rethinking Schools http://www.rethinkingschools.org

The Universal Black Pages http://www.ubp.com/

University of Virginia—Multicultural Pavilion http://curry.edschool.Virginia.EDU/go/multicultural/

U.S. Census Black Facts http://www.thuban.com/census/index.html

Computer Software

Some may see it as a stretch, but somewhere in the very near future, with the aid of every conceivable technology—artificial intelligence, interactive computers, virtual reality, hypermedia—the following classroom scenario may become common in schools.

A classroom somewhere in the USA.
Teacher: Good morning class. Here's next month's world history assignment. Write a 3,000-word newspaper article comparing the freedom

movements led by Martin Luther King Jr. in the United States and Nelson Mandela in South Africa. Major emphasis should be placed on the tactics both used to achieve voting rights for their people. Your article must be based on the following activities:

1. Interviews with Martin Luther King Jr. and Nelson Mandela
2. Interviews with three of King's and Mandela's co-workers
3. Shadowing King a year prior to the 1963 March on Washington, D.C.
4. Shadowing Mandela on his 1994 presidential election campaign

One more thing class. Your completed article must appear on the school's network by the last day of next month. No excuses! No paper copies!

If today's virtual reality technology can make us believe we are actually driving a car, flying an airplane, or playing a game of one-on-one basketball, then the possibility of conducting a simple face-to-face interview with King or Mandela is a sure thing.

Today's computer technology cannot deliver face-to-face interviews with important historical figures [5]; however, present-day computer software titles offer quite a few creative solutions for teaching tolerance, exploring other cultures, or exploring important U.S. historical events such as the mass migration of Southern blacks to the industrial North and the civil rights movement.

The American People: Fabric of a Nation. National Geographic Society. (202) 828-5664.

> National Geographic's claim that its interactive videodisc series *The American People* "brings textbooks (and your students) to life" is not just idle promotional talk. The series does a thorough job of dealing with important social and historical issues such as immigration, slavery, the Ku Klux Klan, racism, civil rights, and religious freedom.

History of the Blues. QUEUE, Inc. (800) 232-2224.

> This CD-ROM program traces the African roots of the blues (including chants and field hollers) and explores the many different musical styles associated with the blues.

Eyes on the Prize Part I, 1954–65. Public Broadcasting Service. (800) 344-3337.

> The award-winning film series on the civil rights movement has been converted to videodisc. The videodisc version is packed with materials that add greater depth and context to the video, including photographs, profiles of people and

organizations, documents, charts and graphs, music, news, and advertising of the period.

Struggle for Justice. Scholastic, Inc. (800) 325-6149.

The history of the disenfranchised—African Americans, Native Americans, Latinas and Latinos, women, and immigrants—is told in comprehensive detail in this two-volume, interactive videodisc.

Black American History: Slavery to Civil Rights. QUEUE, Inc. (800) 232-2224.

This CD-ROM is divided into eight 20-minute segments that include the Colonial Period, the Civil War, Reconstruction, the Harlem Renaissance and Black Protest Movements.

Cultural Reporter. Tom Snyder Productions. (800) 342-0236.

This interdisciplinary kit sends students into their communities to investigate, document, and better appreciate the diversity of the areas in which they live.

Annotated Guides

Annotated guides are extremely useful and time saving because they provide teachers with specific book recommendations. A number of annotated guides worth considering in a search for quality African American materials follow. Most are updated periodically, so no specific publication dates are noted; however, a telephone number for either the publisher or organization responsible for the guide is listed. The *Guide to Multicultural Resources; Our Family, Our Friends, Our World;* and *The African-American Experience: An HBJ Resource Guide for the Multicultural Classroom* are highly recommended.

The African-American Experience: An HBJ Resource Guide for the Multicultural Classroom. Orlando: Harcourt Brace Jovanovich. (800) CALL-HBJ.

Black Images in Contemporary Children's Books. Nashville: Edit Cetera Company. (615) 665-0404.

Guide to Multicultural Resources. Fort Atkinson, WI: Highsmith Press. (800) 558-2110.

Journey Home. Rochelle Park, NJ: The Peoples Publishing Group. (800) 822-1080.

Kaleidoscope: A Multicultural Booklist for Grades K–8. Urbana, IL: National Council of Teachers of English. (217) 328-3870.

Our Family, Our Friends, Our World: An Annotated Guide to Significant Multicultural Books for Children and Teenagers. New Providence, NJ: R. R. Bowker Company. (800) 521-8110.

The Spirit of Excellence Resource Guides. Washington, DC: National Black Child Development Institute. (202) 387-1281.

Curriculum Guides

The marvelous thing about curriculum guides is that they not only list resources but they also present specific instructional guidelines on how to teach those materials. Since many guides are updated periodically, no specific publication dates are noted in what follows. A telephone number for either the publisher or organization responsible for the guide is listed.

America's Civil Rights Movement. Montgomery, AL: Teaching Tolerance. (334) 264-0286.

America's Original Sin: A Study Guide on White Racism. Washington, DC: Sojourners. (800) 714-7474.

Anti-Bias Curriculum: Tools for Empowering Young Children. Washington, DC: National Association for the Education of Young Children. (800) 424-2460.

Freedom's Unfinished Revolution. New York: The New Press. (800) 233-4830.

Malcolm X in Context: A Study Guide to the Man and His Times. New York: PACE. (212) 274-1324.[6]

Many Voices. Jefferson City, MO: Scholastic, Inc. (800) 325-6169.

Nat Turner's Slave Revolt—1831. Amawalk, NY: Jackdaw Publications. (800) 789-0022.

Planning and Organizing for Multicultural Instruction. Menlo Park: Alternative Publishing Group. (800) 447-2226.

Ready-to-Use Multicultural Activities for Primary Children. Des Moines, IA: Prentice-Hall. (800) 288-4725.

Rethinking Our Classrooms: Teaching for Equity and Justice. Milwaukee, WI: Rethinking Schools. (414) 964-9646.

"Teacher, they called me a _____!" Hohakus, NJ: The Anti-Defamation League. (800) 343-5540.

Teaching about Haiti. Washington, DC: Network of Educators on the Americas. (202) 429-0137.

WE: Lessons on Equal Worth and Dignity, the United Nations and Human Rights. Minneapolis: United National Association of Minnesota. (612) 333-2824.

Documentary Film

On occasion, a particular book or an instructional kit or a film simply overwhelms us in that we immediately recognize the value of the material for teaching important lessons on racial and cultural harmony or tolerance. While every medium has its impact, films often seem to make a lasting impression. Clearly, the realistic nature of films, as well as their immediacy, have everything to do with their potential to captivate.

Teachers searching for films on African Americans have a variety of outstanding places to turn. What follows is a brief list of our favorite documentary film distributors. Most of the distributors listed below have sizable collection of films on African American culture and history. In many cases, films are accompanied with lesson plans, teacher guides, and supplemental materials and readings.

No attempt is made here to pick Hollywood-produced commercial films. We believe that well-known, critically acclaimed commercial films need no real endorsement. Films such as *A Raisin in the Sun* (1961), *Sounder* (1972), *Roots—the TV Series* (1977), *The Color Purple* (1985), *Glory* (1989), *The Long Walk Home* (1990), *Malcolm X* (1992), *Once Upon a Time When We Were Colored* (1995), *Ghosts of Mississippi* (1996), *Rosewood* (1997), and *Amistad* (1997) have a place in the classroom, and where appropriate we see value in showing these films. We do, however, offer one warning: Hollywood films sometimes stray from important historical facts. Take for example the Civil War film *Glory*. In the Hollywood version the all-black Massachusetts 54th, one of the first regiments of black soldiers recruited for the Union army, is made up of ex-slaves. In reality, the regiment was composed of free men. In fact, many of the men were skilled and literate. The actual letters of one of these soldiers, twenty-six-year-old seaman James Henry Gooding, are recommended reading, and are found in the 1991 book *On the Altar of Freedom: A Black Soldier's Civil War Letters From the Front.*[7]

California Newsreel
149 Ninth Street
San Francisco, CA 94103
(415) 621-6196

Canada Film Board
1251 Avenue of the Americas
New York, NY 10020
(800) 542-2164

Carousel Film and Video
260 Fifth Avenue, Suite 405
New York, NY 10001
(212) 683-1660

Cinema Guild
1697 Broadway
New York, NY 10019-5904
(800) 723-5522

First Run/Icarus
153 Waverly Place
New York, NY 10014
(800) 876-1710

Georgia Humanities Council
50 Hurt Plaza S.E., Suite 440
Atlanta, GA 30303-2936
(404) 523-6220

Knowledge Unlimited
P. O. Box 52
Madison, WI 53701
(800) 356-2303

Media Projects
5215 Homer Street
Dallas, TX 75206
(214) 826-3863

Public Broadcasting Service Video
1320 Braddock Place
Alexandria, VA 22314
(800) 344-3337

Teaching Tolerance
400 Washington Avenue
Montgomery, AL 36104
(334) 264-0286

Women Made Movies
462 Broadway, Suite 500-F
New York, NY 10013
(212) 925-0606

Awesome Anthologies

One expeditious way to cover the rich tradition of African American literature is to turn to anthologies. Certainly, anthologies do not survey all works, and in many cases the anthologies only print a selection of a particular work; nonetheless, they stand out as valuable for those in search of quality literary works—poetry, plays, short stories, essays, novels. Teachers sometimes can turn to anthologies for critical analyses of particular bodies of work. Practically all of the anthologies listed below assist readers in understanding the importance of the work presented.

Abrahams, Roger D., ed. 1983. *African Folktales: Traditional Stories of the Black World: Selected and Retold.* New York: Pantheon Books.

Adedjouma, Davida, ed. 1996. *The Palm of My Heart: Poetry By African American Children.* New York: Lee & Low.

Asante, Molefi Kete, and Abu S. Abarry, eds. 1996. *African Intellectual Heritage: A Book of Sources.* Philadelphia: Temple University Press.

Courlander, Harold, ed. 1996. *A Treasury of Afro-American Folklore.* New York: Marlowe & Co.

Cunard, Nancy, ed. 1996. *Negro: An Anthology.* New York: Continuum.

Gates, Henry Louis, and Nellie Y. McKay, eds. 1997. *The Norton Anthology of African American Literature.* New York: Norton.

Gillan, Maria M., and Jennifer Gillan, eds. 1994. *Unsettling America: An Anthology of Contemporary Multicultural Poetry.* New York: Penguin Books.

Hamilton, Virginia. 1995. *Her Stories: African American Folktales, Fairy Tales and True Tales.* New York: The Blue Sky Press/Scholastic, Inc.

Hudson, Wade, and Cheryl Hudson, eds. 1995. *How Sweet the Sound: African-American Songs for Children.* New York: Scholastic, Inc.

Killens, John Oliver, and Jerry Ward, eds. 1992. *Black Southern Voices: An Anthology of Fiction, Poetry, Drama, Nonfiction, and Critical Essays.* New York: Meridian.

Lewis, David L., ed. 1994. *The Portable Harlem Renaissance Reader.* New York: Penguin.

Long, Richard, and Eugenia Collier, eds. 1985. *Afro-American Writing: An Anthology of Prose & Poetry.* University Park, PA: The Pennsylvania State University Press.

Rowell, Charles, ed. 1995. *The Ancestral House: The Black Short Story in the Americas and Europe.* New York: Westview Press.

Slier, Deborah, ed. 1991. *Make a Joyful Sound: Poems for Children by African-American Poets.* New York: Scholastic, Inc.

Books and Literature

It is impossible to offer readers here an exhaustive list of all available African American literature; however, it is possible to offer readings which fall into three general time periods: the Middle Passage/Slavery/Civil War Years; Reconstruction/Jim Crow Years; and the Civil Rights Era. There are recent attempts to be inclusive beyond these suggested categories of study. For example, readers certainly are encouraged to turn to the 1997 *Norton Anthology of African American Literature* for a lesson in comprehensiveness.[8] Every English teacher who desires to teach about African Americans should have this outstanding collection on his or her desk.

The Middle Passage/Slavery/Civil War Years

Adams, Virginia M., ed. 1991. *On the Altar of Freedom: A Black Soldier's Civil War Letters from the Front.* Amherst, MA: The University of Massachusetts Press.

Barrett, Tracy. 1993. *Nat Turner & the Slave Revolt.* Brookfield, CT: The Millbrook Press.

Bisson, Terry. 1995. *Nat Turner: Slave Revolt Leader.* New York: Chelsea House.

Douglass, Frederick. 1993. *Narrative of the Life of Frederick Douglass: An American Slave, Written by Himself.* New York: St. Martin's.

Everett, Gwen. 1993. *John Brown: One Man against Slavery.* New York: Rizzoli.

Hamilton, Virginia. 1992. *The People Could Fly: American Black Folktales.* New York: Knopf.

Johnson, Dolores. 1994. *Seminole Diary: Remembrance of a Slave.* New York: Macmillan.

Lawrence, Jacob. 1993. *Harriet & the Promised Land.* New York: Simon & Schuster.

McKissack, Patricia. 1992. *The Dark-Thirty: Southern Tales of the Supernatural.* New York: Knopf.

Pinkney, Andrea D. 1994. *Dear Benjamin Banneker.* Orlando, FL: Harcourt Brace.

Ringgold, Faith. 1993. *Aunt Harriet's Underground Railroad in the Sky.* New York: Crown.

Schroeder, Alan. 1996. *Minty: A Story of Young Harriet Tubman.* New York: Penguin USA.

Stepto, Michele, ed. 1994. *Our Song, Our Toil: The Story of American Slavery as Told by Slaves.* Brookfield, CT: The Millbrook Press.

Sullivan, George. 1994. *Slave Ship: The Story of the Henrietta Marie.* Bergenfield, NJ: Penguin USA.

Wright, Courtni C. 1994. *Jumping the Broom.* New York: Holiday House.

Reconstruction/ Jim Crow Years

Bland, Celia. 1995. *The Conspiracy of the Secret Nine.* New York: Silver Moon Press.

Carnes, Jim. 1995. *Us and Them: A History on Intolerance in America.* New York: Oxford University Press.

Cooper, Floyd. 1994. *Coming Home: From the Life of Langston Hughes.* New York: Philomel.

Hamilton, Virginia. 1992. *Drylongso.* San Diego: Harcourt Brace Jovanovich.

Hughes, Langston. 1994. *The Dream Keeper and Other Poems.* New York: Knopf.

Katz, William L. 1995. *Black Women of the Old West.* New York: Atheneum.

Lawrence, Jacob. 1993. *The Great Migration: An American Story.* New York: The Museum of Modern Art/The Phillips Collection/HarperCollins.

Myers, Walter Dean. 1997. *Harlem.* New York: Scholastic, Inc.

Ritter, Lawrence S. 1995. *Leagues Apart: The Men & Times of the Negro Baseball Leagues.* New York: Morrow Junior Books.

Schlissel, Lillian. 1995. *Black Frontiers: A History of African American Heroes in the Old West.* New York: Simon & Schuster.

Taylor, Mildred D. 1991. *Roll of Thunder, Hear My Cry.* New York: Dial Books for Young Readers.

Washington, Booker T. 1997. "Up from Slavery." In *The Norton Anthology of African American Literature.* New York: Norton.

Weatherford, Carole Boston. 1995. *Juneteenth Jamboree.* New York: Lee & Low.

Civil Rights Era

Bray, Rosemary L. 1995. *Martin Luther King.* New York: Greenwillow.

Coles, Robert. 1995. *The Story of Ruby Bridges.* New York: Scholastic, Inc.

Duncan, Alice F. 1995. *The National Civil Rights Museum Celebrates Everyday People.* Mahwah, NJ: Bridge Water Books.

Feelings, Tom. 1993. *Tommy Traveller in the World of Black History.* New York: Black Butterfly Children's Books.

Gotenbock, Peter. 1990. *Teammates.* Orlando, FL: Harcourt Brace Jovanovich.

Haskins, Jim. 1997. *Rosa Parks: My Bus Ride to Freedom.* New York: Dial Books for Young Readers.

Igus, Toyomi, ed. 1993. *Great Women in the Struggle: Book of Black Heroes.* Orange, NJ: Just Us Books.

King, Sarah E. 1993. *Maya Angelou: Greeting the Morning.* Brookfield, CT: Millbrook Press.

Levine, Ellen. 1993. *Freedom's Children: Young Civil Rights Activists Tell Their Own Stories.* New York: The Putman & Grosset Group.

Parks, Rosa. 1992. *Rosa Parks: Mother to a Movement.* New York: Dial Books for Young Readers.

Ringgold, Faith. 1995. *My Dream of Martin Luther King.* New York: Crown.

Rochelle, Belinda. 1994. *When Jo Louis Won the Title.* Boston, MA: Houghton Mifflin.

Siegel, Beatrice. 1994. *Murder on the Highway: The Viola Liuzzo Story.* Riverside, NJ: Macmillan.

———. 1992. *The Year They Walked: Rosa Parks and the Montgomery Bus Boycott.* Riverside, NJ: Macmillan.

Walter, Mildred P. 1992. *Mississippi Challenge.* Riverside, NJ: Macmillian.

Woodson, Jacqueline. 1990. *Martin Luther King, Jr., and His Birthday.* Englewood Cliffs, NJ: Silver Press.

Notes

1. Just to keep up, one must resort to a variety of reference books, for example, the recently published *Oxford Companion to African American Literature* (William L. Andrews, Frances S. Foster, and Trudier Harris, eds., 1997. New York: Oxford University Press). Currently, the Du Bois Institute at Harvard University is in the process of putting together an *Encyclopedia Africana.*

2. There are many definitions of tolerance, and our recommended readings explore the concept thoroughly. A discussion of how we define the concept is best captured in the following article: Heller, Carol, and Joseph A. Hawkins, 1994, "Teaching Tolerance: Notes from the Front Line." *Teachers College Record* 95: 337–68.

3. Bennett's success extends beyond his 1993 *The Book of Virtues.* His other "virtue" books—*The Book of Virtues for Young People: A Treasury of Great Moral Stories* and *The Moral Compass: Stories for a Life's Journey*—are also recommended.

4. See Clifford Lynch, 1997, "Searching the Internet." *Scientific American* 276 (March): 53.

5. This limitation, however, is about to end. For example, during Black History Month, February 1997, Scholastic, Inc., allowed school children across the country to interview Rosa Parks live online. One can visit Scholastic at http://scholastic.com.

6. This guide is based on teaching the book *The Autobiography of Malcolm X* by Alex Haley.

7. Adams, Virginia M., ed. 1991. *On the Altar of Freedom: A Black Soldier's Civil War Letters from the Front.* Amherst, MA: The University of Massachusetts Press.

8. Gates, Henry Louis, and Nellie Y. McKay, eds. 1997. *The Norton Anthology of African American Literature.* New York: Norton.

20 How Long Will Dennis Still Be a Menace? Teacher Resources for Deregulating Gender Roles in Elementary Classrooms

Judith P. Robertson
University of Ottawa

Bernard W. Andrews
University of Ottawa

According to Brabant and Mooney (1997), the apron as the traditional symbol of the domestication of women is still alive and well in the Sunday comics. The researchers report on the disturbing trend that comic strip images of male and female appearances and roles have returned in the late 1990s to 1974 levels of gender stereotyping. Should elementary language arts educators be concerned about the relationship between media and stereotypes? And if so, what resources are available to teachers to help them learn more about the impact of stories and images on children's gender attitudes, perceptions, and behaviors?

Often used as a synonym for *sex* (i.e., biological maleness or femaleness), *gender* refers to the socially imposed dichotomy of masculine and feminine roles and character traits. Sex is physiological, where gender is cultural. As Mary Anne Warren writes in *A Feminist Dictionary* (1985, 174), "The distinction is a crucial one which is ignored by unreflective supporters of the status quo who assume that cultural norms of masculinity and feminity are 'natural,' i.e., directly and preponderantly determined by biology." What is important in terms of schooling is that the categories through which young (and not so young) children imagine themselves as strong or weak, assertive or passive, rational or illogical, or *something* or *nothing* shape themselves in concrete, historically changing ways. The social fabric that constructs children's ideals as masculine or feminine persons (and that regulates everything from desired characteristics, behavior, talk, appearance, dress, expectations, and roles) is continually socially managed through institutions, language, and texts, including those used in elementary language arts classrooms.

Problematically, the linguistic and cultural markers of gender in storybooks and language often make girls and women either appear as "less than," or disappear altogether. For example, using content analysis as a technique, Brabant and Mooney (1997, 273) report that "in each of the comics studied, the female was portrayed in the traditional stereotypical role. She was less likely to appear in the strip, and when she did, more likely to remain in the home engaged in home or child care." *The Cambridge Encyclopedia of the English Language* (Crystal 1995, 368–69) makes the disturbing point that the analysis of gendered discourse in patterns of English reveals a framework of thought and belief in operation that is often so deep-rooted that it remains unquestioned by females and males alike.

The authors of this bibliography hold an activist view in the support of social change. We are teacher educators who believe that the eradication of sexism in language and practice should be a goal that permeates all aspects of education. Without being meant to represent a complete or finished set of resources, the annotations we present focus teacher attention directly and immediately on both the theoretical aspects of and activist responses to the problem of words, texts, gender, and education. Suggestions include books and articles from educational research about K–6 children's learning of gender from picture books, novels, popular culture, and computer programs. As well we signal those journals we have found most nourishing for our own learning, and the addresses and phone numbers of Canadian and American associations devoted to the goal of sex equity in education.

Readings on Gender and Education for Teachers

As staff teaching in a faculty of education, we have found the following texts valuable for learning about gender. We hope that classroom teachers who are working to understand the relationships between language and gender oppression will also find the resources useful as a starting point for further thinking. We suggest readings in three main areas: Foundations and Curriculum, Arts (dance, drama, music and visual arts), and Language Arts and Popular Culture. Space limitation allows us to provide detailed annotations of our favorite books, with only the titles and sources given for professional readings from journals.

Books on Gender and the Foundations of Education

Connell, R. W. 1995. *Masculinities.* Berkeley, CA: University of California Press.

Examines masculinities as social constructs that are institutionally made and historically produced; explores how gender conditions and conflicts have diminished possibility for persons of both sexes.

Gaskell, Jane. 1992. *Gender Matters from School to Work.* Toronto, ON: OISE Press.

Examines the impact of gender relations on work and schooling and examines how classrooms and careers have been organized by historical and continuing patterns of gender and class inequality.

Grumet, Madeleine R. 1988. *Bitter Milk: Women and Teaching.* Amherst: The University of Massachusetts Press.

A poetic and scholarly analysis of women's lives and struggles in teaching, including their ambivalences and lived tensions in negotiating the shifting boundaries between private and public worlds.

hooks, bell. 1994. *Teaching to Transgress: Education as the Practice of Freedom.* London: Routledge.

A powerful book that combines knowledge of teaching with deeply felt emotions to raise critical questions about love and rage, grief and reconciliation, and the future of teaching; explores how teachers should deal with sexism and racism in the classroom and encourages transgression against sexual, racial, and class boundaries.

Kohli, Wendy, ed. 1995. *Critical Conversations in Philosophy of Education.* New York: Routledge.

Presents essays from leading feminist thinkers in educational philosophy. Explores questions of social constructions of self, alternatives to dominant masculinist versions of truth, redefinitions of educational aims in light of women's knowledge, criticisms of rationality as an educational aim, the role of spirituality and moral education in children's learning, and gender and the shaping of public school teaching.

Nemiroff, Greta Hofmann, ed. 1996. *Matters of Gender.* Toronto, ON: McGraw-Hill Ryerson.

An anthology of popular articles, poetry, and short stories that relate to the experiences of boys and girls growing up, having bodies, loving, hoping, experiencing disappointments, and being in affectionate relation with others.

Orenstein, Peggy. 1994. *School Girls: Young Women, Self-Esteem and the Confidence Gap.* New York: Doubleday.

Examines the devastating social and intellectual consequences of simply letting "girls be girls" and "boys be boys" by recounting raw scenes of young girls' lives in classrooms; encourages readers to fight for change.

Stone, Lynda, ed. 1994. *The Education Feminism Reader.* New York: Routledge.

A companion text to Kohli (1995) for explorations of gender, knowledge, self, and learning, and a must-have for every teacher education foundations course.

Articles on Gender and Education for Use in Foundations Courses

Fennema, Elizabeth, and C. Leder Gilah. 1988. "Sexuality, Schooling and Adolescent Females: The Missing Discourse of Desire." *Harvard Educational Review* 58(1): 29–53.

Grant, Linda. 1985. "Race-Gender Status, Classroom Interaction and Children's Socialization in Elementary School." In *Gender Influences in Classroom Interaction,* edited by Louise Cherry Wilkinson and Cora B. Marrett, 57–77. Orlando, FL: Academic Press.

Harper, Helen. 1996. "Reading, Identity, and Desire: High School Girls and Feminist Avant-Garde Literature." *Journal of Curriculum Theorizing* 12(4): 6–13.

Laird, Susan. 1988. "Reforming 'Woman's True Profession': A Case for 'Feminist Pedagogy' in Teacher Education?" *Harvard Educational Review* 58(4): 449–63.

Sadker, David, and Myra Sadker. 1985. "Sexism in the Classroom: From Grade School to Graduate School." *Phi Delta Kappan* 66(5): 358–361.

Walkerdine, Valerie. 1994. "Femininity as Performance." In *The Education Feminism Reader,* edited by Lynda Stone, 57–75. New York: Routledge.

Books on Gender and Social Studies/History

Barfoot, J. 1997. *A Time Apart: Letters of Love and War—Norah & Frank Egener.* Toronto: Umbrella Press.

This book is excerpts from four years of letters between a young Owen Sound housewife and her husband who was stationed overseas. It charts the critically important emotional bonds which sustained these two people during a protracted period of crisis. The book illustrates one unrecognized strength typically associated with women, and would be a fine backdrop for students completing family histories.

Bradbury, B., R. Heap, F. Iacovetta, K. McPherson, B. Mehta, C. Morgan, and J. Sangster, eds. 1995. *Teaching Women's History: Challenges and Solutions.* Athabasca, Alberta: Athabasca University Press.

This compendium of resources, ideas, and problems in teaching women's history emerged from a conference at Trent University in 1993. The questions addressed in the book include how to create a more inclusive history, approaches in integrating class, race, ethnicity, and sexual orientation into history, clarifying the meaning and implications of feminist pedagogy, and making women's history exiting.

Cruikshank, Julie, in collaboration with Angela Sidney, Kitty Smith, and Annie Ned. 1990. *Life Lived Like a Story: Life Stories of Three Yukon Native Elders.* Lincoln: University of Nebraska Press.

This prize-winning example of oral history provides many examples of legends and family tales as told by three remarkable women elders. *Becoming a Woman, Potlatches,* and *The Resourceful Woman* all demonstrate the centrality of women in Yukon culture, the rights and responsibilities of family members as well as the broader contours of Native Canadian life in this region.

Prentice, A., P. Bourne, G. C. Brandt, B. Light, W. Mitchinson, and N. Black. 1988. *Canadian Women: A History.* Toronto: Harcourt Brace Jovanovich.

This book is the single best resource for the teaching of women's history/social studies at any level. Authored by Canada's first-ranking historians and delightfully written, the book is used as a course text in some secondary-level classrooms and many undergraduate courses.

Staton, P., and P. Bourne. 1994. *Claiming Women's Lives: History and Contemporary Studies.* Toronto: Green Dragon Press.

This resource book is intended to fill the gap of usable materials to teach women's history to junior and intermediate-level students. Keyed to the Ontario History/Social Science Ministry of Education and Training Guidelines, the resource book offers a wide variety of documents and short interpretative articles. Each section provides a sampling of published print resources, easily obtained audiovisual resources, and museum and other resources.

Top Picks of Gender-Equitable Social Studies Resources for Children

The Heritage Post: History in the Classroom Series. Produced by The CRB Foundation and Canada Post Corporation. Produced and sent free of charge to interested persons monthly.

The Heritage Post is keyed to the Heritage Minutes, and produced by the same trust as is the *We Are Canadian* educational kit. All of these materials introduce women's history in a naturalistic, organic fashion. Pitched to children from grades 3 to senior secondary grades, the materials are dramatic and highly entertaining, with women's experiences—albeit women from an elite class—reasonably well represented.

Inkwell Learning Materials, including *Ornamental Toys and Other Pastimes, Nineteenth-Century Christmas Presents,* and several activity booklets which are gender sensitive and representative of historical artifacts. Suitable for children from kindergarten to grade 6.

Merritt, S. E. 1993. *Her Story: Women from Canada's Past.* St. Catharine's: Vanwell Publishing Limited.

The book surveys many well-known Canadian women between the seventeenth and twentieth centuries, including women in such varied fields as fort defender (Marie Jacquelin de la Tour), war refugee (Shawnadithit), artist (Emily Carr), and member of the "Alberta Five" (Emily Murphy).

The Ontario Historical Society. *Discovering Your Community: Activities and Suggestions for Developing Local History Projects for Young People.* Toronto, ON.

Although intended to profile local history more than women's contribution, the Ontario Historical Society's many publications, including this compendium of curriculum ideas and resources, is unusually rich in materials which allow a balanced view of women's pioneer role. The sections devoted to food and clothing are especially useful.

Sadlier, R. 1997. *Tubman: Harriet Tubman and the Underground Railroad—Her Life in the United States and Canada.* Toronto: Umbrella Press.

Although representative of the "great woman" approach to gender-sensitive history, this book fills an obvious need in elementary classsrooms' resource base in providing a source about an outstanding woman of color. Also from this publisher, see *Mary Ann Shadd* and *Women of Vision* as well as *Women Who Gave $$$$.*

Angel, Barbara, and Michael Angel. 1981. *Letitia Hargreaves and Life in the Fur Trade.* Agincourt: The Book Society of Canada.

Wright, Helen K. 1980. *Nellie McClung and Women's Rights.* Agincourt: The Book Society of Canada, Limited.

Both of the preceding booklets, part of the *We Built Canada* series, are representative of an earlier stage of historiography which admitted women into the pantheon of luminaries if they were sufficiently "worthy." These "women worthies" are interpreted as being in no sense representative of their era, but heroines. Given this obvious limitation, however, the series offers rich social history with women at the center of the process. Chapters are supplemented with visuals and guiding questions for students at the junior or intermediate level.

Books on Gender and Curriculum

Acker, Sandra. 1989. *Teachers, Gender, and Careers.* New York: Falmer Press.

Looks at gender divisions in teaching and analyzes the impact of identity on teachers' lives, including an assessment of the potential for feminist educational reform.

Casey, Kathleen. 1993. *I Answer With My Life: Life Histories of Women Teachers Working for Social Change.* New York: Routledge.

Presents the voices of women teachers and implications of their life histories for schooling; the women's narratives create alternative discourses of strength and beauty that stand in opposition to dominant stories of schooling.

Cole, Michael, David Hill, and Shan Sharanjeet. 1997. *Promoting Equity in Primary Schools.* London: Cassell.

Contributors are educators who deplore the devastating effects of conservative economic policies on the school curriculum, and the marginalization of equity issues from the social agenda; examines the need for equity policies in school curriculum and teacher education.

Grant, Carl A., and Christine E. Sleeter. 1998. *Turning on Learning: Five Approaches for Multicultural Teaching Plans for Race, Class, Gender and Disability.* Upper Saddle River, NJ: Prentice-Hall.

A practical text that shows the implications of theory for practice in a multicultural curriculum; presents classroom concerns related to race, class, gender, disability, language, and sexual orientation.

Robertson, Judith P., Bernard W. Andrews, Sharon Anne Cook, and Timothy J. Stanley. 1998. *Words Can Change the World: a Gender Education Manual for Pre-Service Teaching.* Toronto: Ministry of Ontario Publishers.

Contents include detailed analyses of the experiences of preservice teachers (e.g., fear, anger, resistance, and optimism) in learning to teach gender equity; a discussion of the relationship between language, gender, and schooling; and suggested pedagogical interventions into gender stereotyping in teacher education. 112 pp. Copies available from Dr. Judith Robertson, Faculty of Education, 145 Jean Jacques Lussier Blvd., Ottawa, ON, K1M 6N5; fax: 613-562-5146; e-mail: jrobert@uottawa.ca.

Siraj-Blatchford, Iram. 1993. *Race, Gender and the Education of Teachers.* Bristol, PA: Open University Press.

Confronts sexism and privilege directly by exploring the negative impact of inappropriate curriculum content, teacher stereotyping, and the use of sexist and racist resources in the classroom; intended as a practical introduction to issues of concern for teacher educators; reviews the policies, strategies, and changes required to promote equity in teacher education.

Siraj-Blatchford, John, and Iram Siraj-Blatchford. 1995. *Educating the Whole Child: Cross-Curricular Skill, Themes and Dimensions.* Bristol, PA: Open University Press.

Identifies aspects upon which educational practice may be developed in the interests of children, their families, and communities; argues that children need to be able to make meaningful connections in learning, and that the culture of schooling needs to connect with the social worlds of children as the basis for organizing a curriculum.

WEEA Publishing Center. 1995. *Gender Equity for Educators, Parents and Community.* Newton, MS: Education Development Center.

Explains the purpose of equity education; assists teachers, administrators, and the community in understanding gender issues and gives examples of how to recognize and respond to gender bias; illustrates the effect of gender stereotyping on student performance; provides activities for elementary and secondary classrooms.

Weiler, Kathleen. 1988. *Women Teaching for Change: Gender, Class and Power.* Amherst, MA: Bergin and Garvey.

An inspirational account of feminist struggle in public school teaching.

Articles on Gender and Curriculum

Bergsgaard, Michael. 1997. "Gender Issues in the Implementation and Evaluation of a Violence-Prevention Curriculum." *Canadian Journal of Education* 22(1): 33–45.

Bourne, Paula, Liza McCoy, and Myra Novogrodsky, eds. 1997. *Orbit: Special Issue on Gender and Schooling.*

A must-have for teachers, this special edition has twenty-eight articles meant to raise teacher hope, awareness, and understanding of the issues involved in delivering gender equitable education.

Coffey, Amanda J., and Sandra Acker. 1991. "Girlies on the Warpath: Addressing Gender in Initial Teacher Education." *Gender and Education* 3(3): 249–61.

Cook, Sharon C., and Jacqueline Riley. 1994. "The Case for a Gender Issues Course in Teacher Education." *Multicultural Education* 54/55. Edited by F. Schultz. Guilford, CT: Dushkin Publishing Group.

Lafrance, M. 1991. "School for Scandal: Different Educational Experiences for Females and Males." *Gender and Education* 3(1): 3–13.

Lenskyj, H. 1990. "Beyond Plumbing and Prevention: Feminist Approaches to Sex Education." *Gender and Education* 2(2): 217–30.

Lenskyj, H. 1994. "Going Too Far? Sexual Orientation(s) in the Sex Education Curriculum." In *Sociology of Education in Canada,* edited by L. Erwin and D. MacLennan. Toronto: Copp Clark Longmans.

Skelton, C. 1987. "A Study of Gender Discrimination in a Primary Programme of Teacher Training." *Journal of Education for Teaching* 13(2): 163–75.

Books That Challenge Gender Normativity in Arts Education—Dance

Ancona, George. 1981. *Dancing Is.* New York: Dutton.

Photo-essay presenting dance as an art shared by all cultures; illustrates men and women expressing their emotions through a wide variety of dance forms.

Collard, Alexandra. 1984. *Two Young Dancers: Their World of Ballet.* London: Messner.

Recounts the lives of two ballet students, a girl and a boy, and their aspirations and frustrations; realistic and unromanticized account of the challenges in the world of dance.

Martin, Bill Jr., and John Archambault. 1986. *Barn Dance!* New York: Henry Holt.

A rollicking tale about a skinny boy lured by the scarecrow's fiddle to the barn at midnight. The book features gender-breaking images of toe-tapping, hand-clapping, square-dancing fun in the dark of the night against a full moon.

Walker, Katherine, and Joan Butler. 1979. *Ballet for Boys and Girls.* Englewood Cliffs, NJ: Prentice-Hall.

A comprehensive introduction to ballet, including technique, routines, and a synopsis of several major ballets; examines the differences in technique for female and male dancers; presents viewpoints of female choreographers and discusses their personal lives.

Zeck, Gerry. 1982. *I Love to Dance!* New York: Carolrhoda Books.

Recounts the story of a ten-year-old boy and his life as a dance student, including the issue of peer ridicule and how he copes with pursuing what society often deems to be an unconventional career for males; photographs of dancing, family, and friends.

Journal Articles about Gender and Dance

Alderson, E. 1987. "Ballet as Ideology." *Dance Chronicle* 10(3): 290–304.

Berringer, J. 1986. "Dancing across Borders." *The Drama Review* 30(2): 85–97.

Boyer, J., A. Daly, B. T. Jones, and C. Martin. 1988. "Movement and Gender: A Roundtable Discussion." *The Drama Review* 32(4): 82–102.

Caddick, A. 1986. "Feminism and the Body." *Arena* 74: 60–89.

Daly, A. 1986. "Classical Ballet: A Discourse." *The Drama Review* 30(2): 85–97.

Books about Gender and Drama Education

Finney, Gail. 1989. *Women in Modern Drama*. Ithaca, NY: Cornell University Press.

Overview of women's roles in modern theater from the turn of the century until the present; contrasts the earlier view that women were fundamentally different from and subordinate to men with the emerging feminist view that challenged this thinking and increased women's involvement in theater; tells the story of how women figures have come to populate the stage in larger numbers and with greater power than at any previous point in theatrical history.

Hart, Lynda, and Peggy Phelan, eds. 1996. *Acting Out: Feminist Performances*. Ann Arbor, MI: University of Michigan Press.

Collection of essays that critically examines the impact of feminist theater troupes, playwrights, comedians, and performance artists who have challenged conventions, raised consciousness, and provoked controversy; essays discuss alternative theater, the diversity of feminist aesthetic strategies, stand-up comedy, and the politics of gender, lesbian sexualities, anti-feminists, and anti-abortionists.

Laughlin, Karen, and Catherine Schuler, eds. 1995. *Theater and Feminist Aesthetics*. London: Associated University Press.

Intended to broaden readers' perspectives on what feminists have done in the theater, and on how feminism and feminist aesthetics have changed theatrical practices.

Women's Studies. 1988. *Snakes and Snails*. Toronto, ON: Toronto Board of Education.

Book of activities that encourages students to think about male sex stereotyping; examines the rigid sex role stereotyping that has constricted males and females alike; tableaux, role-playing, and improvisations are utilized to provide students with the opportunity to try on new roles.

Journal Articles on Gender and Drama Education

Butler, Judith. 1988. "Performative Arts and Gender Constitution." *Theatre Journal* 40: 519–31.

Daniels, Sarah. 1984. "There Are Fifty-two Percent of Us." *Drama* 152: 23–25.

Lott, Eric. 1991. "'The Seeming Counterfeit': Racial Politics and Early Blackface Minstrelsy." *American Quarterly* 43(2): 223–51.

Wilt, Judith. 1980. "The Laughter of Maidens, the Cackle of Matriarchs: Notes on the Collision between Comedy and Feminism." *Women and Literature* 1: 173–90.

Books on Gender and Music Education

Bowers, Jane, and Judith Tick, eds. 1986. *Women Making Music: The Western Art Tradition 1150–1950*. Urbana: University of Illinois Press.

This collection of historical studies of women in Western art music explores the process through which women's contributions have been shaped, and documents achievements of outstanding individual artists; explores women as a distinct political group within the music world.

Clement, Catherine. 1988. *Opera, or, The Undoing of Women*. Translated by Betsy Wing. Minneapolis: University of Minnesota Press.

Flinn, Caryl. 1992. *Strains of Utopia: Gender, Nostalgia, and Hollywood Film Music*. Princeton, NJ: Princeton University Press.

Herndon, Marcia, and Joan Ziegler. 1990. *Music, Gender and Culture*. New York: Floriaz, Noetzel, Verlag and Wilhelmshaven.

Compilation of articles from the Music and Gender Study Group of the International Council for Traditional Music with an ethnomusicological emphasis; designed to encourage an understanding of gender in terms of the roles it plays in music and society.

Kivi, K. Linda. 1992. *Canadian Women Making Music.* Toronto: Green Dragon Press.

Koskoff, Ellen. 1987. *Women and Music in Cross-Cultural Perspective.* New York: Greenwood Press.

Introduction to women, music, and culture; focuses on women's cultural identity and musical activities and includes historical accounts, genre studies, and descriptions in a variety of cultural/musical settings; good for learning about cross-cultural issues of women in music.

McClary, Susan. 1991. *Feminine Endings: Music, Gender and Sexuality.* Minneapolis: University of Minnesota Press.

Pendle, Karin, ed. 1991. *Women and Music: A History.* Bloomington, IN: Indiana University Press.

A historical survey of women's activities in music performance, composition, teaching, and patronage with an emphasis on art music in Europe and the Americas; includes chapters on women in popular music and jazz, women as financial supporters of the arts, and women's roles in non-Western music; helpful introduction to a study of women in music.

Reich, Nancy B. 1985. *Clara Schumann: The Artist and the Woman.* Ithica: Cornell University Press.

Solie, Ruth, ed. 1993. *Musicology and Difference: Gender and Sexuality in Music Scholarship.* Berkeley: University of California Press.

Subotnik, Rose R. 1991. *Developing Variations: Style and Ideology in Western Music.* Minneapolis: University of Minnesota Press.

Zaimont, Judith Lang, Catherine Overhauser, and Jane Gottlier. 1994. *Musical Women: An International Perspective.* Westport, CT: Greenwood Press.

Chronicles women's achievements around the world as composers, conductors, critics, commentators, scholars, and entrepreneurs; includes surveys of composers and essays on women's contributions to music; reviews women's economic difficulties in musical careers and describes the challenges of balancing family responsibilities with artistic pursuits.

Articles about Gender and Music Education

Andrews, Bernard W. 1996. "Women in the Arts: Supporting Aspirations." *The Recorder* 38(3): 115–16.

Caputo, Virginia. 1995. "Add Technology and Stir: Music, Gender and Technology in Today's Classroom." *The Recorder* 37(2): 61–66.

Citron, Marcia. 1990. "Gender, Professionalism and the Musical Canon." *The Journal of Musicology* 8: 102–117.

Comber, C., D. J. Hargreaves, and A. Colley. 1993. "Girls, Boys and Technology in Music Education." *British Journal of Music Education* (July): 123–34.

Flinn, Caryl. 1986. "The Problem of Femininity in Theories of Film Music." *Screen* 27(6): 56–72.

Gates, E. 1994. "Where Are All the Women Composers?" *Canadian Music Educator* 35(5): 17–20.

Green, Lucy. 1994. "Gender, Musical Meaning and Education." In *Critical Reflections on Music Education.* Edited by Lee R. Bartel and David J. Elliott, 229–36. Toronto, ON: University of Toronto.

Lamb, Roberta. 1990. "Are There Gender Issues in School Music?" *Canadian Music Educator* 31(6): 9–13.

———. 1991. "Medusa's Aria: Feminist Theories and Music Education." In *Women and Education,* edited by Jane Gaskell and Arlene McLaren, 299–319. Calgary, AB: Detselig.

———. 1994. "Feminism as Critique in Philosophy of Music Education." In *Critical Reflections on Music Education,* edited by Lee R. Bartel and David Elliott, 237–63. Toronto, ON: University of Toronto.

Pegley, Karen. 1995. "Places Everyone: Gender and the Non-Neutrality of Music Technology." *The Recorder* 37(2): 55–60.

Shepherd, John. 1989. "Music and Male Hegemony." In *Music and Society: The Politics of Composition, Performance and Reception,* edited by R. Leppert and S. McClary, 151–72. Cambridge, UK: Cambridge University Press.

Wood, Elizabeth. 1980. "Women in Music." *Signs* 6(2): 283–97.

Books about Gender and the Visual Arts

Elliott, Bridget, and Janice Williamson. 1990. *Dangerous Goods: Feminist Visual Art Practices*. Edmonton, AL: Edmonton Art Gallery.

This book explores the work of Canadian feminist visual artists and recounts the influence of the women's movement on feminist artistic production and criticism; discusses women's relation to various institutions, such as educational systems and gallery networks.

Hedges, Elaine, and Ingrid Wendt. 1980. *In Her Own Image: Women Working in the Arts*. New York: McGraw & Hill.

Illustrates the nature, breadth, and diversity of women's work in painting, graphics, sculpture, photography, ceramics, and needlework; focuses on the subjective reality of the woman artist from the viewpoint of the artist; represents artists from diverse national, ethnic, racial, and economic backgrounds and traces important relationships between women's art and women's social conditions.

Kelley, Caffyn. 1991. *In My Country: An Anthology of Canadian Artists*. Vancouver, BC: Gallerie Publications.

Recounts the personal lives of Canadian women artists from across the country and chronicles their reactions to recent current events; considers the impact on the artist's psyche of the Aboriginal peoples' challenge to decades of subservience and Quebec's demands for sovereignty.

Lucky, Natalie. 1983. *Visions and Victories: 10 Canadian Women Artists 1914–1945*. London, ON: London Regional Art Gallery.

Stories of women artists who share the ability to interpret Canada's physical and spiritual landscapes with a unique sensibility; recounts the excellence of women in the visual arts and the hardships they endure to succeed, including lack of recognition and family responsibilities; provides inspiration to contemporary girls and women pursuing their creativity through the visual arts.

Meskimmon, Marsha. 1996. *The Art of Reflection: Women Artists' Self-Portraiture in the 20th Century*. New York: Columbia University Press.

Historical overview of women artists' differing strategies of self-portraiture throughout the twentieth century; analyzes why this area has proven so fruitful and inspiring for women; questions of gender, sexualities, and maternity are considered through self-representation; addresses how women have contested traditional art practice.

Journal Articles on Gender and the Visual Arts

Anderson, Heather. 1992. "Making Women Artists Visible." *Art Education* 45(2): 14–22.

Butler, S. 1987. "So, How Do I Look? Women before and behind the Camera." *Photo Communique* 9(3): 24–35.

Favorite, M. 1987. "Portrait of Self Contemplating Self: The Narrative of a Black Female Artist." *SAGE* 4: 34–40.

Jack, M., and J. Sang. 1989. "Using Original Paintings with Young Children." *Journal of Arts and Design Education* 8(3): 257–73.

Johnson, C. 1992. "Issues Surrounding the Representation of the Naked Body of a Woman." *Feminist Arts News* 3(8): 12–14.

Nicely, N. T. 1992. "A Door Ajar: The Professional Position of Women Artists." *Art Education* 15(2): 6–13,

Spence, J. 1989. "Disrupting the Silence: The Daughter's Story." *Women Artists State Library Journal* 29: 14–17.

Books on Gender and Language Arts

Barrs, Myra, and Sue Pidgeon. 1993. *Gender and Reading in Elementary Classrooms.* Markham, ON: Pembroke.

This well-focused discussion of gender in reading achievement encourages teachers and caregivers to look more deeply into gender implications for children's reading development.

Best, Raphaela. 1983. *We've All Got Scars: What Boys and Girls Learn in Elementary School.* Bloomington: Indiana University Press.

Clark, M. 1990. *The Great Divide: Gender in the Primary School.* Melbourne: Curriculum Corporation.

Davies, Bronwyn. 1989. *Frogs and Snails and Feminist Tales: Preschool Children and Gender.* Sydney: Allen and Unwin.

Fascinating study of children's play, conversations, responses, and resistances to feminist stories; details the social construction of children's gendered fantasies; explores how young children use fairy tales to construct fantasy versions of who they want to be. Excellent bibliography of feminist children's picture books.

Durkin, Kevin. 1985. *Television, Sex Roles and Children: A Developmental Social Psychological Account.* Milton Keynes: Open University Press.

Evaluates the research on television and sex role acquisition, and addresses central questions of media influences on gender.

Jacobs, James S., and Michael O. Tunnell. 1996. *Children's Literature, Briefly.* Englewood Cliffs, NJ: Merrill/Prentice-Hall.

An excellent basic resource book that presents the best of the best in children's literature, with helpful annotations, information about authors and artists, and addresses of publishing companies. No separate chapter on nonsexist or feminist literature, but good representation of diverse genres and communities.

Lehr, Susan, ed. 1985. *Battling Dragons: Issues and Controversy in Children's Literature.* Portsmouth, NH: Heinemann.

This resource book for teachers confronts questions about how and why "risky stories" can be used to support children's learning in elementary language arts classrooms.

Lynch-Brown, Carol, and Carl M. Tomlinson. 1993. *Essentials of Children's Literature.* Boston: Allyn & Bacon.

A useful and accessible resource text for language arts teachers in search of good books for kids. No separate category for feminist or nonsexist literature, but widely representative of diverse genres, authors, and communities, with helpful annotations.

Paley, Vivian G. 1984. *Boys and Girls: Superheroes in the Doll Corner.* Chicago: University of Chicago Press.

The first few sentences of this book speak to its power: "Kindergarten is a triumph of sexual self-stereotyping. No amount of adult subterfuge or propaganda deflects the five-year-old's passion for segregation by sex. They think they have invented the differences between boys and girls and, as with any new invention, must prove that it works. The doll corner is often the best place to collect evidence. It is not simply a place to play; it is a stronghold against ambiguity."

Tutchell, Eva, ed. 1990. *Dolls and Dungarees: Gender Issues in the Primary School Curriculum.* Milton Keynes: Open University Press.

Walkerdine, Valerie. 1990. *Schoolgirl Fictions*. London: Verso.

> A frank series of reflections on the effects of gender on learning by a leading British feminist educator, mathematics researcher, former primary school teacher, and working-class woman.

Articles on Gender and Language Arts

Anti-Sexist Working Party. 1985. "'Look, Jane, Look': Anti-Sexist Initiatives in Primary Schools." In *Just A Bunch of Girls: Feminist Approaches to Schooling,* edited by G. Weiner. Milton Keynes: Open University Press.

Anyon, J. 1983. "Intersections of Gender and Class: Accommodations and Resistance by Working Class and Affluent Families to Contradictory Sex-role Ideologies." In *Gender, Class and Education,* edited by S. Walker and L. Barton. London: Falmer Press.

Cleary, Linda Miller. 1996. "'I Think I Know What My Teachers Want NOW': Gender and Writing Motivation." *English Journal* 85(1): 50–57.

Davies, Bronwyn, and Chas Banks. 1992. "The Gender Trap: A Feminist Poststructuralist Analysis of Primary School Children's Talk about Gender." *Journal of Curriculum Studies* 24(1): 1–25.

Hannan, Dennis J. 1995. "Gender Equity in the American Classroom: Where Are the Women?" *English Journal* 84(6): 103–117.

Hanson, Trudy L. 1995. "Teaching Gender Issues in Storytelling and the College Teaching Class." Paper presented at the Annual Meeting of the Southern States Communication Association, New Orleans, Louisiana, April 5–9. ERIC Document 385867.

Henkin, Roxanne. 1995. "Insiders and Outsiders in First-Grade Writing Workshops: Gender and Equity Issues." *Language Arts* 72(6): 429–34.

Hill, Laura. 1992. "Visions for Problem Resolution in Eating Disorders." *Journal of Counseling and Development* 70(5): 584–87.

Labbo, Linda D., and Sherry L. Field. 1996. "Celebrating Culturally Diverse Families." *Language Arts* 73(1): 54–62.

Martinez, Miriam, and Marcia F. Nash. 1995. "Talking about Children's Literature—Special Relationships." *Language Arts* 75(5): 368–75.

Trousdale, Ann M. 1995. "I'd Rather Be Normal: A Young Girl's Response to 'Feminist' Fairy Tales." *The New Advocate* 8(3): 167–82.

Westland, Ella. 1993. "Cinderella in the Classroom: Children's Responses to Gender Roles in Fairy Tales." *Gender and Education* 5(3): 237–49.

Yokota, Junko. 1994. "Books that Represent More than One Culture." *Language Arts* 71(3): 212–19.

Top Picks in Feminist and Nonsexist Picture Books

Cole, B. 1986. *Princess Smartypants*. London: Hamish Hamilton.

Cooney, B. 1982. *Miss Rumphius*. London: Julia MacRae Books.

Cox, D. 1985. *Bossyboots*. London: The Bodley Head.

Denton, K. 1985. *Felix and Alexander*. Oxford: Oxford University Press.

de Paola, T. 1980. *The Knight and the Dragon*. London: Methuen.

Gaspar, T. 1974. *Yolanda's Hike*. Berkeley: New Seed Press.

Munsch, R., and M. Marchenko. 1980. *The Paper Bag Princess*. Toronto: Annick Press Ltd.

Suroweicki, S., and P. Lenthall. 1977. *Joshua's Day*. Chapel Hill, NC: Lollipop Power Inc.

Turin, A., and N. Bosnia. 1976. *A Fortunate Catastrophe*. London: Writers and Readers Publishing Cooperative.

Wells, R. 1975. *Benjamin and Tulip*. Harmondsworth: Kestrel Books.

Williams, J. 1978. *The Practical Princess and other Liberating Fairy Tales*. London: The Bodley Head.

Zipes, J. 1986. *Don't Bet on the Prince: Contemporary Feminist Fairy Tales in North America and England*. Aldershot: Gower.

Zolotow, Charlotte. 1985. *William's Doll*. New York: HarperCollins.

Novels on Gender and Language Arts

Ackerman, Karen. 1995. *The Night Crossing*. New York: Random House.

A fictional introduction to the Holocaust useful for raising questions of girls' and women's roles in political resistance;

the story takes place during the Nazi occupation of Austria and recounts the experiences of young Clara, whose quick thinking assists the Jewish family's survival. [Editor's note: See the essay by Karen Shawn, this volume, for important qualifications regarding the use of this book for Holocaust education.]

Coerr, Eleanor. 1979. *Sadako and the Thousand Paper Cranes.* New York: Putnam.

Recounts the irrepressible lifeforce and dreams of athletic Sadako, who was two in 1945 and ten years later died from leukemia as a result of radiation from the bomb dropped on Hiroshima; useful for addressing issues of hope, resistance, courage, friendship, and the strength of friendship and community. A rich array of Web sites makes this book ideal for early investigations into female authorship, female heroism, international communities of hope, and war and patriarchy.

Coerr Web Sites
Sadako Resource List
http://www.he.net/~sparker/resource.html

Sadako Homepage
http://www.sadako.org/

Paulsen, Gary. 1993. *Nightjohn.* New York: Delacorte Press.

Artistically crafted portrayal of the grim past of the American South told from the point of view of a black preadolescent female slave, Sarney; graphic portrayal of the struggle of black Americans for literacy and emancipation. Useful for exploring themes of black female heroism, the strength of community, and female leadership within black communities. Rich links to Web sites stimulate student research into authorship, the Civil War period of American history, black African female heroines such as Harriet Tubman and Rosa Parks, and white patriarchal laws affecting the right to literacy.

Paulsen Web Sites

Gary Paulsen's Homepage
http://www.ksu.udu/agronomy/FACULTY/PAULSEN/

Biographical information on Paulsen
http://falcon.imu.edu/~ramseyil/paulsen.htm

Gary Paulsen curriculum materials
http://www.plconline.com/ccenter/gpcurr/html

Journal Articles on Gender and Popular Culture (Children's Toys, Popular Reading Choices, Video Games, and Motion Pictures)

Abraham, Kitty G., and Lieberman, Evelyn. 1985. "Should Barbie Go to Preschool?" *Young Children* 40(2): 12–14.

Brabant, Sarah, and Linda A. Mooney. 1997. "Sex Role Stereotyping in the Sunday Comics: A Twenty Year Update." *Sex Roles* 37(3/4): 269–81.

Brown, R. Michael, Lisa R. Hall, Roee Holzer, Stephanie L. Brown, and Norma L. Brown. 1997. "Gender and Video Game Performance." *Sex Roles* 36(11/12): 793–812.

Burwell, Hope E. 1995. "Nancy Drew, Girl Detective, Nascent Feminist, and Family Therapist." *English Journal* 84(4): 51–53.

Cesarone, Bernard. 1994. "Video Games and Children." ERIC Document EDO-PS-94-3.

Chavez, Deborah. 1985. "Perpetuation of Gender Inequality: A Content Analysis of Comic Strips." *Sex Roles* 13(1/2): 93–103.

Cumming, Peter. 1996. "Disney's *Pocahontas*: The Emptiness Inside." *Canadian Children's Literature* 83: 142–43.

DiPietro, Janet Ann. 1981. "Rough and Tumble Play: A Function of Gender." *Developmental Psychology* 17(1): 50–58.

Galloway, Margaret E. 1987. "American Indian Women in Literature: Stereotypical Self-Determination." Paper presented at the 10th Annual American Indian Conference, Mankato, Minnesota, May 7, 1987. ERIC Document 287 793.

Gibson, James William. 1989. "Paramilitary Culture." *Critical Studies in Mass Communication* 6(1): 90–93.

Green, Rayna. 1975. "The Pocahontas Perplex: The Image of Indian Women in American Culture." *The Massachusetts Review* (Autumn): 698–714.

Greenberg, Harvey R. 1987. "Dangerous Recuperation: Red Dawn, Rambo, and the New Decaturism." *Journal of Popular Film and Television* 15(2): 60–70.

Hanlon, Heather, Judy Farnsworth, and Judy Murray. 1997. "Ageing in American Comic Strips: 1972–1992." *Ageing and Society* 17(3): 293–304.

Hughes, Renee M. 1995. "The Inclusion of Fantasy Play through the Use of Barbie Dolls in a Developmentally Appropriate Learning Environment for Preschool Three and Four Year Olds." ERIC Document 388 415.

Jackson, Kathy Merlock. 1997. "From Mouse to Mermaid: The Politics of Film, Gender, and Culture." (Book Review). *Journal of Popular Film and Television* 25(1): 48.

Jordan, Ellen. 1995. "Fighting Boys and Fantasy Play: The Construction of Masculinity in the Early Years of School." *Gender and Education* 7(1): 69–86.

Keller, Suzanne. 1992. "Children and the Nintendo." Research report. ERIC Document 405 069.

Kent, Steven. 1997. "Super Mario Nation." *American Heritage* 48(5): 65–77.

Kubey, Robert, and Reed Larson. 1990. "The Use and Experience of the New Video Media Among Children and Adolescents." *Communication Research* 17(1): 107–130.

Leadbeater, Bonnie J., and Gloria Lodato Wilson. 1993. "Flipping Their Fins for a Place to Stand: 19th- and 20th-Century Mermaids." *Youth & Society* 24(4): 466–86.

Mackey, Margaret. 1990. "Filling the Gaps: The Baby-sitters Club, the Series Book, and the Learning Reader." *Language Arts* 67(5): 484–89.

MacLeod, Anne Scott. 1987. "Nancy Drew and Her Rivals: No Contest Part II." *The Horn Book Magazine* (July/August): 442–51.

Magro, Albert M. 1997. "Why Barbie Is Perceived as Beautiful." *Perceptual and Motor Skills* 85: 363–74.

Meier, Terry, and Peter C. Murrell Jr. 1996. "'They Can't Even Play Right!' Cultural Myopia in the Analysis of Play." In *Playing for Keeps: Supporting Children's Play.* Topics in Early Childhood Education, Vol. 2. ERIC Document 405 106.

Mitchell, Claudia, and Jacqueline Reid-Walsh. 1995. "And I Want to Thank You Barbie: Barbie as a Site for Cultural Interrogation." *The Review of Education/Pedagogy/Cultural Studies* 17(2): 143–55.

————. 1996. "Reading on the Edge: Serious Series Readers of Nancy Drew and Hardy Boys Mysteries." *Changing English* 3(1): 45–55.

Molesworth, Charles. 1986. "Rambo, Passion, and Power." *Dissent* 33(1): 109–111.

Nelson, Claudia. 1990. "The Beast Within: *Winnie-the-Pooh* Reassessed." *Children's Literature in Education* 21(1): 17–22.

Ohanian, Susan. 1997. "Some Are More Equal than Others." *Phi Delta Kappan* 78(6): 471–74.

Provenzo, Eugene R. Jr. 1992. "The Video Generation." *Educating for Results* 179(3): 29–32.

Rollin, Roger B. 1970. "Beowulf to Batman: The Epic Hero and Pop Culture." *College English* 31(5): 431–49.

Schroeder, Randy. 1996. "Playspace Invaders: Huizinga, Baudrillard and Video Game Violence." *Journal of Popular Culture* 30(3): 143–53.

Simons, Martin. 1988. "Montessori, Superman, and Catwoman." *Educational Theory* 38(3): 341–49.

Smoodin, Eric. 1997. "From Mouse to Mermaid: The Politics of Film, Gender, and Culture." (Book Review). *Film Quarterly* 50(3): 54–55.

Snyder, Eldon E. 1997. "Teaching the Sociology of Sport: Using a Comic Strip in the Classroom." *Teaching Sociology* 25 (July): 239–43.

Sugarman, Sally. 1995. "The Mysterious Case of the Detective as Child Hero: Sherlock Holmes, Encyclopedia Brown and Nancy Drew as Role Models." Paper presented at the Annual Joint Meetings of the Popular Culture Association/American Culture Association, Philadephia, Pennsylvania, April 12–15. ERIC Document 382 935.

Journals and Newsletters on Gender and Education

Association for Women in Mathematics Newsletter
Box 178
Wellesley College
Wellesley, MD 02181

Canadian Journal of Mathematics and *Canadian Mathematical Bulletin*
Canadian Mathematical Society/Société Mathématique du Canada
577 King Edward, Suite 108
Ottawa, ON K1N 6N5

Girls in Science Newsletter
American Association for the Advancement of Science
Directorate for Education and Human Resources Programs
1333 H Street NW
Washington, DC 20005

Mentor
P. O. Box 4382
Overland Park, KS 66204

NCSEE News
A Publication of the National Coalition for Sex Equity in Education
Theodora Martin, NCSEE Business Manager
One Redwood Drive
Clinton, NJ 08809

*News from the Center for Children and Technology and the Center for
    Technology in Education*
Bank Street College of Education
610 West 112th St.
New York, NY 10025

Woman'space Magazine
Women's Guide to the Internet
R. R. # 1
Scotsburn, NS B0K 1R0

**Associations That
Support Education
about Gender**

Association of Black Women Entrepreneurs
1301 Kenter Avenue
Los Angeles, CA 90049
(310) 472-4927

Society for Canadian Women in Science and Technology/Société des
    Canadiennes dans la Science et Technologie (SCWIST/SCST)
#417
535 Hornby Street
Vancouver, BC V6C 2E8
(604) 895-5814

Women Inventors Project
107 Hom Crescent
Thornhill, ON L3T 5J4
(905) 731 0328

FC Feminist Collections
Women's Studies Librarian
430 Memorial Library
728 State Street
Madison, WI 53706

National Women's History Project
7738 Bell Road
Windsor, CA 95492-8518
(707) 838 6000

Acknowledgments   The authors gratefully acknowledge the financial support of the Ontario
Women's Directorate and the Ontario Association of Deans of Education.
Thanks to Diana Shaffer for tracking down resources, and to Deanne
Bogdan for her assistance with music and gender resources. The research
out of which this article originated (Gender and Equity Research in Teacher
Education) was supported by Sharon Cook, Diana Masny, Donatille
Mujawamariya, Tim Stanley, and Mariette Théberge at the University of
Ottawa.

21 From Cupboard to Classroom: First Nations Resources

Elspeth Ross

It is vital that First Nations resources be included in a book on educating about genocide and intolerance. Too often the world and school leave out the indigenous peoples, who in the United States are called Native Americans, and in Canada called First Nations, Aboriginal, or Native People, and include Indians, Inuit, and Métis Peoples.

Images of Indians, Inuit, and Métis are all around us. The stereotypic Indian is found in common knowledge and folk image, public opinion, literature and magazines, newspapers, school textbooks, movies and television. The image is, on the balance, negative. The Indian is both noble and savage, and somehow symbolic of Canada and the United States. The stereotypic Indian is "different," a being outside the ordinary daily lives of non-Indians[1].

Everyone knows the bloodthirsty savage; brave, stoic, loyal follower; noble child of nature; wise old chief; squaw; Indian princess; Eskimo hunter. "Indians" are all the same, frozen in time, artifacts in museums with teepees and totem poles, bows and arrows, Plains Indian headdresses, Hollywood Tonto, Disney Pocahontas, textbook Indian at the very beginning of History, "woo-woo" Indians, "a bunch of wild Indians," "Ten Little Indians," sports mascot Indian, souvenir carving Indian or Eskimo, street Indian, drunken Indian, militant Indian.

Today First Nations people continue to have to put up with racist remarks. Native writers and actors say that the white world continues to fashion Native people. They are told "You're not Indian enough"; "It doesn't look Indian"; "Make it more Indian."[2] A stereotype is a fixed idea about what people are like. Racialized stereotyping means that some teachers expect all Native children to be quiet and withdrawn. Stereotypes limit how children see others and how they see themselves. Stereotypes rob individuals and their cultures of human qualities and promote no real understanding of social realities. Native heritage is viewed as a relic of the past belonging to some earlier phase of human development with no part in the present.[3]

Who are the real Indians and Inuit? Children ask: "Are all the Indians dead?"; "Where do the Indians live? Do they live in the hills?" Many children still view Indian people as far removed from their own way of life, for example, historic and traditional or warlike and hostile. Most children do not recognize the great diversity among Indian people which existed in the past and continues today."[4]

Most students and teachers know few if any Aboriginal people. Many teachers don't know how to inform themselves about First Nations issues and don't know how to find appropriate learning materials. Some people are so unsure about how to present Native literature and issues that they do not present them at all. Mainstream publishers, bookstores, bookfairs, Web sites, and libraries are often not the best sources to use to educate teachers about First Nations people. Many books and movies for general consumption are still made without Native input. Books like *The Indian in the Cupboard* (Reid Banks 1980), which is well written but widely condemned as racist, and movies like *Pocahontas* (Walt Disney Pictures 1995), with its gross distortions, are wildly popular.

We are all enriched by learning about the living cultures of First Nations peoples. First Nations children gain in self-esteem and come to take pride in their rich artistic and creative heritage and their flourishing modern arts through role models, posters, videos, and writings. Books are not merely frivolous entertainment:

> They are part of society's general culture . . . and reinforce and perpetuate its racism . . . To the extent that Native people continue to become inhuman, objectified "Indians" . . . peoples of the past or creatures of fantasy . . . all alike . . . to the extent that children are taught to fear "Indians" . . . to that extent continued aggression against Native people is supported.[5]

The challenges are to educate ourselves about First Nations peoples, to counter the prevalent stereotypes by discussion and by presenting today's First Nations in the classroom, and to know where to get good materials. For this, we need realistic stories of modern life, and sensitive historic and community portrayals. We should study Native people by using their own literature, instead of social studies texts which frequently present romantic, demonizing, or colonizing perspectives. We should also incorporate the legends into the main curriculum as teaching stories for us today. Since these are adaptations of traditional tales told orally, we should check to see that they come from reliable sources with permission.

There are numerous places to go for help in finding information about First Nations peoples and anti-biased, anti-racist education and classroom resources. There is a flowering of writing and artistic expressions of all forms by First Nations peoples. Canada produces a wealth of materials from small presses, especially the First Nations publishers Pemmican and Theytus, First Nations cultural education centers, and independent booksellers.

Teachers and librarians should consider the evaluation criteria and order posters, videos, and books on contemporary First Nations, Indian, Inuit, and Métis life. Teachers should check to see that Native publishers, authors, consultants, illustrators, and reviewers are used and that resources are relevant to modern life. The resources we use can perpetuate myths or open up possibilities.

How the Recommended Resources Are Presented

The contacts and resources suggested here come from a wide variety of sources. Every effort has been made to find Canadian material. Resources for educating teachers are presented first: Readings, Organizations, Journals and Newspapers, Web Sites and Publishers in Education, Anti-bias/Anti-racist Teaching, First Nations Anti-bias Teaching, First Nations Culture and Education, and Book Sources. Classroom resources suggested for use are First Nations Anthologies, Posters, Videos, and Books for primary and junior children from kindergarten to grade 6. Most have Native involvement in their production or have been approved by Native people. All books are believed to be in print.

There is so much information, especially on the Internet, and much can be obtained full-text. The western Canadian provinces and northern territories have a project with a common approach to Native education. There is some sharing of curriculum materials. Educators must select from a vast array of documentation. Readers of this chapter are invited to dip into the resources on the Web, and to contact some of the organizations for materials.

Readings for Teachers

General Anti-bias/ Anti-racist Teaching Readings

Campbell, Patricia, and Jeana Wirtenberg. 1980. "How Books Influence Children: What the Research Shows." *Interracial Books for Children Bulletin* 11(6): 3–6.

Cheng, Maisy. 1994. *Anti-Racist Education: A Literature Review.* Research Report no. 206. Toronto: Board of Education.

Council on Interracial Books for Children. *10 Quick Ways to Analyze Children's Books for Racism and Sexism.* Pamphlet. 1841 Broadway, New York, NY, 10023.

Derman-Sparks, Louise. 1989. *Anti-bias Curriculum: Tools for Empowering Young Children.* A. B. C. Task Force. Washington: National Association for the Education of Young Children. 1509 16th St. NW, Washington, DC, 20036-1426.

———. 1993–94. "Empowering Children to Create a Caring Culture in a World of Differences." *Childhood Education* 70(2): 66–71.

Derman-Sparks, Louise, Maria Gutiérrez, and Carol B. Phillips. *Teaching Young Children to Resist Bias: What Parents Can Do.* Pamphlet. Washington, DC: National Association for the Education of Young Children, 1509 16th St. NW, Washington, DC, 20036-1426. Phone: (800) 424-2460 and (202) 232-8777.

Elliott, Anne, and Joyce Castle. 1997. "Canadian Children's Literature: Building Connections Across Cultures." *Multiculturalism/ Multiculturalisme* 17(1): 34–39.

Hull, Nadia. 1995. *The Affective Curriculum: Teaching the Anti-Bias Approach to Young Children.* Toronto, ON: Nelson Canada.

Manitoba Education and Training. 1997. *Anti-Racist Education: A Bibliography.* Winnipeg. http://www.gov.mb.ca/metks4/instruct/iru/iruinfo/index.html#anti-racist

———. 1994. *Bias in Learning Materials: A Bibliography of Resources Available from the Library, Instructional Resources.* Winnipeg: Manitoba Education and Training, Instructional Resources.

Muse, Daphne, ed. 1997. *The New Press Guide to Multicultural Resources for Young Readers.* New York: New Press.

Saskatchewan Education. 1991. *Selecting Fair and Equitable Learning Material.* Regina: Guidelines for Recognizing Bias.

Smith, Karen. 1993. "The Multicultural Ethic and Connections to Literature for Children and Young Adults." *Library Trends* 41(3): 340–53.

First Nations Anti-bias Teaching Readings

Almeida, Deirdre. 1996. *Countering Prejudice against American Indians and Alaska Natives through Antibias Curriculum and Instruction.* Charleston, WV: ERIC Clearinghouse on Rural Education and Small Schools. ED400146.

Billman, Jane. 1992. "The Native American Curriculum: Attempting Alternatives to Teepees and Headbands." *Young Children* 47(6): 22–25, and *Young Children* 48(2): 3, 77–80.

Caldwell-Wood, Naomi, and Lisa Mitten. 1991. "Selective Bibliography and Guide: 'I' Is Not for Indian: The Portrayal of Native Americans in Books for Young People." *Multicultural Review* 1(2): 26–35; also Program of the ALA/OLOS Subcommittee for Library Services to American Indian People, American Indian Library Association, Atlanta. http://info.pitt.edu/~lmitten/ailab.htm

Canadian Alliance in Solidarity with Native Peoples. 1990. *Resource Reading List 1990: Annotated Bibliography of Resources by and about Native People.* Catherine Verrall, Patricia McDowell, and Lenore Keeshig-Tobias, compilers. Toronto, ON: CASNP. Includes "Evaluating Books about Native Peoples" and "What Is a Stereotype?"

———. 1996. *Resource Reading List: An Annotated Bibliography of Recommended Works by and about Native Peoples.* Jonathan Van Etten, compiler. Toronto, ON: CASNP. Much shorter children's section; does not pretend to be comprehensive.

Charles, Jim. 1996. "Out of the Cupboard and into the Classroom: Children and the American Indian Literary Experience." *Children's Literature in Education* 27(3): 167–79.

Cooke, Katie. 1984. *Images of Indians Held by Non-Indians: A Review of Current Canadian Research.* Ottawa, ON: Indian and Northern Affairs Canada, Research Branch.

Council on Interracial Books for Children. 1977. *Unlearning "Indian" Stereotypes: A Teaching Unit for Elementary Teachers and Children's Librarians.* New York: Racism and Sexism Resource Center for Educators.

Dowd, Frances. 1992. "Evaluating Books Portraying Native American and Asian Cultures." *Childhood Education* 68(4): 19–24.

Grant, Agnes, and Lavine Gillespie. 1992. *Using Literature by American Indians and Alaska Natives in Secondary School.* Charleston, WV: ERIC Clearinghouse on Rural Education and Small Schools. ED348201.

Greenberg, Polly. 1992. "Ideas That Work with Young Children. Teaching about Native Americans? Or Teaching about People, Including Native Americans." *Young Children* 47(6): 27–30, 79.

Gregg, Alison. 1996. "Political Correctness or Telling It Like It Is: Selecting Books about Australia's Indigenous People." *Emergency Librarian* 23(4): 9–13. Also published as ERIC Document 400844.

Haukoos, Gerry, and Archie Beauvais. 1996/97. "Creating Positive Cultural Images: Thoughts for Teaching about American Indians." *Childhood Education* 73(2): 77–82.

Hirschfelder, Arlene. 1982. *American Indian Stereotypes in the World of Children: A Reader and Bibliography.* Metuchen, NJ: Scarecrow Press.

———. 1993. "Native American Literature for Children and Young Adults." *Library Trends* 41(3): 414–36.

Horning, Kathleen. 1993. "The Contributions of Alternative Press Publishers to Multicultural Literature for Children." *Library Trends* 41(3): 524–40. Section on Native American presses.

Kuipers, Barbara. 1991. "Understanding the Evaluation Criteria for American Indian Literature." Chap. 2 in *American Indian Reference Books for Children and Young Adults.* Englewood, CO: Libraries Unlimited.

LaBonty, Jan. 1995. "A Demand for Excellence in Books for Children." *Journal of American Indian Education* 34(2): 1–9.

McDonald, Peter. 1993. "Selecting Books for and about Native Americans for Young People." *Multicultural Review* 2(1): 16.

McIvor, Betty-Ann. 1992. "Not 'Indians': Selecting Native Literature from a Native Perspective." *CM: Canadian Materials* 20(4): 193–95. http://www.mbnet.mb.ca

Mihesuah, Devon. 1996. *American Indians: Stereotypes and Realities.* Atlanta, GA: Clarity.

Moore, Kathryn. 1992. *Racial Bias in Children's Textbooks.* Toronto: University of Toronto. M.A. Thesis.

Moore, Opal, and Donnarae MacCann. 1988. "The Ignoble Savage: Amerind Images in the Mainstream Mind." *Children's Literature Association Quarterly* 13: 26–30.

Pauls, Syd. 1996. "Racism and Native Schooling: A Historical Perspective." In *Racism in Canadian Schools,* edited by M. Ibrahim Alladin, 22–41. Toronto: Harcourt Brace Canada.

Pohl, Ann. 1996. "First Things First: Anti-Racist Education on Turtle Island." *Our Schools/Our Selves* 8(1): 61–80.

Reese, Debbie. 1996. *Teaching Young Children about Native Americans.* Urbana, IL: ERIC Clearinghouse on Elementary and Early Childhood Education. ED394744; also at http://www.nativechild.com

Saskatchewan Education. 1993. *Diverse Voices: Selecting Equitable Resources for Indian and Métis Education.* Regina.

Slapin, Beverly, and Doris Seale. 1992, 1988. *Through Indian Eyes: The Native Experience in Books for Children.* Philadelphia: New Society. Includes "How to Tell the Difference: A Checklist."

Stott, Jon. 1995. *Native Americans in Children's Literature.* Phoenix, AZ: Oryx Press. Foreword by Joseph Bruchac.

Tjoumas, Renee. 1993. "Native American Literature for Young People: A Survey of Collection Development Methods in Public Libraries." *Library Trends* 41(3): 493–523.

Zarate, Jose. 1994. "Indigenous Knowledge and Anti-Racist Education: Reaching Out to People and Culture." *Orbit* 25(2): 35–36.

First Nations Readings and Resource Lists

Alberta Department of Education. 1992. *Native Library Resources for Elementary, Junior and Senior High Schools.* Edmonton. 4th ed. ERIC ED393627.

Bagworth, Ruth. 1995. *Native Peoples: Resources Pertaining to First Nations, Inuit and Métis.* Winnipeg: Manitoba Department of Education and Training. Also available from ERIC ED400143.

Dowd, Frances. 1992. "An Annotated Bibliography: Recent Realistic Fiction and Informational Books for Young Children Portraying Asian-American and Native American Cultures." *Multicultural Review* 1(2): 26–35.

Dwarka, Diane. 1992. "Aboriginal Books: A Selected Bibliography of Recommended Titles." *CM: Canadian Materials* 20(4): 195–97. http://www.mbnet.mb.ca

Manitoba Education and Training. 1995. *Native Studies: Early Years (K–4): A Teacher's Resource Book.* Winnipeg.

————. 1995. *Native Studies: Early Years (K–4): A Teacher's Resource Book Framework.* Winnipeg.

Mukwa Geezis: Resource Guide to Aboriginal Literature in Canada. 1997. Toronto: Wabanoong Multimedia Publications ANDPVA. Includes a recommended Booklist for "Children and Young Adults."

Sutton, Sue. 1995. "First Nation's New Shoots: Stacks of Books Have Been Published about Native People, Now They're Being Published by Them." *Quill & Quire* 61(12): 10, 20.

Young-Ing, Greg. 1995. "Regaining Our Voice." *Quill & Quire* 61(12): 12–13.

Organizations

Education Organizations

Manitoba Education and Training Instructional Resources Library, Box 3, Main Floor
1181 Portage Ave.
Winnipeg, MB R3G 0T3
(204) 945-7830/7851/4015

National Film Board of Canada
P. O. Box 6100
Station Centre-Ville, Montreal, QC H3C 3H5
(800) 267-7710

Ontario Institute for Studies in Education of the University of Toronto (OISE)
252 Bloor St. W.
Toronto, ON M5S 1V6
(416) 923-6641

Saskatchewan Education
Resource Centre
7th floor
2220 College Ave.
Regina, SK S4P 3V7
(306) 787-2259

Anti-bias Organizations

Anti-racism Campaign
Canadian Heritage
15 Eddy St.
Hull, QC K1A 1K5

Annual contest for young people on how to stop racism; teachers' guides, posters, kits.

Ontario Education Alliance
238 Davenport Rd.
P. O. Box 89
Toronto, ON M5R 1J6
(416) 322-3185

> Opens possibilities in the classroom and community.

Urban Alliance on Race Relations
675 King St. W., Suite 202
Toronto, ON M5V 1M9
(416) 703-6607

> Education programs to address racism in society.

First Nations Cultural Educational Organizations

Aboriginal Multi-media Society
15001 112 Ave.
Edmonton, AB T5M 2V6
(403) 455-2700

> Facilitates the exchange of information reflecting Aboriginal culture.

Alberta Native Education Project
11160 Jasper Ave.
Edmonton, AB T5K 0L2
(403) 427-2043

Learning Resources Distributing Centre
12360 142 St.
Edmonton, AB T5L 4X9
(403) 427-2767

Canadian Alliance in Solidarity with Native Peoples
39 Spadina Rd.
Toronto, ON M5R 2S9
(416) 972-1573

First Nations Confederacy of Cultural Education Centres
191 Promenade du Portage, Suite 500
Hull, QC J8X 2K6
(819) 772-2331

> Coordinating body for First Nations cultural centers across Canada.

First Nations Education Centre
3430 Sparks St.
Terrace, BC V8G 2V3
(250) 638-6394

> Works to integrate First Nations content and materials into K–12 curriculum.

Four Worlds International Institute for Human and Community
    Development Four Directions International
1224 Lakemount Blvd. South
Lethbridge, AB T1K 3K1
(403) 320-7144

> Resource Catalogue of holistic, culturally based curriculum materials.

Gabriel Dumont Institute of Native Studies and Applied Research
505 23rd St. E.
Saskatoon, SK S7K 4K7
(306) 934-5073

> Publishes books with Métis and First Nations content, K–12 and all levels.

Manitoba Indian Cultural Education Centre
119 Sutherland Ave.
Winnipeg, MB R2W 3C9
(204) 942-0228

> Lists of children's books, films, VHS tapes, educational kits, cassette tapes, adult books.

Métis Resource Centre
506-63 Albert St.
Winnipeg, MB R3B 1G4
(204) 956-7767

> Preserves, shares, and promotes culture and history.

National Native Role Model Program
P. O. Box 1440
Kahnawake, QC J0L 1B0
(800) 363-3199, (514) 638-3199

> Free posters for schools.

Native Book Centre
150 York Hill Blvd.
Thornhill, ON L4J 2P6
(905) 881-7804

> Over 1,100 titles in thirty-five categories. Mostly adult and U.S.

North American Native Authors Catalog
The Greenfield Review Press
P. O. Box 308
2 Middle Grove Road
Greenfield Center, NY 12833
(518) 583-1440.

Oyate
2702 Mathews St.
Berkeley, CA 94702
(510) 848-4815

> Evaluates texts, resource materials, and fiction by and about
> Native peoples, conducts teacher workshops, distributes
> books and materials, emphasizing writing and illustration by
> Native people. Includes a large number of Canadian titles.

Saskatchewan Indian Cultural Centre
120 33rd St. E.
Saskatoon, SK S7K 4K7
(306) 244-1146

> Publishes books in four Native languages and English.

Wabanoong Multimedia Publications ANDPVA [Association for
     Native Development in the Performing and Visual Arts]
39 Spadina Rd., 3rd floor
Toronto, ON M5R 2S6
(416) 972-0871

Yinka Dene Language Institute
P. O. Box 7000
Vanderhoof, BC V0J 3A0
(250) 567-9236.

Anti-bias Journals

Multicultural Review. Dedicated to a better understanding of ethnic,
     racial, and religious diversity. Greenwood Publishing Group,
     88 Post Rd. W., Westport, CA. (203) 226-3571.

Multiculturalism/Multiculturalisme. Canadian Council for Multicultural Intercultural Education, 200-124 O'Connor St., Ottawa, ON. (613) 233-4916.

Our Schools, Our Selves: A Magazine for Canadian Education Activists. Our Schools/Ourselves Education Foundation, Toronto, ON. (416) 463-6978.

First Nations Journals, News-papers

Aboriginal Voices. 116 Spadina Ave., Suite 201, Toronto, ON M5V 2K6. (416) 703-4577.

Bimonthly magazine dedicated "to bring[ing] Native creative visions and accomplishments to a wide audience."

Akwesasne Notes: A Journal of Native & Natural Peoples. Mohawk Nations, P. O. Box 196 via Rooseveltown, NY 13683-0196. (518) 358-9531; P. O. Box 30, St. Regis, QC H0M 1A0. (613) 575-2063.

First Perspective Online: Canada's Source for Aboriginal News & Events. http://www.mbnet.mb.ca/firstper/

Gatherings: The En'owkin Journal of First North American People. Theytus Books, P. O. Box 20040, Penticton, BC V2A 8K3.

"The only known journal of literary writings by Aboriginal people in North America."

Windspeaker. 15001 112th Ave., Edmonton, AB Y6M 2V6. (403) 455-2700.

Canada's national Aboriginal news publication. Has Classroom edition. Includes book reviews.

Web Sites

Educational Web Sites

Canadian Education on the Web
http://www.oise.utoronto.ca/~mpress/eduweb.html

Canadian Information by Subject (CAN)
http://www.nlc-bnc.ca/caninfo/ecaninfo.htm (National Library of Canada)

CanGuide (CAN)
http://www.oise.utoronto.ca/canguide
Provincial and territorial curriculum guides and resources.

Anti-bias Web Sites

Equal Opportunity Education
http://www.equalopp.web.net/
Resources on many subjects, including Race/Native. (Ontario Education Alliance and Urban Alliance on Race Relations)

Multicultural Bibliography (U.S., some CAN)
http://falcon.jmu.edu/~ramseyil/mulnativ.htm
Native Americans divided by area.

Multicultural Book Review homepage (U.S.)
http://www.isomedia.com/homes/jmele/homepage.html
Includes Native American and Eskimo Literatures.

First Nations Cultural Educational Web Sites

Ableza: A Native American Arts and Film Institute (U.S.)
http://www.ableza.org/
Includes "Do's and Don'ts When Teaching about Native Peoples."

Aboriginal Directors (CAN)
http://www.nfb.ca/aboriginal99/
National Film Board. Children and youth; cultural diversity.

Aboriginal Multi-media Society (CAN)
http://www.ammsa.com/ammsa.html
Includes text of *Windspeaker* (Classroom Edition).

Aboriginal Super Information Highway (CAN)
http://www.abinfohwy.ca/

Aboriginal Voices (CAN)
http://www.aboriginalvoices.com/

Aboriginal Web Links (CAN)
http://euronet.nl/~fullmoon/aborig.html
Especially, but not exclusively, Canadian.

Aboriginal Youth Network (CAN)
http://ayn-0.ayn.ca/

American Indian Library Association (U.S.)
http://info.pitt.edu/~lmitten/aila.html
Includes President's Column on Stereotypes and "'I' Is Not for Indians."

American Indian Science and Engineering Society (U.S.)
http://www.aises.org/
Includes a link to *Winds of Change: A Magazine for Indian Education and Opportunity* (http://aises.uthscsa.edu/winds/index.html).

**First Nations
Studies Guide for
Teachers K–10**

B. C. Ministry of Education—Aboriginal Education Team (CAN)
http://www.bced.gov.bc.ca/abed/

Canadian Alliance in Solidarity with Native Peoples
http://www.cyberglobe.net/~casnp/

Canadian First Nations
http://indy4.fdl.cc.mn.us/~isk/maps/cantreat.html
Part of the large site: Native American Indian.

Cradleboard (U.S.)
http://www.cradleboard.org/
Promotes public education about Native American culture.

First Nations Confederacy of Cultural Education Centres (CAN)
http://www.schoolnet.ca/aboriginal/fnccec/

First Nations Education Centre (CAN)
http://www.cmsd.bc.ca/schools/fnec/main.html
School District no. 82 (Coast Mountains), Terrace, B. C.

First People's Curriculum & Educational Resources on SchoolNet
(CAN)
http://www.schoolnet.ca/aboriginal/curri-e.html

First Perspective Online: Canada's Source for Aboriginal News &
Events
http://www.mbnet.mb.ca/firstper/
Has digest on education.

Four Worlds Institute for Human and Community Development
(CAN)
http://nucleus.com/4worlds

Gabriel Dumont Institute (CAN)
http://www.saskpublishers.sk.ca/publisher/gdi.htm

Index of Native American Resources on the Internet (U.S.)
http://www.hanksville.org/NAresources/
Includes Native American Teachers Resources on the Internet,
Storytellers, Native American Authors.

Indian and Northern Affairs Canada
http://www.inac.gc.ca/
Includes Aboriginal Peoples; Definitions; Statistics.

Indigenous Education Network (CAN)
http://www.oise.utoronto.ca/other/ien/ienpage.html
Promotes the development of Aboriginal curricula.

Indigenous Peoples' Literature (U.S. and CAN)
http://www.whitestareagle.com/natlit/
Includes Canada and Stereotypes.

Kids from Kanata (CAN)
http://www.stellar.inf.ca/1997-1998/district6/rlacol2.html
National telecommunications project linking urban and rural First
Nations and non-Native students and teachers via the Internet.

Line in the Sand (U.S.)
http://www.hanksville.org/sand/sand.html
Issues of cultural property; stereotypes of Native Americans.

Métis Resource Centre (CAN)
http://www.metisresourcecentre.mb.ca/

Native American Authors: Internet Public Library (U.S.)
http://ipl.org/ref/native/

Native American Book Sources on the Internet (U.S.)
http://www.hanksville.org/NAresources/

Native American Books (U.S., some CAN)
http://indy4.fdl.cc.mn.us/~isk/mainmenu.html
Part of the large site includes Canadian; many books are rated.

Native American Indian Art, Culture, History, Science (U.S.)
http://indy4.fdl.cc.mn.us/~isk
Over 300 Web Pages: Bookstore, Native Maps, Stories, Authors,
Stereotypes. These pages not maintained since the author's death in
1997.

Native American Sites (U.S.)
http://www.pitt.edu/~lmitten/indians.html
Native Studies Programs and Indian Education.

Native Child (U.S.)
http://www.nativechild.com
Preschool curriculum material; promotes multicultural understanding. Includes Stereotypes, Pocahontas, "Teaching Young Children
about Native Americans."

Native Lit (U.S.)
http://www.uwm.edu/~mwilson/lit.htm
Listserv for discussion of Native American literature.

Native Web (U.S., some CAN)
http://www.nativeweb.org/
An Internet community. Includes Arts, Literature by Region: Canada.

North American Native Authors Catalog (U.S.)
http://www.nativeauthors.com/
Native nonprofit organization. Cassettes, books, posters, Education, Stories & Legends, Children, Fiction.

Ontario Native Literacy Coalition
http://www.nald.ca/onlc.htm
Learning materials.

Oyate (U.S., includes CAN)
http://oyate.org

Saskatchewan Indian Cultural Centre
http://www.sicc.sk.ca

Siksik (CAN)
http://siksik.learnnet.nt.ca/
Northwest Territories Educational Resources.

Voices (CAN)
http://www.oise.utoronto.ca/~jib-project/voices.html
E-mail listserv for Aboriginal teachers.

Windspeaker classroom edition (CAN)
http://www.ammsa.com/classroom/index.htm
Includes Teaching Respect for Native Peoples: Do's and Don'ts: "When Teaching about Aboriginal Peoples . . ." and Education Resources on the Internet

Book Web Sites for First Nations

Amazon Online Bookstore
http://www.amazon.com/
Thousands of Native American books; includes reviews.

Association of Book Publishers of British Columbia First Nations Catalogue (CAN)
http://www.books.bc.ca/

Native Book Centre (CAN)
http://www.nativebooks.com/

Pemmican Publications (CAN)
http://www.pemmican.mb.ca

Bookstores   Two examples of independent bookstores.

Another Story Bookshop
164 Danforth Ave.
Toronto, ON M4K 1N1
(416) 462-1104

> Gender, race, and class issues, progressive children's books, and First Nations titles.

Prairie Sky Books
871 Westminster Ave.
Winnipeg, MB R3G 1B3
(204) 774-6152

> Booklist: Native American history, society, and spirituality.

**Publishers of
First Nations
Children's
Books
(Selected)**

Annick Press
15 Patricia Ave.
Toronto, ON M2M 1H9
(416) 221-4802

Arsenal Pulp Press
103 - 1014 Homer St.
Vancouver, BC V6B 2W9
(604) 687-4233

Blizzard Publishing
73 Furby St.
Winnipeg, MB R3C 2A2
(204) 775-2923

Children's Book Press
246 First St., Suite 101
San Francisco, CA 94105
(415) 995-2222

Coteau Books
2206 Dewdney Ave., Suite 401
Regina, SK S4R 1H3
(306) 777-0170

Douglas & McIntyre
1615 Venables St.
Vancouver, BC V5L 2H1
(604) 254-7191, 254-8218; (800) 667-6902

Fifth House Publishers
6125 11 Street S.E. #9
Calgary, AB T2H 2L6
(403) 571-5230

Fitzhenry & Whiteside
195 Allstate Parkway
Markham, ON L3R 4T8
(905) 477-9700

Hancock House Publishers
Blaine, Washington, and Surrey, BC
(800) 938-1114

Highway Bookshop
R.R.1
Cobalt, ON P0J 1C0
(705) 679-8375

Hyperion Press
300 Wales Ave.
Winnipeg, MB R2M 2S9
(204) 256-9204

Nightwood Editions
R.R. 5
S-26, C-13
Gibsons, BC V0N 1V0
(604) 885-0212

Pacific Edge Publishing Ltd.
R.R.2, Site 21, C-50
Gabriola Island, BC V0R 1X0
(250) 247-8806

Pacific Educational Press
Faculty of Education
University of British Columbia, Vancouver, BC
V6T 1Z5
(604) 822-5385

Peguis Publishers
100 - 318 McDermot Ave.
Winnipeg, MB R3A 0A2
(204) 987-3500

Pemmican Publications Inc.
Unit 2 - 1635 Burrows Ave.
Winnipeg, MB R2X 0T1
(204) 589-6346
Métis publishing house.

Penumbra Press
1225 Potter Drive
Manotick, ON K4M 1C9
(613) 526-3232

Plains Publishing
15879 116 Ave.
Edmonton, AB T5M 3W1

Polestar Book Publishers
103 - 1014 Homer St.
Vancouver, BC V6B 2W9
(604) 488-0830

Pottersfield Press
83 Leslie Rd.
East Lawrencetown, NS B2Z 1P8
(902) 827-4517

Reidmore Books
11523 100 Ave.
Edmonton, AB T5K 0J8

and

10109 106 St.
Edmonton, AB T5J 3L7
(403) 424-4420; (800) 661-2859

Sister Vision Press
P. O. Box 217, Station E
Toronto, ON M6H 4E2
(416) 533-9353

Theytus Books
P. O. Box 20040
Penticton, BC V2A 8K3
(250) 493-7180.
Native-run publishing house.

Tundra Books Inc.
481 University Ave., Suite 802
Toronto, ON M5G 2E9
(416) 598-4786

Waapoone Publishing & Promotion
Box 1358
67 Hunter Street
Lakefield, ON K0L 2H0
(705) 652-7947

Suggested Resources

Anthologies/Collections for Children and Young People

Ahenakew, Freda, Brenda Gardipy, and Barbara Lafond, eds. 1993. *Native Voices*. Toronto: McGraw-Hill.

The Issues Collection. Also *Teacher's Guide.*
Poems, stories, plays and articles by Native writers. For use in grades 7, 8, 9.

———. 1993. *Voices of the First Nations*. Toronto: McGraw-Hill.

The Issues Collection. Also *Teacher's Guide.*
Secondary level.

Archibald, Jo-ann, Val Friesen, and Jeff Smith, eds. 1993. *Courageous Spirits: Aboriginal Heroes of Our Children*. Penticton, BC: Theytus. Mokakit Education Research Association.

Also *Teacher's Guide.* Aboriginal children write about their everyday heroes.

Caduto, Michael, and Joseph Bruchac. 1991a. *The Native Stories from Keepers of the Animals*. Saskatoon: Fifth House.

From *Keepers of the Animals: Native Stories and Wildlife Activities for Children.*

———. 1991b. *The Native Stories from Keepers of the Earth*. Saskatoon: Fifth House.

From *Keepers of the Earth: Native Stories and Environmental Activities for Children.*

———. 1991c. *The Native Stories from Keepers of the Night.* Saskatoon: Fifth House.

From *Keepers of the Night: Native Stories and Nocturnal Activities for Children.*

———. 1994. *The Native Stories from Keepers of Life.* Saskatoon: Fifth House.

Mythical tales from *Keepers of Life: Discovering Plants through Native Stories and Earth Activities for Children.*

Dolan, Marlena, ed. 1994–96. *Just Talking about Ourselves: Voices of Our Youth.* Penticton, BC: Theytus. 3 vols.

Stories, poetry, and visual art by First Nations youth of British Columbia reflecting often harsh realities.

Elston, Georgia, ed. 1985. *Giving: Ojibwa Stories and Legends from the Children of Curve Lake.* Lakefield, ON: Waapoone.

———. 1991. *In Honour of Our Elders: Essays by the Children of Curve Lake and Quotations from the Elders.* Lakefield, ON: Waapoone.

Roman, Trish Fox, ed. 1994. *Voices Under One Sky: Contemporary Native Literature: Reflections in Fiction and Non-Fiction.* Scarborough, ON: NelsonCanada.

Also *Teacher's Guide.* Stories, poems, and memoirs by today's Native storytellers.

Verrall, Catherine, and Lenore Keeshig-Tobias. 1988. *All My Relations: Sharing Native Values through the Arts.* Toronto: Canadian Alliance in Solidarity with Native Peoples.

Kit of poetry, activities, lessons, and songs.

White, Ellen. 1981. *Kwulasulwut: Stories from the Coast Salish.* Penticton, BC: Theytus.

Original and traditional stories.

———. 1997. *Kwulasulwut II: More Stories from the Coast Salish.* Penticton, BC: Theytus.

Williams, Lorna. 1991. *Sima 7: Come Join Me.* Vancouver: Pacific Educational Press.

Also *Teacher's Guide.* Stories about First Nations cultures set at a youth gathering.

First Nations Posters

Role-Model Posters. Series of 9. National Native Role Model Program, Kahnawake Resource Centre, P. O. Box 1440, Kahnawake, QC J0L 1B0; (514) 638-3199; (800) 363-3199. Free posters for schools.

Teaching Respect for Native Peoples. A list of suggestions about how—and how not—to teach about Native peoples in the classroom from Oyate. 2702 Mathews St., Berkeley, CA 94702; (510) 848-6700.

First Nations Videos

Children of Canada Series. 1994. National Film Board (NFB). 3 videos. Ages 8+. #2 is set on the Fountain Reserve near Lillooet, BC.

First Nations, the Circle Unbroken. 1993. NFB. 4 videos. Ages 9+. Topics include artists, education, the environment, racism, spirituality, and Aboriginal title to the land.

For Angela. 1991. NFB. Ages 10+. A bus ride changes lives. Story of racism's impact and empowerment.

Great Wolf and Little Sister. 1989. Four Worlds Institute. Children go for a walk in the woods with their grandfather.

Many Voices Series. 1991. TV Ontario. Ontario Educational Communications Authority. (800) 463-6886 and (416) 484-2600. Send orders to (800) 561-4300; U.S. orders to (919) 380-0740. Grade 4 to Senior.

Moccasin Flats. 1991. "It's Okay to Be Who You Are." NFB. Ages 8+.

Native Awareness: Behind the Mask. 1989. Grade 5+. Edmonton: Access Network. (403) 440-7777.

Native Legends. 1994. NFB. Indian and Inuit legends.

Playing Fair Series. 1991. NFB. Directed by Alanis Obomsawin, produced by Wolf Koenig, Colin Neale, and Penny Ritco. Ages 7 to 12.

Walking with Grandfather. 1988. Four Worlds Institute. Six-part video stories about ordinary people meeting extraordinary challenges.

First Nations Children's Books

Primary K–Grade 3 (Picture Books)

Andrews, Jan. 1985. *Very Last First Time*. Vancouver: Douglas & McIntyre.

In Ungava Bay a girl collects mussels alone on the bottom of the sea.

Armstrong, Jeannette. 1991. *Neekna and Chemai*. Penticton, BC: Theytus.

Life for Okanagan children before the coming of the white man.

Bouchard, Dave. 1994. *The Meaning of Respect*. Winnipeg, MB: Pemmican.

A Cree boy learns from his grandfather on the reserve.

Bruchac, Joseph. 1993. *Fox Song*. Don Mills: Oxford University Press.

Family stories are shared by a girl bereaved by the death of her grandmother.

Brynjolson, Rhian. 1996. *Foster Baby*. Winnipeg, MB: Pemmican.

What children need from their families.

Capek, Peggy. 1993. *Mirrna and the Marmots*. Penticton, BC: Theytus.

A Vancouver Island story with an environmental message.

Crow, Allan. 1989. *The Crying Christmas Tree*. Winnipeg, MB: Pemmican.

A heartbroken grandmother gets a surprise.

Cumming, Peter. 1993. *Out on the Ice in the Middle of the Bay*. Toronto, ON: Annick.

A little girl and a young polar bear discover each other, to the concern of both their parents.

Eyvindson, Peter. 1984. *Kyle's Bath*. Winnipeg, MB: Pemmican.

———. 1986. *Old Enough*. Winnipeg, MB: Pemmican.

A father dreams of the things he will do with his son.

———. 1987. *The Wish Wind*. Winnipeg, MB: Pemmican.

A boy wishes to be in another time and another place.

———. 1988. *Chester Bear, Where Are You?* Winnipeg, MB: Pemmican.

A missing stuffed bear requires a household search.

———. 1992. *The Yesterday Stone.* Winnipeg, MB: Pemmican.

A child wants to share her learning from her grandmother.

———. 1993. *The Missing Sun.* Winnipeg, MB: Pemmican.

In Inuvik the sun disappears for many days.

———. 1994. *The Night Rebecca Stayed Too Late.* Winnipeg, MB: Pemmican.

Two girls see dangers in the shadows.

———. 1996. *Red Parka Mary.* Winnipeg, MB: Pemmican.

A growing friendship between a little boy and an old neighbor.

Goodtrack, Kim Soo. 1994. *ABC's of Our Spiritual Connection.* Penticton, BC: Theytus.

Keeshig-Tobias, Lenore. 1991. *Bineshiinh Dibaajmowin/Bird Talk.* Toronto, ON: Sister Vision.

Feelings brought by playing Cowboys and Indians lead to teachings on Native tradition and pride.

———. 1996. *Emma and the Trees/Emma minwaah mtigooh.* Toronto, ON: Sister Vision.

Friendship with nature.

Klassen, Dale. 1994. *I Love to Play Hockey.* Winnipeg, MB: Pemmican.

Kusugak, Michael Arvaarluk. 1990. *Baseball Bats for Christmas.* Toronto, ON: Annick.

Children of Repulse Bay make use of a gift.

———. 1992. *Hide and Sneak.* Toronto, ON: Annick.

A game with an Ijiraq.

———. 1993. *Northern Lights: The Soccer Trails.* Toronto, ON: Annick.

The Northern Lights are watched by a child whose grandmother's wisdom guides her.

————. 1996. *My Arctic 1, 2, 3*. Toronto, ON: Annick.

An Inkuktitut counting book shows some animals that a boy has watched.

Littlechild, George. 1997. *This Land Is My Land*. San Francisco: Children's Book Press.

Pictures and stories of humor and healing.

Loewen, Iris. 1986. *My Mom Is So Unusual*. Winnipeg, MB: Pemmican.

A girl and her mother live alone.

————. 1993. *My Kokum Called Today*. Winnipeg, MB: Pemmican.

A girl expects a special experience on the reserve.

Mosionier, Beatrice. 1996. *Christopher's Folly*. Winnipeg, MB: Pemmican.

A dream lesson about not taking without giving something back.

Munsch, Robert, and Michael Kusugak. 1991. *A Promise Is a Promise*. Toronto, ON: Annick.

A girl and her mother are more than a match for the wily Qallupilluit.

Pelletier, Darrell. 1992a. *Alfred's First Day at School*. Regina, SK: Gabriel Dumont Institute.

————. 1992b. *Alfred's Summer*. Regina, SK: Gabriel Dumont Institute.

————. 1992c. *The Big Storm*. Regina, SK: Gabriel Dumont Institute.

————. 1992d. *Lisa and Sam*. Regina, SK: Gabriel Dumont Institute.

A girl and a pet snake.

————. 1992e. *The Pow-wow*. Regina, SK: Gabriel Dumont Institute.

Plain, Ferguson. 1988. *Eagle Feather—An Honour*. Winnipeg, MB: Pemmican.

A boy grows up with his grandfather's teachings.

————. 1992. *Little White Cabin*. Winnipeg, MB: Pemmican.

An Elder passes along life's lessons.

————. 1993. *Amikoonse (Little Beaver)*. Winnipeg, MB: Pemmican.

Amikoonse takes a journey to find himself.

————. 1996. *Rolly's Bear*. Winnipeg, MB: Pemmican.

A young friend hears a bear hunt story from an Elder.

Poirier, Thelma. 1993. *The Bead Pot*. Winnipeg, MB: Pemmican.

A young girl inherits the role of making moccasins.

Sanderson, Esther. 1990. *Two Pairs of Shoes*. Winnipeg, MB: Pemmican.

A child is given shoes for different occasions.

Speare, Jean. 1991. *A Candle for Christmas*. Toronto, ON: Douglas & McIntyre.

A boy eagerly awaits his parents' return.

Swamp, Chief Jake (Tekaronianeken). 1995. *Giving Thanks: A Native American Good Morning Message*. New York: Lee & Low.

Based on the Thanksgiving Address of the Six Nations.

Tappage, Mary Augusta. 1973. *The Big Tree and the Little Tree*. Winnipeg, MB: Pemmican.

A young tree grows to honor an older one.

Truss, Jan, and Nancy Mackenzie. 1987. *Peter's Moccasins*. Edmonton, AB: Reidmore.

A boy learns to feel good about his moccasins.

Van Camp, Richard. 1997. *A Man Called Raven*. San Francisco: Children's Book Press.

Canadian illustrator George Littlechild. A mysterious man teaches the meaning of respect for nature.

Waterton, Betty. 1986, 1978. *A Salmon for Simon*. Vancouver, BC: Douglas & McIntyre.

A boy who goes fishing lets a fish swim free.

Weber-Pillwax, Cora. 1989. *Billy's World*. Edmonton, AB: Reidmore.

A boy and his grandfather visit a cabin.

Wheeler, Bernelda. 1984. *I Can't Have Bannock but the Beaver Has a Dam*. Winnipeg, MB: Peguis.

A child learns the cause of a power failure.

———. 1986. *Where Did You Get Your Moccasins?* Winnipeg, MB: Peguis.

A child describes how his grandmother made his moccasins.

Wheeler, Jordan. 1994. *Just a Walk*. Penticton, BC: Theytus.

A humorous story of misadventures to be used interactively.

Yerxa, Leo. 1993. *Last Leaf First Snowflake to Fall*. Toronto, ON: Douglas & McIntyre.

A dreamlike voyage into nature

Primary Classrooms/ Nonfiction

Adams, Dawn. 1984. *Island Fun*. Vancouver, BC: Pacific Educational Press.

A Queen Charlotte Islands reader.

———. 1985. *Potlatch*. Vancouver, BC: Pacific Educational Press.

Bates, Mary-Ann, and Millie Jones. 1989. *Exploring Carcross*. Vancouver, BC: Douglas & McIntyre.

Children of La Loche and Friends. 1990. *Byron through the Seasons/ Byron Bel Haet'azi Luk'é Sine: A Dene-English Story Book*. Saskatoon, SK: Fifth House.

Students write about and illustrate their own community.

Clark, Karin. 1996. *Long Ago in Victoria*. Victoria, BC: Greater Victoria School District #61.

Coast Salish history.

Jacobs, Sharon, and Heather Jones. 1985. *Exploring Haines Junction*. Vancouver, BC: Douglas & McIntyre.

Manywounds, Muriel, Dolores Schultz, and Wendy Soderberg. 1987. *Sarcee Reserve: An Indian Community*. Edmonton, AB: Reidmore.

Meekins, Del. 1989. *Exploring Old Crow.* Vancouver, BC: Douglas & McIntyre.

Ortiz, Simon. 1988. *The People Shall Continue.* San Francisco: Children's Book Press.

An overview of Native history.

Thompson, Sheila. 1994. *Cheryl Bibalhats/Cheryl's Potlatch.* Vanderhoof, BC: Yinka Language Institute.

Junior Grades (4–6)

Bear, Glecia (Nêhiyaw). 1991. *wanisinwak iskwêsisak: awâsisasinahikanis: Two Little Girls Lost in the Bush: A Cree Story for Children.* Saskatoon, SK: Fifth House.

Fiction

Blades, Ann. 1984. *A Boy of Taché.* Montreal, QC: Tundra.

A boy chooses to live with his grandparents in a cabin by a lake.

Culleton, Beatrice. 1993, 1985. *Spirit of the White Bison.* Winnipeg, MB: Peguis.

A story of deliberate decimation.

Dorion, Betty. 1995. *Melanie Bluelake's Dream.* Regina, SK: Coteau Books.

A Cree girl finds it hard to move to a city school.

Eyvindson, Peter. 1997. *Chubby Champ.* Winnipeg, MB: Pemmican.

Will a boy be able to live up to his nickname?

King, Edna, and Jordan Wheeler. 1991. *Adventure on Thunder Island.* Toronto, ON: James Lorimer.

Contemporary short stories where the supernatural is everywhere.

King, Thomas. 1992. *A Coyote Columbus Story.* Toronto, ON/ Vancouver, BC: Douglas & McIntyre.

How Coyote fixed up the world without concentrating on what she was creating.

Mamchur, Carolyn Marie, with M. Zola. 1993. *In the Garden.* Winnipeg, MB: Pemmican.

A Métis girl grows vegetables from her grandmother's seeds.

Sterling, Shirley. 1992. *My Name is Seepeetza*. Toronto, ON: Douglas & McIntyre.

A child's account of the racism of residential schools.

Students of G. T. Cunningham Elementary School. 1996. *We Are All Related: A Celebration of Our Cultural Heritage*. Vancouver, BC: Polester Book Publishers.

Students from many countries and cultures make collages and describe their histories and heritages with words from elders.

Umpherville, Tina. 1995. *The Spring Celebration*. Winnipeg, MB: Pemmican.

A girl's involvement in an annual picnic at Brochet.

———. 1997. *Jack Pine Fish Camp*. Winnipeg, MB: Pemmican.

A girl describes events at the annual fish camp.

Waboose, Jan Bourdeau. 1997. *Morning on the Lake*. Toronto, ON: Kids Can Press.

In three linked stories of an Ojibway grandfather and grandson, the child learns about nature and his place in the world.

Junior Classrooms: Biography, Memoirs, Society, History, Photographs

Bragg, Lynn. 1995. *A River Lost: A Message from Grandma Toopa*. Surrey, BC and Blaine, WA: Hancock House.

A story of ancient lifeways forever changed by the Grand Coulee Dam.

Campbell, Maria. 1976. *People of the Buffalo: How the Plains Indians Lived*. Vancouver, BC: Douglas & McIntyre.

Ekoomiak, Normee. 1990. *Arctic Memories*. Toronto, ON: NC Press.

Paintings and words depicting traditional legends and family life honor an ancient lifeway that continues still.

Gaikesheyongai, Sally. 1994. *The Seven Fires: An Ojibway Prophecy*. Toronto, ON: Sister Vision.

A spiritual history of the Ojibway people.

Haegert, Dorothy. 1989, 1983. *Children of the First People*. Vancouver, BC: Tillacum.

Photos portray Native children of Canada's West Coast accompanied by elders' narratives.

Harper, Maddie. 1993. *"Mush-hole": Memories of a Residential School.* Toronto, ON: Sister Vision.

Experiences in an Indian residential school and escape and recovery.

Hubbard, Jim, ed. 1994. *Shooting Back from the Reservation: A Photographic View of Life by Native American Youth.* New York: New Press.

Children give a camera's-eye view of their lives.

Jensen, Vickie. 1994. *Carving a Totem Pole.* Toronto, ON: Douglas & McIntyre.

Niska wood-carving.

Maracle, Sylvia (Skonaganleh:ra). 1994. *Onkwehonwe-Neha.* Toronto, ON: Sister Vision.

A history of the Haudenosaunee (Mohawk) people.

Plouffe, Vivianne. 1988. *Winds of Change: Indian Government.* Edmonton, AB: Reidmore.

The Kehewin Reserve today and in the past.

Pratt, Neal. 1991. *Place Where the Spirit Lives: Stories from the Archaeology and History of Manitoba.* Winnipeg, MB: Pemmican.

Rempel, David, and Laurence Anderson. 1987. *Annette's People.* Edmonton, AB: Plains Publishing.

A Métis girl learns about her family.

Schreiber, June et al. 1988. *Alberta's Métis: People of the Western Prairie.* Edmonton, AB: Reidmore.

Also *Teacher's Resource.*

Shemie, Bonnie. 1989. *Houses of Snow, Skin and Bones: The Far North.* Montreal, QC: Tundra.

———. 1990. *Houses of Bark: The Eastern Woodlands.* Montreal, QC: Tundra.

———. 1991. *Houses of Hide and Earth: The Plains.* Montreal, QC: Tundra.

———. 1992. *Houses of Wood: The Northwest Coast.* Montreal, QC: Tundra.

———. 1993. *Mounds of Earth and Shell: The Southeast.* Montreal, QC: Tundra.

———. 1995. *Houses of Adobe: The Southwest.* Montreal, QC: Tundra.

Architectural paintings and research.

Steltzer, Ulli. 1990, 1981. *Building an Igloo.* Toronto: Douglas & McIntyre.

A photographer's records.

———. 1994. *Indian Artists at Work.* Vancouver: Douglas & McIntyre.

Tappage, Mary Augusta, and Jean Speare. 1992, 1973. *The Days of Augusta.* Vancouver/Toronto: Douglas & McIntyre.

A woman in her eighties shares memories of her life and her heritage.

Wheeler, Jordan et al. 1992. *Tapping the Gift: Manitoba's First People.* Winnipeg: Pemmican.

Native and Métis biographies.

Legends/ Traditional Stories for All Ages

Traditional stories of Wisahkecahk, Nanabosho, and Raven; heroes learn of the world around them; the courageous are honored; trickery backfires; young children are taught to honor all creatures and listen to their parents; stories of the way things began. Traditional and modern illustrations.

Ahenakew, Freda, ed. 1988a. *How the Birch Tree Got Its Stripes.* Saskatoon, SK: Fifth House.

———. 1988b. *How the Mouse Got Brown Teeth: A Cree Story for Children.* Saskatoon, SK: Fifth House.

———. 1997. *Wisahkecahk Flies to the Moon.* Winnipeg, MB: Pemmican.

Ballantyne, Bill. 1994a. *Wesakejack and the Bears.* Winnipeg, MB: Blizzard.

———. 1994b. *Wesakejack and the Flood.* Winnipeg, MB: Blizzard.

Beavon, Daphne "Odjig." 1971. *Nanabush and the Dancing Ducks.* Cobalt, ON: Highway Bookshop.

———. 1989. *Nanabush and the Spirit of Winter.* Cobalt, ON: Highway Bookshop.

Boreham, Brenda, and Donna Klockars. 1993. *Legends from the Chemainus Tribe: Stories and Teachings from the Oral Tradition of their Elders.* Vancouver, BC: Pacific Edge Publishing.

Fox, May Lou. 1993. *Why the Beaver Has a Flat Tail.* Markham, ON: Fitzhenry & Whiteside.

Higgins, Edwin. 1990. *Grandmother Tell Me a Story.* Cobalt, ON: Highway Bookshop.

Johnston, Basil. 1978. *How the Birds Got their Colours: Gah w'indinimowaut binaesheehnyuk w'idinauziwin-wauh.* Toronto, ON: Kids Can Press.

———. 1981. *Tales the Elders Told: Ojibway Legends.* Toronto, ON: Royal Ontario Museum.

———. 1986. *By Canoe & Moccasin: Some Native Place Names of the Great Lakes.* Lakefield, ON: Waapoone.

Marchand, Barbara. 1991a. *How Food Was Given: An Okanagan Legend.* Penticton, BC: Theytus.

———. 1991b. *How Names Were Given: An Okanagan Legend.* Penticton, BC: Theytus.

———. 1991c. *How Turtle Set the Animals Free: An Okanagan Legend.* Penticton, BC: Theytus.

McLellan, Joseph. 1989. *The Birth of Nanabosho.* Winnipeg, MB: Pemmican.

McLellan, Joseph, and Matrine McLellan. 1990. *Nanabosho Steals Fire.* Winnipeg, MB: Pemmican.

———. 1991. *Nanabosho Dances.* Winnipeg, MB: Pemmican.

Story about the origin of the hoop dance told to modern children.

———. 1993. *Nanabosho, Soaring Eagle, and the Great Sturgeon.* Winnipeg, MB: Pemmican.

———. 1994. *Nanabosho: How the Turtle Got Its Shell*. Winnipeg, MB: Pemmican.

Story told to modern child at aunt's.

———. 1995. *Nanabosho and the Woodpecker*. Winnipeg, MB: Pemmican.

———. 1997. *Nanabosho and Kitchie Odjig*. Winnipeg, MB: Pemmican.

Oliviero, Jamie. 1993. *The Fish Skin*. Winnipeg, MB: Hyperion.

———. 1995. *The Day Sun Was Stolen*. Winnipeg, MB: Hyperion.

Paul-Dene, Simon. 1992. *I Am the Eagle Free (Sky Song): A Six-Nations Legend*. Penticton, BC: Theytus.

Plain, Ferguson. 1994. *Grandfather Drum*. Winnipeg, MB: Pemmican.

Grandfather tells a Nanaboozhoo story.

Rossetti, Bernadette. 1991. *Musdzi 'Udada'/The Owl: A Carrier Indian Legend*. Vanderhoof, BC: Yinka Dene Language Institute.

Scribe, Murdo. 1985. *Murdo's Story: A Legend from Northern Manitoba*. Winnipeg, MB: Pemmican.

Sechelt Nation. 1993a. *How the Robin Got Its Red Breast: A Legend of the Sechelt People*. Gibsons, BC: Nightwood Editions.

———. 1993b. *Mayuk the Grizzly Bear: A Legend of the Sechelt People*. Gibsons, BC: Nightwood Editions.

Spicer, Stanley. 1991. *Glooscap Legends*. Hantsport, NS: Lancelot.

Taylor, C. J. 1990. *How Two-Feather Was Saved from Loneliness*. Montreal, QC: Tundra.

———. 1991. *The Ghost and Lone Warrior: An Arapaho Legend*. Montreal, QC: Tundra.

———. 1992. *Little Water and the Gift of the Animals*. Montreal, QC: Tundra.

———. 1993a. *How We Saw the World: Nine Native Stories of the Way Things Began*. Montreal, QC: Tundra.

———. 1993b. *The Secret of the White Buffalo*. Montreal, QC: Tundra.

Taylor, C. J. 1994. *Bones in the Basket: Native Stories of the Origin of People.* Montreal, QC: Tundra.

————. 1995. *The Monster from the Swamp.* Montreal, QC: Tundra.

Waboose, Jan Bourdeau. 1994. *Where Only the Elders Go—Moon Lake Loon Lake.* Ottawa, ON: Penumbra.

Notes

1. Cook, Katie. 1984. *Images of Indians Held by Non-Indians.* Ottawa: Indian and Northern Affairs Canada Research Branch. P. 65.

2. Taylor, Drew. 1995. "Not 'Native' Enough." *Quill & Quire* 61 (12): 11. Also, his *Funny You Don't Look Like One: Observation of a Blue Eyed Ojibway.* 1996. Penticton: Theytus; and articles by Richard Wagamese in the *Calgary Herald* and in *The Terrible Summer.* Toronto: WarWick, 1996.

3. Canadian Alliance in Solidarity with Native Peoples. 1990. *Resource Reading List 1990.* P. 7. Toronto.

4. Hirschfelder, Arlene. 1993, 1982. *American Indian Stereotypes in the World of Children.* Metuchen, NJ: Scarecrow. Pp. 7–10.

5. Council of Interracial Books for Children. 1997. *Unlearning "Indian" Stereotypes.* New York. Pp. 20–21.

22 What Should They Read, and When Should They Read It? A Selective Review of Holocaust Literature for Students in Grades 2 through 6

Karen Shawn
Moriah School of Englewood, New Jersey

This chapter presents an annotated bibliography of Holocaust literature for young people, a bibliography specifically designed for teachers in elementary schools. *Dimensions* first published such a list in 1994, and this chapter is a partial reprint of an updated list published there in January 1998. The almost yearly increase in legislated recommendations and mandates to teach the Holocaust makes such a document a necessity for those teachers who wish to make informed decisions about the wealth of memoirs and novels long in circulation as well as those recently issued.

This overview, which covers books published between 1971 and 1997, is idiosyncratic, not exhaustive. It includes novels, photo essays, autobiographies, memoirs, and short story collections popular with youngsters and recommended by librarians and other educators. It also covers little-known works, some out of print but still on library shelves. Recommendations for students as young as

This essay originally appeared in 1997 as "What Should They Read and When Should They Read It?: A Selective Review of Holocaust Literature for Students in Grades Two through Twelve: Part II" in *Dimensions: A Journal of Holocaust Studies* 11(2): A-3–A-11. Reprinted with permission.

second grade are included for those who feel the necessity for introducing this subject at that age.

There is a discernable—and disturbing, in my opinion—trend toward publishing Holocaust literature for ever-younger primary grade students. Oddly, many of these works are more graphic and depressing than those aimed at middle and high school students. For this older audience, Holocaust books often focus on the aftermath of the Final Solution and on its themes of rebirth and renewal.

Whether the newest novels are based on bits of testimony, family memories, or historical composites, the majority of authors have made a clear attempt to reach out to today's elementary and middle school reader, either by including vivid and eye-catching graphics, or by writing contemporary (and anachronistic) dialogue.

Criteria Used for Recommended Selections

1. They reflect a historical reality. Even as fiction, they depict the truth of the Holocaust era with a high degree of accuracy.

2. They present the truth without unduly traumatizing the young reader. Books for middle school students that include concentration and death camp scenes are not graphically violent.

3. They present the *Shoah* through limited, recognizable human experiences, thereby fostering involvement and identification with the victims and survivors of the Holocaust and personalizing the abstract statistics of the phenomenon.

4. They engage and involve students, encourage further study of the Holocaust, and help to ensure remembrance.

5. They highlight the Jewish response to events during and after the Holocaust, rather than, for example, the actions of the perpetrators.

6. Books recommended for elementary and middle school offer flexibility in the classroom:

   a. They are highly readable.

   b. They can be used to lay the groundwork for the subsequent teaching of Holocaust history. In the upper grades, they can be used as an introduction to, in conjunction with, or as a culmination of the history unit.

   c. They provide an active learning experience for students, offering opportunities for dramatic reading, active listening, discussion, cooperative learning, responsive writing, and extended, individualized research projects.

   d. They promote opportunities to explore the universal issues and themes evoked by the unique stories of the Holocaust.

All age recommendations listed are, of course, approximate; if I err, it is on the side of caution. They are also theoretical; in practice, educators will take into account not only students' grade level but also their abilities, interests, background, and depth of understanding of this period. However, I strongly suggest that the details of the Final Solution be taught only in high school, and that no book about the Holocaust, even the simplest, be offered to students before second grade.

A final note: Before you begin to teach about the Holocaust and the need for remembrance, you may wish to lay the groundwork by helping children to understand the concept and importance of remembering, and the role that memory plays in the life of individuals and peoples. The following books are perfect choices to assist such a pursuit. They address definitions of memory and their significance; intergenerational relationships; the importance of retelling our personal and collective stories; and recollections of immigration.

Blegvad, Lenore. 1993. *Once upon a Time and Grandma*. New York: Margaret K. McElderry Books.

Bunting, Eve. 1988. *How Many Days to America?: A Thanksgiving Story*. New York: Clarion Books.

Fox, Mem. 1989. *Wilfrid Gordon McDonald Partridge*. Brooklyn: Kane/Miller Book Publishers.

Martin, Bill Jr., and John Archambault. 1987. *Knots on a Counting Rope*. New York: Henry Holt. A Reading Rainbow Book.

Moss, Marissa. 1994. *In America*. New York: Dutton Children's Books.

Oberman, Sheldon. 1994. *The Always Prayer Shawl*. Honesdale, PA: Boyds Mills Press, Inc.

Polacco, Patricia. 1988. *The Keeping Quilt*. New York: Simon & Schuster.

The following children's books address issues of identity and difference, mutual respect and tolerance, group dynamics (in-group, out-group), individual responsibility, and making difficult choices—important themes to explore as part of a Holocaust Education Reading Readiness program.

Alexander, Liza. 1991. *No Red Monsters Allowed!* Racine, WI: Western Publishing Co.

Berenstain, Stan, and Jan Berenstain. 1989. *The Berenstain Bears and the In-Crowd*. New York: Random House.

Bunting, Eve. 1989. *Terrible Things*. Philadelphia: Jewish Publication Society.

Fox, Mem. 1986. *Hattie and the Fox*. New York: Aladdin (Simon & Schuster).

Seuss, Dr. 1989. *Sneetches and Other Stories*. New York: Random House.

Grades 2–4 Adler, David. 1997. *Hiding from the Nazis*. New York: Holiday House.

Four-year-old Lore Baer witnesses her beloved grandfather taken by the Nazis in Holland in 1943. Shortly after, her parents send her to hide in the home of trusted acquaintances. But this couple fears discovery, so they take Lore to the farmhouse of the Schoutens, a courageous, anti-Nazi Dutch family. Lore remains with them for two years, living under an assumed name as a Christian. Cornelia Schouten mothers Lore, and makes her childhood as normal as possible. When Lore's parents come to claim her after the war, Cornelia helps Lore make the difficult transition from the Schouten home to her new life. This true story, told without drama or graphic detail, is a good introduction to the hiding experience and the actions of rescuers.

Grade 4 and Up Adler, David. 1995. *One Yellow Daffodil: A Hanukkah Story*. New York: Harcourt Brace & Company.

Lloyd Bloom's illustrations are reason enough to buy this book. Luminous, almost three-dimensional, they enhance each page. The story is worthy of these paintings. Morris Kaplan is a florist whose family perished in Auschwitz. A generous, gentle man, he takes pleasure in selling flowers. Two of his favorite customers are Ilana and Jonathan Becker, neighborhood children who come each Friday to buy flowers for Shabbat. When they invite him to join them for a Chanukah celebration, he refuses, saying he doesn't celebrate the holiday anymore. But they insist, and his visit forces him to confront long-buried memories and feelings.

"At home he searches in his closet. He brings out an old box. Inside are a metal cup, a torn shirt, a child's hat, and an old menorah. Morris holds the menorah in both hands and cries."

He returns to the Kaplans with the menorah and begins to tell them of his family, and of a yellow daffodil that offered him a symbol of hope, and of his loss.

"After the war . . . I had no one," he says. "Mrs. Becker holds Morris's hand in hers and says, 'Now you have us.'"

I am concerned about the trend to make the Holocaust a part of every Jewish holiday; I hope the connection here is not for the purpose of marketing the book as a Chanukah gift. Assuming it is not, I recommend this book. It is honest in its portrayal of history and authentic in its portrayal of the pain of loss. It is utterly without sensationalism or graphic detail. It is appropriately sad and yet hopeful, allowing young readers a glimpse of one survivor's tragic past and the comfort of feeling the strength of his new life.

Grade 4   Feder, Paula Kurzband. 1995. *The Feather-Bed Journey.* Morton Grove, IL: Whitman.

When Rachel and Lewis destroy Grandma's feather pillow, they don't understand why she tries to gather the loose feathers. "Once this was my mother's featherbed," she tells them, and begins to explain her family's experiences during the Holocaust.

"Sad times came to us. War began. Certain people from Germany, called Nazis, came to Poland. They didn't want Jews in Poland. They didn't want Jews anywhere." In the ghetto, the featherbed keeps her warm. The dangers posed by the Nazis are great and her parents fear for her life, so they send her away to hide with a Christian farmer. For two years she hides in a basement, until a neighbor sees her peering from a window. The farmer, his life now in danger, sends her to the woods, where she hides with others for two more years. She and her mother survive the Holocaust and are reunited. After the war, safe in America, they write to the kind farmer to thank him. In response, he sends them the feather pillow. He had made it from the remains of their featherbed, which he had been given in return for his help.

The plot is contrived, a composite of many stories told to the author by her mother. In addition, the little grandson, Lewis, is a jarring, annoying character. But the story is gentle and imbued with the warmth of a loving, supportive Jewish family. It provides a good introduction to these concepts: the Nazi occupation, the hiding experience, and rescuers, especially when paired with Oppenheim's *The Lily Cupboard.* In an epilogue, Feder concisely summarizes the Holocaust in Poland. Stacey Schuett's excellent paintings help readers see the ghetto, the woods, and the Displaced Persons camp.

Lakin, Patricia. 1994. *Don't Forget*. New York: Tambourine Books.

This life-affirming book, with evocative pastel illustrations by Ted Rand, is a perfect follow-up to Adler's *The Number on My Grandfather's Arm*. It is appropriate for any child who has had the unsettling experience of seeing and learning about the numbers on the arm of a Holocaust survivor.

Sarah is shopping for ingredients for an orange sponge cake to bake for her mother, but she hesitates to go into Singer's. "The Singers were nice. But their secret was not. . . . Sarah knew not to stare at the blue numbers tattooed on the Singers' left arms." Sarah is aware that "the Nazis gave them the blue numbers and put them in the concentration camp— just because they were Jews." That comment is the only reference to the Holocaust.

Mrs. Singer, understanding Sarah's discomfort, helps her to understand that "The numbers should never be a secret. . . . If no one knows about bad things, they can happen all over again. Don't forget." Reassured, Sarah stays with Mrs. Singer and bakes the cake. The strength of this book is that it allows children to acknowledge the discomfort or concerns they may have had in a similar situation.

Second Thoughts: Grades 2–4

Nerlove, Miriam. 1996. *Flowers on the Wall*. New York: Margaret K. McElderry Books.

The first thing that struck me about this book was the age recommendation on its book jacket: ages 5–9. The second was the litany of tragedy summarized directly underneath: life is hard; anti-Semitism is on the rise; Papa's business is forcibly closed; Nat must give up school to help Papa haul heavy loads; Rachel is sick in an unheated, one-room, basement apartment; their situation worsens; Rachel's dreams vanish; finally, she and her family are sent to Treblinka. I read the book, which is an expansion on each of these statements. And on the last page I read, "Rachel's dreams, along with those of thousands of other Warsaw Jews, faded like the flowers on her apartment walls. And then they were gone forever."

This book is unnecessarily harsh, particularly for its intended audience. Because children lost their innocence during the Holocaust, does that mean our children should lose theirs, too? To what end? I appreciated Nerlove's beautiful illustrations, but I am sure that they will mislead parents and teachers into buying this book for the youngest readers, and I feel profoundly sad about that.

What purpose is served by introducing five-year-olds, especially non-Jews, to anti-Semitism and anti-Jewish actions? What purpose is served by introducing Jews as victims? There is nothing positive about being Jewish in this story, no celebrations, no Shabbat prayers, no particular faith, spirituality, or Jewish values—quite the opposite, in fact: for example, the family eats horsemeat, which is not kosher; and instead of underscoring the importance of education in Jewish life, these parents promptly take their son out of school and put him to work. The book ignores the fact that there were clandestine schools throughout the Warsaw ghetto, where teachers risked their lives to teach, and parents gave their own food rations to their children's tutors. This book fails to teach, to illuminate, to give hope; it leaves readers puzzled, bereft, and frightened, mired in a past they did not know they had.

Schnur, Steven. 1995. *The Tie Man's Miracle*. New York: Morrow Junior Books.

Mr. Hoffman sells ties door-to-door. When he visits Seth's house on the last night of Chanukah, he is urged to join the family in their celebration. Slowly he tells of his own wife and children, lost in "a terrible war. Many people were killed, especially Jewish people." Before he leaves, he tells "a happy tale" of his childhood belief in a special Chanukah miracle that could occur only on the eighth night of the holiday. If all nine candles "went out at exactly the same instant, those nine little columns of smoke would rise as one up to heaven, carrying our wishes straight to the ear of God. . . . Watch them carefully," he admonishes Seth. "Perhaps tonight your dreams will come true."

The tie man leaves, and Seth, alone with the dwindling candles, makes a silent wish: "Please give the tie man back his family."

"A moment later the room went black. Nine narrow columns of smoke rose from the silver menorah. A little way above my head they seemed to join in a delicate braid, rising faster. Suddenly the room grew bright. I heard voices shouting, 'Papa, Papa!' Shadows danced on the ceiling, feet scurried across the floor, laughter filled the air. And then all was silent and dark."

Seth waits for the tie man to make his usual visit, but he waits in vain. Has he moved to another city? Or, in a twist like that in the ironic plot of W. W. Jacob's classic "The Monkey's Paw," has Seth's wish inadvertently caused the man's death? And, if so, is his death better than the lonely life he lived?

I appreciate the beautiful writing, a hallmark of a Schnur book. And the immutable sadness of the survivor who has lost his entire family is powerfully presented. But I am troubled by the implications of such "magical thinking," especially for children at the very age when they start feeling guilty for actions they mistakenly believe they have caused.

I am also concerned about the artificial connection between the Holocaust and Chanukah. The trend to touch every Jewish event with the shadow of the Holocaust may sell more books, but it is not appropriate.

The most serious problem of the book for me, however, lies in the offensive drawings by Stephen T. Johnson. His tie man, especially in the cover drawing, is a caricature, a faint echo of the Der Stürmer Jew. These are not the pictures that should be presented to children as their introduction to the people who endured the Holocaust.

Grades 5–6 Abells, Chana Byers. 1983. *The Children We Remember: Photographs from the Archives of Yad Vashem, Jerusalem, Israel.* Rockville, MD: Kar-Ben Copies, Inc.

This is an excellent introduction to learning about the importance of archival photographs in studying the Holocaust. Through these photographs of children, we learn about the Holocaust with an immediacy that transcends anything offered by most history texts. But care must be taken: this book should be used only with the right age group. Because the text is spare and simple, the book is always advertised for very young children. It is *about* very young children, but surely not *for* them. The pictures are painful in their portrayal of loneliness and helplessness, and the text, too, is bleak and distressing, including as it does such facts as that children were taken from their parents and put to death. Middle school seems to be the appropriate time to introduce these photographs to students.

Grade 6 and Up Adler, David A. 1993. *A Picture Book of Anne Frank.* New York: Holiday House.

A factual account of Anne's short life, this brief biography might be useful for those learners unable to tackle the diary in its original or dramatic form. The illustrations by Karen Ritz, unfortunately, don't do justice to the original photos from which they were taken.

Grade 6 and Up for Challenged Readers

Herman, Erwin, and Agnes Herman. 1985. *The Yanov Torah.* Rockville, MD: Kar-Ben Copies, Inc.

This is the beautiful and moving story of the Torah that was smuggled, in sections, into a work camp in Yanov, a town near Lvov, Poland (now Russia), in 1941. Piece by tiny piece, parchment was smuggled in weekly by volunteers—inmates who were allowed to go home. The segments were retrieved and put together at great risk to the inmates. This special Torah survived the Holocaust and, fifty years later, is given to Dr. Orlove, the book's narrator, as he leaves Europe to come to America.

This is a wonderful story of faith, resistance, and hope. It is most appropriate for children in Jewish day or Hebrew schools, even though there is some violence. The strength and faith of the Jews in the book help the reader to feel the power of their spirit, and to understand the centrality of the Torah in the lives of many survivors.

Grade 6 and Up

Hurwitz, Johanna. 1988. *Anne Frank: Life in Hiding.* Philadelphia: The Jewish Publication Society.

Richer in historical detail than Adler's biography of Anne Frank, this fifty-page biography presents a thorough account of Anne's life in hiding, and includes a historical overview of Dutch life just before and after Anne's experiences in the attic at 263 Prinsengracht in Amsterdam. It is a sober, straightforward treatment without photographs (they would have added immensely to the text). This may be a good choice for a unit on biographies, and may well persuade a child who has not yet read Anne's diary to do so. But it is in no way, nor was it intended to be, a substitute for the original *Diary.*

Grades 5–6

Jules, Jacqueline. 1993. *The Grey Striped Shirt.* Los Angeles: Alef Design Group.

This large-print, sixty-three-page story begins with nine-year-old Frannie's discovery of a wartime grey striped prison uniform tucked away in Grandma Trudie's cedar closet. Frannie doesn't know what her grandparents endured during the war, but she does know from her parents that "what Grandma Trudie and Grandpa Herman had suffered during the war was the kind of thing of which nightmares were made." She doesn't want nightmares, so she doesn't tell them quite yet of her discovery. But little by little, over an entire year, Frannie asks questions and gets gentle, direct answers.

She learns about the ghetto, and about work in a concentration camp. "I don't want to hear any more," she says, and Grandma says no more until the next time Frannie asks. When Grandpa Herman tells her that 1.5 million Jewish children were killed during the Holocaust, Frannie waits a whole year before asking another question on the subject.

In form and content, Jules presents a wonderful model for teaching the Holocaust: answer the inevitable questions in a simple, straightforward way; don't volunteer additional information; give children permission to say stop, or to talk about their fears and sadness; discuss the strength, courage, and faith of the Jews ("A Jew believes in the future," Grandma says. "No matter how bad it was, we kept faith that one day the war would be over"); explain the various kinds of resistance they offered ("We fought the Nazis by staying alive," Grandma tells Frannie). Finally, tell the story in a context that also offers the richness of Jewish life today. (Frannie goes to shul regularly and celebrates Shabbat.)

This book has a brief explanation of Auschwitz and mentions gas chambers, but the references are muted. If you feel an introductory overview of these topics is necessary in the fifth or sixth grade, I recommend this book highly.

Kerr, Judith. 1971. *When Hitler Stole Pink Rabbit.* New York: A Dell Yearling Book.

This ALA Notable Book has long been a favorite of sixth- and seventh-grade girls, and for good reason. It is 1933: nine-year-old Anna has a warm and loving family, and Hitler is just a face on Berlin posters. Within a year, however, Anna and her family are refugees in Switzerland. Later they move to France and, just when Anna has mastered French, they move yet again to England.

Anna struggles with the problems most refugees face, including poverty. Yet her strong sense of self and her optimism endow her experiences with an engaging sense of adventure. When her cousin Otto says, "It must be quite difficult to spend one's childhood moving from country to country," Anna wonders, "Could her life since she had left Germany really be described as a difficult childhood? . . . No . . . Some things had been difficult, but it had always been interesting and often funny—and she and Max and Mama and Papa had nearly always been together. As long as they were together she could never have a difficult childhood."

This autobiographical novel is an excellent choice to begin a unit on the Jewish family during the Holocaust.

Grade 6 and Up

Silton, Faye. 1997. *Of Heroes, Hooks, and Heirlooms.* Philadelphia: The Jewish Publication Society.

Mia, age twelve, wants to be a hero because her parents are: "They survived Hitler's war and started a family all over again." She will be a hero, she believes, if she can make her mom "be less sad, to make up to her something of what she lost" in the Holocaust. When her class is assigned a Heritage Project and an Heirloom Fair, Mia despairs. "How could I ask Mom and Dad to fill out a tree that had lost so many of its branches?" She realizes she has nothing to display; the only treasure left to her mother is one family photograph.

With affectionate guidance from two teachers, she ultimately crochets her own heirloom, a copy of a lace collar worn by her grandmother in the one photo she has, and, wearing it, she explains to her classmates the story of the last Shabbat of her grandmother's life. The book is short—ninety-nine pages of large print—but the plot is detailed, the conversation realistic, and the survivors deftly drawn. Tonia, Mia's mother, hoards groceries; she wakes with night terrors. She cares nothing for possessions; their apartment "aches with drabness." She warns her daughter "not to shine too much." But the house is filled with quiet love, and the family is religiously observant.

Through other characters we learn of the uniqueness of a multitude of cultures. The Irish Potato Famine, customs of the Ojibway Indians, the beauty of a generations-old Christian Bible, the sounds of a Russian balalaika, and the strength of early American settlers in the Nebraska prairie engage the reader.

Winner of the Sydney Taylor Manuscript Competition Award, Silton's book is both authentic to the Second Generation experience and appropriate for multicultural studies, an important accomplishment in this decade of mandated Holocaust and genocide studies. This excellent book might well be the impetus for a Heritage Project in your own classroom.

Second Thoughts: Grades 5–6

Ackerman, Karen. 1994. *The Night Crossing.* New York: Knopf.

This simple, fifty-six-page novel presents the story of Clara and her family, who are forced by the Nazi occupation of Austria to leave their home in Innsbruck and travel at night across the foothills of the Swiss Alps to the safety of Switzerland. They sell their belongings to raise money to pay their way during the dangerous journey. Clara, however, is allowed to keep two of her dolls, which play a crucial role at the Swiss border. The tone is extremely gentle; even Elizabeth Sayles's black-and-white illustrations are soft and reassuring.

If only Ackerman had read a history book! She misuses the symbol of the Jewish star, planting it on Clara's coat in 1938 instead of 1941. Moreover, she writes about a nonexistent 1938 war between Germany and Austria that ruined neighborhoods and forced Clara's family to sell their piano for firewood. There is no justification for such easily avoided historical inaccuracies, and I feel compelled to reject books that include them.

Adler, David A. 1995. *Child of the Warsaw Ghetto.* New York: Holiday House.

This is an odd book, with gray pages dense with print and murky illustrations by Karen Ritz. Survivor Froim Baum has told Mr. Adler his story, and Adler uses it to tell young readers the story of the Warsaw ghetto. Part testimony, part history, the narrative does justice to neither. The sentences are short, apparently because Adler is writing for a juvenile audience. But the subject demands more than simple sentences: it is not appropriate for an audience that cannot follow the complexity rendered by subordinate clauses. The historical narrative, intended to be brief and coherent, is instead superficial and confusing.

The book jacket blurb, in reviewing another of Adler's books, notes, "Teachers and librarians are faced with the formidable task of finding titles that present a complex, horrifying subject for primary graders' listening or independent reading." Adler's book illustrates the near impossibility of succeeding in this search. Doesn't anyone question the rationale for finding material about a "complex and horrifying" topic for "primary graders"?

Adler, David A. 1994. *Hilde and Eli: Children of the Holocaust.* New York: Holiday House.

Adler again teams with Karen Ritz to craft a picture book about the true story of two children who died in the Holocaust. Hilde Rosenzweig and Eli Lax did not know each other; their countries and backgrounds were different. Both were Jewish, however, and thus both were targets of the Nazis. If their stories had been kept separate, the book may have been better. But Adler arbitrarily interweaves the children's experiences, confusing young and adult readers alike. Furthermore, the large drawings will encourage unwary teachers to recommend the book to young children. However, the text, though sparse, is not appropriate for elementary readers. Eli, hearing screams, is "too frightened to sleep at night." Hilde and her mother, along with a trainload of prisoners, are gassed. The unsuspecting reader, having read just one paragraph earlier that Hilde was ordered to wear a yellow star on her clothing, is totally unprepared for her murder. Eli and his family are chased with clubs and gassed in the showers; their bodies are burned. Such information demands a more appropriate format and an older audience.

Hoestlandt, Jo. 1995. *Star of Fear, Star of Hope.* New York: Walker.

This prize-winning, age-appropriate book made me wonder if I should stop reviewing for a while, since none of my colleagues shared my discomfort with parts of this story, set in the north of France in 1942.

Helen, the narrator, is best friends with Lydia. Lydia wears a yellow star, because "every Jew must wear it. It's the new law." That is the sole mention of the word *Jew.*

The girls are sleeping at Helen's house on the eve of Helen's ninth birthday, when they hear strangers in the hall. A frightened woman tells the girls that people are being arrested. When Lydia sees the yellow star on the woman's coat, she insists on going home. Early the next morning in front of Helen's apartment building, police surround long lines of people wearing yellow stars and carrying suitcases. Helen and her mother rush to Lydia's house, but, "There wasn't anybody in her apartment. Their neighbors didn't know anything. Had Lydia's family been arrested? Had she escaped? There was no telling." Helen's mother explains that Lydia's "bad luck . . . comes from people, from the wickedness of some and the weakness of others. Sometimes it can be so hard to live to-gether. . . ."

But who are the weak people, I wondered uneasily. Those who didn't try to stop the deportations? Or does she mean the Jews? And with whom is it hard to live together? And what is the implication of that unfinished sentence?

The book ends with Helen, now an old woman, hoping that Lydia lived, waiting for her call. But is this "hope" in reality a form of denial?

Perhaps my discomfort with this beautifully illustrated (by Johanna Kang) story arises from the recognition of the difficulties we adults face when we try to explain to children aspects of the Holocaust that we do not yet understand.

Perl, Lila, and Marion Blumenthal Lazan. 1996. *Four Perfect Pebbles: A Holocaust Story.* New York: Greenwillow Books.

These words are from the first three paragraphs: "concentration camp . . . muffled noises . . . gasps and moans . . . rattling coughs . . . piercing cries . . . ever-present stench . . . unwashed bodies . . . disease . . . death . . . prisoners . . . thin straw mattresses . . . died . . . tumbled from their bunks . . . crude stretchers . . . bodies taken away . . . burned . . . buried . . . mass graves." If you were a child, would you want to continue reading?

This graphic introductory flashback is one problem with this book, which, with its large type and cover photo of a child, is presented as appropriate for early middle school students. The remainder of the as-told-to testimony recounts the Blumenthals' experience in transit and concentration camps in a somewhat more appropriate tone.

But Perl is determined to fit in as much grim description as she can. Although the Blumenthals were not in Auschwitz, for example, young readers are given the details of the killing process there.

In addition, Perl's historical accounts may lead to continued stereotyping. She doesn't explore the concepts of anti-Semitism and racism, for instance, but writes instead, "True, Jews didn't run the giant industries of Germany . . . But they were involved in business and professions. . . . In . . . Berlin . . . the major department stores were Jewish-owned. . . . Whatever abilities, talents, influence, or wealth the Jews of Germany possessed were seen as a threat by the Nazis."

If this were the Blumenthals' story alone, it would be acceptable. But attempting to weave history around an occasional quote from a survivor requires far more scholarship than is evident here.

Index

Editor

Judith P. Robertson is associate professor in the Faculty of Education and the Department of Women's Studies at the University of Ottawa, where she teaches foundations and cultural studies. Her work uses psychoanalytic concepts and methods to rethink the uses and effects of symbolizing practice, including narrative production and reception. Her publications have appeared in *Canadian Social Studies* (1993), *The Canadian Journal of Education* (1997), *Rereading English* (1997), *Taboo: A Journal on Culture and Education* (1997), *Language Arts* (1997), *English Quarterly* (1997), *Canadian Children's Literature* (1999), and *Literature Interpretation Theory* (1999). She is the author of *Cinema and the Politics of Desire in Teacher Education,* forthcoming from SUNY Press. She began her career as an elementary school teacher.

Contributors

Bernard W. Andrews is a member of the Faculty of Education at the University of Ottawa. He has presented research papers at provincial, national, and international conferences on arts education and program evaluation. Current research is focused on describing gender differences in arts education, evaluating the effect of multimedia on arts learning, developing an arts skills profile for elementary and secondary educators, and assessing the impact of restructuring on arts curricula. He teaches in preservice teacher education and curriculum studies at the graduate level.

Wendy Armitage Simon has taught in elementary classrooms in inner-city schools in Toronto, Canada, for over thirty years. She has served on curriculum writing teams, as an adjunct professor supervising teachers in training, and as an instructional development and curriculum resource teacher for a project devoted to enhancing social justice and academic excellence. Armitage Simon retired in the spring of 1998 and now enjoys a mix of study, gardening, and long-term occasional work in the Toronto system.

Anne C. Bell is a doctoral student in the Faculty of Environmental Studies, York University, Toronto. She works in environmental education, advocacy, and ecological restoration initiatives, and is a director of the Wildlands League Chapter of the Canadian Parks and Wilderness Society. Supported by the Social Sciences and Humanities Research Council of Canada, her work has appeared in *Alternatives, The Trumpeter: Journal of Ecosophy, Pathways, Undercurrents, Journal of Environmental Education, Canadian Issues in Environmental Ethics, Women's Voices in Experiential Education* and *Common Ground: Feminist Collaboration in the Academy*.

Deborah P. Britzman teaches at York University, Toronto, Canada. She is the author of *Practice Makes Practice: A Critical Study of Learning to Teach* (1991) and *Lost Subjects, Contested Objects: Toward a Psychoanalytic Inquiry of Learning* (1998).

Grace M. Caporino has taught English for twenty-four years at Carmel High School in Carmel, New York. She has served as an educational consultant to the U.S. Holocaust Memorial Museum and to the College Board. In 1991 she was awarded the Regents of the State University of New York, Louis Yavner Award for Teaching about the Holocaust and Human Rights. She has been named to *Who's Who among America's Teachers* and to *Who's Who of American Women*. She is a member of the NCTE Committee on Teaching about Genocide and Intolerance. Caporino has been the recipient of several grants including those funded by the National Endowment for the Humanities, which funded her program "Holocaust Perspectives: The Word and the Image," in 1989 and again in 1995. She is listed in *Who's Who in America 1998* and was a Mandel Fellow for 1998–99 with the United States Holocaust Memorial Museum.

Christine D. Connelly was a teacher education student in the Faculty of Education at the University of Ottawa, Canada, at the time of writing her chapter. She struggles to voice possibilities beyond the silences and in/visibilities from, with/in, and outside of sociocultural margins. In attempting to invite/support collaboration toward social justice, she actively attends to creating spaces for negotiating "difference." She is currently a doctoral candidate in education at the Ontario Institute for Studies in Education, University of Toronto.

Michelle R. Dunlap was born and raised in Detroit, Michigan. She earned her Ph.D. degree in social psychology from the University of Florida in 1993. She is assistant professor of human development at Connecticut College in New London, Connecticut. She has taught a variety of courses in the child development, human development, and social and psychological sciences areas over the past eight years in Connecticut and Florida.

María E. Fránquiz is assistant professor in the School of Education at the University of Colorado in Boulder. She teaches classes on literacy and multiethnic education. Her doctoral dissertation (UC-Santa Barbara), entitled *Transformations in Bilingual Classrooms: Understanding Opportunity to Learn within the Change Process,* was awarded first place in the National Association of Bilingual Education's Outstanding Dissertation Competition. Her work appears in *TESOL Quarterly* (Spring 1997). Her current research focuses on bilingualism and the literacy development of Chicana/Chicano youth.

Anne K. Goudvis is a staff developer with the Public Education and Business Coalition, a nonprofit educational organization that works to improve teaching and learning in Denver-area schools. She has a doctorate in curriculum and instruction, with an emphasis in reading, from the University of Illinois.

Joseph A. Hawkins Jr. received his B.A. from Boston University and his M.A. from Howard University. He has worked in the Peace Corps and served as a teacher in Africa, and has taught at Howard University. He started working for the Montgomery County Public Schools (Maryland) in 1979. As an evaluation specialist, he manages research projects covering a wide variety of topics such as teacher training, discipline, and technology use. His work has appeared in *Teacher Magazine, Education Week, Teachers College Record, Teaching Tolerance Magazine, The Journal of Reading,* and the *College Board Review.* For many years, he wrote a column—"HawkTalk"—for the Montgomery *Journal.*

Dona J. Helmer is currently associate professor at Montana University-Billings, where she is the Education Librarian and teaches courses in children's literature. Dona has served on both the Newbery and Caldecott Award Committees for the American Library Association.

Before completing her doctoral work at the University of Southern Mississippi, she taught for fifteen years in Alaska. Her recent publications include "Using Picture Books to Combat Racism" (*Teaching Tolerance* Fall 1996). She has received three National Endowment for the Humanities grants to work with K–12 educators on the images of Native Americans in literature and film.

Louise B. Jennings is assistant professor at the University of South Carolina in the College of Education, where she teaches qualitative research methods and social/cultural foundations of education. Her doctoral dissertation (UC-Santa Barbara), *Multiple Contexts for Learning Social Justice,* was an ethnographic study of Irene Pattenaude's class. Central to her current research interests are principles and practices for promoting tolerance and equity in and through education. She has published with Sabrina Tuyay and Carol Dixon, "Classroom Discourse and Opportunities for Learning: An Ethnographic Study of Knowledge Construction in a Bilingual Third Grade Classroom" in *Discourse Processes* (January, 1995).

Belinda Yun-Ying Louie is associate director of teacher education at the University of Washington, Tacoma. Her scholarly interest is in developing interdisciplinary studies using literature, especially in promoting multicultural understanding. She has contributed to *The Reading Teacher, Journal of Reading, English Journal* and other publications.

Douglas H. Louie is a clinical assistant professor at the University of Washington, Tacoma. His scholarly interest is in enhancing health knowledge among teachers, students, and his patients. He has initiated a series of conflict-resolution projects in classrooms to promote mental health among school-aged children.

Debbie Miller has been a teacher in the Denver Public Schools for twenty-five years. She has a master's degree from Regis College and works throughout the Denver metro area as a staff developer and teacher trainer.

April D. Nauman recently completed her doctorate in literacy education and masters degree in creative writing at the University of Illinois-Chicago. She currently teaches graduate and undergraduate courses in reading and writing instruction in the Chicago area. Her research interests include literary response, the influences of fictional characters on children's understandings of themselves and others, and the teaching of fiction writing to students at all grade levels. Her publications explore reading-writing connections. In addition, she has published several works of short fiction in U.S. literary journals.

Yeuk Yi Pang graduated with a Ph.D. in philosophy of education from the University of British Columbia in 1994. Her dissertation was in moral education. She has worked as an Education Assistant at the Vancouver School Board on policy and administrative issues. Currently on leave from that position and living in Heidelberg, Germany, Yi is concentrating on improving her proficiency in German.

Her developing interest is to help educators better understand the importance of philosophical questions on their work, and to find a philosophical perspective that allows philosophy of education to contribute to the living philosophical wisdom of educators.

Sarah-Hope Parmeter teaches composition at the University of California, Santa Cruz. She is a founding member and past chair of the Lesbian and Gay Caucus of the CCCC; former co-director of the Central California Writing Project; coordinator of a bilingual early-outreach program providing Spanish-speaking fifth-grade students with university mentors; co-author of pieces on lesbian/gay/bisexual education in *Social Issues in the English Classroom* and *Voices in English Classrooms: Honoring Diversity and Change* (both NCTE) and co-editor of *The Lesbian in Front of the Classroom*.

Irene Pattenaude is a fifth-grade teacher in a bilingual (Spanish/English) classroom at McKinley Elementary School in Santa Barbara, California. She is a Fellow with the South Coast Writing Project (UCSB), and has been a teacher researcher member of the Santa Barbara Classroom Discourse Group since 1993. Pattenaude is currently compiling data regarding students' understanding of the classroom as a community. She is also currently writing with Louise Jennings an article examining literate strategies that influenced one student's learning of tolerant actions.

Elspeth Ross has an M.A. in Canadian Studies and an M.L.S. and is a researcher, librarian, and information provider in the fields of racism, First Nations children's literature, child welfare, adoption, and permanency planning. She and her husband are parents to two Cree teenage boys.

Rose A. Rudnitski is Chair of the Department of Elementary Education and Presiding Officer of the Faculty of the State University of New York at New Paltz. After teaching for eighteen years, she earned a doctorate in education from Columbia University in 1991. Since then her scholarship has focused on the history of education, social justice, and gifted education. The co-author of the textbook *Integrated Teaching Methods* and author of many articles in the field, Rudnitski is the editor of the middle school volume in the *Teaching for a Tolerant World* series. She also serves on the editorial review boards of *The Gifted Child Quarterly* and *Roeper Review*.

Constance L. Russell teaches in the Faculty of Environmental Studies at York University. To investigate the role of experiential learning in the social construction of nature and other animals, she has conducted research on the educational aspects of whalewatching and orangutan ecotourism. Other interests include critical environmental education, ecofeminism, and collaboration between academics, activists, and teachers. Her work appears in the *Journal of Experiential Education, Journal of Environmental Education, Holistic Education Review, Society and Animals, The Trumpeter: Journal of Ecosophy, Tourism Recreation*

Research, Women's Voices in Experiential Education, Common Ground: Feminist Collaboration in the Academy, and *Pathways.*

P. J. Nomathemba Seme, assistant professor at Old Dominion University in Norfolk, Virginia, teaches in the Educational Curriculum and Instruction department. She has presented numerous papers and written articles in *Language and Literacy, Curriculum and Teaching,* and *Classroom Research.* Her recent review of *Languages of Learning* by Karen Gallas (1994) appeared in the *Harvard Educational Review.* The *Who is Who in the South and Southeast* recently recognized her outstanding achievements in the Silver 25th edition of Marquis.

Karen Shawn is an assistant principal of the Moriah School of Englewood, a Hebrew Day School in New Jersey. She is the Regional Director of Educational Outreach for the American Society for Yad Vashem, and teaches the pedagogical component of the Yad Vashem Summer Institute for Educators from Abroad. She is also consultant to the Ghetto Fighters House and co-author of the teacher's guide for the GFH International Book-Sharing Project. She is the author of *The End of Innocence: Anne Frank and the Holocaust* and editor of *In the Aftermath of the Holocaust: Three Generations Speak.* She has written articles on teaching about the Holocaust for such journals as *Dimensions, Ten Da'at,* and *Judaica Librarianship.* Her most recent publication, "What Makes a Good Book Good? Choosing Literature for Students in Grades Two through Nine," will appear in *Teaching about the Holocaust,* edited by Samuel Totten and Steven Feinberg.

Roger I. Simon is a faculty member in the Department of Curriculum, Teaching and Learning at the Ontario Institute for Studies in Education, University of Toronto. Much of his recent teaching and writing has been devoted to the study of commemorative pedagogies and the development of public memory. He is research director of the University of Toronto Testimony and Historical Memory Project.

Timothy J. Stanley is associate professor of educational foundations at the Faculty of Education, University of Ottawa, Canada. His work examines the history of racism in British Columbia, the production of nationalism, and Chinese-Canadian experience. He is active in anti-racist education and has published in *Discourse: Studies in the Cultural Politics of Education* and *The Canadian Historical Review.*

Sharon Todd is assistant professor in the Faculty of Education, York University, Toronto, Canada. She is the editor of *Learning Desire: Perspectives on Pedagogy, Culture, and the Unsaid* (1997), a book that examines the ways in which desire intersects with knowledge, fantasy, and embodiment.

Samuel Totten is professor of curriculum and instruction at the University of Arkansas at Fayetteville. He is a member of the Council of the Institute on the Holocaust and Genocide (Jerusalem, Israel). Among his publications on genocide are *First-Person Accounts of Genocidal*

Acts Committed in the Twentieth Century: An Annotated Bibliography (1991); *Guidelines for Teaching About the Holocaust* with William S. Parsons (1993); *Genocide in the Twentieth Century: Critical Essays and Eyewitness Testimony* with William S. Parsons and Israel W. Charny (1995); and *Century of Genocide: Eyewitness Testimony and Critical Essays* with William S. Parsons and Israel W. Charny (1997).

Glenda K. Valentine is associate director of the Teaching Tolerance Project of the Southern Poverty Law Center in Montgomery, Alabama. A native of Riverside, California, and an alumna of California State University, Sacramento, Valentine holds a master of science in counseling and human development. She is an experienced trainer and diversity facilitator and a member of the American Society for Training and Development, the American Counseling Association, and the Association for Multicultural Counseling and Development. Valentine conducts diversity workshops for educators across the country. She has written several articles and most recently wrote the introduction to *Of Many Colors: Portraits of Multiracial Families.*

Beth Yeager is a fifth-grade teacher in a bilingual (Spanish/English) classroom at McKinley Elementary School in Santa Barbara, California. She received her master of arts degree in education from the University of California, Santa Barbara. Yeager is a Fellow and teacher consultant with the South Coast Writing Project (UCSB) and has been a teacher researcher member of the Santa Barbara Classroom Discourse Group since 1992. She co-authored "Learning to See Learning in the Classroom: Developing an Ethnographic Perspective" with Judith Green and Ana Floriani in *Students as Ethnographers,* edited by David Bloome and Anne Egan-Robertson (1998). Her work examines the social construction of communities of learners and equitable access to learning for all students.

Vicki Zack has served for the past seven years as a teacher researcher in a fifth-grade classroom. There she pursues a long-standing interest begun in her doctoral work of the ways in which peers interacting together can contribute to the construction of their knowledge. Her research involves exploring children's discussions, in both literature and mathematics. Most pertinent to the work that appears in this volume, Zack is the daughter of survivors, a student of the Holocaust in literature and history, and has taught children's literature at McGill University's Faculty of Education (1979–1985). The essay in this volume is one of three in which she explores children's responses to intolerance and genocide in children's literature.

This book was typeset in Palatino and Avant Garde by Electronic Imaging.
Typefaces used on the cover were Gill Sans and Gill Sans Bold Extra Condensed.
The book was printed by Edwards Brothers, Inc.